The Post-War Compromise, 1945-64

The Post-War Compromise: British Trade Unions and Industrial Politics, 1945–64

Edited by

ALAN CAMPBELL
NINA FISHMAN
JOHN McILROY

MERLIN PRESS

© Editors and contributors, 2007
First published 1999 by Ashgate
First paperback edition published in 2007
by The Merlin Press
96 Monnow Street
Monmouth
NP25 3EQ
Wales

www.merlinpress.co.uk

ISBN. 9780850366013

British Library Cataloguing in Publication Data
is available from the British Library

The editors and contributors have asserted their moral rights
under the Copyright, Designs and Patents Act 1998 to be identified
as the editors/authors of this work.

All rights reserved. No part of this publication may be
reproduced, stored in a retrieval system, or transmitted,
in any form or by any means, electronic, mechanical,
photocopying, recording or otherwise, without the
prior permission of the publisher.

Cover photo: Grunwick strike, © and with thanks to TUC Library Collections.

Printed in Great Britain by Lightning Source UK, Milton Keynes

Contents

List of Tables   vii

List of Abbreviations   viii

Contributors   xiii

Introduction to the Paperback Edition:
Reflections on British Trade Unions and Industrial Politics
John McIlroy   xiv

Preface to the 1999 Edition   xli

Introduction: Approaching Post-War Trade Unionism   1
John McIlroy, Alan Campbell, Nina Fishman

PART ONE Overviews, 1945–79

1   The Role of Industrial Correspondents   23
         Geoffrey Goodman

2   Making Trade Unionists: the Politics of Pedagogy, 1945–79   37
         John McIlroy

PART TWO Survey

3   The Post-War Compromise: Mapping Industrial Politics, 1945–64 69
         Alan Campbell, Nina Fishman, John McIlroy

PART THREE Case Studies, 1945–64

4   'Shut Your Gob!': the Trade Unions and the Labour Party   117
         David Howell

5 The Trades Union Congress in the International Labour
  Movement 145
  Anthony Carew

6 Cold War Politics: Communism and Anti-Communism in the
  Trade Unions 168
  Richard Stevens

7 Social Democracy and Anti-Communism: Allan Flanders and
  British Industrial Relations in the Early Post-War Period 192
  John Kelly

8 The Shop Floor Politics of Productivity: Work, Power and
  Authority Relations in British Engineering, *c.*1945–57 222
  Alan McKinlay and Joseph Melling

9 'The Most Serious Crisis since 1926': the Engineering and
  Shipbuilding Strikes of 1957 242
  Nina Fishman

10 'Spearhead of the Movement?' The 1958 London Busworkers'
  strike, the TUC and rank Cousins 268
  Nina Fishman

11 Democracy and Trade Unionism on the Docks 293
  Jim Phillips

Afterword 311
Eric Hobsbawm

Index *317*

Tables

Table 3.1	Index of real wages and percentage unemployed in the United Kingdom, 1945–64	102
Table 3.2	Aggregate union membership and density in the United Kingdom, 1945–64	103
Table 3.3	The ten largest TUC affiliates, 1945 and 1963	104
Table 3.4	Political classification of trade unions in the 1950s	104
Table 3.5	Trends in recorded strikes, 1946–64	105
Table 4.1	Some trade union affiliations to the TUC and Labour Party, 1946	119
Table 4.2	Trade union affiliations to the Labour Party, 1946, 1947	120
Table 4.3	Sponsored candidates and Members, 1945–59	122
Table 4.4	Sponsorship of MPs: the predominant unions	123
Table 6.1	Communist union membership in various industries, 1945–62	183
Table 6.2	Workplace organization in the London District of the CP, 1952–58	184

Abbreviations

ACAS	Advisory, Conciliation and Arbitration Service
ACP	Advisory Committee on Policy
ACTT	Association of Cinematograph and Allied Technicians
ACTU	Association of Catholic Trade Unionists
AEF	Amalgamated Engineering and Foundry Workers' Union
AES	Alternative Economic Strategy
AESD	Association of Engineering and Shipbuilding Draughtsmen
AEU	Amalgamated Engineering Union
AFL	American Federation of Labor
AFL-CIO	American Federation of Labor - Congress of Industrial Organizations
APEX	Association of Professional Executive, Clerical and Computer Staff
ASLEF	Associated Society of Locomotive Engineers and Firemen
ASSET	Association of Supervisory Staffs, Executives and Technicians
ASTMS	Association of Supervisory, Technical and Managerial Staffs
ASW	Amalgamated Society of Woodworkers
AScW	Association of Scientific Workers
ATTI	Association of Teachers in Technical Institutions
ATUA	All Trade Union Alliance
AUCCTU	Soviet All Union Central Council of Trade Unions
AUEW	Amalgamated Union of Engineering Workers
AUEW(E)	Amalgamated Union of Engineering Workers, Engineering Section)
AUFW	Amalgamated Union of Foundry Workers
BBC	British Broadcasting Corporation
BDC	Biennial Delegate Conference
BEC	British Employers' Confederation
BISAKTA	British Iron, Steel and Kindred Trades' Association
BL	British Leyland; Broad Left
BMC	British Motor Corporation
BTC	British Transport Commission
CATU	Ceramic and Allied Trades Union
CAWU	Clerical and Administrative Workers' Union
CBC	Central Bus Committee of the Transport and General Workers' Union

CBI	Confederation of British Industry
CCU	Civil Contingencies Unit
CEU	Constructional Engineering Union
CGT	Confédération Générale du Travail
CIR	Commission on Industrial Relations
CLP	Constituency Labour Party
CND	Campaign for Nuclear Disarmament
Confed	Confederation of Shipbuilding and Engineering Trade Unions
CP	Communist Party of Great Britain
CPC	Conservative Political Centre
CPS	Centre for Policy Studies
CPSA	Civil and Public Services Association
COHSE	Confederation of Health Service Employees
CRD	Conservative Research Department
CSEU	Confederation of Shipbuilding and Engineering Unions
CWU	Chemical Workers' Union
DATA	Draughtsmen's and Allied Technicians' Association
DC	District Committee
DE	Department of Employment
DEA	Department of Economic Affairs
DGB	Deutscher Gewerkschaftsbund
DMA	Durham Miners' Association
DO	Divisional Organizer
DPC	District Party Committee of the CP
EATSSNC	Engineering and Allied Trades Shop Stewards' National Council
EEC	European Economic Community
EEF	Engineering Employers' Federation
EETPU	Electrical, Electronic, Telecommunication and Plumbing Union
EIS	Educational Institute of Scotland
EPEA	Electrical Power Engineers' Association
ERO	European Regional Organization of the ICFTU
ETU	Electrical Trades Union
ETUC	European Trade Union Confederation
EVWs	European Volunteer Workers
FBI	Federation of British Industry
FBU	Fire Brigades' Union
Fed	South Wales Miners' Federation
F&GP	Finance and General Purposes Committee

FTAT	Furnishing Timber and Allied Trades Union
GC	General Council
GCA	Glasgow City Archives
GEC	General Executive Council
GMWU	General and Municipal Workers' Union (see also NUGMW)
HRM	Human Resource Management
ICFTU	International Confederation of Free Trade Unions
IEA	Institute of Economic Affairs
IGF	International Graphical Federation
ILO	International Labour Organisation
ILP	Independent Labour Party
IMG	International Marxist Group
IRD	Information Research Department
IRIS	Industrial Research and Information Services
IRSF	Inland Revenue Staff Federation
IS	International Socialists
ISF	International Solidarity Fund
ITF	International Transport Workers' Federation
ITS	International Trade Secretariats
IWC	Institute for Workers' Control
JPC	Joint Production Committee
JSS	Joint Shop Stewards
KFL	Kenya Federation of Labour
KPD	Kommunistische Partei Deutschlands (German Communist Party)
LCC	London County Council
LCDTU	Liaison Committee for the Defence of Trade Unions
LGOC	London General Omnibus Company
LISSDC	London Industrial Shop Stewards' Defence Committee
LO	Landsorganisationen i Sverige
LPC	Local Party Committee of the CPGB
LPCR	Labour Party Conference Report
LRC	Labour Representation Committee
LRD	Labour Research Department
LTE	London Transport Executive
MDW	measured day work
MFGB	Miners' Federation of Great Britain
MLSA	Ministry of Labour Staff Association
MRC	Modern Records Centre, University of Warwick
NAFF	National Association for Freedom

NALGO	National Association of Local Government Officers
NAPE	National Association of Port Employers
NASD	National Amalgamated Stevedores and Dockers
NCB	National Coal Board
NCLC	National Council of Labour Colleges
NDLB	National Dock Labour Board
NEC	National Executive Committee
NEDC	National Economic Development Council
NEDDY	National Economic Development Council (see also NEDC)
NEDDYS	sector- or industry-based economic development committees serviced by NEDC secretariat
NF	National Front
NGA	National Graphical Association
NIC	National Incomes Commission
NIRC	National Industrial Relations Court
NJC	National Joint Council
NMLH	National Museum of Labour History
NPWU	National Passenger Workers' Union
NSSM	National Society of Metal Mechanics
NSP	National Society of Painters
NUAW	National Union of Agricultural Workers
NUB	National Union of Blastfurnacemen
NUBSO	National Union of Boot and Shoe Operatives
NUDAW	National Union of Distributive and Allied Workers
NUDBTW	National Union of Dyers, Bleachers and Textile Workers
NUFTO	National Union of Furniture Trade Operatives
NUGMW	National Union of General and Municipal Workers (see also GMWU)
NUHKW	National Union of Hosiery and Knitwear Workers
NUJ	National Union of Journalists
NUM	National Union of Mineworkers
NUPE	National Union of Public Employees
NUR	National Union of Railwaymen
NUS	National Union of Seamen (later Seafarers)
NUSMW	National Union of Sheet Metal Workers and Braziers
NUT	National Union of Teachers
NUTGW	National Union of Tailors and Garment Workers
NUVB	National Union of Vehicle Builders
OECD	Organization for Economic Co-operation and Development
PEP	Political and Economic Planning

PLP	Parliamentary Labour Party
POEU	Post Office Engineering Union
PPS	Parliamentary Private Secretary
PTU	Plumbing Trades Union
RCP	Revolutionary Communist Party
RSL	Revolutionary Socialist League
RTUO	Revolutionary Trade Union Opposition
SDP	(British) Social Democratic Party
SEEA	Scottish Engineering Employers' Association
SLL	Socialist Labour League
SOGAT	Society of Graphical and Allied Trades
SPGB	Socialist Party of Great Britain
SS	steamship
STA	Socialist Teachers' Alliance
STUC	Scottish Trades Union Congress
SWP	Socialist Workers' Party
TASS	Technical and Supervisory Section of AUEW
TGWU	Transport and General Workers' Union (also T&G)
TSSA	Transport Salaried Staffs Association
TUC	Trades Union Congress
TWU	Tobacco Workers' Union
UCATT	Union of Construction, Allied Trades and Technicians
UCS	Upper Clyde Shipbuilders
UPW	Union of Post Office Workers
USB	United Society of Boilermakers
USDAW	Union of Shop, Distributive and Allied Workers
UTFWA	United Textile Factory Workers' Association
WEA	Workers' Educational Association
WETUC	Workers' Educational Trade Union Committee
WFTU	World Federation of Trade Unions
WLBTU	Watermen, Lightermen, Tugmen and Bargemen's Union
WRP	Workers' Revolutionary Party
WSL	Workers' Socialist League

Contributors

Alan Campbell is Reader in Labour and Social History, University of Liverpool. He is the author of the two-volume *The Scottish Miners, 1874–1939* (2000).

Anthony Carew recently retired as a Reader in Industrial Relations, University of Manchester. He co-edited *The International Confederation of Free Trade Unions* (2000).

Nina Fishman is Honorary Research Professor in History, University of Swansea, and author of *The British Communist Party and the Trade Unions, 1933-45* (1995).

Geoffrey Goodman was the industrial correspondent of the *Daily Mirror*. He is the author of *The Awkward Warrior: Frank Cousins, his life and times* (1979).

Eric Hobsbawm is one of Britain's most eminent historians. His recent books include his autobiography, *Interesting Times: a twentieth century life* (2002).

David Howell is Professor of Politics, University of York, and the author of *MacDonald's Party: Labour identities and crisis, 1922–1931* (2002).

John Kelly is Professor of Industrial Relations at Birkbeck College, London. His books include *Rethinking Industrial Relations: mobilization, collectivism and long waves* (1998).

John McIlroy is Professor of Industrial Relations at Keele University. His books include *Industrial Politics and the 1926 Mining Lockout: the struggle for dignity* (2004).

Alan McKinlay is Professor of Management, University of St Andrews. His latest book is *Inside the Factory of the Future* (2007).

Joseph Melling is Reader in Economic and Social History at the University of Exeter. He is the co-editor of *Management, Labour and Industrial Politics in Modern Europe* (1996).

Jim Phillips works in the Department of Economic History, University of Glasgow. He is the author of *The Great Alliance: economic recovery and the problems of power, 1945-51* (1996).

Richard Stevens wrote his doctoral thesis on Communism and trades councils.

Introduction to the Paperback Edition:
Reflections on British Trade Unions and Industrial Politics

John McIlroy

The two companion volumes addressing industrial politics in the post-war era, *The Post-War Compromise* and *The High Tide of British Trade Unionism*, were first published in 1999.[1] They attracted both commendation and criticism. Most of the reviewers were kind. Neville Kirk, a professor of labour history, felt that the texts constituted 'a major contribution towards filling the many gaps in our understanding of post-war trade unionism and politics. They also provoke many new questions and open up important areas of research.'[2] The economic historian Alan Fowler described *The Post-War Compromise* as 'a most welcome addition to the literature ... this volume will provide future scholars with a far greater understanding of the post-war period than has yet been available.'[3]

The insightful student of the politics and sociology of industry Colin Crouch found the books 'deeply empirical and detailed, scrupulously scholarly ... They tell it how it was.'[4] Mike Terry, a professor of industrial relations, characterized *The High Tide of British Trade Unionism* as 'scholarly and precise ... [the essays] add greatly to our knowledge of the period under review, extending our understanding of the familiar and exposing much that lay hidden ... It is a fascinating volume that will engage all readers with its mix of meticulous research and lucid exposition. Together with its companion volume it will no doubt come to serve as one of the definitive assessments of post-war trade unionism.'[5]

In the introduction to the two books we were at pains to stress that they made no claim to provide a comprehensive account of the trade unionism of this period, still less its social and political context and its impact on the economy. Eric Hobsbawm believed that we were excessively modest in characterising much of the work as 'first accounts of neglected byways'.[6] Needless to say, at least one reviewer succumbed to the perennial malady of that trade by suggesting that we should have edited two very different books covering, *inter alia*, globalization; class mobility; popular attitudes; 'sheer [*sic*] generational change'; the role of trade unionists as consumers; and 'the changing developmental role of government'.[7] More reasonable was the observation that the activities of black and Asian trade unionists, women employees and 'white-collar workers in general' during these years merited greater attention.[8]

Within the confines of our texts there should certainly have been more on the link between the unions and the Labour Party which by 1979 contributed so much to the discourse of 'ungovernability'; on labour legislation and the role of the judiciary, a topic of undoubted political importance throughout the period; on industrial democracy, not only on the Bullock Report of 1977 but also on initiatives from below; as well as greater attention to the alternative economic strategies, predicated as a means of mobilizing trade unionists for radical change, which transcended existing approaches to reform. A rounder treatment of the period would need to pay fuller attention to the context and content of social change, the changing culture of working-class communities and the lives and experiences of political and industrial activists, as well as those they represented.[9]

* * * * *

Lord Morgan generously praised many of the contributions. He claimed that others were too concerned with 'justifying rank-and-file militancy as a reasonable response to anti-inflation policies'.[10] Morgan was particularly perturbed at McIlroy and Campbell's discussion of the 'Winter of Discontent', 1978–9, in their survey, 'The High Tide of Trade Unionism', omitting to inform readers that, among other things, that chapter critically engages with his own examination of those events.[11] In his account, the Labour Prime Minister James Callaghan, the subject of a major biography by Morgan, is a tragic hero brought down by the trade unions, personified by the irresponsibility of Moss Evans, general secretary of the Transport and General Workers' Union (TGWU), and Alan Fisher, general secretary of the National Union of Public Employees.[12]

In his biography, Morgan notes the risk that Callaghan ran in unilaterally imposing a 5 per cent pay limit against the opposition of both the TUC and the Labour Party when inflation was running at almost twice that amount. He records Callaghan's miscalculation in refusing to call a general election in autumn 1978. He even recognizes that beneath the high politics that he chronicles 'lay the pent-up anger of public sector service workers after three years of pay restraint'.[13] He is very clear who the villains of the piece are. In Morgan's narrative, exercise of 'the irresponsible power of the over mighty unions' paves the way for Thatcherism. Trade unionists succumb to a 'feverish madness' and 'commit hara kiri', in the process derailing a government 'helpless in the face of the undisciplined brute force of union power'.[14] Evans and Fisher are found wanting, judged by the ahistorical standards of Callaghan's and Morgan's model union leaders, Ernest Bevin, Arthur Deakin, Sir William Lawther and the later Jack Jones.[15]

In their essay McIlroy and Campbell looked at matters differently and, we would submit, rather more convincingly. They commenced not with explanations in terms of pathology or the death wish of irresponsible union leaders but with analysis rooted in the structural situation constraining the actors of 1978–9 and the interplay of agency with context. The power of the unions, even at their high tide, and their leaders' ability to mobilize it for agreed objectives, remained limited, secondary and, it should be stressed, diffuse.[16] Until the end of our period the decentralization of union structure and collective bargaining, and the confines of sectoral and workplace consciousness as well as the weaknesses of state policy, and persisting economic pressure, militated against concertation and social contracts. Whatever else they are in business for, union leaders are essentially preoccupied with securing real wage increases. Real wages had fallen in 1976 and fallen sharply in 1977. Attributed to government policy, this aroused understandable resentment among trade unionists. Yet a new wage limit of 5 per cent for 1978–9 was introduced when prices were rising at around 9 per cent.[17] As Andrew Thorpe comments in his chapter in *The High Tide*: 'To most informed observers, the new limit seemed utterly unrealistic.'[18] Faced with further initiatives to control wages, trade unionists, often far from militant, responded with industrial action to an inflationary situation which was not of their making and over which they possessed little control.[19]

In explaining rank-and-file action, McIlroy and Campbell stated (although not in direct reference to 1978–9), that 'economic rationality provides a plausible explanatory starting point'.[20] But not, we hasten to add, a concluding point. Politics is part of the business of union leaders and union leadership requires relating wage policy to other issues including the social wage, public expenditure and the welfare state. By 1978, although there was as always differentiation within the unions, the trade-off between the pay packet and the social wage was deteriorating; the turn to monetarism supervised by the Chancellor, Dennis Healy, was emerging. Fundamentally, in terms of what happened the union leaders of 1978–9 were neither autocrats nor simply conduit pipes for their members' aspirations. There are always limits to the most vigorous leadership over wages in economic organizations which, to one degree or another, acknowledge the demands of democracy and which were at the time relatively fragmented and often decentralized as far as decision-making and action went.[21]

The firm smack of government of Bevin, Deakin and Lawther resounds nostalgically from the 1930s through the 1950s. But those were different times and different unions. The writ of the grandees of the past was perhaps more contested than Morgan allows. Moreover, as Thorpe observes of Morgan's contemporary exemplar, Jack Jones, by 1977 he 'had no choice but to back away from the kind of "one-way" incomes policy which came to dominate the scene after 1976'.[22] Ultimately he had to accept the mandate of the TGWU conference. In the end, despite some politicking, he had to respect his members' rejection of wage controls. Evans was more sceptical about government policy; the constraints of union democracy were again paramount.

Trade unionists are not, as far as we are concerned, above criticism. The Labour government had its achievements and it was operating within the rigours of the changing world economy and intensifying international competition. But explanation – and judgement – of the 'Winter of Discontent' has to start with the policy of that government and its leaders and the choices made by Callaghan and his Cabinet in the troubled context of 1978, as well as the difficult inheritance of the earlier 1970s. Our understanding is not greatly furthered by interdictions against 'over mighty unions' and the 'irresponsibility' of union leaders who failed to impose their will against their members' wishes.[23]

Morgan asserts that McIlroy and Campbell 'attempt to deny that the Winter of Discontent … had much impact on the unions' reputation. They also believe that the poll evidence that Labour could handle the unions better half justifies the strikes …'.[24] We refer readers to what we wrote. The episode, we emphatically concluded, 'undoubtedly played a role in the Conservative victory at the polls'.[25] But rigorous explanation needs to register the nuances. If the 'Winter of Discontent' was in itself the unique, transformative agent of much mythology and not a little history, it is difficult to understand why, in April 1979, Labour once more headed the Conservatives in the polls. It is hard to comprehend why, during the election campaign itself, Labour was still judged more capable than the Conservatives of handling the unions.[26] And if Morgan consults the contributions which he claims refute our views, he will discover that he is mistaken: they do not dissent from our comments and conclusions.[27]

* * * * *

Specific strictures apart, the only largely hostile review of the two volumes came from the journalist John Lloyd.[28] It was embedded in reflection on the decline of the trade unionism he had reported on as an industrial correspondent during the 1980s. It is, he contends, a reverse for which the unions bear a significant share of the blame.[29] Within this problematic, Lloyd is exercised by our critical probing of New Labour's mythmaking about the trade unionism of the 1960s and 1970s. He overlooks our rider: '… we should remain alert to the recrudescence of currently less influential left-wing fables such as the inevitability, despite everything that has happened, of the revival of labour's progress or the essential, if presently invisible, revolutionary instincts of the rank and file trade unionist.'[30]

All history, Lloyd pronounces, is partisan and 'the majority' of the essays in these two volumes are not only 'militantly partisan' but further a particular political agenda.[31] This verdict is at odds with the judgements of other reviewers. One of them recognised 'a disparate group of labour historians, political scientists, management studies and industrial relations specialists'.[32] Another registered 'the diversity of approach and coverage in the contributions'.[33] The latter approved the editors' restraint in declining to produce a directed text 'smoothed for consistency'.[34] A glance at the contributors and what they have written here and elsewhere sustains this assessment. They hold different views in relation to history and politics: if they are united, it is only, in differing degrees, by their critical, sometimes very critical, advocacy of trade unionism.

In a broader sense Lloyd is repeating a commonplace of historiography: the values, preconceptions and politics of the historian are there in the writing of history, in selection, analysis and evaluation. Reconstruction inevitably includes an element of construction. Perhaps, as Lloyd claims, a critical stance towards New Labour (or, in Lloyd's case, a supportive stance) may influence matters. We measure this by the extent to which the historian's product, whatever the historian's commitments, passes the scholarly tests of evidence, interpretation and analysis. Here Lloyd is less than convincing. His assertions are rarely encumbered by evidence and sometimes elide history. Take this example: '… the unions again and again spurned the opportunity, in whatever guise it was offered, to take any responsibility for production, or to be party to any agreement in which a Labour government would plan output and growth.'[35]

Quite apart from the evasive grandiloquence, 'responsibility for production', something that was never on offer, this is caricature. A terse correction might go: the evidence discloses that between 1964 and 1966 trade unionists agreed to support Harold Wilson's National Plan, the National Economic Development Council (NEDC), the work of the National Prices and Incomes Board and the government's proffered 'planned growth of incomes'. Whatever their divisions, deficiencies – in terms of the structures of collective bargaining and trade unionism– and doubts, they supported government projects for planning prices, profits, wages, income and wealth. Blown off course in 1966, the government placed deflation and statutory control over pay, at the expense of control over prices, profits and redistribution, at the centre of economic management. Planned growth of incomes dwindled into rhetoric; consensual restraint transmuted into coercion. Recent research perhaps goes too far in contending that confusion in the government over the purpose of incomes policy was more important than the response of trade unions and employers and that by 1970 'there were very few proponents of wage and price control left within government'.[36]

In opposition the unions worked closely with Labour's leadership to produce the Social Contract strategy. Between 1974 and 1976 it had its successes, particularly with pay restraint. Again a sterling crisis struck and again radical designs were deserted. The 1975 Industry Act, the National Enterprise Board, planning agreements, redistribution of income and wealth – in sum the radical edge of Labour's strategy – were overshadowed by emphasis on wage controls, fiscal rectitude, tightening of public expenditure and a turn to monetarism. Union leaders continued to cooperate. But by 1978 pressure from below rendered this precarious. Some opportunities were in retrospect disregarded, notably Lord Bullock's proposals on industrial democracy. But that was 1977–1978 not 1974 or 1964. Despite helpful reforms, the overarching reality that trade unionists ultimately faced in 1964–70 and again in 1974–9 was downward pressure on wages from governments retreating from radicalism.[37]

A not uncritical reviewer acknowledged: '… as Dave Lyddon points out in an essay that sets out to rescue the 1972 high point of militancy from inaccurate accounts by lazy historians, what deserves our attention is at least as much that "glorious summer" as the all too often remembered "winter of discontent" seven years later.'[38] Lloyd, in contrast, takes exception to Lyddon's admiration for the militancy of 1972. This does not take us very far. Those of a different persuasion may object to Lloyd's aversion to it. Unlike Hinton, Lloyd takes issue with Lyddon's criticism of the depiction of key events of the 1970s by politicians, union leaders and 'lazy historians'. The difference is that Lyddon provides quotation and citation of 'inaccuracies': Lloyd does not.[39]

One reviewer felt that: 'The excellent survey chapters make the editors' case for the need for far more detailed narrative work on the post-war period. The accounts here are balanced and reflective.'[40] Another declared that both surveys 'nicely provide an integrative core and balance to the broad and diverse concerns of other contributors'.[41] Lloyd again disagrees. The only evidence he deploys to explain his dissent is a single sentence from McIlroy and Campbell's survey, 'The High Tide', to the effect that incomes policies were generally temporary expedients centred on wage restraint while their articulation with prices, profits, the social wage and the redistribution of income and wealth was slight and rhetorical.[42] Lloyd claims this as evidence for the view, which he again attributes to the majority of contributors, that Labour governments 'were never serious about running a corporatist policy'.[43] The sentiments in our sentence are, he asserts, not substantiated elsewhere in the text; indeed, they are, he believes, contradicted in the essays by Thorpe and Andrew Taylor and Robert Taylor in the same volume.[44]

The test of the seriousness of Labour governments is what they did, or what they assiduously endeavoured to do, in terms of developing corporatism. The pages from which Lloyd extracts McIlroy and Campbell's sentence detail, with extensive reference, how incomplete and fragile corporatist initiatives in Britain were. These pages remark on successive governments' attention to controlling labour at the expense of controlling capital, the absence of any *dirigiste* National Economic Forum or National Economic Assessment with teeth, and the inadequacies of the NEDC as an instrument of decision-making and intervention. They go on to note that both employers and unions were ill-equipped to play a viable part in long-term, strategic concertation; and they record that by the end of the period capital was moving away from corporatist solutions to its problems.[45]

Thorpe certainly, as Lloyd suggests, opens his account with the pronouncement that in 1974, '... there was an explicit commitment that pay restraint would not be a one-way street'.[46] But Thorpe then rehearses Labour's policies on the social wage before concluding that the cuts and fiscal stance adopted in autumn 1976 'effectively marked the end of the government side of the Social Contract ... the restraint of income growth would provide more of a priority than ever. In this sense *incomes policy once again became a one-way street ...*'[47] (emphasis added). Andrew Taylor does indeed observe that in 1972 the Conservative Prime Minister Edward Heath attempted to draw the unions into corporatism. But he adds: '... the Industrial Relations Act and the TUC's insistence on statutory price control and voluntary pay restraint remained insuperable obstacles to an agreement.'[48] This was not the spurning of an opportunity. In the prevailing circumstances union leaders could do little else: the Act was an insuperable obstacle of Heath's making. Robert Taylor, Lloyd's third supposed witness, has nothing of substance to say on the matter. While Taylor does not exonerate union leaders he presents a rather more nuanced account of their difficulties quite distinct from simplistic 'the unions were to blame' paradigms.[49]

Trade unionists wielded restricted, reactive, fragmented, largely negative, power over the market, which they were unable to co-ordinate and develop into positive political power over the state. They cannot be artificially extrapolated from the matrix of inter-relating actors and interactive pressures configuring the crisis of the labour movement in the late 1970s and 1980s, still less conjured into a major contributory factor for the decline of collectivism at the expense of more qualitatively powerful protagonists. To take a further step and blend explanation with blame compounds the error. James Hinton's review endorses one message of our books in providing an antidote to the 'it's largely the unions' fault' approach: 'The most important explanations of the inability of the unions to translate their growing power into structural reform lie with the state and capital – forces beyond their control and largely beyond the brief of these volumes. Labor governments proceeded on the basis of incomes policy devised as short-term crisis management rather than any fundamental thinking about the refashioning of the state.'[50] As Brian Towers, another reviewer, put it: 'it is laying "very rough hands on history", as the late and much missed Henry Phelps Brown would have said, to find villainy in only one place.'[51]

* * * * *

Our purpose in these volumes was to record the marginal as well as the mainstream. In that context we readily concede the point made by Hinton that we could have made more room for discussion of the 'new social movements', which emerged from the late 1960s.[52] Vietnam, the peace movement, what became the green movement, the women's liberation movement, the Working Women's Charter Campaign, the National Abortion Campaign, a range of movements centred on sexual orientation, black consciousness, international solidarity, tenants' associations, theatre groups and alternative newspapers, all had an impact on contemporary trade unionism. They sometimes criss-crossed with union campaigns and initiatives, such as the workers' alternative plans discussed by Richard Hyman in his 'Afterword' to *The High Tide of British Trade Unionism*.[53] They enriched, sometimes belatedly, aspects of trade unionism. The women's movement, particularly its more radical varieties, laid the basis for growing consciousness of the diversity of oppression in the unions and their extensive institutional restructuring to counter inequality in the last years of the century. As Chris Wrigley concludes in his chapter on women in the same volume, external forces stimulated internal change.[54]

In this sense the women's movement was 'a social force'. As a movement – diffuse, disparate, minimally organized – it existed on a different plane to organized labour which arguably offered the best arena for pressing and realising its demands. Like trade unionism, social movements have their limits. Nor can oppression based on gender or ethnicity –significant as this is, it remains patterned by class – in itself stand convincing comparison with class as a potential motor for transformative social change. Capitalism can never terminate, although it may ameliorate, class exploitation. It can and it has assimilated movements based on gender and ethnicity.[55]

In the writing of labour and social history there is, as we noted in our 1999 introduction to these volumes, a deficit in work on gender and ethnicity. Hinton's view that in repairing it class analysis and gender analysis should be seen as 'complementary' is imprecise and may be perceived as denying the ultimate paramountcy of class as an analytical tool and conciliating identity history. In his recent writing, Hinton is similarly reticent: 'Much recent scholarship has been concerned to downgrade the explanatory power of the concept of class …

xxii

the category of gender cannot usefully be given precedence over the category of class ... if class was gendered then gender was also "classed".'[56] Certainly they interact. But which category is analytically prior? The task, surely, is to structure the intersections and integrate gender into the concept of class.[57]

Several reviewers recognised and endorsed our desire to examine the post-war years on their own terms. We wanted to convey how things were then for actors whose formative experiences stretched even further back into the past, men and women who did things differently in the topography of 'a foreign country'. This was a reaction to narratives in which 'the period has typically been viewed as a necessary preface to the demise of the British labour movement'.[58] We wanted to avoid teleologies and meta-narratives, whether of the 'irresistible rise and rise of neo-liberalism' or 'the forward march of labour halted' genre, in which the downfall of the unions in the 1980s was largely determined by the events of the post-war period. Partly because of this we essayed terse counterfactuals. Rejecting pristine and conservative conceptions of balance and relevance, utility and public policy, we included essays on the Communist Party and the Trotskyists. History is about the losers as well as the winners.

Nonetheless, we glanced towards the future in assessing the strengths and weaknesses of trade unionism in 1979. So did several of our contributors, on whom no particular approach was incumbent. Despite this, Colin Crouch, who acknowledged 'it is not the primary task of the authors ... to provide answers to how what was in 1945 arguably the world's most important trade union movement, came to such a pass',[59] and Mike Terry, both suggested the need for further consideration of the direction which trade unionism was taking in 1979, and whether and how the impasse of the late 1970s 'paved the way for the 1980s'.[60]

It is important to re-emphasise that what happened in the 1980s depended crucially on the circumstances and struggles of that decade and can only be understood through a proper historical account of that decade. It is a truism that Thatcherism was neither *ab initio* a fully fledged ideology nor a *blitzkrieg*: it represented, despite preparations, increasingly confident groping towards a new politics; it developed and unfolded incrementally in sustained engagement with the labour movement; it was different in 1989 than in 1979; and it was never fully coherent. The reverses unions suffered occurred on the terrain of that decade, on territory newly treacherous to trade unionism, reconfigured by economic policy, large-scale unemployment, industrial restructuring, the increasing marginalization of the Labour Party and the Falklands War. They had more to do with the printworkers' dispute of 1982 than the strikes of 1972, more to do, even more crucially, with the miners' strike of 1984–5 than the miners' strike of 1974.[61] The recent past remained relevant. So, too, did the more distant past and *la longue durée* of British industrial relations, a largely evolutionary trajectory which the state was increasingly determined to rupture.[62]

It is important to recognise the elements of truth in the arguments, most powerfully proposed by Colin Crouch, that as the 1970s moved to their turbulent close, the potential of existing trade union ideologies of mission and mobilisation was becoming exhausted.[63] Like others, we have been educated by subsequent experience. We understand to a far greater degree than we did the complexities and limitations of industrial struggle within never to be underestimated capitalisms as well as the inadequacy of much that once passed for radicalism and militancy as a road to socialist change. We appreciate the need for deeper, more extensive, transformative ideological shifts as a condition for progress and the necessity for greater control and co-ordination within the labour movement, as well as critical but ambitious engagement with the state. We can learn but we cannot go back. And some of these arguments appear pessimistic in relation to the 1970s, overly informed and sometimes flawed by hindsight and backward projection of what we know now. If we compare British trade unionism at that time with its position both earlier and later in the twentieth century, it is difficult to agree (without over-estimating their influence) that unions were already Emperors with no clothes.[64]

There was unity and class consciousness as well as fragmentation, solidarity as well as sectionalism. In 1979 British trade unionism was, in one sense, moving in the direction of a stronger, more inclusive collectivism, better able to provide, albeit still inadequate, protection to workers against the vicissitudes of an inequitable, exploitative class society. If restricted, variable and contingent, its reach, its legitimacy, its social presence, measured by membership, density, legislation and access to government, its potential to mobilize its members and its ability to bargain successfully with the state, were greater than at any other time in its history. What was in question was its structure, its purpose, its politics, and the nature of its power, as well as its impact on capital and profit levels.

Post-war labourism and post-war trade unionism tried but failed to secure a satisfactory trade-off between planning capitalism efficiently, voluntarism and 'free collective bargaining'. The results, an uneasy mix of flaking collective *laisser-faire* and incomplete corporatism, were increasingly viewed as stifling economic regeneration. Strong, uncoordinated collective bargaining was seen as economically dysfunctional. Trade unionism was increasingly perceived as generating inflation, constricting the freedom of business and the market, and obstructing government. Its specific strengths and weaknesses are outlined in the survey chapter in *The High Tide of British Trade Unionism*.[65] The latter were differently elaborated by other contributors, particularly by Richard Hyman in his 'Afterword'.[66]

They ranged from problems of sectional bargaining, organization and consciousness, failure to develop structures and strategies of co-ordination adequate to articulate either successful antagonism or political exchange with the state, the unevenness of militancy, its tensions with concertation and its singular failure to produce substantial political radicalisation, to the enrolment of members, often by management in closed shops, rather than the ideological making of trade unionists, and the brittleness of solidarity between them. They included incapacity to effectively link the trade union and Labour Party left, take industrial democracy and new forms of workers' control over production sufficiently seriously, and appreciate the significance of internationalism and Europe.

Both strengths and weaknesses must be weighed within an understanding of the nature and historic limits of British trade unionism: it has been an agency of real but circumscribed class cohesion, an agency of real but restricted social change.[67] And they must be assessed in the context of the power of the state and capital and their historic inhibitions about strategic co-ordination, inhibitions which could not be reassured by the confused choreography of concertation during the 1960s and 1970s. There developed increasing awareness among elite opinion makers, employers and politicians beyond the ranks of Conservatism that it was time to turn from the post-war compromise, time to turn instead towards the liberation of the corporation and the remaking of the market, time to turn towards privatization, deregulation and globalization.[68]

If the debilities of the trade unions pre-Thatcher played a role in the events of the 1980s, they did not play a primary role. The leading actors in the drama were not trade unionists but politicians and capitalists. We also recorded that by 1979 management was harvesting the fruits of more strategic approaches to regaining control of the workplace, formalizing single-employer bargaining at company and enterprise level, weakening union workplace organization and eroding the sinews of mobilization.[69] It was moving away from its never powerful belief in co-ordination, and even employer coalitions, towards freedom and company autonomy. The prolonged crisis of planning, the faltering corporatist experiment, the periodic challenges to the state, the pressure on profits, the resilience, unpredictability and economic consequences of fragmented collective bargaining, recurring stagflation: all of this, in the context of Britain's decline in a changing world economy, made strong trade unionism appear a liability. Politically packaged, this perspective influenced the turn to Thatcherism and the construction of consent.

It was, in retrospect, the moment of neo-liberalism, just as 1945 had been the moment of social democracy. We must not lose sight of national particularities and national tempos as one kind of international capitalism turns into another. But 'future historians may well look upon the years 1978–80 as a revolutionary turning point in the world's social and economic history'.[70] Few saw it then.[71]

Suitably amplified, the problems of post-war trade unionism stimulated change. They did not help in combating it, although the resistance of the 1980s should not be passed over lightly. Without disregarding the necessity for a detailed history of the period, what was ultimately involved was perhaps something more fundamental: the fragility of trade unionism nurtured by a collectivist, consensual state when confronted by capitalist restructuring and a hostile, confrontationist, market-oriented state. In the 1960s and 1970s, myth maintained that significant curtailment of trade unionism was too costly: it had to be moulded, integrated or for some placated. As the 1980s demonstrated, that only went for the social democratic state, for the post-war compromise, for a certain balance of class forces, for a relatively benign attitude towards collectivism and coercion.

Conservative neo-liberalism 'affirmed that in the twentieth century as in the nineteenth, it has proved immensely difficult – perhaps impossible – for organized labour to defeat a strategic attack led by the state which fused politics and economics in an extended, sophisticated assault.'[72] The degree to which British trade unionism had been fostered by the state became apparent as the state withdrew support and legitimacy. This is not to deprecate the creative power of workers' self-activity. It is rather to acknowledge that agency operates in contexts facilitative or constrictive, to judge that in the face of neo-liberalism British trade unionism was 'confirmed as the bearer of a secondary, derivative, negative, limited power, severely circumscribed by economic change and state initiatives'.[73]

* * * * *

Since 1999 a variety of texts relevant to the history of post-war trade unionism have appeared.[74] Popular histories still arguably pay inadequate attention to the subject despite its contemporary significance. Dominic Sandbrook's *Never Had It So Good* is very much in tune with current pre-occupations, with cultural history of the popular kind and representations mixed with a dash of high politics.[75] Most of the relatively little it has to say about trade unionism is drawn from popular contemporary sources while it has rather a lot to say about *I'm All Right, Jack,* admittedly a marvellous film. The same goes, on the whole, for Sandbrook's engaging companion volume dealing with 'the swinging sixties', while Peter Hennessy's fascinating history of the 1950s is also relatively restrained on trade unions.[76]

Three general surveys of trade union history have been published. Chris

Wrigley's brief synopsis of the years since 1933 is effectively organized around issues such as strikes, incomes policies and legislation and is strong on the economic impact of trade unionism.[77] In contrast, Hamish Fraser traverses the three centuries from 1700. This is well-researched, accessible, empirical history, enlivened by examples from Scotland, which centres on collective bargaining and industry sometimes at the expense of the unions' political role. Some forty-three pages are devoted to 1945–79 and this makes for broad sweep treatment, more descriptive than analytical, with occasional over-emphasis on 'restrictive practices' and unofficial strikes.[78]

Alistair Reid's *United We Stand* is the successor volume to Henry Pelling's durable *History of British Trade Unionism*: it covers developments from the late 1600s to the present in less than 450 pages.[79] Like Fraser, Reid is constrained by the difficulty of doing justice to three packed centuries in a single text. Moreover, his eschewal of Pelling's chronological approach and his attempt to separate out the stories of different types of trade unionists – contentiously defined – and narrate them sequentially, produces fragmentation, overlap and sometimes neglect of the commonality and centrality of key episodes. Reid's examination of post-war events can be cursory. *In Place of Strife* and the struggles around the Industrial Relations Act 1971 each receive a couple of paragraphs and the miners' strikes of 1972 and 1974 take up a couple of pages in total.[80] His attempt to rehabilitate moderation and bread-and-butter trade unionism amongst the alarums and excitements of mobilization is laudable if occasionally intrusive. It is a truism that trade unionism reflects a variety of goals and is, in essence, neither militant nor moderate. At times authorial antipathy towards the struggles and socialist alignments which co-existed with, and in certain periods transcended, acquiescence, ensures that co-operation is emphasised against conflict.[81]

The field of industrial relations continues to benefit from the work of scholars in adjacent disciplines. The political scientist Chris Howell has written an important overview of the role of the state in British industrial relations.[82] Revising conventional accounts of state abstention, voluntarism and collective *laisser-faire*, Howell rehabilitates the interventionist role of the state from the cautious initiatives of the 1890s through Whitley and Donovan to neo-liberalism. He highlights the importance of the institutions the state created in constituting industrial relations systems, if not their outcomes. The corporatist experiment – is it more useful, as Howell does, to see it as a distinctive system or regime, rather than a tendency within, although pushing against, the limits of the regime of collective *laisser-faire*? – broke down because of its contradictions. The state's strategic sponsoring of trade unionism was increasingly perceived as dysfunctional in terms of economic efficiency and productivity and, as international competition intensified, employers turned to undermine both corporatism and collective bargaining. By depriving trade unionism of its props, they demonstrated that its autonomous strength had been exaggerated. We made similar points earlier.

Explorations of trade unionism need to transcend the conventional treatment of the state by industrial relations scholars: they should consider its role in legitimation and coercion and, pertinently here, taxation, social security and welfare regimes. This is one of the numerous lessons reinforced by reading Simon Deakin and Frank Wilkinson's imposing *Law of the Labour Market.*[83] A labour lawyer and labour economist respectively, their book represents a wide-ranging synthesis which, like Howell's work, foregrounds the creative role that the state and social regulation have played, in interaction with private regulation, in developing the role of the market and influencing industrial relations. Focusing on the historical development of the contract of employment, they examine the interplay of labour law, the welfare state and collective bargaining in the formation of employment relations. They stress the limitations of collective bargaining in terms of trade union objectives, wider economic planning and counter-inflation policy, and eschew both neo-liberal policies and the lost world of corporatism in favour of a middle way, a system of social rights which far from impairing market regulation can complement it.

In a different vein, the industrial relations academics Ralph Darlington and Dave Lyddon have extended the latter's study of that *annus mirabilis* of militancy, 1972, in *The High Tide of British Trade Unionism*, into a meticulously detailed, book-length account of events. If some will question its emphasis on rank-and-file activism and belief in militancy as a precursor or necessary component of class-based political action, it provides a valuable addition to the literature on strikes and strike strategy.[84] Paul Smith's research into road haulage has resulted in an impressive study of the evolution of industrial relations at national and local level illuminated by analysis of theories of trade unionism. For our purposes it is particularly useful on the 'Winter of Discontent'. Like much work in industrial relations it is underpeopled.[85] The political scientist Andrew Taylor writes top-down, institutional history. His two volumes on the National Union of Mineworkers (NUM) shed new light on the experience of nationalization and the impact of state policy, NUM policy, the development of factionalism and the important internal as well as the significant external conflicts of the 1960s and 1970s.[86] Keith Gildart's volume on the tiny North Wales coalfield usefully rounds out our knowledge of miners' activities in the regions during the post-war years.[87]

Understanding the development of the TUC is indispensable to comprehending the reconstruction of collective *laisser-faire* after 1945, the detail of the post-war compromise and the burgeoning of corporatism from the early 1960s. Building on his analysis of George Woodcock in *The High Tide of British Trade Unionism*, Robert Taylor has provided us with an extended, accessible analysis of TUC initiatives throughout the period. Replete with shrewd and vivid portraits of protagonists, it is perhaps stronger on the conflicts of the later years.[88]

The advent of New Labour provoked a spate of publications, some of which interrogated its antecedents, and this was reinforced by a number of books published to mark the party's centenary. Recent scholarship on the Labour Party sometimes suffers from a constriction of focus. It is difficult to deny that the trade unions were part of the marrow of labourism or that trade unionists were key actors in the party. It is, consequently, hard to understand why some of these volumes treat trade unionism in perfunctory fashion. There is nothing of substance about it in the history of the Labour Party in Wales while in *Labour's First Century* a few pages in a single chapter cover the period 1945–79, a time when trade unionism constituted an unavoidable landmark in the landscapes of labourism, not to speak of the wider polity.[89] Despite the centrality of 'the trade union question' to the concerns of the Wilson administrations, a recent three-volume history of the 1964–70 Labour governments contains sparse address of trade unions and their links with the party.[90] Its revisionist claims to rehabilitate the limited achievements of the Wilson administrations in economic policy may have some merit. They are questionable with regard to industrial relations.[91]

The more comprehensive centenary volume edited by Brian Brivati and Richard Heffernan has a valuable chapter on 1945–64 and a slighter survey of the rest of the century.[92] The position may be different today but in the 1950s and 1960s trade unionism was an integral part of the culture of the left. Nonetheless, a recent monograph on the subject has scarcely anything to say about it.[93] In contrast, James Cronin makes a valiant attempt to integrate analysis of the unions' role into his assessments of the Wilson and Callaghan governments. He emphasises the extent to which moving away from the intractabilities of 'the contentious alliance' with the unions, perceived as antagonistic to winning elections, good policy and good government, distancing the party from the unions and repudiating class, was central to defining the New Labour project. Cronin provides insightful reading on the economic dilemmas, the incomes policies and the confrontations over legislation of the post-war years.[94]

The final two volumes of the 'official' history of the Communist Party add to the detail of the industrial politics of the period,[95] although there has been little new on Trotskyism.[96] Attention to factional organization and the political process in trade unions[97] and the role of political activists in the unions and the workplace,[98] has been sustained, but slight. In terms of serious investigation of the circumstances that mould militants and militancy, make moderates and moderation, the literature remains vestigial and undeveloped. The influences that created activism in different periods, the forces that maintain or transform the trajectories of individual activists, the interactions and tensions between their union activities and their political allegiances, require further exploration.[99] We need more biographies, more prosopographies and greater address of the varieties of militancy and moderation as well as the attitudes towards them of union members. Conventional biographies continue to appear in abundance. In contrast with the multiplying lives of politicians – Clement Attlee, Harold Macmillan, Barbara Castle, Wilson, Heath, Callaghan, Michael Foot – extended studies of union leaders, let alone activists, have remained at a premium.[100] However the *Dictionary of Labour Biography* maintains its useful role.[101]

* * * * *

This brief survey suggests that, whatever its difficulties, the history of labour and industrial politics remains very much alive. We conclude with a plea for breadth, range and historical imagination in research and writing, and recognition of values as well as acknowledgement of variety and commonality in trade unionism. An emphasis on industrial politics, as we suggested in our 1999 introduction, requires an inter-disciplinary approach. Historians are often at their best when they work across boundaries and synthesize the insights of different fields and disciplines. If the labour movement has often seemed a pallid simulacrum of what the words conjure up, the term is suggestive of the integration necessary in historical writing about industrial politics. To take one example, in telling the story of the Labour Party, historians cannot, at least not with any conviction, treat trade unionism as playing a minor part nor can they treat it as a monolith: they need to address trade unionism and its complexities and divisions as an integral aspect of the party narrative. What is connected should not be sundered.

Eric Hobsbawm remarked, '... *even the recorded past* changes in the light of subsequent history.'[102] (original emphasis) Some of the studies discussed above were written in the context of the emergence of New Labour, a development which has led historians to reconsider Labour's past. If for some the triumphant advent of New Labour represented, like Hobsbawm's illustration, the collapse of the Soviet Union, the closure of an historic period or 'the strange death of social democracy', others stressed its continuity with earlier phases of labourism and Labour's links with liberalism.[103]

Caution may be in order. If there are continuities between today and yesterday – and the Labour Party and the trade unions have unquestionably reinvented aspects of their ideology, politics and political practice throughout their history

– New Labour may be persuasively represented as a novel reaction to a novel context, the brave new world of neo-liberalism. To assimilate recent innovation to the liberalism or even the revisionism of Labour's past risks entering the realm of the ahistorical.[104] It may also be premature: how rooted is 'Blairism'? Is Old Labour dead and gone, with Nye Bevan in the grave? An evanescent present can be an unreliable guide to such questions. Those who prophesied a renewal of the radical Liberalism of the early twentieth century, the dissolution of the party's alliance with the unions and the success of Tony Blair, already have much to think about.[105]

But looking at the past with an eye on the present is not, as Herbert Butterfield had it, the greatest of all historical sins.[106] Current pre-occupations can be a stimulus to reconstructing the past and informing us about the present. So long as we accept that the past possesses its own integrity. If we impose our vision of the present onto the past we run the risk of violating that integrity. Historians should travel across time as well as across boundaries. They should treat the past on its own terms. If we employ historical imagination to reconstruct it, rather than too easily understanding it in terms of today and ransacking it for contemporary parallels, lessons may still emerge. They are likely to be complex, conditional, contingent and contradictory.

Relevance is contested and changing. What some perceive as relevant today may not have been perceived as relevant yesterday nor appear relevant tomorrow.[107] Acknowledgement of forgotten movements and lost causes, recognition of the Digger, the Leveller, the stockinger, the handloom weaver, is more than antiquarian whimsy: it is a central aspect of the heritage of labour and social history. In the same spirit, the casual docker, the aristocratic tool-room worker, the black-coated clerk, the female sewing machinist, the black bus conductor and the Trotskyist militant of the post-war period, demand rescue from the condescension of posterity and, in some cases, the twenty-first century historian.[108]

For the wheel turns bringing new fashions, new professional cultures, new academic networks, new gatekeepers.[109] This may militate against certain subjects and certain approaches. One wonders how the work of Edward Thompson, Eric Hobsbawm, Christopher Hill and John Saville would be received if it was published for the first time today.[110] A fair assessment would honour its breadth, its analytical insight and its vindication of the use of an open and creative Marxism. Contemporary critics are worried by its teleological aspects, the socialist values which impregnate it and their impact on subsequent historians of labour.[111] Reappraisal is healthy and history should not ultimately be measured against what ought to have happened, whatever we think that should have been. But all historians mediate between themselves, their readers and the 'facts'. Evaluation is not exclusive to socialist historians. It is inescapable.[112] The temptation to depict assessments, which employ criteria that we find disagreeable, as illegitimate intrusions into the province of the value-free historian may miss the point in making a partisan point. Commitments, conceptions of progress, yardsticks of one kind or another are pervasive. They can be creative if open to scrutiny, conscious and controlled. If we remember this then the history of labour may possess not only a path breaking past but a vibrant future.

Notes

This paperback edition has been produced using images of the original pages published in 1999.
Place of publication is London unless otherwise indicated.

1   A. Campbell, N. Fishman and J. McIlroy (eds), *The Post-War Compromise: British trade unions and industrial politics, 1945–64* (2007) first published by Ashgate as A. Campbell, N. Fishman and J. McIlroy (eds), *British Trade Unions and Industrial Politics, vol. 1: the post-war compromise, 1945–64* (Aldershot, 1999); J. McIlroy, N. Fishman and A. Campbell (eds). *The High Tide of British Trade Unionism: trade unions and industrial politics, 1964–79* (2007) first published by Ashgate as J. McIlroy, N. Fishman and A. Campbell (eds), *British Trade Unions and Industrial Politics, vol. 2: the high tide of trade unionism, 1964–79* (Aldershot, 1999).

2   N. Kirk, review, *International Labor and Working-Class History*, 63, 2003, p. 166.

3   A. Fowler, review, *Historical Studies in Industrial Relations*, 9, 2000, pp. 171, 175.

4   C. Crouch, 'Once upon a time, trade unions …', *Political Quarterly*, 71, 2000, p. 362.

5   M. Terry, review, *Historical Studies in Industrial Relations*, 11, 2001, pp. 148, 155. See also the reviews by I. Aitken, 'New Labour may not like us …', *Guardian*, 26 April 2000, J. Tomlinson, 'Rough and tumble on the shop floor', *The Times Higher Education Supplement*, 29 September 2000, R. Darlington in *Socialist Review*, January 2001 and H. Ratner in *Revolutionary History*, 8, 2, 2002. See also *Labour Research*, May 2000.

6   E. Hobsbawm, 'Afterword', in Campbell *et al.*, *Post-War Compromise*, p. 314, and J. McIlroy *et al.*, 'Introduction: approaching post-war trade unionism', p. 13.

7   K. O. Morgan, review, *Labour History Review*, 65, 3, 2000, p. 387.

8   Kirk, review, pp. 166–7 and T. Bergholm, review, *Scandinavian Economic History Review*, xlix, 2, 2001, p. 100

9   Cf Hobsbawm, 'Afterword'.

10 Morgan, review, p. 386. His distaste for the many index entries referring to the Communist Party and the Trotskyists is suggestive of the allegiance to top-down history and high politics evident in his published work.

11 J. McIlroy and A. Campbell, 'The high tide of trade unionism: mapping industrial politics, 1964–79' in McIlroy *et al.*, *High Tide*, pp. 116–18.

12 K. O. Morgan, *Callaghan: a life* (Oxford, 1997), pp. 626–76.

13 Ibid., p. 673.

14 Ibid., pp. 664, 657, 650, 672.

15 Ibid., pp. 343, 658.

16 Cf McIlroy and Campbell, 'High tide', p. 101.

17 Cf ibid., pp. 113 and 123, Table 4.4.

18 A. Thorpe, 'The Labour Party and the trade unions', in McIlroy *et al.*, *High Tide*, p. 145: '... it was to assert a fairly naked truth to argue that, for many workers, years of pay restraint had brought few real benefits and not a few costs ... This time there was no question of union agreement' (ibid.).

19 Cf McIlroy and Campbell, 'High tide', pp. 110–11.

20 Ibid., p. 110.

21 Cf The 5 per cent norm 'certainly put any trade union leader who wished to support government policy in an extremely difficult position. Few would have the authority to control the demands of their members to this degree and their position would be impossible if other union leaders had not even the will to support the policy' (D. Barnes and E. Reid, *Governments and Trade Unions: the British experience, 1964–79* (1980), p. 214).

22 Thorpe, 'Labour Party', p. 146.

23 Cf 'While the 1979 "winter of discontent" was certainly less decisive than is claimed by subsequent mythologies, there is little doubt that Callaghan's political miscalculations (which more than any "irresponsibility" on the part of union leaders or members, was, as Andrew Thorpe shows, largely responsible for the crisis) contributed to the Tories' eventual success ...' (J. Hinton, review, *Albion*, 33, 2, 2001, p. 357).

24 Morgan, review, p. 386.

25 McIlroy and Campbell, 'High tide', p. 117.

26 Ibid., pp. 117–8.

27 Cf Thorpe, 'Labour Party', pp. 145–7; A Taylor, 'The Conservative Party and the trade unions', in McIlroy *et al.*, *High Tide*, pp. 176–8 and p. 180, Table 6.2, which confirms that the indicators of the public esteem for trade unions recorded in opinion polls were the same in August 1977 as in August 1979. There is no reference to the 'Winter of Discontent', let alone refutation of McIlroy and Campbell's views, in R. Taylor, '"What are we here for?" George Woodcock and trade union reform', in McIlroy *et al.*, *High Tide*, although they take issue with some of the comments he has made elsewhere – see McIlroy and Campbell, 'High tide', pp. 116–17.

28 J. Lloyd, 'All together now', *London Review of Books*, 19 October 2000. Lloyd commends Nina Fishman's chapters in *Post-War Compromise* and appears to exclude from censure those by Geoffrey Goodman (ibid.), Alan McKinlay and Joseph Melling (ibid.) and Robert Taylor (*High Tide*) and to some extent that of Mike Savage (ibid.).

29 Lloyd states that the contention 'that it was the unions' own fault – contains something of the truth ... organised labour bears part of the responsibility for its

own marginalisation' (Lloyd, 'All together now', pp. 32–3). But the thrust of his essay indicts the unions and nowhere does he refer to any other actor or any other factor as playing a part in union decline.

30 McIlroy *et al.*, 'Introduction', p. 2.

31 Lloyd, 'All together now', p. 33.

32 B. Towers, review, *Industrial Relations Journal*, 32, 4, 2001, p. 349.

33 E. Sullivan, 'Chronicling labour: recent writings', *Journal of Contemporary History*, 40, 2, 2005, p. 402.

34 Ibid., pp. 402–3. Cf 'Most tastes are well catered for': Kirk, review, p. 166.

35 Lloyd, 'All together now', p. 32.

36 G. O'Hara, '"Planned growth of incomes" or "emergency gimmick": the Labour Party, the social partners and incomes policy, 1964–70', *Labour History Review*, 69, 1, 2004, p. 59. O'Hara's insistence that 'agreement was fleeting mainly because the Labour Party in government was uncertain in its theoretical outlook as to what prices and incomes policy was actually for' and that in assessing policy failure this confusion was 'just as important as the structure of British capital, industrial relations and labour politics' (ibid., pp. 61, 62) remains unconvincing.

37 See Thorpe, 'Labour Party', pp. 133–50; see also L. Panitch, *Social Democracy and Industrial Militancy: the Labour Party, the trade unions and incomes policy, 1945–74* (Cambridge, 1976); Barnes and Reid, *Governments and Trade Unions*; D. Coates, *Labour in Power?: a study of the Labour Government, 1974–79* (1980); J. Cronin, *Labour and Society in Britain, 1918–79* (1984), pp. 193–205; D. Coates, *The Crisis of Labour: industrial relations and the state in contemporary Britain* (1989), pp. 37–159; J. McIlroy, *Trade Unions in Britain Today* (2nd edn, Manchester, 1995), pp. 186–207; P. Bell, *The Labour Party in Opposition, 1970–74* (2003); J. E. Cronin, *New Labour's Pasts: the Labour Party and its discontents* (Harlow, 2004), pp. 1–202.

38 Hinton, review, p. 360.

39 Lloyd, 'All together now', p. 33; D. Lyddon, '"Glorious summer": the high tide of rank and file militancy', in McIlroy *et al.*, *High Tide*.

40 Towers, review, p. 349.

41 Kirk, review, p. 166.

42 McIlroy and Campbell, 'High tide', p. 96.

43 Lloyd, 'All together now', p. 33.

44 Ibid.

45 McIlroy and Campbell, 'High tide', pp. 96–7.

46 Thorpe, 'Labour Party', p. 142.

47 Ibid., p. 144.

48 Taylor, 'Conservative Party', p. 161.

49 Taylor, 'What are we here for?' Some of Lloyd's extensive engagements are with straw men: '… it's wrong to argue that the unions hadn't benefited from Labour legislation or that there was nothing to gain from further cooperation …' ('All together now', p. 33). It remains unclear whom he is arguing against. He also notes that Harold Wilson's 'National Dividend' of 1967 is not mentioned in our book and implies that the unions 'killed it off'(ibid., p. 32). Wilson's vague suggestion was for the long term (unlike his contemporary proposals for the statutory restriction

of wages) and met with immediate opposition from the Confederation of British Industry as well as the TUC. The latter deemed it 'administratively impractical' but nevertheless remained committed to voluntary wage vetting (*The Times*, 4, 6 March, 3 April 1967; Panitch, *Social Democracy*, pp. 141, 296, n.9).

50 Hinton, review, pp. 357–8.

51 Towers, review, p. 348.

52 Hinton, review, p. 359. And I readily concede Hinton's point that my dismissal was unduly peremptory given the 'admirably balanced commentaries' on other marginal movements (ibid.).

53 R. Hyman, 'Afterword', in McIlroy *et al.*, *High Tide*, p. 359.

54 C. Wrigley, 'Women in the labour market and in the unions', in McIlroy *et al.*, *High Tide*, pp. 60–1. But the distance of feminism then from feminism now may be evoked by reading S. Rowbotham, L. Segal and H. Wainwright, *Beyond the Fragments: feminism and the making of socialism* (1979).

55 For the contemporary relevance of class analysis from a range of perspectives, see E. Meiksins Wood, *Democracy Against Capitalism: renewing historical materialism* (Cambridge, 1995); G. Marshall, *Repositioning Class: social inequality in industrial societies* (1997); R. Crompton, *Class and Stratification: an introduction to current debates* (2nd edn, Cambridge, 1998); F. Devine *et al.*, *Rethinking Class: culture, identities, lifestyle* (Basingstoke, 2005). For discussions of gender, see, for example, A. Baron (ed.), *Work Engendered: towards a new history of American labor* (Ithaca, NY, 1991); A. Kessler-Harris, 'Treating the male as "other": redefining the parameters of labor history', *Labor History*, 34, 2/3, 1993, pp. 190–204.

56 J. Hinton, *Women, Social Leadership and the Second World War: continuities of class* (Oxford, 2002), p. 9.

57 Our doubts as to his position are intensified by Hinton's apparent rejection of class as a structure: 'It is not however my intention to reassert a foundational concept of class as a precursive reality structuring social and political life ... class was, amongst other things, a matter of identity' (ibid., p. 10).

58 McIlroy and Campbell, 'High tide', p. 113.

59 Crouch, review, p. 362.

60 Terry, review, p. 150.

61 For a brief summary see McIlroy, *Trade Unions in Britain Today*, particularly pp. 194–222.

62 See, for example, A. Fox, *History and Heritage: the social origins of the British industrial relations system* (1985).

63 Crouch, review, p. 63. This was, of course, the contemporary position of Hobsbawm although, as discussed in McIlroy *et al, High Tide,* his evidence was contentious.

64 Crouch, review, p. 364. He invokes Richard Hyman in support, quoting Hyman's observation that 'by the 1970s unions seem to have lost their former status as influential components of civil society'. Hyman, 'Afterword' p. 362 was referring specifically to England, and excluding Scotland and 'perhaps' Wales. Again, if we compare the 1970s with the rest of the century this judgement seems questionable.

65 McIlroy and Campbell, 'High tide', pp. 106–19.

66 R. Hyman, 'Afterword'. pp. 355–9; see also Thorpe, 'Labour Party', pp. 142–7.

67 For a recent discussion, see P. Smith, *Union Organization and Union Leadership: The Road Haulage Industry* (2001), pp. 7–30.

68 G. Duménil and D. Lévy, *Capital Resurgent: roots of the neo-liberal revolution* (Cambridge, Mass., 2004); D. Harvey, *A Brief History of Neo-Liberalism* (Oxford, 2005); A. Glyn, *Capitalism Unleashed* (Oxford, 2006).

69 McIlroy and Campbell, 'High tide', pp. 97–8; Hyman, 'Afterword', pp. 357–8; J. McIlroy, Notes on the Communist Party', in McIlroy *et al.*, *High Tide*, pp. 245–8; J. McIlroy, '"Always outnumbered, always outgunned": the Trotskyists and the trade unions', in ibid., pp. 279–83.

70 Harvey, *A Brief History*, p. 1.

71 Hyman refers to Hugh Clegg and Royden Harrison, well known professors of industrial relations and social and labour history respectively. To take another example, Colin Crouch hazarded some 'combination of monetarism and attempts at straightforward corporatism' would characterize the 1980s (C. Crouch, *The Politics of Industrial Relations*, Manchester (1979), pp. 195–6).

72 J. McIlroy, 'Still under siege: British trade unions at the turn of the century', *Historical Studies in Industrial Relations*, 3, 1997, p. 103.

73 McIlroy, *Trade Unions in Britain Today*, p. 398. Unemployment was important in weakening the unions. But the state can influence or refuse to influence the level of unemployment. Adoption of neo-liberal economics restrained inflation, real wages rose for key groups of workers, employment levels and compositional changes in the labour force, in the context of union exclusion, restrictive legislation and economic policy, shifted the balance of forces. Cf H. Gospel, 'Markets, firms and unions', in S. Fernie and D. Metcalf, *Trade Unions: resurgence or demise?* (2005), pp. 35–9.

74 Lack of space does not permit address of recent periodical literature; for this see, particularly, the annual bibliographies published in *Labour History Review* and the indexes to *Historical Studies in Industrial Relations*.

75 D. Sandbrook, *Never Had It So Good: a history of Britain from Suez to the Beatles* (2005). Sandbrook draws largely on A. Sampson, *Anatomy of Britain* (1962) and also on M. Shanks, *The Stagnant Society* (Harmondsworth, 1961). There are isolated references to the work of academics Hugh Clegg and Henry Phelps Brown.

76 D. Sandbrook, *White Heat: a history of Britain in the swinging sixties* (2005); P. Hennessy, *Having It So Good: Britain in the fifties* (2006) presents a portrait of trade unions as political actors, drawing usefully on Cabinet papers but not on academic work, saving R. Taylor, *The Trade Union Question in British Politics* (Oxford, 1993).

77 C. Wrigley, *British Trade Unions since 1933* (Cambridge, 2002).

78 W. Hamish Fraser, *A History of British Trade Unionism, 1700–1998* (Basingstoke, 1999), pp. 191–235.

79 A. J. Reid, *United We Stand: a history of Britain's trade unions* (2004).

80 Ibid., pp. 301–2, 327–8.

81 Reid warns readers that the growth of shop floor bargaining after 1945, 'had very little to do with any mood of revolutionary revolt' (ibid., p. xv). Moreover, the

miners' strikes of the 1970s were 'less a result of popular insurgency than of the excessively confrontational attitudes of those managing the industry' (ibid.) Some historians may be surprised to learn that: 'Most previous discussions of the history of trade unions in Britain have portrayed a unitary figure of "the working class" in either a heroic or sinister light, implying that its members came from somewhere different from the rest of the population and may indeed have been not quite human' (ibid., p. ix).

82　C. Howell, *Trade Unions and the State: the construction of industrial relations institutions in Britain, 1890–2000* (Princeton, NJ, and Oxford, 2005). Similar points have been made in earlier literature; see K. D. Ewing, 'The state and industrial relations: "collective laissez-faire" revisited', *Historical Studies in Industrial Relations*, 5, 1998; N. Fishman, 'A vital element in British industrial relations: a reassessment of Order 1305, 1941–51', *Historical Studies in Industrial Relations*, 8, 1999. But Howell's work constitutes a powerful, synthetic elaboration.

83　S. Deakin and F. Wilkinson, *The Law of the Labour Market: institutions, employment and legal evolution* (Oxford, 2005).

84　R. Darlington and D. Lyddon, *Glorious Summer: class struggle in Britain, 1972* (2001).

85　Smith, *Unionization and Union Leadership*.

86　A. Taylor, *The NUM and British Politics, vol. 1: 1947–1968* (Aldershot, 2003); *vol. 2: 1968–1995* (Aldershot, 2005).

87　K. Gildart, *The North Wales Miners, 1945–1996: a fragile unity* (Cardiff, 2001).

88　R. Taylor, *The TUC: from the general strike to new unionism* (Basingstoke, 2000). On the neglected area of trade union education, see J. Fisher, *Bread on the Waters: a history of TGWU education, 1922–2000* (2005), pp. 92–209.

89　D. Tanner *et al* (eds), *The Labour Party in Wales, 1900–2000* (Cardiff, 2000); A. Reid, 'Labour and the trade unions', in D. Tanner *et al.* (eds), *Labour's First Century* (Cambridge, 2000), pp. 230–33.

90　S. Fielding, *The Labour Governments, 1964–70, vol. 1: Labour and cultural change* (Manchester, 2003); J. W. Young, *The Labour Governments, 1964–70, vol. 2: international policy* (Manchester, 2003; J. Tomlinson, *The Labour Governments, 1964–70, vol. 3: economic policy* (Manchester, 2003). For example, *In Place of Strife* attracts little over a page in volume 1 (pp. 105–6) and four pages in volume 3 (pp. 142–5). For a recent analysis, see R. Tyler, '"Victims of our history"? Barbara Castle and *In Place of Strife*', *Contemporary British History*, 20, 3, 2006.

91　A possible example is the long-term impact on industrial relations reform of the proposals of the Donovan Commission. But Wilson was not prepared to wait for the voluntary implementation of these recommendations. *In Place of Strife* was 'In Place of Donovan'. P. Jenkins, *The Battle of Downing Street* (1970), pp. 26–43.

92　R. Taylor, 'Trade union freedom and the Labour Party: Arthur Deakin, Frank Cousins and the Transport and General Workers' Union, 1945–64', in B. Brivati and R. Heffernan (eds), *The Labour Party: a centenary history* (Basingstoke, 2000); S. Ludlam, 'Norms and blocks: trade unions and the Labour Party since 1964', in ibid. See also A. Seldon and K. Hickson (eds), *New Labour, Old Labour: the Wilson and Callaghan governments, 1974–79* (2004), particularly the chapters by Robert Taylor and Jim Tomlinson.

93 L. Black, *The Political Culture of the Left in Affluent Britain, 1951–64: old Labour, new Britain* (Basingstoke, 2003).

94 Cronin, *New Labour's Past*. See also S. Ludlam, 'Too much pluralism, not enough socialism: interpreting the unions-party link', in J. Callaghan *et al.* (eds), *Interpreting the Labour Party: approaches to Labour Party history* (Manchester, 2003); E. Shaw, 'Lewis Minkin and the party-unions link', in ibid.

95 J. Callaghan, *Cold War, Crisis and Conflict: the history of the Communist Party of Great Britain 1951–68* (2003); G. Andrews, *End Game and New Times: the final years of British Communism 1964–91* (2004). The former makes no reference to R. Stephens, 'Cold War politics: Communism and anti-Communism in the trade unions', in Campbell *et al.*, *Post-War Compromise*. Other pertinent publications also go uncited, for example, J. McIlroy, 'Reds at work: Communist factory organisation in the Cold War 1947-56', *Labour History Review*, 65, 2, 2000; J. McIlroy, ' "Every factory our fortress": Communist Party workplace branches in a time of militancy, 1956-79, part 1: history, politics, topography', *Historical Studies in Industrial Relations*, 10, 2000; and J. McIlroy, 'Every factory our fortress": Communist Party workplace branches in a time of militancy, 1956-79, part 2: testimonies and judgements', *Historical Studies in Industrial Relations*, 12, 2001. In contrast, Geoff Andrews generously acknowledges McIlroy, 'Notes on the Communist Party', and other relevant work: 'The first in-depth study of the party's industrial strategy during the 1960s and 1970s, carried out by John McIlroy, has made a major contribution towards understanding the complexities of this period, by bringing much new evidence to light …'. (ibid., p. 106).

96 There is some material in T. Cliff, *A World to Win: life of a revolutionary* (2000), and T. Grant, *History of British Trotskyism* (2002); and see, for example, J. McIlroy, 'The revolutionary odyssey of John Lawrence', *Revolutionary History*, 9, 2, 2006; J. McIlroy, 'A Communist historian in 1956: Brian Pearce and the crisis of British Stalinism', *Revolutionary History*, 9, 3, 2006

97 G. Gall, *The Meaning of Militancy? Postal workers and industrial relations* (Aldershot, 2003).

98 S. Cohen, *Ramparts of Resistance: why workers lost their power and how to get it back* (2006). R. Darlington, 'The agitator 'theory' of strikes re-evaluated', *Labor History*, 47, 2006.

99 Cf McIlroy, 'Notes on the Communist Party', p. 216. A number of largely uncritical autobiographies have been published: for example, F. Westacott, *Shaking the Chains: a personal and political history* (Chesterfield, 2002); N. Harding, *Staying Red: why I remain a socialist* (2005).

100 See, for example, A. Perkins, *Red Queen: the authorized biography of Barbara Castle* (2003); D. Howell, *Attlee* (2006); F. Beckett, *Macmillan* (2006); H. Conroy, *Callaghan* (2006); D. McShane, *Heath* (2006); P. Routledge, *Wilson* (2006); K. O. Morgan, *Michael Foot* (2007).

101 K. Gildart *et al.*, (eds), *Dictionary of Labour Biography, vol. 11* (Basingstoke, 2003); K. Gildart and D. Howell (eds) *Dictionary of Labour Biography, vol. 12* (Basingstoke, 2005). Volume 11 has entries relevant to this period on the engineering workers' leader, Jack Tanner, by Nina Fishman, the TGWU officials, Huw Edwards and Thomas Jones, and the mining trade unionist Tom Stephenson,

by Keith Gildart. Volume 12 has entries on the Scottish miners' leader, Abe Moffat, by myself and Alan Campbell as well as my piece on the Trotskyist and trade union educator, Jock Haston. See also my entry on the engineering union's Reg Birch and myself and Campbell on miners' leader Michael McGahey in volume 13 (forthcoming, Basingstoke, 2008). Also of interest is Joe Melling's work on the white-collar trade unionist, Clive Jenkins: see, for example, J. Melling, 'Leadership and factionalism in the growth of supervisory trade unionism: the case of ASSET, 1939–1956', *Historical Studies in Industrial Relations*, 13, 2002; J. Melling, 'Managing the white-collar union: salaried staff, trade union leadership and the politics of organised labour in post-war Britain, c1950-1968', *International Review of Social History*, 48, 2003.

102 E. Hobsbawm, 'The past as history', in E. Hobsbawm, *On History* (1997), p. 235.

103 S. Fielding, *The Labour Party: continuity and change in the making of 'New' Labour* (Basingstoke, 2003).

104 R. Toye, '"The smallest party in history"? New Labour in historical perspective', *Labour History Review*, 69, 1, 2004.

105 In a different way we may note the persistent attempts by industrial relations scholars to predicate the resurgence of contemporary trade unionism on the basis of short-term, sometimes ephemeral, indicators. See, for example, E. Heery, J. Kelly and J. Waddington, 'Union revitalization in Britain', *European Journal of Industrial Relations*, 9, 1, 2003; for a corrective, see A. Charlwood, 'The new generation of trade union leaders and prospects for union revitalization', *British Journal of Industrial Relations*, 42, 2, 2004.

106 H. Butterfield, *The Whig Interpretation of History* (1931), pp. 11–14, 62–3, 111.

107 Cf S. Fielding, 'Interesting but irrelevant', *Labour History Review*, 60, 3, 1995; J. Saville, 'The crisis in labour history: a further comment', *Labour History Review*, 61, 3, 1996.

108 Cf. The invocation of 'quirkiness' to characterise our attention to Stalinists and Trotskyists in Crouch, review, p. 364

109 Cf R. J. Evans, *In Defence of History* (1977), pp. 191–203.

110 Cf Fielding, 'Interesting but irrelevant'; Saville, 'The crisis in labour history'.

111 Cf D. Howell, 'Reading Alastair Reid: a future for labour history?', in N. Kirk (ed.), *Social Classes and Marxism* (Aldershot, 1996). For self-styled revisionism see A. Reid, 'Marxism and revisionism in British labour history', *Bulletin of the Society for the Study of Labour History*, 52, 3, 1987; A. Reid and E. F. Biagini, 'Currents of radicalism 1850-1914' in A. Reid and E. F. Biagini (eds), *Currents of Radicalism: popular radicalism, organised labour and party politics in Britain, 1850-1914* (Cambridge, 1991). A. Reid, 'A new paradigm for British labour history', *History Compass*, 3, 2005, pp. 2, 19–20.

112 Alistair Reid, who emphasises continuity and the resilience of liberalism in British labour history and contends that scholars in the Marxist tradition are handicapped in writing history by their politics, may provide a case in point. For example, he summarises the agitation against the 1971 Industrial Relations Act thus: 'Since this was a campaign of industrial and extra-parliamentary action, it could be portrayed as having extremist overtones, but in reality it showed marked continuities with

all the most respectable traditions of craft unionism and parliamentary liberalism, earlier enshrined in the statutory provisions of 1871, 1875 and 1906.' ('A new paradigm', p. 11). Reid makes a judgement, and it is partial. The drive to restore voluntarism and its continuity with the past and with liberal values is evaluated as significant and real. But this is at the expense of what was strikingly new and startling different. Militant political strikes, often organised from below, which challenged the state, were at the heart of the events that Reid characterises here. Allowing for the fact that craft unionists were sometimes not quite as respectable as they led liberals to believe, the strikes of the early 1970s hardly 'showed marked continuities with all the most respectable traditions of craft unionism and parliamentary liberalism'. Strikes, not to say strikes of this kind and on this scale, were absent from the campaigns of the 1870s and 1906. Reid's one-sided evaluation – underlining what was similar at the expense of what was distinctive – may be read as reflecting his predispositions and determination to discern 'the persistence of liberalism' (ibid., p. 20).

Preface to the 1999 Edition

The idea of this book and its companion volume, *British Trade Unionism and Industrial Politics: the high tide of trade unionism, 1964–79*, came from a conference we organized on the theme of 'British Trade Unionism, Workers' Struggles and Economic Performance, 1940–1979', held at the University of Warwick in September 1997. The event strengthened our belief that it was more than time for historians to begin taking stock of the trade unionism of these decades in more detailed and extensive fashion. The war years are of great significance but constitute a discrete period. The literature discussing the elusive relationships between trade unions and national economic performance is a burgeoning industry. Hence our emphasis in these texts upon the politics of trade unionism, conceived not only in terms of relations with the state but in terms of factionalism, the dynamics of industrial struggles and the allegiances of union activists.

Many of our chapters started life as conference papers; others were specially commissioned for these volumes. These two collections of essays make no claim to be comprehensive. We have revisited well-trodden ground and also provided first accounts of neglected byways, although we are under no illusions that key areas still require excavation and others more research. We have attempted to sketch in some of the background to the period in the survey chapters which preface the case studies. The books are most profitably read together but each stands independently in its own right.

We would like to express our gratitude to Dave Lyddon, Paul Smith, Richard Storey and Chris Wrigley who were involved with us in organizing the Warwick conference. Thanks are also due to the Modern Records Centre and the School of History, University of Warwick, the Society for the Study of Labour History, *Historical Studies in Industrial Relations*, the Barry Amiel and Norman Melburn Trust and the University of Stirling, who all supported the conference in a variety of ways. We are personally indebted to the Society for commissioning these texts as part of the Studies in Labour History series, and to Chris Wrigley, its President, who has supported us through a difficult gestation period. As a publisher, Alec McAulay has given unique and enduring support to labour history and we wish to thank him for his tolerance, good humour and hospitality.

Trade unionism, most particularly British trade unionism, is about people, people as volunteers and the personal efforts and sacrifices they are prepared to make; it is made by its activists. Over the years, in both our teaching and research, we have enjoyed the enriching experience of encountering hundreds of those lay officials and full-time officers who, often at great personal cost, forged trade unionism in the post-war period. It was, for all its undoubted problems and weaknesses, a major social achievement, a progressive, civilizing force which protected millions from the vicissitudes of capitalism. It is to these activists that the book is dedicated.

John McIlroy, Alan Campbell, Nina Fishman, December 1998

Introduction:
Approaching Post-War Trade Unionism

John McIlroy, Alan Campbell, Nina Fishman

In the last decade of the twentieth century myths about the role of trade unions in the preceding post-war era were extended and lodged themselves deeper in public consciousness. The common sense of Thatcherism had long held the 1950s to be the locust years of lost opportunity in which Conservative administrations embraced social democracy and legitimized and stimulated collectivism and union power in ways inimical to the economic and political health of the nation. The 1960s and 1970s were depicted as a period of hedonism, indiscipline, appeasement. Edward Heath's 'U-turn' in 1971–2, his subsequent succumbing to the miners in 1974 and the 'Winter of Discontent' of 1978–9 were foundation legends of the new Conservatism. As the 1990s developed, Labour Party leaders began to subscribe to similar readings of history, signalling their own adaptation to neo-liberalism. Finally union leaders, traditionally renowned for celebratory accounts of labour's past, nailed their colours to the same mast. The 'magnificent journey', it seemed, had crashed into the buffers in 1979. A completely new beginning was necessary and timely.

From 1994, TUC leaders questioned the rationale and value of union policy in the 1960s and 1970s, branded the period 'the bad old days' and suggested that the central thrust of TUC strategy in the post-war era – the drive to secure working-class influence over the state – was 'a mistake, one which should never be repeated'.[1] For New Labour leader Tony Blair, Conservative governments since 1979 had improved industrial relations and moulded more responsible and efficient trade unionism. If the language employed was furtive in comparison with the saloon bar hyperbole of Thatcherism, its purposes in determining the parameters of policy and reducing the currency of debate were all too clear. In Blairspeak, the negative pre-1979 and positive post-Thatcher properties of trade unionism were asserted, unargued, unevidenced but coded: on the one hand, 'flying pickets ... closed shop ... relations with the state too close for comfort', and on the other, 'ballots ... fairness not favours'. The union struggles of recent history and their protagonists were, for Blair, his government and supporters, simply 'ghosts of time past ... it is time to leave them where they lie'.[2]

Just as much as Thatcherism, New Labour and New Unionism have defined their projects in opposition to a past selectively rendered. All these rhetorics underline once more the intense relevance of interpretations of the past for politicians and trade unionists, members as well as leaders, as a source of meaning and validation for action in the present. This development suggests again the value of close scrutiny of contemporary history, and the essential role of scholars in recreating and analysing the complexities of yesterday's issues, events and personalities, failures and successes. It foregrounds the necessity to recover the diminishing role of historians in assessing and challenging appropriations and partisan recovery of the recent past which may close off alternatives and provide a false basis for future strategy and policy by political and union activists. It is worth adding that we should remain alert to the recrudescence of currently less influential left-wing fables such as the inevitability, despite everything that has happened, of the revival of labour's progress or the essential, if presently invisible, revolutionary instincts of the rank and file trade unionist.

The hazards of engagement with the history of our own times have been recently and eloquently re-argued.[3] The problems – from our own proximity and personal experience, which can constrain detachment, to the difficulties of access to participants and documentation – are numerous. Yet the dangers of leaving the field to self-interested mythmakers justify the preliminary work of clearing the ground and beginning a more rigorous scrutiny of the fortunes of post-war trade unionism. If the labour movement is to have a future, it requires a more detailed, more balanced account of its past.

This aspiration is reinforced by the general neglect of trade unionism by social scientists and historians in recent years and specifically the relative paucity of work on the post-war era, 1945–79. The interest sociologists took in this area in the 1970s has diminished.[4] With the exception of Lewis Minkin's monumental work on relations between unions and the Labour Party and the extended survey edited by Pimlott and Cook, covering the period from the early eighteenth century but containing several chapters dealing with the period 1945–79, much the same could be said about political scientists. As with sociology, there is only a sparse periodical literature devoted almost wholly to developments in trade unionism in the 1980s.[5] In contrast, economists continue to take an interest in trade unionism, if largely through a specialized literature dealing with wage movements, bargaining models, the consequences of state policy and the impact of unions on the firm and the national economy. The totalized, problem-centred synthesis associated most recently with the labour economist, the late Henry Phelps Brown, is rarely emulated today.[6]

Industrial relations has continued to constitute the heartland for the study of trade unionism. It still produces a rich periodical and monographic literature dealing with diverse aspects of current trade union organization and practice. Yet it is adjudged by leading practitioners as a subject in some disarray. It has proved unable to come to terms with central questions: the role of the state; the political alignments of trade unions; power, conflict and change in the workplace; and the social processes of worker mobilization. Since the 1980s its core concerns, always broadly managerialist and pre-occupied with public policy but set within a pluralist framework which privileged collectivism, have shifted. Industrial relations, in the workplace and in the university, has been in decline. It has been beset, within and without, by the growth of Human Resource Management (HRM) which, with its crude unitarist paradigm, reduces trade unionism to the margins. The growth of HRM has unfortunately overshadowed a more beneficial, novel strand in the discipline which has involved more sophisticated interest in enterprise organization and managerial strategy.[7]

Industrial relations academics, an observer faithfully recorded forty years ago, 'think in constricted terms, nearly always in the present tense ... the sense of history, with its depth, reach and contemplative spirit, fails to stir.'[8] Texts addressing the past, even the post-war period, have been rare and have constituted a small fraction of the output of industrial relations, as a glance at its major journals will confirm. Alan Fox's magisterial *History and Heritage* deals with the years after 1945 in broad sweep; the late Hugh Clegg brought his three-volume *History of British Trade Unions* up to 1951; and Terry and Edwards have produced a valuable collection of essays on the hidden history of union workplace organization in the post-war decades. Valuable histories of individual unions which cover this period have continued to appear in healthy numbers, although they are sometimes overlooked.[9]

Nor has the study of trade unionism found a safe refuge in labour history. Here too there has been much talk of 'crisis'.[10] The shift in disciplinary concerns in the 1960s from an institutional emphasis on unions and political parties to a new concern with working-class experience and culture, stimulated by the publication of Edward Thompson's *The Making of the English Working-class* in 1963, was increasingly questioned by the 1980s. Concerned at the direction the discipline had taken, critics indicated the hazards inherent in the redefinition of labour history as the social history of the working-class, and worried about the extent to which labour history's political concerns had been dissolved in the 'general celebration of working-class life'. Selective appropriation from Thompson's own highly politicized writing had led to a de-politicization of the subject,

and a radically de-institutionalised understanding of politics, in which the possible sources of working-class oppositional impulse are displaced from the recognized media of political parties and trade unions into a variety of non-institutional settings, embracing behaviour previously regarded as 'non-political' – eg. crime, street violence, riots, industrial sabotage, mental illness, etc.[11]

In this context, Zeitlin urged a return to the institutional history of industrial relations while Kimeldorf argued for bringing the analysis of trade unionism back to the centre of historical exploration.[12]

None the less, studies of working-class experience, housing, education, gender, ethnicity, and of course language, continue to proliferate to the relative neglect of scholarship on trade unions. In the *Labour History Review's* annual bibliographies for recent years, far fewer contributions are listed under 'trade unionism' – quite widely defined – than under 'popular culture, leisure, sport and religion'.[13] For the post-war period, there have been some attempts to address areas of trade union development but much remains to be done. The late Henry Pelling updated his classic survey, *A History of British Trade Unions*, to cover the 1960s and 1970s. There has been a new general study by Laybourn, and Wrigley has published a valuable collection of documents on mainstream trade unionism. Writing in the aftermath of the decisive defeat of the 1984 miners' strike, John Saville delivered a concise, insightful critique of the twentieth century labour movement. More specialised studies have been provided by Hyman on unions in the late 1940s and by Tomlinson on the high politics of union-government relations under the Attlee administration, while Tolliday, Zeitlin and Lyddon have begun to examine workplace organization. One of the most impressive contributions, out of print and often overlooked, is Cronin's synthetic, rounded history of *Labour and Society* which devotes most of five chapters to the post-war period and tells us a great deal, albeit sometimes indirectly, about the predicament of trade unionism and its essential context.[14] But despite rhetorical attention, neglected areas have continued to be uncultivated: recent decades have seen few significant studies of the experiences of women and black workers in trade unions between 1945 and 1979. Nor has the role of political activists in the post-war unions yet been fully addressed. Although general surveys of the Communist Party (CP) have appeared by Thompson and Branson (whose book ends in 1951), as well as a case study of engineering in the 1940s by Hinton, we still lack an appreciation, based on detailed archival excavation, of the role of the CP in industry throughout the post-war period comparable with studies of the party's earlier activities.[15]

Economic and social history more generally has neglected the study of trade unionism over the last decade. Symptomatic of this tendency is a recent collection of essays on *Twentieth Century Britain: economic, social and cultural change*, a 500-page volume with clear ambitions to be seen as an authoritative text (the authors were assembled by the Economic History Society). There is no reference to the shop stewards' movement of the First World War; there is no index entry on the Communist Party, although it is briefly mentioned in a chapter on inter-war unemployment which contains two inconclusive paragraphs on the National Unemployed Workers' Movement. In the chapter 'Crisis and turmoil? 1973–93', two pages are devoted to industrial relations: they mention neither shop stewards nor the 1984–5 miners' strike.[16] Such deficiencies have been partially repaired by inter-dis-

4

ciplinary work and by contributions from outside the universities. We are referring here to Chris Wrigley's edited *History of Industrial Relations*, the third volume of which covers the period 1940–79 and draws on contributions from historians and industrial relations scholars, and the well-known journalist Robert Taylor's volume in the series sponsored by the Institute of Contemporary British History.[17]

This uneven but overall far from impressive picture must be set within a general sense of malaise in labour studies in the 1990s, which has produced some heart-searching. The decline of class and the social weight of trade unionism; the political shift to the right; the collapse of the Soviet bloc; labour history's neglect of women and ethnic minorities; and the firm yoking of research funding to managerial agendas: all are commonly implicated.[18] It is far from obvious why the decline of trade unionism and socialist radicalism should of itself cause committed scholars to lose interest in serious research concerns. The alleged decline of class constitutes a good positive example: it has been vigorously combated in a growing inter-disciplinary literature.[19] The secular decline of labour in the United States since the 1950s has not stemmed a fertile stream of labour studies there. One wonders whether for some the essential historical sense of time, and the intuitive feeling for history's upturns and downturns has become coarsened and attenuated. Are Edward Thompson's and Christopher Hill's concern with lost causes and Eric Hobsbawm's belief that nothing sharpens the historical mind like defeat merely residues from a more principled era?[20] The events of 1956 stimulated the intellectual and political revitalization of many of labour history's formative spirits. It is difficult to understand in the context of labour history and industrial relations why the collapse of Stalinism should have dissipated interest in these fields unless there were many more closet Stalinists than we previously conceived. Labour history's neglect of women and minorities is indubitable: what is in contention is the means by which this should be redeemed. Once more the reinvigoration of class analysis suggests that, on any account, the revitalization of traditional approaches has more to offer the committed historian than emphases on patriarchy and identity. Heralded as an alternative to the durable duality of class and labour movement as the subject of politics and history, social movements based on gender and ethnicity have demonstrated sectionalism, subordination and compatibility with capitalism. Despite their incalculable educational impact, they are no substitute for the potential universality of movements and history rooted in class.

As for research funding, academics play some role in setting its parameters and are under no direct or overpowering compulsion to take the neo-liberal shilling. Their freedom in this sphere alerts us to a missing element – somewhat ironically, given the emphasis potential protagonists place upon it in their academic work – human agency. An increasingly overlooked but central factor since 1979 has been the refusal of resistance to trends in the universities – trends inimical not only to radically committed scholarship but to the liberal academy itself – by social scientists and historians who once eagerly supported struggle in factories and offices. As David Howell has pointed out, the 'Third Way' – the attempt to subvert the assumptions, language and priorities of the funding agencies by critically emulating them – usually leads to the appropriation of the would-be appropriators.[21]

The debilities of labour studies in terms of both coverage and method have to be located within state policies and academic responses to them. Both have influenced diminished autonomy, reinforced cultures of deference to power, conformity and managerialism and stimulated a growing allegiance to 'relevance', increasingly defined as contributing to the state's political agendas and the resurgence of British capital. The competing post-modernist tendency to take refuge from reality and seek solace in 'virtual' control of events, play and 'discourse', has been only minimally apparent here. In its more moderate variants, post-modernism can help counteract simplistic ideas about human progress, the natural advance of labour, the inevitability of trade unionism. We can retrieve from post-modernism – as from older philosophies of history – reaffirmation of the tenuousness of our recovery of the past as it was, the space for competing narratives and interpretations, the importance of language. Critical engagement with the literary techniques of post-modernism, its passion for buried episodes, lost lives and storytelling, as practised by, say, Orlando Figes in *A People's Tragedy*, his enthralling, if for some of us politically dubious and over-inventive, study of the Russian revolution, may help to produce richer history and better writing.

There remains, nevertheless, the intellectual necessity to confront and reject post-modernism's epistemological core and its approach to history. Here we encounter the mistaken view – vigorously rebuffed by the post-modernists themselves – that labour historians should welcome and utilize the post-modernists' 'exciting' contribution to modern labour history. Some have urged that in resisting post-modernism's 'theoretical pretensions', we should accept that, in spite of its nihilism, epistemic relativism, rejection of class, 'its focus and practice ... should be embraced within the widening agenda of labour history'. The specific contention, based upon, in this case, an unwarranted division between post-modernists' theory and practice, is that recent work, notably by Patrick Joyce and James Vernon, helps us 'to appreciate the complex interaction of language and social structure, to examine more thoroughly the link between structure and action, the medium between material conditions and consciousness'.[22] If historians have always struggled with these relationships, they are precisely what post-modernists are *not* about. As one incisive review of their recent contributions to labour history put it,

What is disappointing, however, is that the prominence given to language in these new accounts does not actually help to meet the need to examine these complex connections. The stress on language all too easily slides into a form of linguistic

6

determinism, in which the historical impact of any non-linguistic realm is obscured, denied or declared unknowable. The turn against social class, in favour of a form of historical research in which only the concepts, idioms and grammars used in discourse are regarded as open to examination, is profoundly disabling.[23]

The more popular labour history is, the better, provided, of course, this is consonant with its rigour and integrity. But the health of a discipline must not be confused with its popularity or its ability to adapt to, as distinct from take the measure of, the latest intellectual fashion. Identity history which deserts universalism and privileges the particular, whether ethnicity, gender, sexuality, whatever, is subversive of good history.[24] The lure of post-modernist novelty should not lead us to trim, still less desert, basic touchstones, from class to the reality of the past and our ability to know it. There are incontestably real difficulties and fundamental problems in labour history – not least in the lack of recent attention to labour movements, with their aspiration and, sometimes, ability to transcend particularism – even if it is a little premature to speak of fatal crisis. New work of diversity and originality is still being produced, if on a smaller scale than we would like. The stream of studies of trade unionism has not yet dried up. Academics are still taking ambitious initiatives, witness the revamping of the *Labour History Review*, the recent establishment of the already thriving journal *Historical Studies in Industrial Relations*, the continuing vigour of the *International Review of Social History* and the welcome attention which *Twentieth Century British History* is paying to the labour movement.[25]

Our purpose in these two volumes is to extend this existing work and to fill gaps within it. But we also want to begin to build on strengths and compensate for weaknesses in its method and approach. Willman and Winch's *Innovation and Management Control: labour relations at BL Cars* (1985) may be taken as exemplifying the problems with even more sophisticated industrial relations research.[26] Unlike many of the surveys which dominate the industrial relations literature and which de-emphasize social action, it promises an in-depth historical analysis based on research conducted over three years. The study, focused on the development of the Metro model which was intended to restore profitability to the crisis-ridden British Leyland, covers the period from the early 1970s to the early 1980s. The account starts from, and remains heavily weighted towards, management's perspective. In terms of the relative absence of emphasis on management strategies from industrial relations research in the past, this rehabilitation is healthy.

However, it is achieved at the expense of adequate treatment of trade unionism. While fourteen stewards and three full-time officials were interviewed, this contrasts unfavourably with thirty-two BL managers, and footnote references to sources are biased towards the latter group. The texture is thin, the writing brusque and flesh and blood actors largely non-existent. Internal divisions amongst stewards in the plant and their relation, on the one hand, to members, and, on the other, to the AUEW and the TGWU, as well as the politics of these two unions, are briefly mentioned but far from fully developed. The BL Combine Committee is given a few lines, the victimization of Derek Robinson a page, in an account which contrasts unfavourably with those proffered by managers and trade unionists.[27] Robinson is typically referred to anonymously as 'the Longbridge convenor'. His membership of the Communist Party and the significant role CP members played in building and sustaining the stewards' organization in the plant is simply not mentioned.

The book's central section is referred to by Zeitlin as ' a detailed account of industrial relations at British Leyland in the late 1970s and early 1980s'.[28] It merits this evaluation only in an institutionalized and historically impoverished way. The narrative's connection with conflicts outside the plant to which the struggles depicted here were intimately related – the sharp conflict over the role of the state between corporatist and neo-liberal tendencies, internal union politics, the collapse of the Social Contract – is tenuous. Although the plant battles over participation, productivity and the activity of the National Enterprise Board were an integral part of wider agendas and struggles, these are only dimly echoed here. Strong on accounts of bargaining structures and procedures, management strategy and technological innovation, the text has difficulty in dealing with human agency, with alternatives and choices, with politics and with history. Whilst the authors are concerned to demonstrate 'how deep rooted historically were the trends that fostered labour relations problems', their histories of union organization and its protagonists are pallid and sometimes unsure: 'Another characteristic of the industry, the reliance on the shop steward system to express union demands may have originated in the wartime period'. Comparisons with Richard Croucher's well peopled, thick textured, wide canvassed *Engineers at War* (1982) are irresistible. More space is devoted by Willman and Winch to the engineering process of constructing the Metro than the political processes of the joint shop stewards' committee.[29] We make these criticisms at some length, not to dismiss what remains a valuable case study in industrial relations, but to illustrate that discipline's lack of a historical imagination even in its better work.

Some of these problems – from industrial relations' engagement with trade unions rather than labour movements, its neglect of the state, the influence of the past, the values and motivations of its actors, suggest the need for a multi-disciplinary approach. They have received attention in the past and it has recently been renewed. Lyddon and Smith have asserted the importance of history in industrial relations and, with their colleagues, have sought to remedy its absence through the important publication of *Historical Studies in Industrial Relations*.[30] However the question remains: what kind of history, what kind of conceptual framework? It is, of course, possible, at least 'in principle', to insert class struggle into the mechanical categories of

Dunlop's system of industrial relations as David Brody has suggested, though it is not necessarily desirable. Or, as Lyddon more fruitfully argues, by developing the insights of the Webbs, Allan Flanders and Hugh Clegg and in opposition to the neo-institutionalism of Jonathan Zeitlin, to centrally locate the history of trade unions within 'a very comprehensive classification of internal and external job regulation'. Although Lyddon is 'mindful' of Montgomery's caution regarding the dangers of 'an exclusive focus on industrial relations', this remains a potential hazard of such a strategy. A historical vision confined to the processes of regulation in the workplace and the industry, even one encompassing the role of the state, may remain in practice unnecessarily limited.[31] For, at least to date, the history of industrial relations has tended to address the historicized problematics of contemporary industrial relations. Thus we get Clegg's immensely valuable but nevertheless restricted history of industrial relations from above. Even Terry and Edwards' pioneering collection has, on close scrutiny, too little to say either about workplace politics or politics beyond the factory, and still feels the need to justify itself as 'a guide to good policy making'.[32] Even the class struggle component of industrial relations literature has possessed a restrictive bias towards the workplace and a partial, circumscribed and, for many, esoteric conception of politics.

We would endorse the sentiments of Alan Fox (and the scope of his essay in realizing them) which insists on an integrated approach in examining historically the social context of industrial relations but also,

> involves dwelling at some length upon matters not normally discussed in industrial relations literature. Political theory, upper class strategies of rule, the nature of the British state, the nature of English law, the Victorian middle class concept of service, social imperialism, the personality and political convictions of Stanley Baldwin, the reasons for the failure of British fascism: these are among the themes I have found relevant for understanding why the industrial relations system grew as it did and not in some other way.[33]

This is essentially and extensively a political agenda, if one which conceives of a politics deeper than many contemporary political scientists envisage. We would embrace but go beyond this formulation to argue for a multi-layered concern with social and economic, as well as political, factors. We are looking for a totalized approach, a return to the broad vision of political economy. We would agree with Richard Price: advocacy of the primacy of politics in writing history, and certainly politics as discourse, politics autonomous and free-floating from structure, may be self-defeating. He remarks that it is unclear how strikes fit entirely into 'that lockbox' and observes pertinently that 'politics tends to be confined to institutions rather than action and behaviour'.[34] But whilst we need to embed our analysis in economics, politics plays an intrinsic role in the mobilization of industrial action, in the form that action takes, in its progress, its resolution and its consequences. There is no need at all for politics to be confined to institutions – although let us not downplay the importance of institutions. Whilst we must address the wide range of factors stimulating and constraining social action, politics is certainly there, very close to its heart, in the values of protagonists and in the structures they make and confront.

What appears to us most fruitful in writing the history of trade unions and trade unionists, a history soaked in politics, is thus a multi-factor approach which emphasizes politics. The traditional, essential subject of history is politics, for it is through politics that change takes place, it is through politics that change in other realms, economic, technological, social, is mediated. It seems artificial and constricting to conceive of the history of trade unions or industrial relations as a distinct field, set apart from labour history. To attempt to press this necessarily diverse subject matter solely into the boundaries of job regulation or an industrial relations history demarcated from the wider field of labour history appears to deny its breadth and its freedom. This is not to reject the utility of a dedicated journal but to address its scope. The kind of approach Fox offers is most fruitfully conceived of, we would argue, as the history of industrial politics, essentially imbricated with the broader field of labour history.[35]

To adopt this emphasis is consciously to redress the conventional focus of industrial relations by a consideration of industrial politics, from above and from below. This necessitates an examination of politics not only at the level of the state, but inside unions and parties. It requires address of politics not only inside these institutions but also inside the workplace, and in the values and actions of trade unionists. Our concern must be not only with the politics of the labour movement, its activists and the broader working-class but with the politics of capital and the management of labour, an area that has been relatively ignored.[36] David Marsh recently reproached industrial relations scholars for their limited interest in political issues and the literature of political science – ironically in a study of trade unionism with scarcely a word to say about politics inside unions. Political scientists, for their part, have neglected trade unions and their history. When unions have attracted their attention they have all too often been examined in a shallow fashion, their relations with the state being considered to the virtual exclusion of most other aspects of union activity.[37]

But Marsh has a point. Some years ago a monograph appeared analysing conflicts inside the AUEW, centred on a study of one district committee from the 1940s to the 1970s. The limited and disparate literature on factionalism in trade unions was outlined. There were brief references to 'the left-wing faction' and CP members. Indeed factional membership was stated to be one of the 'four structural dimensions of Committee membership'. Although the district and the committee researched – Manchester –

were perhaps the strongest base of 'the Broad Left' in Britain, the organization of the faction and the manner in which membership of it impinged upon
the actions of the committee's members went unexamined. This was despite
the existence at the time of a detailed study of the Broad Left in Manchester,
a rich fugitive literature and the availability of key protagonists. Important
political actors, right-wing as well as left, occasionally intrude into the text;
but their voices are mute, their politics, and the impact of those politics on
their trade unionism, are scarcely mentioned. In terms of their contribution
to understanding conflict, it is instructive to place the institutional, impersonal account given of the Platts (Barton) Ltd closure in 1956 alongside the
later view of politics from below embodied in the testimony of the Trotskyist
senior steward, who of course is absent from the academic text. The politics
of internal conflict in unions is, at least in recent literature, generally neglected.[38]

When industrial relations writers have addressed the political aspects of
trade unions, they have largely operated one-dimensionally, employing a
partial focus on politics which sometimes eschews consideration of the practice and organization of reformism – which is politics for most trade unionists
– and which primarily discusses the potential contribution which tendencies
in trade unionism may make to revolutionary change.[39] Conventional, 'actually existing' politics have been judged in practice as peripheral to industrial
relations. Yet exchange with the state and political parties, the political process inside unions, factionalism, the political allegiances of activists, the role
of political parties and their impact in the workplace should surely constitute an integral, indispensable component of the study of trade unionism.

At least some contributions to the long debate on writing labour history
are tinged with a somewhat dogmatic prescription of particular paths and
panaceas. We are instead pointing towards a framework which we feel will
produce fruitful work without detracting from diversity and pluralism, a di-
rective emphasis on the history of trade unionists rather than trade unionism.
But this framework draws our attention to related silences. The need for
studies of the organizational culture of unions, how the values of trade unionists and the structures and ethos which these values shape change over
time and the factors which influence the forms they take, has been urged but
not realized. Long-running debates on bureaucracy and rank and file have
far outpaced empirical studies.[40] No writer in recent decades has sought to
expand the boundaries of the history of the single union, to develop general
theory with the ambition deployed by Turner in the 1960s. There has been
no attempt to ponder the life and career of union leaders for similar purposes in the style once essayed by Vic Allen. Writing in 1964, Eric Hobsbawm
highlighted the dearth of studies of union leadership.[41] The absence remains
acute. Despite their importance, we have no published studies on Jack Jones
or Hugh Scanlon – or any other leader of the period with the exception of
Arthur Scargill.[42]

Despite the sterling efforts of John Saville, Joyce Bellamy and their contributors to the multi-volume *Dictionary of Labour Biography*, the lack of sufficiently extensive materials for rigorous, comparative prosopography has circumscribed the use in practice of important theoretical tools such as generational analysis. We still have inadequate information on the lay activists, despite acknowledgement of their importance, along with national leaders, in working-class mobilization. The stress on the active – not always militant – minority is sometimes criticized on the grounds that they were untypical and exceptional. Again the problem is one of integration. The active minority's importance lies precisely in their immense significance to the development and sustenance of consciousness and action. What made them, what motivated them, as well as the complex processes of interaction, in the workplace and beyond it, between members, representatives and officials are central to understanding trade unionism. And of course we cannot understand these relationships of power, authority and legitimacy unless we relate them to wider processes involving political parties, capital and the state.[43]

David Montgomery asserts that 'what needs to be kept in mind is that unions are but one instrument – one extremely important instrument – of working-class mobilization ...'.[44] We would rebalance his specification. Our claim for twentieth-century Britain is that trade unionism, grasped in its industrial and political dimensions, has been the primary, fundamental instrument for attracting workers' allegiance and realizing workers' goals. By far the largest voluntary movement and with a strong associational culture, it has been the key means of creating class unity and action. We would, however, endorse Montgomery's plea for a history which situates unions within the complex web of community associations, parties, employers, economy and state.[45] *Starting from* trade unionism as the bedrock, the animating core of the labour movement, still seems to us the most fruitful way to proceed.

In beginning to develop these approaches we have related our two volumes to the existing work covering the period 1945–79. Pelling's treatment justifiably emphasizes high politics to a greater degree than for the earlier period of his study. The same is true of Fox as he develops the compelling themes of his probing interrogation of two centuries. Robert Taylor likewise largely addresses 'the complex relationship between governments and organized labour and narrates the flow of events'.[46] Wrigley and his colleagues cover similar ground although their volume also provides valuable analyses of strikes and social welfare as well as case studies of the docks, car manufacture and road haulage. The breadth of Cronin's fertile treatment of these decades prohibits him from any detailed address of developments within individual unions. As he is addressing a packed century and four countries, Phelps Brown's discussion of the post-war era requires re-examination and expansion. Pimlott and Cook's collection contains several valuable chapters

12

ot relevance: an essay by Robert Taylor on 'the trade union problem' and a brief overview by Ken Coates of 1945–60.

In the light of this literature, we have included in these volumes more detailed analyses by authoritative scholars of the industrial politics of the Conservative and Labour Parties. But we also have studies of the relatively obscure industrial activities of the Communist Party and the Trotskyists. There are contributions on ethnicity, gender and internationalism, as well as case studies of neglected but important strikes, individual unions and the role of the TUC. There is novel analysis of the use of language by militants to mobilize support; of class and work culture; the role of the labour correspondent; workers' education; the politics of academics and their influence on state policy.

Our contributors are drawn from a range of disciplines – industrial relations, sociology, labour history, political science, management studies. Our hope is that these texts will appeal to students of each of these subjects. The essays are thus diverse and far reaching, dealing anew with ground previously tilled as well as with neglected areas. We attempt to address the mainstream and the marginal. Our subject is the politics – in the fullest sense of the term – of trade unionism, treated as an autonomous and still exciting subject for study which may provide lessons for future architects of labour movements. Perhaps unfashionably, the diverse activities and complex experience of trade unionists have not been winnowed here to provide evidence of their impact upon productivity, the enterprise and the fortunes of national capital, an exercise currently popular with academics from a variety of disciplines, nor re-interpreted in such a way that they might be accommodated, however imperfectly, within contemporary economic theories.[47] Neither do we make any claim to provide a full account of the trade unionism of these years, although the survey chapters in each volume map out brief overviews. A comprehensive, panoramic history requires as a preliminary the deep quarrying of its component blocks; it is in this spirit that we offer these essays, as a further step towards constructing both a broad and detailed picture of industrial politics during these years. If the labour movement is to continue to be relevant to working people, its partisans must understand what happened to it and why. Labour history still has a vital role to play in this process.

Notes

1. See, for example, J. Monks, 'No shopping list', *New Statesman*, 8 September 1995; 'Interview with John Monks', *New Statesman*, 6 September 1996; J. Monks, 'Gains and losses after twenty years of legal intervention', in W. McCarthy (ed.), *Legal Intervention in Industrial Relations: gains and losses* (1992).
2. Quoted in J. McIlroy, 'The enduring alliance? Trade unions and the making

of New Labour, 1994–97', *British Journal of Industrial Relations*, 36, 4, 1998, p. 542.

3. E. Hobsbawm, 'The present as history', in E. Hobsbawm, *On History* (1997).

4. See, for example, the studies of trade unionism in the workplace, notably T. Lane and K. Roberts, *Strike at Pilkingtons* (1971); H. Beynon, *Working for Ford* (Harmondsworth, 1973); A. Pollert, *Girls, Wives, Factory Lives* (1981); T. Nichols and P. Armstrong, *Workers Divided* (1976); and wider attempts to analyse trade unionism such as A. Fox, *A Sociology of Work and Industry* (1971); R. Hyman, *Marxism and the Sociology of Trade Unionism* (1971) and *Industrial Relations: a Marxist introduction* (1975); V. L. Allen, *The Sociology of Industrial Relations* (1971); J. A. Banks, *Trade Unionism* (1974); S. Hill, *Competition and Control at Work* (1981); C. Crouch, *Class Conflict and the Industrial Relations Crisis* (1977) and *Trade Unions: the logic of collective action* (1982); not to speak of the influential work of Goldthorpe and his colleagues – see J. Goldthorpe et al., *The Affluent Worker: industrial attitudes and behaviour* (Cambridge, 1968), *The Affluent Worker: political attitudes and behaviour* (Cambridge, 1968), and *The Affluent Worker in the Class Structure* (Cambridge, 1969); but see now F. Devine, *Affluent Workers Revisited: privatism and the working-class* (Edinburgh, 1992) and D. Gallie, R. Penn and M. Rose (eds), *Trade Unionism in Recession* (Oxford, 1996).

5. L. Minkin, *The Labour Party Conference* (Manchester, 1980) and *The Contentious Alliance: trade unions and the Labour Party* (Edinburgh, 1991); B. Pimlott and C. Cook (eds), *Trade Unions in British Politics: the first 250 years* (2nd edition, 1991): whereas the balance of the first edition of this book, published in 1982, was tilted towards the period before 1945, additions to the second edition focused on the years after 1979. See also M. Moran, *The Union of Post Office Workers: a study in political sociology* (1974) and *The Politics of Industrial Relations* (1977); A. Taylor, *Trade Unions and the Labour Party* (1987); D. Marsh, *The New Politics of British Trade Unionism* (1992).

6. Recent surveys include J.H. Pencavel, *Labour Markets under Trade Unionism* (Oxford, 1991); A.L. Booth, *The Economics of the Trade Union* (Cambridge, 1995). An outstanding, wide-ranging analysis is H. Phelps Brown, *The Origins of Trade Union Power* (Oxford, 1983).

7. J. Kelly, 'Does the field of industrial relations have a future?', unpublished paper to the British Universities Industrial Relations Association Annual Conference, Oxford 1994, and see now J. Kelly, *Rethinking Industrial Relations* (1998). Industrial relations academics have produced books on aspects of trade unionism in the 1990s which contain some historical material; see, for example, P. Ackers et al., *The New Workplace and Trade Unionism* (1996); J. Kelly and E. Heery, *Working for the Union: British trade union officers* (Cambridge, 1994); R. Darlington, *The Dynamics of Workplace Unionism* (1994); R. Undy et al., *Managing the Unions: the impact of legislation on trade unions' behaviour* (Oxford, 1996). General accounts of contemporary trade unionism have come from the margins of the industrial relations field; see, for example, R. Taylor, *The Future of the Trade Unions* (1994) and J.

McIlroy, *Trade Unions in Britain Today* (Manchester, 1995).

8. M. Neufeld, 'The sense of history and the annals of labor', *Proceedings of the American Industrial Relations Research Association*, 1961, quoted in D. Brody, 'Labor history, industrial relations and the crisis of American labor', *Industrial and Labor Relations Review*, 43, 1, 1989, p. 7.

9. A. Fox, *History and Heritage: the social origins of the British industrial relations system* (1985); H.A. Clegg, *A History of British Trade Unions since 1989, vol. 3, 1934–51* (Oxford, 1994); M. Terry and P. Edwards (eds), *Shop floor Politics and Job Controls* (Oxford, 1988). For individual union histories see, for example, J. Gennard, *A History of the National Graphical Association* (1990); J. Gennard and P. Bain, *A History of the Society of Graphical and Allied Trades* (1995); A. Marsh and V. Ryan, *The Seamen: a history of the National Union of Seamen, 1887–1987* (Oxford, 1988); J. E. Mortimer, *History of the Boilermakers' Society, volume 3: 1940–89* (1994); A. Marsh, *The Carpet Weavers* (Oxford, 1995). Perhaps the most successful recent work in this genre is K. Coates and T. Topham, *The Making of the Labour Movement: the formation of the Transport and General Workers' Union* (Nottingham, 1994).

10. See, for example, D. Howell, 'Editorial', *Labour History Review* (*LHR*), 60, 1, 1995; 'Comments' by M. Chase, S. Fielding, K. Flett and J. Halstead & D. Martin, *LHR*, 60, 3, 1995; J. Saville, 'The "crisis" in labour history: a further comment', *LHR*, 61, 3, 1996.

11. G. Eley and K. Neild, 'Why does social history ignore politics?', *Social History*, 5, 2, 1980, pp. 264, 267. See also R. Price, 'The future of British labour history', *International Review of Social History*, 34, 1991, for a renewal of such concerns.

12. J. Zeitlin, 'From labour history to the history of industrial relations', *Economic History Review*, 40, 2, 1987; H. Kimeldorf, 'Bringing the unions back in (or why we need a new old labour history)', *Labor History*, 32, 1, 1991. As is apparent below, we do not endorse the narrowing of labour history's agenda implicit in Zeitlin's prescriptions.

13. In 1990, for example, there were 29 entries under 'trade unionism' compared with 81 on 'popular culture, leisure, sport and religion', (*LHR*, 55, 2, 1990); in 1993 the comparable figures were 11 and 45 (*LHR*, 58, 2, 1993); in 1997, 25 and 56 (*LHR*, 62, 2, 1997), although the former figure was inflated by 8 entries relating to articles in *Historical Studies in Industrial Relations*: see below, note 35.

14. H. Pelling, *A History of British Trade Unionism* (5th edition, Harmondsworth, 1992); K. Laybourn, *A History of British Trade Unions, 1770–1990* (Stroud, 1992); J. Saville, *The Labour Movement in Britain* (1988); R. Hyman, 'Praetorians and proletarians: unions and industrial relations', in J. Fyrth (ed.), *Labour's High Noon: the government and the economy, 1945–51* (1993); J. Tomlinson, 'The Labour government and the trade unions, 1945–51', in N. Tiratsoo (ed.), *The Attlee Years* (1991); S. Tolliday and J. Zeitlin (eds), *Shop Floor Bargaining and the State: historical and comparative perspectives* (Cambridge, 1985); D. Lyddon, 'The car industry, 1945–79: shop

stewards and workplace unionism', in C. Wrigley (ed.), *A History of British Industrial Relations, 1939–79: industrial relations in a declining economy* (Cheltenham, 1996); C. Wrigley (ed.), *British Trade Unions, 1945–95: documents in contemporary history* (Manchester, 1997); J. Cronin, *Labour and Society in Britain, 1918–79* (1984).

15. On ethnicity there is very little by labour historians, although useful material is contained in general works such as R. Ramdin, *The Making of the Black Working-class in Britain* (Aldershot, 1987) and top-down surveys such as R. Miles and A. Phizacklea, 'The TUC and black workers', *British Journal of Industrial Relations*, 16, 2, 1978. There is a similar absence of substantial historical studies of women trade unionists, 1945–79. For surveys see S. Boston, *Women Workers and the Trade Unions* (1980); S. Lewenhak, *Women and Trade Unions* (1977); A. Wilson, 'Finding a voice: Asian women in Britain', in Feminist Review, *Waged Work: a reader* (1986). For the experience of one industry, see C. Cockburn, *Brothers: male dominance and technological change* (1983). W. Thompson, *The Good Old Cause: British Communism, 1921–91* (1992); N. Branson, *History of the Communist Party of Great Britain 1941–51* (1997); J. Hinton, *Shop floor Citizens: engineering democracy in 1940s Britain* (Aldershot, 1994). For studies of the CP before and during the Second World War, see N. Fishman, *The British Communist Party and the Trade Unions, 1933–45* (Aldershot, 1995) and R. Croucher, *Engineers at War* (1982).

16. P. Johnston (ed.), *Twentieth Century Britain: economic, social and cultural change* (1994).

17. Wrigley, *History*; R. Taylor, *The Trade Union Question in British Politics: government and unions since 1945* (Oxford, 1993).

18. Howell, 'Editorial'; Kelly, 'Does the field of industrial relations have a future?'; A. Campbell, 'The pasts and the futures of British labour history', unpublished paper delivered to the Ninth British-Dutch Conference on Labour History, Bergen, September 1994.

19. See, for example, the essays in N. Kirk (ed.), *Social Class and Marxism: defences and challenges* (Aldershot, 1996).

20. Hobsbawm, *On History*, p. 239.

21. Howell, 'Editorial'.

22. J. Belchem, 'Reconstructing labour history', *LHR*,.62, 3, 1997, pp. 320–1.

23. M. Savage and A. Miles, *The Remaking of the British Working-class, 1840–1940* (1994), p. 17. We don't address post-modernism in history further here, not because we feel it is not worthy of detailed attention but because of its minimal impact so far on our specific subject matter. Most of the historical writing influenced by post-modernism which is relevant to labour history is concerned with the nineteenth century. Labour history's encounter with post-modernism has been belated and limited. For example, the only contribution in *LHR* over the last decade which specifically engages with it has been Belchem, 'Reconstructing labour history'. Post-modernism has imposed only tangentially on industrial relations, and then largely in terms of related analyses of 'post-Fordism' and 'new times' which posit epochal change in

16

capitalism since the 1970s: see, for example, S. Crook et al., *Post-modernization: change in advanced societies* (1992). For a rare attempt to write the history of industrial relations in a post-modernist vein see, C. Hay, 'Narrating crisis: the discursive construction of the winter of discontent', *Sociology*, 30, 2, 1990. For an excellent general assessment of post-modernism's contribution to historical endeavour, see R.J. Evans, *In Defence of History* (1997).

24. E. Hobsbawm, 'Identity history is not enough', in *On History*; Evans, *Defence of History*, pp. 215–18.

25. Although the fickleness of fashion has ensured the loss of *History Workshop Journal* as a major support for labour studies. Recent work on trade unions from labour historians includes Hinton, *Shop floor Citizens*; Fishman, *The British Communist Party and the Trade Unions;* A. Campbell, N. Fishman and D. Howell (eds), *Miners, Unions and Politics, 1910–47* (Aldershot, 1996). For work in industrial relations which suggests an historical approach, see J. Kelly, 'Long waves in industrial relations: mobilization and counter-mobilization in historical perspective', *Historical Studies in Industrial Relations* (*HSIR*), 4, 1997; D. Lyddon, 'Industrial relations theory and labor history', *International Labour and Working-class History*, 46, 1994. However one must be concerned at the fact that the 3 volumes and 9 issues of *LHR* published since its revamp have included 21 articles, only 1 of which was a study of trade unionism: R. Stevens, 'Containing radicalism: the Trades Union Congress Organization Department and trades councils, 1928–53', *LHR*, 62, 1, 1997.

26. P. Willman and G. Winch, *Innovation and Management Control: labour relations at BL Cars* (Cambridge, 1995).

27. See, for example, the detailed and gripping account in M. Edwardes, *Back from the Brink* (1983); for a superior account of developments from the union side, see A. Thornett, *Inside Cowley. Trade union struggle in the 1970s: who really opened the door for the Tory onslaught* (1998).

28. Zeitlin, 'From labour history', p. 171, n. 47.

29. Willman and Winch, *Innovation*, pp. 1, 67. Compare their detailed treatment of industrial engineering, pp. 194–9, with their superficial attention to aspects of steward organization, pp. 159–61, 180–2.

30. D. Lyddon and P. Smith, 'Editorial', *HSIR*, 1, 1996.

31. Brody, 'Labor history', pp. 12–13; Lyddon, 'Industrial relations theory', pp. 136–7.

32. Terry and Edwards, *Shop floor Politics*, p. 3; of the case studies in this volume, only S. Jefferys, 'The changing face of conflict: shop floor organization at Longbridge, 1939–80' touches, and then only briefly, on the role of the Communist Party in the plant.

33. Fox, *History and Heritage*, p. xii, quoted, slightly abbreviated, in Lyddon and Smith, 'Editorial', p. 8.

34. Price, 'Future of British labour history', p. 256.

35. The value of *HSIR* is attested by its coverage of trade unionism in comparison with other journals. Its first 5 issues contained 16 articles, 11 of which

dealt with aspects of trade unionism. This understates the position as other articles dealing with management have been of relevance and trade union issues have also been addressed in review essays.

36. But see, for example, C. Crouch, *The Politics of Industrial Relations* (1978), pp. 148–58; S. Tolliday and J. Zeitlin (eds), *The Power to Manage? Employers and industrial relations in comparative-historical perspective* (1991); W. Grant, *Business and Politics in Britain* (1993); J. Melling and A. McKinlay (eds), *Management, Labour and Industrial Politics in Modern Europe* (Cheltenham, 1996).

37. Marsh, *New Politics of British Trade Unionism*, pp. xvii–xix. For his examples of the writing of political scientists on trade unionism in the 1980s, Marsh has to rely on brief references to D. Kavanagh, *Thatcherism and British Politics* (1987); A. King, 'Mrs Thatcher as political leader' in R. Skidelsky (ed.), *Thatcherism* (1988); and A. Gamble, *The Free Economy and the Strong State* (1988). For the earlier period he relies on Minkin and writers outside the mainstream of British political science such as K. Middlemas, *Politics in Industrial Society* (1979) and G. Dorfman, *British Trade Unionism against the TUC* (1983).

38. L. James, *Power in a Trade Union: the role of the District Committee in the AUEW* (Cambridge, 1984), pp. 3–5, 46; M. Armstrong, 'The History and Organization of the Broad Left in the AUEW (Engineering Section) until 1972, with special reference to Manchester', unpublished MA thesis, University of Warwick, 1978; see also J. McIlroy, 'Notes on the Communist Party and industrial politics', in J. McIlroy, N. Fishman and A. Campbell (eds), *British Trade Unionism and Industrial Politics, vol. 2: the high tide of trade unionism, 1964–79* (Aldershot, 1999). James thanks Eddie Frow for his help with this work. Frow was one of the architects of the faction and interviewed as such by Armstrong (*Power in a Trade Union*, p. vii). For the Platt's closure, see James, *Power in a Trade Union*, pp. 75–8, and H. Ratner, *Reluctant Revolutionary: memoirs of a Trotskyist, 1936–60* (1994), pp. 172–84.

39. See, for example, Hyman, *Industrial Relations*; J. Kelly, *Trade Unions and Socialist Politics* (1988).

40. E. Heery and J. Kelly, 'Professional, participative and managerial unionism: an interpretation of change in trade unions', *Work, Employment and Society*, 8, 1, 1994; P. Smith, 'Change in British trade unions since 1945', *Work, Employment and Society*, 9, 1, 1995; J. Zeitlin, '"Rank and filism" in British labour history, *International Review of Social History*', 34, 1989, and the responses by Richard Price and James Cronin in that same volume and by Richard Hyman in the subsequent issue; for one attempt at a sustained empirical examination of some of the issues raised in that debate, see M. Leier, *Red Flags and Red Tape: the making of a labour bureaucracy* (Toronto, 1995).

41. H. A. Turner, *Trade Union Growth, Structure and Policy: a comparative study of the cotton unions* (1962); V. Allen, *Trade Union Leadership: based on a study of Arthur Deakin* (1957); E. Hobsbawm, 'Trade union historiography', *Bulletin of the Study for the Society of Labour History*, 8, 1964, p. 33.

42. P. Routledge, *Scargill: the unauthorized biography* (1993). On Jones there is only J. Jones, *Union Man: an autobiography* (1986), and on Scanlon, K. Ryan, 'The power of the presidency: an evaluation of Hugh Scanlon's early leadership', unpublished paper delivered to the conference on British Trade Unionism 1940–79, University of Warwick, 1997.

43. On this point see D. Montgomery, *The Fall of the House of Labor: the workplace, the state and American labor activism, 1865–1925* (New York, 1987), p. 2; J. McIlroy, 'Still under siege: British trade unions at the turn of the century', *HSIR*, 3, 1997, pp. 118–21; Saville, 'The "crisis" in labour history', pp. 322–3.

44. D. Montgomery, 'The limits of union-centred history: responses to Howard Kimeldorf', *Labor History*, 32, 1, p. 116.

45. Ibid; J. McIlroy, review of Wrigley, *History*, in *HSIR*, 2, 1996, pp. 169–70.

46. Taylor, *Trade Union Question*, p. 4.

47. There is a voluminous literature on the general topic of economic decline which is usefully surveyed by M. Dintenfass, *The Decline of Industrial Britain, 1870–1980* (1992); see also D. Coates and J. Hillard (eds), *The Economic Decline of Modern Britain: the debate between left and right* (1986); D. Coates (ed.), *Industrial Policy in Great Britain* (Basingstoke, 1996); Melling and McKinlay, *Management, Labour and Industrial Politics*.

PART ONE

Overviews, 1945–79

CHAPTER ONE

The Role of Industrial Correspondents

Geoffrey Goodman

To describe the role and function of industrial correspondents in the post-war world, from the end of the Second World War in 1945, it is necessary first of all to describe the climate and the ambience of that post-war world. I was a young journalist just returning from nearly six years in the armed forces. My pre-war world, then, seemed as far removed as the immediate post-war period does to a contemporary generation. Everything had changed; most of all ourselves as individuals.

Memory plays tricks with time. But one thing remains very vivid; we all lived, then, in a kind of battlefield timewarp. Normality was not peacetime – but the battlefields, on land, sea and in the air. The new battlefield was adjustment to a non-war (rather than peaceful) environment. For, although we had moved away from the 'big bang' operation of wartime activities, the damage and the disrepair was still being assessed, in our own minds as well as in society at large. The public psyche itself was being newly formed or, at least, reformed.

Millions had returned to 'civvy street', or were still in the process of doing so when I came back to post-war journalism. That extraordinary act of demobilization was well under way, transferring something like 6 million – or was it 7 million? – people out of uniform or war factories into a post-war world of work and reconstruction. The dead were mourned and the war graves still being labelled. The mix of casualties – the partly-fit, the moderately well, the seriously unfit – still being categorized even as the newly-fledged Welfare State was being created; all the limited resources of that post-war Attlee government trying, magnificently and often absurdly amateurishly, to cope with the near-impossible. All of that provided the atmospherics against which we have to analyse the role of any journalist, not merely the industrial reporters, trying to cover the Britain of the late 1940s and early 1950s. It was a strange, incomplete, still largely disoriented post-war period, deeply unsure of itself, weakened, a touch arrogant in its uncertainties – always full of paradox. The big guns were silent, or so it then seemed. Only peacetime battlefields remained to be conquered in this new land in which a Labour government had been elected to power for the first time, with a landslide majority. History seemed to be beckoning.

Of course everyone needs some kind of battlefield to demonstrate their fantasies; to discover, or as it was then, to re-discover, their identity. That was part of the problem. The need was to fit into the new world that was being born out of the ashes of war. It is quite difficult, now, to look back at that epoch of 1945–50; and still more difficult to describe it to generations in the 1990s to whom that far-away country of post-war Britain must seem as far removed from their perception of reality as the Napoleonic wars.

It was then that I became an industrial correspondent. Or, as the role was then more correctly and modestly described, an industrial reporter. Most of us young journalists returning from war service preferred that description rather than the more grandiloquent label of journalist. Such grandness seemed absurdly inappropriate to most of us seeking entry into the legendary heights of Fleet Street. At that time I was not an industrial reporter. I was a general reporter covering everything from flower shows to murders. I moved around from provincial papers (that is, regional newspapers in modern argot) and then to the focal point of all ambitions, the grand alleyway to stardom, Fleet Street. Finally I reached the reporters' room at the *News Chronicle* – that marvellous national daily paper of the radical middle ground which, in modern terms, means a paper of the distinctly radical left. Of course even that very title probably sounds like something from the far away mists of time. The *News Chronicle* died in October 1960.

It was by pure accident that I became an industrial reporter. It was sometime around 1950–51 when, after about two years as a general reporter on the *News Chronicle*, I was given the opportunity to become a political reporter, standing in at first for the paper's distinguished lobby correspondent, Geoffrey Cox (now Sir Geoffrey) who was going on holiday. That was a magical break of luck for which I was scarcely equipped. The truth was that I was the only available spare hand around at the time who had an interest in political affairs. So it sort of came up with the rations. And, as I was told later, I did surprisingly well. That, too, was a surprise to me.

Then chance played its role again. The industrial correspondent of the paper, at the time, was the great Ian Mackay, arguably the best industrial writer in the land – indeed he later became an outstanding essayist for the paper. After some eighteen years as an industrial correspondent, the editor of the *News Chronicle* (Robin Cruikshank) wisely decided to let Mackay concentrate on his thrice-weekly essay and to leave the routine of industrial reporting to Mackay's then deputy (and indeed his mistress) Margaret Stewart. She then required a deputy and, as I was already listed as a potential specialist, I was drafted in to help out. It was my baptism as an industrial correspondent and I attended my first Trades Union Congress (TUC) at Brighton in 1950. Of course it was all pure magic for a young, politically minded, somewhat war-scarred reporter. The TUC was then at the peak of its authority (albeit not its membership). The war years, with Ernest Bevin at the Ministry of Labour and a key figure in Churchill's war cabinet, had led to the trade union movement becoming firmly cemented into the fabric of the state even if it was sometimes a painful experience because of the pressures of war-time legislation and the way in which Bevin was prone to use his vast powers. None the less the TUC was a power in the land, fully augmented by the Attlee government's six years in office. At that first Congress in September 1950 the Prime Minister, Clem Attlee, was a main speaker; so, too, was the legendary former general secretary of the TUC, Walter Citrine (then Lord Citrine). The great figures of the 1950s trade union movement, were all on display: Arthur Deakin, Sir William Lawther, Tom Williamson, Lincoln Evans. The attack on the establishment came from the then Communist-led Electrical Trades Union (ETU) whose President, Frank Foulkes, and General Secretary, Walter Stevens, presided over the defeat of the pay deal (effectively a wage freeze) that had been agreed between the Attlee government and the TUC the previous year. There were scenes of extraordinary rejoicing by the left-wing trade unions and incandescent rage emerging from the established order, led, primarily, by Arthur Deakin as General Secretary of the Transport and General Workers' Union (TGWU), the largest union in the country and, of course, Bevin's creation.

To have had such a baptism for my inaugural TUC was a piece of remarkable good fortune for this budding industrial correspondent. But there was much more in the pipeline during the next few years. My first full year as an industrial reporter, 1951, was exceptional as a year of political drama: the Gaitskell–Bevan conflict exploded throughout the political and trade union wings of the labour movement; Aneurin Bevan was appointed Minister of Labour in January 1951; the death of Sir Stafford Cripps in the autumn of 1950 had put Gaitskell into the Chancellor's job as Cripps's successor; the Attlee government was riven with dissent about the £4,700 million re-armament programme linked with the Korean war; then Bevan resigned in April 1951 – an action which was to dominate both the political and industrial wings of the labour movement throughout the whole of the 1950s and which penetrated almost every zone of the field covered by the industrial/labour reporters at that time. Indeed, it is important to emphasize that at that time the role of the industrial correspondent (labour correspondent was the by-line used by only a few of the broadsheet newspapers such as *The Times, Manchester Guardian, Financial Times* and several major regional daily papers) was predominant in most political stories involving the Labour Party outside the House of Commons and, oft times, even inside Parliament. At Labour Party Conferences the industrial correspondent almost always wrote the main stories while the political (lobby) correspondent tended to play a secondary role. Only in the mainstream of Westminster political stories did the political correspondent carry an automatic precedence in covering Labour Party affairs. Invariably this led to often quite severe tension within some newspaper offices and between the rival journalists; yet the personality battles were almost always won by the industrial correspondent whose status, in those days, was at least equal if not senior to any other specialist journalist on a national newspaper.

All that changed after 1979. But until then the industrial/labour correspondent (elevated in many offices to the status of industrial or labour editor) was one of the key posts in the national press, on television and radio. To be sure it was a role and status already beginning to be eroded at the margins during the 1970s, not least because of the growth in importance and status in financial coverage by the media, as well as the growing predominance of the political lobby. Even so it wasn't until Margaret Thatcher's government changed the entire landscape of the industrial and trade union scene that the role of the industrial correspondent suffered a gradual, then sharply, diminishing importance – a process due as much to the influence of the Downing Street 'spin doctors' as to the preferences of the editorial command in newspapers and television.

But let us return to the conditions and the climate of the 1950s and the situation at the end of the Attlee governments, after the election in October 1951 which brought the return of the post-war Conservatives, still led by Winston Churchill. Let us also reflect again on the political condition of Britain at that time which, by definition, determined the way journalists behaved and what their newspapers required of them. It is also important to recognize that newspapers were still the predominant source of national information, at national, regional and even local district levels. Television was still in its infancy and radio confined to the BBC's standard routine coverage which hardly ever took risks with speculative stories of any kind and certainly not with political/industrial affairs. So, the role of the national newspapers' industrial journalists was crucial and, without exaggeration, of real national importance.

Much of the industrial news of the day tended to emanate from the nationalized industries. From 1946 through to 1950, the Attlee government had transformed the industrial landscape of Britain. The great Acts of nationalization started with the Bank of England and swept through an entire range of basic industries – coal, gas, electricity, railways. All of them within the range of industrial journalists and all of them containing enough political and social drama to provide a cascade of news stories which often seemed endless as well as fascinating. When Manny Shinwell as the Minister for Fuel and Power (as the Energy Minister was then labelled) hauled up the flag of public ownership over the pitheads in January 1947, he signalled a new epoch in British industrial and political relations. Moreover the creation of the National Health Service in 1948 and the entire development of the welfare state dovetailed into the story of a Britain undergoing a massive social and economic revolution – a revolution in which it was the role of the industrial correspondents to play the part of war correspondents in the midst of an enormous physical, practical and emotional upheaval. It was also quite new territory. There were few ground rules except those the journalists created themselves as they went about their daily business. It was exciting, immensely challenging and, I believe for most of us involved, greatly fulfilling.

It was also an uneasy period for everyone actually involved in trying to transform those industries and give them a quite new and distinctive image from the one they had under private ownership. Trade union leaders were appointed to many of the new nationalized boards along with retired generals and former civil servants. The mix was strange and often ill-conceived. There were innumerable personal tensions to go along with the internal changes taking place at every level in the newly nationalized industries. The relations between workers, management and the public was a difficult, often critical one. At all points in this process the industrial reporters were at hand to report, comment, pursue.

The most fascinating part of it all was the developing, sometimes fractious, relationship between workers and management – and the resultant explosion of disputes, especially in the coal industry. Coal was, of course, the centrepiece of the whole programme. Over 700,000 miners in more than 800 collieries were on parade on Vesting Day in 1947. The demand for coal as the main energy resource for British industry was at its peak. The Attlee government begged the miners to extend the working week and increase productivity because the life-line of the nation rested on that output. Every dispute in the pits was regarded as a crisis. New systems of industrial relations and arbitration methods were drawn up, enshrined in the nationalization Acts themselves and put into operation – often with serious defects, some of which were actually identified from the outset. Never a day went by but that a national newspaper carried some story of crisis (and occasionally success) in one or more of the newly nationalized industries. Workers and management, unsure and untested, were struggling constantly with a new environment in which practicalities were so often in conflict with ideals. The same was true of the trade union leadership. Shinwell, as the minister responsible for drawing up plans for coal nationalization, invited the National Union of Mineworkers (NUM), newly formed out of the pre-war Miners' Federation of Great Britain, to play an active part in making the industry a shining example to all others in worker–management cooperation. Shinwell wanted the NUM to play a joint role in managing the coal industry. The NUM President, Sir William Lawther, awkward and gruff as they used to chisel them in the Durham coalfield, told Shinwell to go to hell. It was, he said, the job of the NUM to protect their members regardless of nationalization and they could best do that by remaining outside the managerial function. They wanted no part in running the industry, Lawther told a deeply saddened Shinwell. That was, and remains, a historic negative. The trade unions have probably paid a very high price for that decision since it established a mantra of adversarial relations which continued throughout the years of nationalized industries. It undoubtedly played a part in conveying the wrong image of public enterprise to the general public at large and was certainly seized on by hostile newspapers to generate the feeling that nationalization had failed. Of course there were many other elements to this conflict and tension; but the truth is that it was very much the conflict between workers and management in the public sector of industry which became the daily routine diet of industrial correspondents – probably right up to the miners' strike of 1984–5. These were the great issues that were already starting to burn across the land, and across the dreams of generations of socialist and trade union thinkers, when I began my industrial reporting days.

Not that the public sector was alone, or even primarily, responsible for industrial strife; the private sector was at least as much, sometimes even more, involved, notably the car industry. The two industries then at the top of the disputes' league table were mining and motor cars, with industries such as transport, shipbuilding and general engineering some way behind. Inevitably the daily news of strikes and strife in one part of industry or another led to the belief that the only function of the industrial reporter was as a conveyer belt of information about conflict on the shop floor. The industrial correspondent was widely seen as 'the strike reporter'. The deeper elements were then rarely investigated. I remember trying hard to impress my editors of the time with the need to broaden our vision and therefore our coverage. My argument was that there were social, economic and certainly psychological forces at work which required investigation and careful analysis and that the simplistic and conventional style of reporting disputes as if they were nothing more than open warfare battles between the shop floor and management was simply inadequate. To be fair, most of my editors agreed with this view but argued that the practicalities of day-to-day coverage demanded so much time and energy that there simply wasn't enough scope to carry out the longer-term and time-consuming operation I was advocating. So for a long time – far too long in my opinion – we remained, largely, strike and strife reporters.

There were odd times when I was able to break away from this remit and conduct longer-vision, in-depth reporting. One example was in the docks industry. Throughout most of the 1950s the docks were the focal point of widespread conflict. The industrial atmosphere in the docks was as bad as anywhere in the land – arguably, in some areas, even worse than in the pits or the motor factories. London docks, then situated around the inner Port of London, West India docks and the Royal group of docks further up river – Tilbury then occupied a somewhat marginal role in the port – were the heartland of trouble. So too were Liverpool docks and occasionally Hull, Glasgow and at odd times Southampton. The Transport and General Workers' Union had the biggest share of members in all the ports; but in the North-East the General and Municipal Workers also had strong membership and in London docks the 'blue' union (named because of the colour of the union's card), the National Amalgamated Stevedores and Dockers (NASD), was very strong in parts of the docks and its members regarded themselves as craftsmen, a cut above the semi-skilled or unskilled TGWU members. The two unions, the NASD 'blue card' union and the TGWU 'white card' members, were in constant conflict. Many of the dock disputes at that time were due to inter-union rivalry, more so than any clear argument with management. Days on end would be spent by industrial reporters in London (or Liverpool) docklands.

It seemed to me a rather futile operation, so I embarked, in the mid-1950s, on a tour of all the docks – Liverpool, Bristol, Manchester, Hull, Glasgow – to try to find out more about the tensions between the unions (the NASD had begun to penetrate TGWU strongholds in Liverpool and Hull) as well as the social and economic problems throughout the industry. I suppose I spent the best part of three weeks on this piece of 'investigative journalism' (which incidentally we then regarded as ordinary, albeit concentrated, reporting). When I came back to the office (the *News Chronicle*) and discussed the findings with the editor, he was as shocked as I was with the results. I had discovered astonishing inefficiencies, poor management bordering on the absurd, corrupt trade union practices and a bewildered workforce. It was dynamite material in those days – and probably would be even now. The editor agreed to three major feature pieces in the paper. But, before any of this appeared, I insisted that I ought to put my findings to the TGWU General Secretary, Arthur Deakin, for his comment. I went to see Deakin and put the story in front of him. He eyed me with great suspicion and demanded to know my sources for what he regarded as 'scandalous inventions'. Of course he knew I would not, could not, divulge any names, so he simply dismissed the whole business as a 'load of malicious anti-T and G lies', and warned me against publishing the material. The paper ignored his threats and did publish my stuff – though making sure that it was all carefully legally vetted. It caused a bit of a sensation at the time but I would like to think, however modestly, that those pieces played some small part in helping to clear the air in the docks industry – at least for a time. I make a point of this because it was not usual for such in-depth coverage to appear in the national press at that time. There were other colleagues on different newspapers who were also developing this technique – notably the highly competent staff of industrial reporters on the *Financial Times*, *Manchester Guardian* (John Anderson and later John Cole come to mind) and on the *Daily Express*, where the outstanding Trevor Evans presided over a splendid team of industrial reporters.

Part of the problem then, and indeed later, was the casual, lazy assumption that all disputes and certainly all unofficial strikes, were the work of the Communist Party (CP) and its army of industrial activists. It was often the first conclusion reached for by the average news desk anywhere. A strike in almost any industry led to an automatic assumption that the cause was some form of Communist 'conspiracy', if not worse – such as the hand of Moscow. Most of this, if not all, was pure nonsense. To be sure the CP was at its strongest and most influential in some of the main trade unions. What the Party lacked in electoral support it seemed to possess in its industrial influence on the shop floor. But the truth was that the vast majority of industrial disputes were based on genuine, or perceived-to-be-genuine, cases of injustice or managerial stupidity. It did not require any 'conspiracy' to generate the friction; it was there to be seen and palpably felt by any observer or reporter worth his salt. None the less it was always a problem for most industrial correspondents, even the most senior and experienced ones, to beat off the superficial assumptions of their news desks that the only reason for strife in the factories or coal mines or docks of Britain was the existence of an 'international Communist conspiracy'. I often wondered whether this naïve over-simplification actually played its own particular role in helping to encourage such a conspiracy where they existed at all.

Of course it would be idle to deny that the CP, along with other left-wing (and sometimes right-wing) organizations used the industrial climate of that period to exploit the situation to their advantage. But even where the influence of the CP was at its most powerful, the results of their activities were almost always exaggerated – not least by themselves. Nor is this to disguise the baleful example of CP practice at its most self-destructive – as in the case of the ballot-rigging episode in the Electrical Trades Union during the late 1950s and early 1960s. It was a situation in which I had more than a mere ringside seat. At a very early stage in the ETU ballot-rigging affair, I ran several stories in the *News Chronicle* revealing how a leading ETU official who had left the CP, the late Leslie Cannon, was being hounded by the union hierarchy. Cannon, who was an exceptionally able officer, was in charge of the union's pioneering education college at Esher. He was also standing for election to the executive in the face of severe opposition from his old comrades. When his election took place I had access to information, via Cannon, which convinced me that the election result had been deliberately falsified. I broke that story in the *News Chronicle* – the first hint that there was a ballot-rigging conspiracy at the centre of ETU power. From that story flowed the entire saga which was to become a classic case of misdirected power in a modern trade union. To be sure that was a Communist conspiracy – there could be no doubting that.

Even so it would be quite wrong to convey the impression – which some newspapers, of course, did at the time – that ballot-rigging was a monopoly of the communists. Most industrial correspondents knew perfectly well that ballot-rigging was a frequent, if not regular, practice in a number of trade unions, of the right as well as the left. In those days of unregulated trade union elections it was quite simple practice for local, as well as national, union officials to stuff the ballot boxes. Indeed I know of one major trade union which, at that time, operated a nationally ordained policy of instructing branch officials how ballot-rigging should be conducted. That particular union, one of the most respected in the Labour establishment, was under the control of a firm right-wing leadership. The practice to my knowledge went on for years without any press disclosure. Why, one might justifiably now ask? The only reason was that the leadership of that particular union had numerous 'friends' in the press who simply refused to investigate the evidence. When I sought to do so, every obstacle was placed in my path. It was very different with the case of the ETU.

Ballot-rigging, wherever it occurred, just like boardroom conspiracies, ought to have been pursued by my generation of industrial correspondents as sedulously as one would hope is now the case. Sadly that diligence was not common during the period I have been describing here.

Probably the most exciting, and demanding, period for industrial/labour correspondents was the 1960s. The closing years of the Macmillan governments brought the birth of a number of new institutions, such as the National Economic Development Council (NEDDY) which set a completely new course in the dialogue between a Conservative government, employers and the trade unions – and, of course, in the relationship with industrial correspondents. The years of the post-war Labour governments established a link between government, Whitehall and the trade unions that had brought the status of the industrial correspondent to new heights – both in terms of how they were viewed by government ministers as well as in their own newspaper offices. The Churchill, Eden and then Macmillan governments of the 1950s and early 1960s did nothing to weaken that status; indeed in many ways the role of the industrial correspondent was enlarged, not least by the growth of trade unionism, numerically and in influence.

The great wage disputes of the 1950s, in the car plants, general engineering and shipbuilding, transport (especially railways) as well as in the docks and coal mines, continued to provide a vast range of material for the industrial journalists. The space they were given in national and regional papers was prodigious. Front-page lead stories in the national dailies were commonplace. Cabinet ministers in the Conservative governments gave frequent briefings to the industrial corps (which then had a long-established and influential specialist group that included pretty well every nationally known industrial journalist). Whitehall's senior civil servants were available for off-the-record briefings at regular intervals; cabinet ministers, along with their juniors, were frequent lunch guests at the tables of industrial correspondents armed with generous expense accounts. The doors of state power were opened, if not completely then certainly to a degree that had not been experienced before. In effect the status of the industrial journalists reflected the role and importance of the TUC as an institution – just as much under the Conservative governments of that period as under Labour.

The search by Macmillan's cabinet for a more rational process with which to settle pay claims and avoid widespread industrial conflict (a philosophy always dear to Macmillan's heart) took on a fresh vigour even before the setting up of NEDDY in March 1962. Macmillan was determined to try to find a coherent system of incomes policy. He had become convinced that the old voluntarist practice of so-called 'free collective bargaining' was no longer workable in a modern economy. But he had no ready-made formula with which to replace that old system. His search for some kind of 'planning' led him to create NEDDY. And that process brought the industrial correspondents into the heart of Whitehall, perhaps on a scale never before experienced. Around the press conference tables of NEDDY the industrial correspondents had precedence not only over their political correspondent colleagues but also, at that time, over the financial journalists.

The city editors of those days had their own separate and important role – but it was distinct and certainly separate from that of the industrial correspondents. Influential though financial news was even then, the fact remains that the period I am now discussing was in so many ways the heyday of the industrial reporters. Moreover it became an increasing practice, during the Macmillan period, for industrial/labour correspondents to do something they had hardly ever done before – attend, and even report on, the Conservative Party annual conference. It was notable during the period of Selwyn Lloyd's term as Chancellor of the Exchequer that industrial correspondents began to attend his briefings at Tory Party conferences and have their stories published, often in preference to the words of their political colleagues.

That was very much the scene when Harold Wilson emerged as leader of the Labour Party – and was certainly one reason why Wilson always carried a special regard for the role of the industrial reporters, sometimes to the consternation and even the detriment of the lobby correspondents. Certainly the Wilson years crowned the developments already under way in the early 1960s and placed the industrial correspondent in a pivotal role. In effect they became parallel political correspondents. And nothing was more reinforcing of this trend than the creation of the Department of Economic Affairs (DEA) after the 1964 general election when Wilson appointed George Brown as his First Secretary at the DEA, effectively Deputy Prime Minister. With Brown's headquarters adjoining the Treasury, the new department of state was very much the power-house of the 1964 innovations. George Brown immediately set about creating his own political lobby of journalists – the industrial correspondents.

For the next two years, until Brown moved to the Foreign Office in 1966, the First Secretary's relations with the press and indeed with television and radio were conducted almost entirely through the channel of his close links with the industrial/labour correspondents. The stream of events and the creation of new centres of influence and activity was non-stop. The Prices and Incomes Board was set up under Aubrey Jones. Then there was the Declaration of Intent, a concordat between government, CBI and TUC to oversee the rejuvenation of British industry and link higher productivity, efficiency and economic growth with a more rational system of pay bargaining (which meant pay restraint) and price regulation. At the same time George Brown set his team of industrial advisers, all newly appointed to his brand new department, working on a National Plan for economic recovery which was scheduled for publication by the end of 1965. Brown's DEA was an absolute beehive in which the First Secretary was the tireless commander-in-chief, urging on his army of officials, industrialists, trade union leaders – and industrial journalist contacts (which were countless) to raise new horizons for national economic ambitions. It was a remarkable period for all involved, not least the corps of industrial correspondents which saw Brown often on a daily basis, and even travelled Europe with him on his various table-thumping missions. Even after his departure from the DEA – after which the new, innovative department effectively went into decline – the Whitehall scene became the natural hunting ground for the industrial correspondent.

This was chiefly due to the prices and incomes policy which, by the late 1960s, came to dominate the entire domestic political and industrial scene. With the TUC playing the part, virtually, of an extension of government and its General Secretary, George Woodcock, effectively enjoying the status of a cabinet minister, the industrial lobby was at its peak of journalistic influence. The Royal Commission on the Trade Unions (and Employers) – the Donovan Commission – added to the overall impetus. New institutions emerging from the Commission's report, like the Commission on Industrial Relations (CIR), all added still further to the thrust and direction of industrial journalism. Barbara Castle's White Paper, *In Place of Strife*, was, perhaps, the final lightning conductor. For years the tensions between the Wilson Government and the unions over pay policy, statutory and voluntary, had dominated the agenda; now came Barbara's plans to follow up on the Royal Commission report by introducing legislation to control strikes. By then Victor Feather had taken over from Woodcock at the TUC (Woodcock becoming the first chairman of the CIR). For nearly two years, up to the general election of 1970, the battle between the government and the trade unions was hardly ever off the front-pages: the Castle versus Feather contest. Frank Cousins, already having resigned from the Wilson government over his opposition to pay restraint, and still very much the leader of the union revolt against the government's pay policy, led the fight from his imperial seat as General Secretary of the TGWU. When he handed over to Jack Jones, his successor as TGWU leader quickly registered in the opinion polls as the 'most powerful man in Britain'. Wilson, fighting to regain some sort of order, brought Jones and Hugh Scanlon, President of the engineers' union, to Chequers one weekend and instructed Scanlon to 'take your tanks off my lawn, Hughie'. For the industrial correspondents, hanging on every move and every word of this extraordinary contest, it was indeed like covering a war zone. Nor did any of this stop with the election of the Heath government in June 1970. Indeed the battlefield grew noisier by the day.

Heath's Industrial Relations Act of 1971 set a formal seal on the warfare. For two years the entire industrial scene seemed to be in perpetual turmoil: national one-day strikes were called by the TUC; days of national protest against the Heath legislation; the trade union hierarchy were in almost constant session. Inside the trade union movement there was equal turmoil as some unions decided to adhere to the new legislation, to avoid costly legal battles, while the majority opposed the new Act with all their force. The TUC, at the centre of this battle scene, was probably in the news more than at any time since the general strike of 1926. The industrial reporters grew in number as newspapers, regional as well as national, and television crews were expanded to cover the picture. If one looks back now at the whole decade of the 1960s, it is possible to detect the pattern of growth in the power and influence of the industrial correspondents and the impact they had, not only on shaping the major news items but also in the development of their own status inside their own newspapers, television and radio networks. There had been nothing quite like this before. And after Margaret Thatcher, from 1979 when the entire scene began to change, there has been nothing like it since.

Everything flowing from that period reinforced, at the time, the role and significance of the industrial journalist. The space and prominence allocated to their stories in broadsheet and popular tabloid papers alike, on all TV and radio networks, commanded a position that hardly any other specialist reporter, in the political lobby or anywhere else, could successfully challenge. When Heath's government performed its remarkable U-turn in 1972, effectively abandoning the Industrial Relations Act and introducing an Industry Act, under Peter Walker (then Secretary of State at the Department of Trade and Industry) which was more interventionist than any piece of legislation since Attlee's nationalization Acts, the continuity of the industrial correspondents' coverage took on yet another lease of life. Indeed there was no significant break in the process through the 1970s.

The oil crisis of September 1973 triggered yet another cycle of dramatic economic and industrial events which engulfed the Heath government and, after the miners' dispute of 1973–4, brought Harold Wilson back to office in February 1974. Immediately there was a new agenda for the industrial correspondents who had scarcely put away their typewriters after the miners' strike and the knock-on effects of that memorable event. Now it was the Social Contract – which, in its way, was a developmental advance from George Brown's days and his Declaration of Intent, albeit this time with the trade unions in a still more commanding role. But the shadows were already falling across this busy scene. As the Wilson days gave way to James Callaghan at No. 10, the tensions grew between government and TUC, or more precisely between Callaghan and his cabinet and the various powerful individual trade unions. Most of us knew in our boots as well as our hearts that something had to give, something was going to snap.

The four years of the Social Contract's pay policy is worth a book in itself. It was the apotheosis of the corporatist concept: the ultimate point, then, in

34

the consensus between government and trade unions. The strain put on trade unionism as an institution was too great. Trade union leaders were asked to carry a responsibility – indeed it was demanded of them – that they simply couldn't sustain, even with the best will in the world. When Callaghan was told this in the mid-summer of 1978, he refused to accept the limitations of trade union power and authority. He told the inner corps of the TUC leadership that he would 'go over their heads' and urge the rank-and-file, their membership, and the voters to back his government's argument about restraint and public spending. Those of us covering those final days of the Callaghan government, through the appalling confusion in that 'winter of discontent', could visibly see the writing on the wall for the Labour government, maybe even for the trade unions, if not for our own role as industrial correspondents. So it was to be.

Margaret Thatcher's victory in May 1979 brought an entire epoch to an end. Just how traumatic it was going to be did not occur to us at the time. She herself had never really trusted the industrial journalists. When she met them collectively for the first time, shortly after her election as leader of the Conservative Party, I well remember her iciness and demonstrable lack of interest in our work. Indeed there was a perceptible contempt for our special field of interest. It ought to have been a warning signal. From the moment of her move into Downing Street, Mrs Thatcher made it her business to weaken and then cut the links that had been established between the industrial correspondents and government, at all levels. At first she was not all that successful in her mission to weaken, perhaps even eliminate, the industrial correspondents and their influence. Her Employment Secretary, Jim Prior, who got on well with the industrial journalists, continued a friendly and informative relationship. So, too, did several other ministers in Thatcher's early cabinets, including the Chancellor, Sir Geoffrey Howe, with whom the industrial reporters had established a mutually useful link when he was drafting Heath's Industrial Relations Act in 1970. But these links were soon to be weakened as Thatcher's control over her Cabinet grew in strength and power.

By the mid-1980s, the links had become severely strained. She regarded the Fleet Street band of industrial correspondents as an extension of the Labour Party and, still worse, the trade unions. Moreover, she conveyed that message to her friends in the press. Her connections with the editors and proprietors of the majority of national newspapers, by then mostly committed Thatcherites, enabled her to convince them that they must change their habits. The demotion of the industrial correspondents had begun and it was soon to develop into a virtual elimination on numerous newspapers, especially the tabloids. One by one the national newspapers moved away from the kind of industrial coverage that had been so profoundly dominant in the decades before. As with the decline of the trade unions, so, too, the industrial correspondent began to disappear from the columns of newspapers. Industrial news as such was played down. The financial journalists were elevated along with the growth of a market economy ambience. Some national newspapers that, for generations, had boasted of the quality of their industrial reporters simply scrapped the appointment. When a story broke requiring attention on the industrial front, a general reporter was put on the task – if indeed the news was reported at all. The door closed on an entire epoch of journalism and effectively, it has yet to be re-opened.

CHAPTER TWO

Making Trade Unionists: the Politics of Pedagogy, 1945–79

John McIlroy

Education within the labour movement may be conceived as a socialization in traditions, values, policies and strategies, as facilitating the engagement and mobilization of members, the selection and development of cadres for leadership and functionaries for service, as a training in ends and means, in the elaboration of desirable objectives and the skills necessary to achieve them. It may be understood as a contribution to developing the culture of the working class, its world view and its political mission. Such education may be formal or informal, based upon organic or self-organized discussion and transmission in the workplace or in union bodies. Pedagogies of labour will certainly reflect and may legitimize and reinforce or alternatively, challenge and consciously seek to change prevailing philosophy, programme and leadership within the movement. They may engender disputation as to the resources committed, who will organize programmes, and the content of the curriculum. Why certain choices are made on these issues while others are rejected will tell us something about the labour movement and its politics. Trade union education is thus part – if a small part – of the agenda of industrial politics. Consideration of its development may cast light on competing conceptions of how labour should organize and act.[1]

The post-war years saw the development of the efforts of Bevin and Citrine to construct a centralized trade union movement marrying Fabianism and economism in the regulation of capitalism.[2] This hybrid labourism continued to be contested. Its central tenets, modulated, 'top-down' political reform, the separation of politics from economics, free collective bargaining and union autonomy, required continual renewal. A review of trade union education demonstrates its relationship to the agenda of modernization and quasi-corporatism in the post-war years. It furnishes insights into conflict, coherence and agency, illuminating how decisions were made, how certain possibilities were pursued and others suppressed. It is highly relevant, given the silence on education and training in contemporary accounts of post-war trade unionism and consequent reliance on a specialist literature largely based on uncontextualized, celebratory accounts.[3]

Post-war visions

The themes which dominated the post-war period had emerged by 1945. There was insistent advocacy from enthusiasts of the necessity of a qualitative extension of workers' education as a contribution to strengthening trade unionism, stimulating industrial efficiency and deepening participatory democracy. Optimistic estimations of the depth of the activism and solidarity engendered in wartime, the work of the Army Bureau of Current Affairs, and the Labour government's commitment to popular education and socialist culture buoyed expectations of expansion. Post-war confidence confronted an enduring neglect of education which is usually related to the pragmatism of Labourism and the pallid culture and restricted corporate life of British trade unionism[4]. Jack Grahl of the Fire Brigades' Union (FBU) informed the 1945 TUC Congress that less than 100,000 members were involved and for most this meant an occasional lecture. The Transport and General Workers' Union (TGWU) led the field with annual expenditure of £8,605, but more typical was the National Union of Public Employee's (NUPE) £450 per annum, spent on courses from the two voluntary organizations, the National Council of Labour Colleges (NCLC) and the Workers' Educational Association (WEA).[5] Union leaders explained the small scale of education programmes in terms of apathy: 'The fundamental problem is not the lack of provision for education but the lack of interest shown by the rank and file'.[6] With classes almost completely in the workers' own time there was indeed an unrelenting struggle to attract students in the 1940s, as in the 1950s. By 1950 only 9 out of 168 affiliated unions were sending students to TUC courses and a year or two later it was remarked the demand was 'negligible'. The emphasis on self-organization and workers' control, with the students selecting syllabus and tutor in the WEA branch or the local labour college, had atrophied.[7]

The centre of gravity moved from the voluntary organizations which flanked the movement into the unions themselves. The conflicting visions of workers' education – independent working-class education purveyed by the NCLC, liberal education proffered by the WEA – now had to compete with the TUC's attempt to universalize a more limited, bureaucratically-delivered, role training. This latter approach flowed from Citrine's conception of the labour movement as an efficient, representative partner for capital and the state. It was privileged as:

> the means by which the Trade Union Movement could be made more efficient, locally and centrally. The trade union leader was expected to be an administrator, a negotiator, to be familiar with trade union law and express himself clearly. A certain amount of wasted effort could be made good by adequate technical training.[8]

The model was the TUC weekend and summer schools which Citrine had fostered before the war in order to encourage identification with the established leadership and its politics. Technical training *provided for* trade unionists made for efficiency and loyalty. The NCLC and WEA, which still adhered to self-organization and student control of classes, were seen as dealing, in contrast, with 'the more *academic* subjects' (emphasis added). Their work was now counterposed to: 'education purely in the work of the union which may have for its purpose the creation of a more enlightened membership or specific training to fit members for office in the union'.[9] Technical training was set against the older conceptions of education for social understanding and political emancipation. It was aimed at office holders rather than in an undifferentiated way at active workers. It was based on a clear division between society and work, politics and trade unionism, between the voluntary organizations and the unions.

Citrine emphasized narrow instrumentalities. Courses should be 'essentially practical in character', for: 'I do not want them to be taught abstractions and then find no relation between these abstractions and their day-to-day administrative work as trade union officers or active members'.[10] This necessitated the assertion, as early as 1945, in response to a bid for partnership by the NCLC, that the TUC must possess 'undivided control' of the courses it sponsored in order to ensure functionaries were 'trained in the concrete application of the policy and principles of our movement'.[11] Trade unionism and collective bargaining were conceived as forming a distinct field of educational endeavour. It was increasingly demarcated from politics, viewed legitimately as the preserve of the Labour Party, and, illegitimately, of the Communist Party (CP), whose members were kept away from tutoring courses in many unions. The NCLC – whose Marxism was viewed as more of an embarrassing relic than a threat – and the WEA were, in their turn, regarded as bearers of social and political education, separated out from the labour movement and increasingly kept at a distance by Congress House. Balance was maintained by the TUC sponsoring the broader trade union studies course at the London School of Economics and evening classes at other universities, and by rhetorical statements on the importance of an all-round education for healthy trade unionism.[12] There was a crying need for:

> a greater provision of that kind of trade union technical education which only the movement itself can provide. There is no desire to compete with the well established work of the NCLC, WEA and Ruskin College. Each has a sphere of work in which it is performing service of great use to the Movement and it is hoped that work will be maintained and extended. The aim of the TUC is to fill a gap.[13]

Empiricist traditions and the cautious, muddled striving to produce a centralized, efficient trade unionism, articulated with the state, encountered little opposition. One delegate to Congress observed evocatively: 'You cannot tackle an administrative job by using the name of Marx, Lenin, Lloyd George or anybody else. You have to get down to brass tacks'.[14] In the TGWU Bevin, always contemptuous of the NCLC, and Deakin espoused a similar philosophy. Education centred on administrative skills, industrial legislation and union history was seen as an instrument of movement building and the creation of hierarchical cohesion. The education scheme, a recent historian of the union observed, was directed:

> towards the greater integration of the active membership into the procedures, the norms and the 'tradition' of the TGWU. An active membership at branch and district levels schooled in the constitution and the objectives of the union might be expected more readily to resist the appeal of sectional and dissident movements ... a well tutored lay membership would strengthen the administrative and organizational efficiency of the union.[15]

Such approaches were strengthened by the educational weaknesses of the voluntary organizations as well as antipathy towards the political and cultural ethos of the NCLC. The latter had perceived itself, at least in embryo, as the educational wing of the labour movement. Its vision and its desired educational territory remained a labour movement, integrated industrially and politically, preparing itself for ideological domination:

> Labour's struggle was not simply an industrial and political struggle. It was also a vast struggle on the field of ideas, an intellectual struggle. To carry through that struggle successfully the Labour Movement required its own educational machine and its own educational policy ... The objects of the Movement are not only to improve social conditions but to bring about a new social order. Consequently the social sciences (eg history and economics) which deal with social problems, are the most important to the working class movement and such subjects form the main part of the NCLC's curriculum ... A system is not changed merely because some people understand it. Steps have to be taken to change it. This requires efficient organization. Thus the NCLC runs classes and postal courses on subjects like chairmanship and public speaking, Trade Union branch administration, Local Government etc.[16]

Seeking to induct workers in both politics and trade unionism, its efforts directed towards both unions and the Labour Party, the NCLC was already in the 1940s in political and financial decline. Its Marxist cutting edge was rusted and its veteran General Secretary asserted in 1947:

> From being principally concerned with fostering an anti-capitalist viewpoint, independent working class education had to concern itself with the more difficult task of engendering a constructive socialist outlook and providing a training necessary to the intelligent grappling of the vast and complex problems confronting the country and the world.[17]

This entailed total support for the Labour government and economic responsibility under its Conservative successors. Marxism was increasingly played down and there was a significant move in classes towards practical skills and current affairs, while even state aid was considered. The limitations of the traditions of independent working-class education were demonstrated when its longstanding supporter, Ellen Wilkinson, became a Minister of Education of impeccable orthodoxy.[18] When the NCLC's debate on reversing its fundamental objections to state financial aid upheld the *status quo*, Wilkinson thanked Millar for saving her from an embarrassing situation. The breadth and disarray of the NCLC were demonstrated in the sustained attempts of its leaders to have the organization taken over by both the TUC, between 1946 and 1957, and the Labour Party, between 1946 and 1951. These episodes affirmed the disregard with which both the TUC and the Labour Party, despite the presence of former NCLC organizers Morgan Phillips and Len Williams at the heart of the party machine, held the post-war NCLC.[19] The decision of the Labour Party to establish, instead, its own small-scale education scheme, based upon the need to train activists and induct members into policy, affirmed the power of centrifugal divisions and the ascendancy of organizational needs.[20] On the left, the pre-war divisions between the NCLC and the CP were reinforced by the President, Arthur Woodburn's membership of the government, by Millar's intelligence-gathering on CP members, his acceptance of the Labour Party's right to question the politics and activities of his organizers, and the CP's left turn from 1947.[21]

Unlike the NCLC, the WEA had always stood, with contradictions, for the melioration of class conflict and the creation of the intelligent, realistic trade union reformist integrated into the political mainstream. Notwithstanding, numerous trade unionists, left and right, had acquired a political and economic education for activism in its classes. Its reformist ethos was at one with Labourism, and like the NCLC it now emphasized education for service in the new social democratic state.[22] Supporters of the WEA at the TUC, such as Harold Clay of the TGWU, occasionally delivered muted criticism of the priority accorded practical instrumentalism: 'We have got to think not only in terms of fitting people to be more technically efficient in the ordinary tasks of the labour movement, but we have in an expanding democracy, to think in terms of education for citizenship'.[23] The WEA's trade union arm, the Workers' Educational Trade Union Committee (WETUC), reasserted its commitment to political education, but again with accompanying genuflection to skills training:

> The WEA has repeatedly stated that in trade union education it is primarily concerned with a broad liberal background of knowledge leaving the more 'specialised' and 'technical' provision to the TUC and to the unions themselves. It would, however, be difficult to distinguish sharply between which is 'liberal' and which 'specialised' and 'technical' and there is undoubtedly something of a no-man's-land which there may be some danger of neglecting.[24]

The WEA was by 1947 providing, in comparison with the 1930s, a diminishing programme of education for trade unionists. It was increasingly concerned with competition from university extra-mural departments, its erstwhile partners, who after 1945 entered the field on their own account. Like the universities, it drew lines against Communists and what was euphemistically termed an 'unbalanced' or 'unprofessional' approach to union education. In a number of incidents, most notably at the Oxford Delegacy for Extra-Mural Studies, the parameters of the permissible were redefined through action against CP members.[25]

By 1950 the Labour Party's decision to create an in-house scheme of education was emulated by the CP, whose history had been marked by oscillations between support for broad based schemes of Marxist education and the assertion of party monopoly and control. In 1945 the CP's emphasis had been on work in the adult education bodies to create a mass socialist education. The party saw the new stress on training loyal, efficient functionaries, as otiose, unless aligned with economic and political studies marked by an anticapitalist approach. The left turn from 1947 saw a retreat to party training and out of hand rejection of 'the flood of class collaboration material that is poured out by the General Council of the TUC, by the Labour Party and through the educational attacks of the WEA and the NCLC'.[26]

The Attlee governments saw no consummation of hopes for a mass, radicalized workers' education taking socialism forward, indeed, workers' education was in decline in the NCLC and WEA, and the unions were failing to fill the gap. The 1940s set the pattern for the twenty years after the war: rhetorical support for growth but a practical failure to generate new resources or make education organic to union concerns; abstention from the state; the hardening of conceptions of workers' education as separate from adult education; the accentuation of practical, specialist, organization-specific, bureaucratically-delivered training. The failure of the projected Labour Party take-over of the NCLC petered out, not, as some have stated, because of the latter's opposition. There was a lack of will inside the party to overcome the technical problems involved and to provide either additional finance or broad based, labour movement education. There was some feeling that labour's educational mission was now accomplished. In the face of conservatism from above, apathy below endured.[27]

From fragmentation to unity?

The TUC's critics in 1945 asserted it was mistaken in limiting its responsibility to technical training. They pointed out that, on its own account, this constituted only one strand in union education and responsibility should not be divided. The General Council should coordinate a comprehensive, unified scheme. A successful 1946 resolution to this effect was not acted upon.

Whilst there were, as the TUC argued in justifying inaction, real financial and organizational problems, the amalgamation of the NCLC and WETUC under TUC aegis was a realistic possibility. There can be little doubt that the TUC 'killed the resolution' and that the rationale was its prioritizing of its own distinctive provision and the desire to insulate it from outsiders, particularly from what it saw as the pretentious, troublesome NCLC.[28] There was visible antagonism towards the NCLC, which was seen as an untrustworthy ally suffering from delusions of grandeur. Funded by the state and with support outside the movement, the WEA was less demanding. Moreover it had its advocates on the TUC Education Committee through the 1950s, whilst the NCLC had no friend at court. Attempts at securing greater cooperation between the NCLC and the TUC in the early 1950s and reopening the question of rationalization of union education were firmly repulsed by Congress House.[29]

The TUC's courses in London remained on a very small scale. Despite a reduction in their length from four to two weeks in 1955, only 73 students attended the general training courses, 66 the production and management courses, and 47 the courses in industrial negotiations – less than 200 trade unionists out of 8 million.[30] Expansion lay elsewhere. The Electrical Trades' Union (ETU) appointed an education officer and then opened a residential college – something that defied the TUC through this period. The General and Municipal Workers' Union (GMWU) began to develop its own courses in 1954, the Union of Shop Distributive and Allied Workers (USDAW) in 1958, with the emphasis once more on the practicalities of organization and bargaining. Again the scope should not be exaggerated: by the middle 1950s the TGWU was devoting in total £80,000 to education, whilst at the decade's end, the TUC spent three times as much on its international work as it did on publicity and education in Britain. Education remained a neglected aspect of union activity.[31]

None the less it was the unions who were now the initiators of change, as the TGWU's relationship with the WEA demonstrated. The drift of the two WEA reports on trade union education in the 1950s was towards acceptance of the view they ascribed to the unions: what was needed was 'a substantial measure of trade union education at a more basic and practical level. This gives priority to elementary training in a variety of practical skills'.[32] Whilst it was claimed that, in its schools with the TGWU, the WEA achieved a successful blend of political education and skills training, by the end of the 1950s training in technique was central. Critics condemned these courses as 'an educational travesty' and staff and students complained of political interference to ensure union policy was not criticized.[33] Whilst innovations were often described as changes in 'teaching methods', what was essentially involved was a change in the *content* of union education. This, and the switch in the centre of gravity, was symbolized by the move of Tony Corfield, the leading WEA figure in these courses, to become the TGWU's Education Officer and his blunt contemporary assessment that what had occurred was a transition from education to training.[34]

That this was not simply a matter of student or union demand can be seen from another important development. Successful day-release courses of up to three years' duration were mounted by university extra-mural departments, notably with the National Union of Mineworkers (NUM), but by the early 1960s with a wide variety of trade unionists. Again there was diversity, related to the different political traditions of both educators and the trade unionists they taught. The courses in Nottinghamshire were more liberal, and in union terms more abstract, those in Derbyshire focused more on the union and were more politically committed. But overall, the two- and three-year courses at Sheffield, Leeds and Nottingham universities provided an alternative model to skills training, seeking to integrate technique within political and economic education. The South Wales Miners experimented from the late 1940s with a scheme at Coleg Harlech and from 1957 appointed a full-time education officer who organized day-release courses 'geared towards the institution of a socialist society'. A further contrast was provided by the Oxford Delegacy's courses for carworkers centred on practical workplace industrial relations.[35]

The NCLC found itself increasingly unable to keep up with its state-resourced competitors, particularly in the universities, and the unions' turn to their own provision. By 1955 it once more resolved on a TUC take-over and the Building Workers were pressing the TUC, yet again, to take on rationalization and a unified scheme. They noted it was, 'increasingly difficult to the NCLC to continue its work on such a wide scale.[36] In fact the scale was declining. The defection of the South Wales Miners and USDAW went hand in hand with failure to win new support. The NCLC's leadership was ageing and there was increasing dependence on postal courses. In 1957 around 90 unions were still affiliated and the NCLC claimed to be running 782 classes with 11,625 students and almost 15,000 correspondence courses. As the TUC had noted earlier, there was some tendency to exaggerate. Much of the provision was short and ephemeral.[37] And by 1959 the unions were spending twice as much on their own schemes as they were disbursing to the NCLC and WEA put together.[38]

Union education constituted a complex mosaic in which the TUC occupied a far from preponderant position but a great deal of authority and legitimacy. The immediate post-war generation of union leaders had little time for political education and were rarely prepared to finance anything half-way adequate from their political funds. The strongest impulse inside the TUC and key unions was to support a restricted view of both the content of education and the students who should be involved in it, with a central focus on the creation of committed functionaries executing established union policy. Yet its realization met with limited success. Continuous pressures on affiliates and initiation of regular meetings of union education officers meant that by 1957 matters had improved somewhat in relation to the Congress House courses. The TUC was able to open its own (non-residential) training college. But the height of its ambition for 1957–8 was the provision of 1,200 one-week places.[39] Nevertheless, when the difficulties facing the NCLC prompted a successful motion at the 1957 Congress calling for a coordinated scheme, the TUC was inclined to look more favourably on the issue.[40]

As the 1950s moved to their close, the demands the state was placing on the unions to speak with a more centralized voice were growing. So was fragmentation within the movement in a range of ways, from the growth of workplace bargaining to the tendency of unions to develop their own education schemes, rather than support TUC provision. A coordinated education scheme could provide the TUC with the opportunity, through the consequent increase in affiliation fees required to finance it, to channel and centralize union spending on education and thus elicit greater support for TUC provision. The creation of loyal lay activists could become another service the TUC could offer unions, and a means of strengthening the voice of the centre in relation to its affiliates, thus influencing the development of British trade unionism.[41] The details of the new TUC scheme were hammered out between 1959 and 1963. The General Council accepted with good grace the decision of the 1959 Congress that, 'the education of active trade unionists must include some sustained study of those subjects which made possible an understanding of the economic, social and political circumstances within which trade unions conducted their work'.[42] And indeed the final scheme accepted in 1964 embraced

the same fourfold educational purpose as those hitherto provided by the NCLC and WETUC, namely
(a) to provide opportunities for active trade union members to undertake systematic social, economic and political studies relevant to their trade union interests
(b) to supplement the direct efforts of trade union organizations to provide 'technical' trade union training
(c) to provide opportunities for active trade union members to remedy to some extent deficiencies of general education which might handicap them in their trade union work, and
(d) to provide directly and indirectly opportunities for trade union students to acquire some knowledge and experience of the techniques of study.[43]

Debate and eventual dissension centred around organization and control. The 1961 Congress was informed that the scheme would be governed by a Joint Trade Union Committee drawing upon not only the TUC Committee, but elected trade unionists and educators.[44] The General Secretary, George Woodcock, was concerned: financial responsibility would rest with the TUC, while this broad-based committee would be technically independent of it,

45

indeed TUC representatives could constitute a minority. Determined there would be no separate educational wing in the movement, Woodcock closely supervised developments and the TUC Education Secretary, Dennis Winnard, attended meetings of the TUC Education Committee and made his views forcefully known. The prestige and sour pugnacity of the General Secretary carried the day. By 1962:

> most of the members of the TUC Education Committee held that control should rest with the General Council directly through the education committee rather than indirectly through a Joint Education Committee in which the General Council's representation would be a minority.[45]

Congress accepted education would become a TUC service and the final scheme provided for no decision-making body outside Congress House. Woodcock perorated on 'the fundamental principle of responsibility from the top down ... if education has become a TUC activity then the TUC must be absolutely in control of it'.[46]

Despite Congress decisions on the need for a broad trade union education, Woodcock's views boded ill for the political heritage of the NCLC and WETUC:

> education is not training, it is a very broad activity intended to stimulate the critical faculties. That is perhaps better done by an organization dedicated exclusively to the task of education and not as a pendant to other activities.[47]

Woodcock, his staff, and particularly his successors who were schooled largely in bureaucratic routinism, with little past experience of shop floor activism, were anxious to avoid political quarrels and treading on the toes of affiliates. His successors took little day-to-day interest in this sphere. Education was another bureaucratic service. Or it should be; so there was a need to circumscribe its potential for controversy and democracy. The TUC did not hold conferences or invite outsiders onto its international or economic committees. This was the path education, or rather training, should follow.

This philosophy marked developments over the next decade. The traditions of the NCLC and WETUC were rooted out in favour of a singular emphasis on the delivery of technical training. The issues were never explicitly debated. And the relatively few Congress speeches and resolutions to the contrary over succeeding years were paid lip-service or ignored.[48] Yet its logic is far from apparent. Given sustained acceptance by Congress of the need for broader education, the TUC's disregard of the clear mandate to produce programmes fusing social and technical education, both of which were viewed by Congress as relevant to union activities, reflected partisan priorities. If there *was* to be a division of labour, it might well appear more rational for affiliates, who were expanding their own provision in the 1950s and 1960s, to train their own activists in the skills and knowledge required in specific organizsational and bargaining contexts, leaving the TUC to address the political and economic issues which faced all unions. The illogical denouement carried its own logic: in the sphere of organizing and bargaining it was necessary to emphasize similarity, if not uniformity, between unions and industries, in the interests of a *specific version* of cohesion. This was bound up with a political context of increased state intervention in collective bargaining and the intensification from the late 1950s of corporatist tendencies, with the demand for a more centralized movement informed with economic rationality and able to deliver wage restraint. The emergence of 'the shop steward problem' coincided with the emergence of the TUC education scheme.

Reforming industrial relations, recreating the shop steward

The development of 'the shop steward problem', centred on the relative autonomy of workplace organization, unofficial strikes and wage drift, saw the steward become the primary object of training to the exclusion of other trade unionists. Hitherto much steward training had been informal or semi-formal. Those who became stewards in the 1940s and 1950s often recall being groomed and advised by established stewards; learning through listening; 'sitting next to Nellie'; emulating the example of their seniors; and pondering everyday experience. Some learned through CP factory branches.[49] There was, at times, suspicion of organized training, its provenance, purpose and effectiveness, although there was semi-formal provision. In the 1940s, it was claimed, the TGWU office in Coventry, 'became a workshop for the exchange of information and training of shop stewards: teach-ins, mock negotiating sessions and educational courses ... we got an informed, collective approach to practical industrial problems'.[50] Twenty years later, the TGWU in the Midlands was taking the initiative in organizing day-release courses, 'sponsored jointly with employers', at universities.[51]

As the unions were drawn into political exchange, training was conceived as one small means of integrating the workplace with national bargains, facilitating incomes policy, signalling something was being done. At the 1960 Congress, the TUC's report on shop stewards suggested unions should discipline recalcitrant representatives. This sparked references to training as a more civilized and potentially successful, integrative solution. This was common ground between unions, employers and the Ministry of Labour. If there was to be qualitative growth in steward training then day-release must be expanded. The employers' control over paid release was an important consideration. To this end, the TUC and unions had few qualms about greater educational collaboration with management. In 1961 the motor industry employers agreed with the Confederation of Shipbuilding and Engineering Unions to jointly support training during working hours 'under independent auspices', in technical colleges and the extra-mural departments of universities.[52] There was criticism from stewards in the car factories who saw the initiative as an imposition and intrusion, intended to undermine them. They argued that neither employers nor outside agencies should be involved in what was a union function; stewards did not train managers, so why should managers train their opponents?[53]

A joint TUC-British Employers' Confederation statement in 1963 asserted that training was predominantly a matter for unions. But in all cases employers should have the right to vet the syllabus whilst more joint management-union courses should be encouraged, 'by bringing about a better understanding of the problems involved, an expansion of this form of training could lead to a marked improvement in industrial relations'.[54] Acceptance of a role for employers, day-release, not of right but as a goodwill concession to achieve common objectives, and improvement of workplace relations as *the* central purpose of courses indicated the contours of future development. Despite reassurances that the union role was primary, the report was fiercely criticized by shop stewards as a fundamental abrogation of union responsibility. It was also pointed out at Congress by veteran Communist Jock Shanley that:

> We have to look at the content of what we are going to teach, because the content of what we teach will determine the character of the people we train. I suggest that if you look at this paragraph from an educational angle, it seems to be saying pretty conclusively that we could not intimidate the stewards by calling them wildcats so we will train them to become lapdogs.[55]

The CP paid continuing attention to union education and what they saw as the dangers, noting: 'The TUC courses on industrial relations, collective bargaining and social security leave out the general overall development [of capitalism] and the Labour Movement, educationally at least, will sink into non-political trade unionism'. But where the party exercised real influence on education programmes, its own approach sometimes encountered criticism.[56]

The strategists of state-led industrial relations reform also took a keen interest in the content of courses. As early as 1952, Allan Flanders commented on the tensions in the renewal of shop-floor organization, between fragmentation and 'factory patriotism' on the one hand, and the desirability of rooting strong trade unionism in the workplace, supplementing the efforts of the full-time apparatus and extending the steward system, on the other. The danger of gaps opening up between leaders and workplace representatives could be minimized by training which would help stewards to internalize and act upon union policies. Flanders became an advocate of technical training based centrally on induction of stewards into procedural agreements, on the model of courses run by the Oxford Delegacy. He observed: 'the contribution which education is able to make to improving industrial relations will be most effective when both sides are well versed in the 'rules of the game' and share a common understanding of what are after all their joint institutions'.[57] This sanitized emphasis, which minimized disparities of power and structural conflict and exaggerated the ability of training to diminish the impact of conflict, found its way into the Donovan Report. Trade unions were urged to concentrate on training junior full-time officers and shop stewards: 'the need for shop steward training is immense'. The state should contribute greater resources 'with a view to using training of stewards as part of the planned move to more orderly industrial relations. This is where shop steward training will be able to make its biggest contribution'.[58]

The TUC had no quarrel with this approach. Trade union education was now explicitly and forcefully redefined as training shop stewards in workplace industrial relations:

> Training means systematic instruction, study and practice that will help union members to be competent as representatives of their union in the workplace. Obviously this excludes consideration of their wider educational needs as citizens or even potential General Secretaries.[59]

A restrictive, static stress on induction and relevance in steward training ran through the TUC's 1968 report. The purpose was to train representatives to deal with workplace problems, not to develop socially aware activists increasingly involved at all levels of the union, as well as politically. Stewards, the TUC insisted, should be trained in what they did at work, not what they did, or might do, beyond it. The TUC viewed the unions' interest in training as threefold: to commit stewards to union policy, to improve their competency and to improve industrial relations and industrial efficiency. Although there might be differences in the motives of managers and trade unionists, they could collaborate fruitfully to achieve these ends,

> whether for the good of the union, the industry or the individual or society, all the parties have a common interest in getting a workplace representative who knows his job. Although success in protecting his members could conflict with management's interest, employers are nevertheless concerned that he should act within the constitutional procedures of his union and industry and observe agreements reached. Training cannot guarantee this but it does give the opportunity for the purpose and nature of all these rules to be examined.[60]

Despite a dash of sexist cant – 'none of these training needs can be fulfilled without also educating the man' – and the need to assert their own primary role in the partnership with employers and state over training, the TUC was at one with the pluralist reformism of the Donovan Commission of which Woodcock was a member. In supporting the Wilson government's efforts at industrial regeneration, TUC leaders had little hesitation in supporting the involvement of the tripartite Industrial Training Boards in sponsoring shop steward training, so long as unions possessed 'a predominant voice'. In 1967 there was a further joint statement with employers emphasizing the pluralist nature of training.[61] Whilst there are no precise figures, it is clear that a substantial amount of steward training in the post-Donovan period was undertaken by management and on joint union–management courses.[62]

The tripartite consensus on training reached by 1970 and the escalation of state intervention was attested by the offer of government funds for steward training in the 1969 White Paper, *In Place of Strife*. The blossoming corporatist conspectus was tested in the final years of the Wilson administration and disrupted by the Heath government's move from voluntary reform to legal regulation of industrial relations. The implications of the TUC's acknowledgement of a role for management were now drawn out, formalized and extended. The Commission for Industrial Relations (CIR), boycotted by the unions, published a report on stewards' training. This separated out the steward's role as workplace representative from the steward's role as a *union* representative. The first, the major object of state concern, should, the CIR recommended, receive the attention of joint union-management courses, financed by the Industrial Training Boards. Such an approach could intensify 'factory patriotism' and stewards' autonomy from their unions. It could enhance fragmentation and company identification, restricting the mediation of the unions in favour of a direct steward-management alignment. Its niche as the major actor in training threatened – to some extent, at least, by its earlier legitimizing of the employers' role – the TUC now recoiled from the logic of 'common interest' as unravelled by the CIR. It condemned the report and asserted for the first time a sole, rather than a primary, responsibility.[63]

This remained rhetorical: even the TUC's own courses, for, of course, it did not employ its own teaching staff, were provided by universities, WEA districts and technical colleges. Attempting to commit independent educational institutions and their teaching staff to approaches sympathetic to TUC imperatives opened up a further set of problems.[64] The growth of the courses themselves was steady but unspectacular. By 1968, the TUC was sponsoring 155 day-release courses, usually of 10–12 days' duration, involving 2,263 students. By 1974, 643 courses enrolled 8,721 students. It was still a fleabite. Unions remained prepared to compromise with employers to secure day-release but pragmatism stopped at direct state aid: this was still rejected.[65]

By the mid-1970s, union education still preserved an ethos of independence from the state. It prioritized collective bargaining, but increasingly formalized, procedure-based, workplace or enterprise bargaining, aligned with Donovan's prescriptions for reform. For, of course – and again this was not explicitly debated – there was little necessity – at least from the vantage point of the stewards involved and much of the political left – to improve the 'efficiency' of workplace bargaining as distinct from other aspects of workplace trade unionism which disclosed real weakness. It was the success, in direct terms at least, of such bargaining, not its failure, that was the problem which training sought to address in the context of TUC-state strategies of incomes policy. Industrial relations training was intended to make collective bargaining more responsible, more amenable to wage restraint and management control and, from the perspective of its immediate beneficiaries, *less* efficient.

The statement, 'For trade unionists industrial relations training is synonymous with trade union education' encapsulated the TUC's priorities in the 1970s.[66] TUC staff were making choices about curriculum which guaranteed the inclusion of skills of communication, grievance handling, negotiating procedures, financial information, and the exclusion, not only of discussion of the unions' relationship to the state, political parties and economic change, but of 'relevant' issues such as union democracy and 'skills' such as organizing industrial action. In the TUC model, the essential context in which collective bargaining was embedded, the economic and political factors which facilitated and constrained workplace bargaining, was simply not the concern of shop stewards. There was, therefore, some disjuncture between, on the one hand, the project of the state and the TUC to make transparent the links between collective bargaining, economics and politics and, on the other hand, the TUC's exclusion of political and economic analysis from its education courses. This in itself suggests the unions' tentative, contradictory, ultimately inadequate, commitment to 'the corporatist project'.

There was undoubtedly a fear of political dissension and challenge which produced a general refusal to conceive of any part of the training system as an explicitly ideological forum, even on the TUC's own terms. Will Paynter put it somewhat baldly – but was undoubtedly onto something – when he remarked of union leaders' attitudes to education: 'they would be afraid that they might create opponents to themselves. They would be afraid of creating a political consciousness amongst the active elements of the membership'.[67] If incomes policies and the reform of collective bargaining were to succeed, then in the eyes of the TUC, it was preferable, pedagogically, to separate them. The priority was to get down to brass tacks by learning how to do reformed industrial relations, rather than discussing its implications for trade unionists, its context and alternative strategies.

There were exceptions. A major departure was the campaign against the Industrial Relations Act. The TUC ran special workshops outside the college courses, but these were structured around specially prepared teaching kits and tutors were advised of the necessity to stick to the materials and their message, and to ensure positions 'contrary to TUC policy' did not develop from the discussion.[68] The lesson that programmed learning could facilitate the structuring of classroom discussion was to be utilized later. On the whole, however, TUC courses reproduced in elitist, paternalist fashion, the absence of the social and political context in recipes for industrial relations reform. As one critic observed:

> Nowhere in the Donovan Report or in the entire tradition of academic industrial relations writing on which it drew so heavily, is there to be found any systematic consideration of how the economic system as a whole, and of its constituent units of production, is founded upon and sustains vast differences in social power and advantage. Nor of how there are then generated, on the one hand, objective oppositions of interest and, on the other, subjective responses of frustration, resentment and antagonism and also, in some degree, aspiration and movements towards an alternative disposition.[69]

And treating the essential context of workplace industrial relations as natural may play some role in legitimizing it. But those who insisted upon the necessity of addressing economy, society, history, also confronted problems of pedagogy and consciousness.

They were not, at least for the most part, dealing with workers thirsting for social understanding and already equipped with the tools of learning. Constructing courses in economics and politics which related to the students' existing levels of education, which linked with their preoccupations and engaged their imagination was no small task. In some cases, as in the miners' courses at Sheffield University which Communists had been influential in establishing and where left-wing tutors played an enduring role, they were dramatically successful.[70] In other contexts such as South Wales, where the NUM education officer was a CP member, a minority criticized the course in a fashion reminiscent of left critiques of TUC and union courses:

> The unfortunate part of any centrally sponsored educational scheme is that a distinct danger of too much control over the subject matter contained in the lectures usually exists. The object of education is to teach a person to think, to enable him to make up his mind with regard to current problems. Immediately the true purpose of education is departed from in the interest of any political or industrial group, it becomes propaganda which can be swallowed in a short time and does more harm than good.[71]

As with education, as with trade unionism, trade union education was a field of political contention. It could be a battleground in which organizational interests were sometimes considered to be at stake, in which factions sometimes contended for control and in which the pure, value-free liberalism which some espoused was unlikely to find substantial purchase. Classes possessed some autonomy but operated within a defined context. Moreover, if the price management exacted for day-release was, in terms of intrusion in courses, limited, patronage, and in some cases interference, was a reality and its possibility a potential constraint.[72]

The Social Contract and state support

The development of the TUC scheme drew criticism from the left, although the issue lay at the margins of their concerns. The CP characterized TUC provision as 'mainly of a narrow practical character and class collaborationist in aim'. The party sought briefly to get stewards to establish their own classes in economics and politics.[73] There was a short-lived attempt involving Ralph Miliband and Ken Coates to regenerate the NCLC through the Centres for Socialist Education in the mid-1960s, whilst the conferences and study groups of the Institute for Workers' Control (IWC) provided a forum for debates amongst left-wing union activists from the mid-1960s to 1979.[74] Some on the Tribunite left put forward a powerful critique of union education as presenting a micro-model of a reconstructed movement, made fit for 'the corridors of power', with top-down delivery of services and restricted democracy in which the stewards had to know their subaltern place. They insisted that the education of trade unionists was too important to be left to union leaders and functionaries.[75] The far left saw training as a means of integrating and professionalizing the steward, re-establishing managerial control and undermining the role of mobilization and self-activity.[76] Tutors organized in the Society of Industrial Tutors, many of whom also participated in the IWC, attempted to develop an approach and a literature which critically examined developments in state policy and trade unionism, provided information and practical advice to stewards, and sought in a small way to create a committed industrial relations from below.[77]

But there was lack of institutional support for realizing left-wing critiques in formal programmes. Hugh Scanlon, for example, acknowledged his debt to the NCLC but appears to have taken little interest in contemporary union education. Jack Jones, a past partisan of the NCLC seems, like many others, to have had, ultimately, an undifferentiated conception of union education, supporting the steward courses at Birmingham University commended by the Ministry of Labour. Both Jones and Scanlon respected labourism's 'great divide' and believed that political education was the job of the Labour Party, not the unions.[78] There is little evidence of left leaders taking any detailed interest and the absence of any counter-conception of a proper union education debilitated critique. Left-wing stewards who had earlier treated courses with suspicion actively participated by the mid-1970s and by the end of the decade in large workplaces, attending courses had become an integral part of being a workplace representative. We must not take too formal or mechanistic a view of the relations between policy and practice. Classrooms produce resistance as well as reproduction and some turned courses to their own purposes. But we hear the voices of students rarely and faintly, usually mediated through questionnaires and reports from organizers and tutors. They record general satisfaction with courses: stewards felt they came out of skills learning as more confident and better representatives. Students on the longer day-release courses at universities reported enhanced activity in the union, the community, politics and education. There were minority critics of the first kind of course who felt that provision should explore the wider context of workplace bargaining. A minority of students on courses which attempted to do this objected that discussions of labour history and politics did not help in negotiating with managers.[79]

The years of the Social Contract and continued dramatic growth in union membership witnessed the climax of earlier tendencies. The Wilson and Callaghan governments sponsored a qualitative extension of steward training and a greater degree of union control over it. This was simultaneously a concession, a lubricant for incomes policy, and an instrument of industrial relations reform. Once again choices were made, alternatives suppressed. Under the Employment Protection Act 1975, stewards were entitled to paid time off for training relevant to the specific industrial relations functions they carried out under agreement at their workplace, subject to 'reasonableness' and 'the operational requirements of the enterprise'. The TUC accepted that paid release would *not* be available for courses which dealt with stewards' wider trade union responsibilities: practical training was privileged over broader courses. The curriculum, indirectly through the conditions placed on paid release, was now largely and legally focused on workplace and employer, with the statutory objective of improving industrial relations. There was no quarrel about this, but the TUC lobbied Ministers to ensure courses required approval by the TUC or individual unions. However, employers were entitled to details of the syllabus and disputes over relevance and release would be finally determined by industrial tribunals and the courts.[80] We need to know more about the *volte face* the TUC executed in relation to important aspects of voluntarism, defended in such measured terms before Donovan in 1966, renounced less than a decade later.[81] There was a clear reversal of position over state aid for steward training. An annual Memorandum of Agreement between the TUC and the government laid down categories of shop steward training for which support – by 1979 worth more than £1 million a year – was available, in return for direct state oversight of curriculum and teaching materials.[82] With all its limitations and contradictions, trade union education had become a mini corporate state.

It was far more professionalized that it had been in 1945 or 1964, and, compared with the years before 1974, the unions possessed a stronger, more protected role, with statutory entitlements to paid release rather than reliance on benign employers. Courses consequently emphasized, to a greater extent, the independence of unions from employers within a pluralist approach to industrial relations which, however, firmly eschewed radical alternatives.[83] Expansion provided a standardized, programmed approach to courses, with Congress House supplying detailed, uniform materials focused on the workplace and bargaining procedures. With the teaching pack as Panopticon, TUC staff took Gradgrind-like pleasure in the belief they knew what every steward on a course was doing at any particular moment of the day. Surveys found courses answered only a partial, TUC constructed version of stewards' needs, failing to connect adequately with the world outside the workplace walls.[84] The benefits of this institutionalization were real if shortlived. For example, TUC basic ten-day courses increased from 684 with 10,640 students in 1975–6 to 1,208 with 15,701 students in 1979–80. There were in addition 383 follow-on courses with 4,542 students and 1,441 Health and Safety courses with 18,700 student places.[85] There were now more than 12 million members, and around 500,000 workplace representatives subject to high turnover. A system providing 40,000 student places a year was an improvement on the past but far from a mass system of training.

The efforts of individual unions, often duplicating TUC provision, made an increasingly significant contribution. Union education remained by the end of the 1970s an unplanned mosaic, with courses often overlapping and competing for students. ASTMS, the NUR, the GMWU and the NUT all opened residential colleges from the mid-1970s. The NGA built up a well-resourced residential scheme based on week-long courses. The POEU operated a four-tier system of basic, intermediate, advanced and specialist one-week courses which explicitly emphasized the need for social and economic education. USDAW's regional training officers specialized in in-plant courses and self learning packages. NALGO, NUPE and the TGWU qualitatively expanded provision which sometimes went beyond the narrow confines of TUC courses. None the less duplication and overlapping of courses continued. Perhaps most important was the appointment in unions like NALGO and the TGWU of regional education officers stimulating education rooted in local membership activities. And of course the longer day-release courses continued to flourish. Miners' leaders could pay tribute to the breadth and radical bent of the NUM's university-based courses whilst researchers reported that these 'political' courses produced activists who were more class conscious and better able to mobilize their members than their counterparts who attended shorter, more 'relevant' provision.[86]

The expansion of steward training with its emphasis upon 'negotiating expertise and orderly procedure rather than membership mobilization' was defined as one factor in 'the bureaucratization of shop stewards' which was proffered as an explanation for the decline in militancy in the mid-1970s.[87] This argument received some sustenance from the 1980 *Workplace Industrial Relations Survey* which found 84 per cent of managers felt training helped stewards and that managers themselves 'tended to derive benefits from shop steward training in the form of the absence of industrial action'.[88] Moreover, if, as Batstone claims, steward training 'was probably less oriented towards a consensual approach to management than in the past', it remained, at least, in its independent TUC variant, firmly in the mould of 'orderly procedure' and technical expertise.[89]

Yet, given the difficulties of establishing the extent of training and its impact on behaviour, the bureaucratization thesis seems exaggerated. Even the TUC figures, which give a far from complete picture, show expansion taking off after the initial decline of militancy in 1974–5 and increasing together with militancy in the last years of the decade. The degree to which there was a qualitative expansion compared with the early 1970s may also be questioned. The government workplace surveys show under 30 per cent of stewards had received training in 1966 and around 40 per cent by the early 1970s.[90] The 1980 survey found 27 per cent of establishments reporting stewards receiving training in 1979, but provided no figures on those already trained.[91] Whilst 33 per cent of stewards in establishments of over 2,000 employees attended courses in 1979–80, earlier research found almost 40 per cent of stewards in workplaces with over 1,000 employees attended courses a decade earlier.[92] What all this means is further muddied by high turnover amongst stewards and the fact that the government surveys include all courses of a day or more duration. Some provision was plausibly superficial and its impact trivial. Fundamentally, there are no satisfactory studies demonstrating the influence of training on the behaviour of stewards.[93] The verdict on the contribution of training to bureaucratization must be 'not proven'.

Despite the lack of conclusive evidence, the TUC had no doubts about the efficacy of its contribution. In 1979 the TUC Education Department exuded confidence. The residential college was at last a reality. Fears of state funding forgotten, they invited the incoming Conservative government to nominate personnel from the Departments of Employment and Education and Science to take seats on the governing body of the new education centre. This confidence in the resilience of corporatism was to prove cruelly misplaced. Hard times were just around the corner.[94]

From workers' education to industrial relations training

In the post-war period, the making of trade unionists became a formalized business focused on union representatives, aligned, though imperfectly, with the professionalization of industrial relations and the drive of the unions to political exchange with the state. Throughout this period it was moulded indirectly and imperfectly by political influences: there was diversity but trade union education increasingly reflected the unions' involvement in state policies. The centre of gravity moved into the unions, eventually underpinned by state support. It moved away from educating labour movement activists to change the world to training stewards to bargain with managers. If collective bargaining overshadowed social transformation, a particular form of collective bargaining was prioritized and articulated, albeit distinctively and inadequately, with state strategies for the reconstruction and 'corporatizing' of industrial relations. By 1979 there was less management involvement and more union control than in the previous decade, but this and the content of courses was set firmly within a pluralist framework of industrial relations with all its limitations. And as the TGWU Education Officer reflected:

> subject matter has tended to be limited to what can be called the non-political or non-controversial aspects of trade unionism. By far the greatest amount of TUC and individual trade union courses concern themselves with what is essentially training in an established role of shop steward or safety representative.[95]

The TUC had succeeded, to a far greater degree than hitherto, in expanding courses and making them more organic to union activities. The nature of the provision meant this was a restricted and tenuous success. State support had been perceived as insecure before 1975. It would prove fragile after 1979. Moreover, the contingent constitution of the steward's role,

> could be said to cast doubt on any very substantial claims being made for shop steward training. Moreover, if it is also accepted that he performs his functions against a complex of largely impersonal factors beyond his control, then it is arguable how far any course of training in itself could hope to affect his behaviour.[96]

Political education, cultural education, intended to provide understanding and ultimately greater control over the universe beyond the workplace, and develop a sense of mission and solidarity, at Ruskin and Northern College, still in university extra-mural and WEA classes, catered only for a small minority. It found little place in mainstream programmes, which concentrated on training for service rather than education for leadership, commitment and ideological renewal. These developments were not predetermined. The form union education took was not the product of inexorable forces or the intrinsic needs of the movement. Tradition, from the comparatively low union dues of British workers to the impoverished internal culture of British unions, shaped change. The trajectory of training was intimately bound up with the TUC's political course and with its uneven, tentative nature, marked by the desire to have both independence from, and collaboration with, employers and the state. Woodcock remarked that union leaders viewed

> trade unionism as a straightforward, routine business. It's as routine as peeling potatoes. I don't know anybody in whom it has induced a mood of reflection. At least not inside the trade union movement. There is this essential conservatism. There is a distrust of what they would call the theorist and the academic – and they would block them altogether.[97]

Woodcock had a point: witness the Yorkshire miners' leaders in the 1960s, hostile to courses on the grounds that the students would take over the union, or the leaders of the steelworkers who, supported by TUC officers, insisted on their right to approve all books recommended to students.[98]

But this world-weariness exaggerates. It tends to the exclusion of change and the role of Woodcock and his supporters in reinforcing and refining particular aspects of tradition. There was a long, albeit minority, tradition of political and cultural education. It was not integral to a pre-war, heroic, golden age; it was as 'relevant' in this period as earlier. The politics of the TUC did not automatically exclude such education. It might have been conceived as inducting representatives in what TUC leaders saw as economic rationality, support for political exchange, closer links with the Labour Party and understanding of its policies. Or alternatively, as developing a new creative force, a distinctive union politics, by equipping grass roots activists to make their own choices between social and economic alternatives. As a means of eliciting acquiescence, or creating a new political constituency to challenge Labour's conservatism, or empowering activists, it was judged, consciously or conventionally, as too great a risk, or too far down the list of priorities compared with training. Or it was simply not considered. Yet, in terms of broad general judgements, what were post-war trade unionists good at? Building workplace organization, bargaining, controlling the labour process, albeit often negatively. Where they were weaker, was in forming political strategies to consolidate and extend these gains, strategic thinking, going beyond the immediate, the local, the urgent, the concrete. Their leaders' conception of 'needs' ensured education was concentrated almost exclusively on areas of strength rather than weakness.

There was to be no third ideological wing to the Labour Movement. In the light of contemporary constraints and possibilities, the General Council could have carried out the mandate Congress gave it in 1964 to develop political and economic education as well as technical training. It could have realistically sought to secure rights to paid release for such education in 1975. That it attempted neither suggests the conservative nature of union leadership, but also the weakness of alternatives. Our story is far from encouraging for the left. The militancy of the 1960s and 1970s, unlike that of the 'Great Unrest' of the early years of the century, produced no resonant alternative pedagogy. Indeed in these years oppositional voices became increasingly muted. After Citrine and his emphasis on administrative and bargaining skills, the construction of union education becomes almost completely the prerogative of union leaders and functionaries, with most leaders taking only an episodic or ritual interest. The voice of the student was largely silent. In classes stewards made contacts, built networks, discussed the challenges facing trade unionism. Side-effects or subversion, informal straying from the curriculum were no substitute for a well prepared explicit pedagogy, designed to effectively maximize exploitation of these issues. But by the 1970s those who conceived of education as a political issue, largely conceived strategy in terms of ensuring that their voice was heard within existing structures, as education officers, tutors or students, rather than questioning

58

organization and curriculum and posing alternatives.[99]

As to the impact on trade union fortunes of this restriction of political vision and refusal to create schools of strategy, we can only guess. Plausibly it cannot have helped equip more activists to make informed choices between corporatist, socialist and neo-liberal politics and their impact on unions. The transformative powers of both training and education are circumscribed, and creating an imaginative, popular fusion of the two was not without difficulties. But the emphasis on skills isolated from context and the insulation of the workplace from the address of the economic and political forces which mould it can have done little to diminish economism and increase cohesion, coherence and political awareness. Those who made post-war union education saw it as making able administrators and responsible collective bargainers. Intriguing light was shed on the uses and limits of this endeavour in early 1979 when Congress House staff, fighting militancy more directly, contacted TUC regional education officers requesting the names of local opponents of the Social Contract.[100] As the 'Winter of Discontent' and Thatcherism demonstrated, trade unionism is not only about collective bargaining. The challenge to trade unionism in the 1960s and 1970s, and even more so in the 1980s, was on an economic and political front which training in workplace and industrial relations failed to penetrate. It could not be answered by collective bargaining. History held that lesson. But by 1979 history, too, was excluded from trade union education.

Notes

1. The fascinating and unexplored question of the informal education of trade unionists is only touched upon in this chapter which deals with organized education and training.

2. K. Middlemas, *Politics in Industrial Society* (1979), particularly pp. 218–303; H. A. Clegg, *A History of British Trade Unions since 1889: volume 2, 1911–1933* (Oxford, 1985), pp. 462 ff.

3. Examples are A. Corfield, *Epoch in Workers' Education* (1969); J. P. M. Millar, *The Labour College Movement* (1979); J. Holford, *Union Education in Britain – A TUC Activity* (Nottingham, 1994).

4. Modern Records Centre, University of Warwick (hereafter MRC), TUC Papers, MSS 292, 817.2/2, *Post-War Education* and NCLC, 'TUC: Post-War Education Plans', 5 October 1944; WEA, *Workers' Education and the Trade Union Movement. A post-war policy* (1944); W. E. Williams, 'Civilian "ABCA"', *Industrial Welfare*, 28, 3, 1946; B. Ford, *The Bureau of Current Affairs, 1946–51* (1951); R. Fieldhouse, 'Adults learning: for leisure, recreation and democracy', in J. Fyrth (ed.), *Labour's Promised Land: culture and society in Labour Britain 1945–51* (1995); J. Jupp, *The Radical Left in Britain 1931–1941* (1983), pp. 131, 197.

5. TUC, *Report*, 1945, p. 329; MRC Mss 292, 817. 2/2, *Post-war Education*.

6. TUC, *Report*, 1946, p. 452.
7. S. Bidwell, Interview with author, 10 February 1987; F. Ward, interview with author, 12 February 1987; TUC, *Report*, 1950, p. 395; TUC, *Report*, 1953, p. 162.
8. TUC, *Report*, 1944, p. 311.
9. J. McIlroy, 'Independent working class education and the trade unions', in R. Fieldhouse *et al.*, *A History of Modern Adult Education* (1996), pp. 277–8; TUC, *Report*, 1944, p. 11.
10. TUC, *Report*, 1944, p. 311; TUC, *Report*, 1945, p. 327.
11. TUC, *Report*, 1945, p. 92; TUC, *Report*, 1946, p. 449.
12. J. McIlroy, 'The demise of the National Council of Labour Colleges', in B. Simon (ed.), *The Search for Enlightenment: the working class and adult education in the twentieth century* (1990), pp. 180–1, 190.
13. TUC, *Report*, 1944, p. 92.
14. TUC, *Report*, 1948, p. 348.
15. T. Topham, 'Education policy in the TGWU 1922–44: a tribute to John Price', *Industrial Tutor*, 5, 5, 1992, pp. 53–4; V. Allen, *Trade Union Leadership: based on a study of Arthur Deakin* (1957), p. 243.
16. J.P.M. Millar, *Education and Power* (Tillicoultry, 1951), pp. 18, 14.
17. Millar, *The Labour College Movement*, p. 132.
18. McIlroy, 'Independent working class education', p. 271.
19. MRC, MSS 292, 814.2(1), D. Winnard, 'Notes on Rationalization of TUE', 1954; National Museum of Labour History, Manchester (hereafter NMLH), Morgan Phillips Papers, Box 7, File GS/NCLC.
20. NMLH, Labour Party Archive, National Executive Committee Minutes, 16 December 1950, H. Morrison, 'Party Education'.
21. NMLH, Morgan Phillips Papers, Box 7, GS/NCLC; National Library of Scotland, NCLC Papers, Accession 5120, Box 22, F2.
22. R. Fieldhouse, 'The Workers' Educational Association', in Fieldhouse, *History*.
23. TUC, *Report*, 1946, p. 452. For contrasting views of the WEA, see Fieldhouse, 'Workers' Educational Association' and J. Rose, 'The workers in the Workers' Educational Association 1903–1950', *Albion*, 21, 4, 1989, pp. 591–608.
24. H. Nutt, *Education Schemes with the WETUC* (1951), p. 1.
25. WEA, *Annual Report*, 1948; R. Fieldhouse, *Adult Education and the Cold War* (Leeds, 1985); L. Goldman, *Dons and Workers: Oxford and adult education since 1850* (Oxford, 1995), pp. 266–86.
26. J. Klugmann, 'Party educational programme for 1952–3', *Communist Review*, September 1952, p. 281.
27. Responsibility is placed squarely with the NCLC in S. Fielding, P. Thompson and N. Tiratsoo, *England Arise! The Labour Party and popular politics in 1940s Britain* (Manchester, 1995), p. 155. There is no evidence for this. It appears from the correspondence in the Morgan Phillips Papers (file GS/NCLC) and the Labour Party NEC minutes that the NCLC leadership was willing and that the problems, legal and political, arose on the party's side.

(See for example GS/NCLC/55/i–iii, 1948; GS/NCLC/13/24 January 1951.)

28. TUC, *Report*, 1948, pp. 155–62; 348. The TUC Education Committee re-sisted continuing overtures from the NCLC for rationalization on the grounds that the NCLC and WETUC were incompatible; that the TUC was involved in 'a different field of work'; that the matter had been fully explored and closed between 1946 and 1948; and that the best field for the TUC's ener-gies was the development of its own courses (MRC, MSS 292, 814.2, G. Thorneycroft to J. Wray, 30 March 1950; 814.2/3, 'Note of Discussion with Deputation from NCLC', 13 December 1949; 811/13, Education Commit-tee, 13 December 1955).

29. Antagonism was re-ignited when the NCLC allegedly breached confidence in its criticisms of the LSE course in 1944–5. It was further fuelled when the TUC refused to establish a joint committee with the NCLC and increased the WEA's grant but not that of the NCLC. Beard, the Education Committee Chair, and other General Council members, such as Ellen McCullough and Florence Hancock, favoured the WEA (Papers in 817.2/3; 814.2, W. Webber to J. Wray, 12 May 1954; 814.2/1, J. P. M. Millar to V. Tewson, 11 April 1947).

30. TUC, *Report*, 1955, p. 167.

31. Political and Economic Planning, *British Trade Unionism: five studies by PEP* (1955), pp. 131–2, 197; D. Butler and R. Rose, *The British General Election of 1959* (1960), p. 28.

32. WEA, *Trade Union Education* (1953), p. 28; H. Clegg and R. Adams, *Trade Union Education. A report for the WEA* (1959), p. 76.

33. Clegg and Adams, *Trade Union Education*, p. 71; J. Mack, 'The education of trade unionists', *Trade Union Education*, 2, July 1955, p. 34; Oxford University Archives, OUDES F/2/9/4, R.J. Enever, 'Report on TGWU Train-ing Course, 21–28 May 1955'.

34. A. J. Corfield, 'Education in the Transport and General Workers' Union', *Rewley House Papers*, 3, 7, 1960, p. 9.

35. A. Burge and K. Davies, 'Enlightenment of the highest order: the education programme of the South Wales miners, 1956–71', *Llafur*, 7, 1, 1996, pp. 111–21; J. McIlroy, 'The triumph of technical training', in Simon, *Search for Enlightenment*, pp. 218–27.

36. MRC, MSS 292, 811/13, Education Committee, 13 December 1955.

37. Clegg and Adams, *Trade Union Education*, pp. 43–6; MRC, MSS 292, 814.2, B. Gallie to J. Wray, 28 December 1944.

38. TUC, *Report*, 1959, p. 383.

39. L. Minkin, *The Contentious Alliance: trade unions and the Labour Party* (Edinburgh, 1991), pp. 184–5; MRC, MSS 292, 817.31/3, 'Training College Special Conference, 27 March 1957'.

40. TUC, *Report*, 1957, p. 390.

41. TUC, *Report*, 1959, pp. 178–9, 383; A. Boyd to author, 6 January 1998.

42. TUC, *Report*, 1959, p. 179; TUC, *Report*, 1960, p. 168; TUC, *Report*, 1961, p. 441.

43. TUC, *Report*, 1964, pp. 198–9.

44. TUC, *Report*, 1961, pp. 79–80.
45. MRC, MSS 292/B/811/1, Education Committee, 18 April, 22 June 1961; 811/2, Education Committee, 13 February 1962; Millar, *The Labour College Movement*, pp. 157–69.
46. TUC, *Report*, 1964, p. 198.
47. TUC, *Report*, p. 484.
48. Ibid.; MRC, MSS 292B/811/6, Education Committee, 8 November 1966; TUC, *Report*, 1967, p. 214; TUC, *Report*, 1973, pp. 497–8.
49. Interview with D. Robinson, Birmingham, 8 January 1998, by J. McIlroy and A. Campbell, transcript in author's possession; interview with K. Halpin, London, 15 April 1998, by J. McIlroy and A. Campbell, transcript in author's possession; interview with Vi Gill, Sheffield, 21 April 1998, by J. McIlroy and A. Campbell, transcript in author's possession; also based on author's conversations over twenty-five years with students on shop stewards' courses.
50. 'Bosses to educate motor stewards', *Metalworker*, April 1961; J. Jones, *Union Man: an autobiography* (1986), p. 93. As late as 1973 the biggest union branch in BL's Cowley plant resolved to replace the courses run in conjunction with BL and Oxford University with classes run by the branch – although nothing came of this. In the 1980s activists in NALGO in the North-West ran their own classes on organizing industrial action.
51. Jones, *Union Man*, p. 147.
52. 'Industrial relations in the motor industry: statement by employers and trade unions', April 1961. (copy in author's possession).
53. *Metalworker*, April 1961.
54. TUC, *Report*, 1963, pp. 190–1.
55. TUC, *Report*, p. 437.
56. J. Klugmann, 'Notes of the month', *Marxism Today*, 8, 10, October 1964, pp. 295–6; Burge and Davies, 'Enlightenment of the highest order', pp. 118–19.
57. A. Flanders, *Trade Unions* (1952), pp. 57–8; A. Flanders, 'Introduction', in A. Marsh, *Industrial Relations in Engineering* (Oxford, 1965), pp. 1–2.
58. Royal Commission on Trade Unions and Employers' Associations 1965–1968, *Report* (Cmnd 3623, 1968), pp. 190–1.
59. TUC, *Training Shop Stewards* (1968), p. 1.
60. TUC, *Training Shop Stewards*, pp. 11–12.
61. MRC, MSS 292B/811/7, 'Industrial Training Boards – Training of Shop Stewards: note by TUC Education Department', 14 March 1967, and 'Statement agreed by TUC and BEC representatives', 8 March 1967.
62. A. Marsh et al., *Workplace Industrial Relations in Engineering* (1971), p. 41; CIR, *Report No. 33 Industrial Relations Training*, 1972, p. 16.
63. *In Place of Strife* (Cmnd 3888, 1969); union leaders were affronted by what they saw as Barbara Castle's macabre suggestion that money collected from unions in fines would be used to train shop stewards (Len Murray, quoted in B. Pimlott, *Harold Wilson*, 1992, p. 530); 'Shop Steward Education and Training: opening statement of the TUC Education Committee chair at meeting

with Parliamentary under Secretary DES May 1973', *Industrial Tutor*, 1, 9, September, 1973, p. 37.

64. See, for example, TUC, *Report*, 1969, p. 292; A. Campbell and J. McIlroy, 'Trade union studies in British universities: changing patterns, changing problems', *International Journal of Lifelong Education*, 5, 3, 1986, pp. 207–40.

65. TUC, *Report*, 1969, p. 292; TUC, *Supplementary Evidence to the Russell Committee on Adult Education 1970*; TUC, *Report*, 1975, p. 159.

66. See note 63.

67. T. Lane, *The Union Makes Us Strong* (1974), p. 260.

68. R. Jackson, 'TUC teaching after the Act', *Industrial Tutor*, 1, 6, March 1972, p. 32. The view that 'achieving nationally approved policies should be a major aim of shop steward training' is asserted in R. Jackson, 'Training shop stewards', *Plebs*, October 1966, pp. 10–14. Jackson was the TUC Education Officer.

69. J. Goldthorpe, 'Industrial relations in Great Britain: a critique of reformism', in T. Clarke and L. Clements (eds), *Trade Unions under Capitalism* (1977).

70. McIlroy, 'Triumph of technical training', pp. 219–24.

71. Burge and Davies, 'Enlightenment of the highest order', pp. 118–19.

72. Corfield's verdict – 'no manager attempted to place any limitation upon the kind of subject taught' – is very wide of the mark (Corfield, *Epoch in Trade Union Education*, p. 142). See J. McIlroy, 'Trade union education for a change', in Simon, *Search for Enlightenment*, pp. 253–4. For one detailed account of interference by union officers in courses, see Sheffield University, 'Closure of trade union courses conducted by Sheffield University Extra-Mural Department and the Workers' Education Association', (n.d., [1972]).

73. NMLH, Communist Party Archive, CP/CENT/PC/08/106, 'Education of Shop Stewards: The TUC Education Scheme', 10 December 1964.

74. *Plebs*, November 1964, May 1965.

75. T. Park 'Trade union education', in K. Coates, T. Topham and M. Barratt Brown (eds), *Trade Union Register* (Nottingham, 1969).

76. T. Cliff, *The Employers' Offensive – productivity deals and how to fight them* (1970), p. 218.

77. The Society of Industrial Tutors (SIT), established in 1969, enrolled a majority of trade union studies tutors for the next decade. A weakness, summed up in the 'Industrial' in its title, was that it also sought, relatively unsuccessfully, to embrace management education. The SIT published a journal, the *Industrial Tutor*, and by 1979 had brought out a series of short books aimed at stewards. The IWC was an even more prolific publisher of pamphlets and short books for tutors and trade unionists. Tutors were also involved in the Pluto Press Workers' Handbook series initiated in 1973.

78. Jones, *Union Man*, pp. 35, 48; Minkin, *Contentious Alliance*, pp. 184–5, 191. Minkin notes that in 1974, an election year, the AUEW spent 1.1 per cent of its political expenditure on 'education and communication', the TGWU 1.8 per cent, and the GMWU 3.2 per cent (*Contentious Alliance* p. 191, n. 102).

79.   For example, A. Warren, 'The aims and methods of the education and train-
        ing of shop stewards: a case study', *Industrial Relations Journal*, 2, 1, 1971;
        T. Smith, 'Trade union education: its past and future', *Industrial Relations
        Journal*, 15, 1, 1985; A.H. Thornton and F. Bayliss, *Adult Education and the
        Industrial Community* (Nottingham, 1965); M. Barratt Brown, *Adult Educa-
        tion for Industrial Workers* (Nottingham, 1969); G. Mee, *Adult Education
        and Community Service* (Nottingham, 1984); Burge and Davies, 'Enlighten-
        ment of the highest order', pp. 118–19.

80.   For a brief accessible guide to the legislation see Lord Wedderburn, *The
        Worker and the Law* (3rd edition, 1986), pp. 310ff.

81.   TUC, *Trade Unionism*, Evidence to the Royal Commission on Trade Un-
        ions, 1966.

82.   For a fuller account of these developments, see TUC, *Report*, 1975, pp. 188–
        207, and *Report*, 1976, pp. 184–6.

83.   For a powerful contemporary critique of the unitary and pluralistic frames
        of reference of industrial relations utilized by employers and the TUC, see
        A. Fox, 'Industrial relations: a social critique of pluralist ideology', in J.
        Child (ed.), *Man and Organization* (1973), pp. 185–234.

84.   J. McIlroy, 'Adult Education and the role of the client', *Studies in the Edu-
        cation of Adults*, 17, 1, 1985, pp. 47–49; Smith, 'Trade Union Education',
        pp. 86–9.

85.   TUC, *Report*, 1980, pp. 166–7.

86.   J. McIlroy and B. Spencer, 'Despatches from a foreign front', *Labor Studies
        Journal*, 17, 2, 1992; P. Rigg, 'Miners and militancy: a study of branch un-
        ion leadership', *Industrial Relations Journal*, 18, 3, 1987.

87.   R. Hyman, 'The politics of workplace trade unionism', *Capital and Class*,
        8, 1979, pp. 54–67.

88.   W.W. Daniel and N. Millward, *Workplace Industrial Relations in Britain*
        (1983), p. 40.

89.   E. Batstone, *Working Order: workplace industrial relations over two dec-
        ades* (1984), p. 101; McIlroy, 'Adult education and the role of the client',
        pp. 47–9.

90.   S. Parker, *Workplace Industrial Relations, 1973* (1975), p. 27.

91.   Daniel and Millward, *Workplace Industrial Relations*, p. 36.

92.   CIR, *Report 33A Industrial Relations Training: statistical supplement*, p.
        37.

93.   T. Schuller and D. Robertson, 'The impact of union education: a framework
        for evaluation', *Labor Studies Journal*, 9, 1, 1984. For an interesting study
        which saw courses as developing a pro-management ideology amongst stew-
        ards, see G.R. Keithley, 'Industrial relations training for shop stewards:
        workplace perceptions of its objectives, impact and consequences', unpub-
        lished PhD thesis, University of Durham, 1982.

94.   TUC, *Report*, 1979, p. 188.

95.   F. Cosgrove, 'Re-shaping trade union education, TGWU proposals for gov-
        ernment support', *Industrial Tutor*, 3, 8, 1983, p. 63.

96.   W. McCarthy, *The Role of Shop Stewards in British Industrial Relations*,

Research Paper 1, Royal Commission on Trade Unions, 1966, p. 111.

97. G. Woodcock, quoted in Lane, *The Union Makes Us Strong*, p. 260.
98. Sheffield University, 'Closure of trade union courses'.
99. cf 'Nineteenth century trade unionism had relied on the solidarity of the members to regulate industrial relations. Citrine by contrast emphasized negotiations and the skills of the negotiator. Converts were therefore to be found primarily among full-time officers and executive members' (Clegg, *A History of British Trade Unions since 1889: volume 2*, pp. 470–1). There are shards of evidence throughout the period suggesting both right and left saw the need to imprint education in their image – see, for example, on the ETU, O. Cannon and J. Anderson, *The Road From Wigan Pier: a biography of Les Cannon* (1973), pp. 141–8, and, for the TGWU, G. Goodman, *The Awkward Warrior. Frank Cousins: his life and times*, (Nottingham, 1984) p. 568. For a later comment on the CPSA, see *The Times*, 5 December, 1985: 'When we have control of the committee we can gain more Broad Left supporters, particularly if we can get the [education] organizer's job and run day schools'.
100. Information from J. Mowatt, former TUC Regional Education Officer.

PART TWO

Survey

CHAPTER THREE

The Post-War Compromise: Mapping Industrial Politics, 1945–64

Alan Campbell, Nina Fishman, John McIlroy

These twenty years saw the apogee of political stability, industrial equilibrium and economic prosperity, fortified by the prolonged absence of ideological or class cleavages in society or the political parties. At any point before 1956, and generally until the mid-sixties, commentators could have been forgiven for concluding that conflict had been institutionalised through a pluralist system of representation. Britain seemed a model of the harmonious relations of governing institutions; and corporate bias a necessary component of a political system in which intelligent economic management ensured that there was no need to defer gratification, and where social change could be achieved without undue distress to any group.[1]

Looking back across the militancy of the 1970s and the Thatcherism of the 1980s, Middlemas' optimistic summary retains considerable force. There were significant continuities over the two decades from 1945. The political accommodation over the welfare state and the mixed economy was underpinned by the long boom and full employment. Throughout the period there was no serious challenge to the settlement of 1945. The structures and cultures of British trade unionism and its links with the Labour Party remained largely unchanged, although the Cold War was divisive. There were fewer strikes in comparison with more turbulent periods in the twentieth century.

There have always been differences as to the nature of the post-war settlement: mainstream political scientists have emphasised consensus between Conservatives and Labour, while others, particularly Marxists, have viewed it more as a compromise over the way capitalism was managed between still hostile classes and parties. Recently contemporary historians, accentuating the conflicts that remained between the parties, have gone on to assert that consensus was a myth. Continuing discord in high politics is highlighted if we focus upon the motivations behind party policies, rather than the policies themselves where what stands out is the expanded degree of agreement. But differences remained, and they were certainly present in industrial relations policies. The Conservatives were reluctant to alienate unions strengthened by the war and a Labour government, and appreciated the electoral importance of winning union members. But the Conservative administrations after 1951 had greater resort to market forces in comparison with their Labour predecessors. This must be kept in proportion: compared to the Conservative's turn to the market after 1979 it was minor. Nevertheless, their reluctance to control prices while demanding wage restraint and cutting Labour's social subsidies caused some strains between union leaders and the state. It also influenced the growth of workplace organization, more aggressive, decentralized bargaining and strikes.[2]

These differences were undoubtedly more than rhetorical. But we should not use them to define a period in which in high politics, relative to other periods, there existed a strong degree of – shall we say without absolutism – *consensus*, whatever its motivations, between the parties. In industrial politics, there was agreement on the legitimacy of unions as economic, social and political actors, as an estate of the realm whose voice should be carefully listened to in the councils of state, whose services should be solicited in regulating the economy. Both parties accepted the unions' special position in industry and politics, and calls for restrictive legislation went unheeded. Consensus was not a myth: it was real and distinctive, if not all-embracing. The areas of agreement were more important than the areas of dispute.[3]

It would be artificial to extend the conception of consensus into industry. It is less useful in defining industrial relations. If conflict was often muted – again in comparison with succeeding decades – in the factories and in the unions it remained a reality. The complex mix of cooperative and antagonistic attitudes which British workers brought to their employment endured. The lives of union activists remained permeated by conflict. Under the surface of the tranquillity evoked by Middlemas, factory lives were lives of struggle. Amongst the political class and wider there was a growing perception of a trade union 'problem' although there was little agreement on its solution. By the 1960s unions were seen as inflationary and restrictive of efficiency, antiquated structurally and culturally. A rather different problem has been identified by those sympathetic to Labour's goals: the electoral defeat in 1951 accelerated developing problems in the movement and the halting of Labour's 'forward march'.[4]

Periodization is an often arbitrary process which can do violence to continuity, to the different tempo of developments in the economic, industrial, social and political spheres and to the different structures of feeling and ethos of particular eras. Different emphases and times of analysis produce different schemas. In a 1979 essay structured by a concern for high politics and organized around what he sees as the decline and fall of the system of industrial relations, Colin Crouch defines four phases: the post-war period from 1945 to the late 1950s; the years of tension to 1968; the collapse of the post-war order, 1969–74; and attempts at renewal, 1974–79. Writing in 1985, Alan Fox sees the industrial relations system undergoing consolidation until

1960 and characterizes the years 1960 to *c.* 1983 as 'the system under strain'. Eight years on, Robert Taylor viewed 1975 as a key turning point separating the post-war period from an evolving neo-liberalism.[5] A variety of defensible dividing lines can be constructed. For example, 1945–51 may justifiably be seen as a distinct period, the years of austerity, rehabilitation of the unions and re-establishment of voluntarism; 1951–7 may be viewed as the era of burgeoning boom, industrial peace and union acceptance; from 1957–64 we can discern growing strains on the economy and industrial relations; the decade 1964–74 can be conceived as one in which the state's attempts to restructure and re-integrate trade unionism are increasingly serious and unsuccessful; finally, 1974–9 may be characterized a time of both creeping corporatism and, in economic policy, creeping neo-liberalism.

We have decided, however, to follow in broad sweep the landmarks of conventional politics. With only a little papering over of the cracks around 1951, the years from 1945 to the early 1960s can be defined as a distinct period. The election of Harold Wilson in 1964, the year after Profumo and the invention of sexual intercourse, the year the Beatles conquered America and the then Cassius Clay vanquished Sonny Liston, seems to us, despite the Conservative's earlier spadework, to finally usher in a new era of state intervention in industrial relations. Whilst granting due weight to the importance of world economic changes from 1973 and their impact on government and unions, particularly from 1975, it appears commonsensical to treat 1979 and the election of Mrs Thatcher as the end of an era, although this judgement is strongly influenced by hindsight. This survey therefore maps the terrain of industrial politics during the years from 1945 to 1964, and situates the individual chapters upon the broader canvas.

Capital and class

The Labour government of 1945 faced enormous economic problems. The national debt had increased threefold; the wartime sale of foreign investment and the sinking of much of the merchant marine reduced invisible earnings; exports had been reduced by two thirds. The sudden termination of American 'lend-lease' economic assistance led Keynes to conjure up the spectre of 'a financial Dunkirk ... and the position of a second class power'. The terms of a new US loan restricted the possibilities of socialist economic policies, which the cabinet itself showed decreasing concern to promote. Both Labour and Conservative governments, under American pressure and delusions of imperial grandeur, maintained extensive defence expenditure which the economy could ill afford: in 1952, defence spending constituted 9.8 per cent of British output.[6]

The weakness of the economy was underlined by balance of payments crises in 1947, 1949 and 1951. That of 1949 was followed by devaluation of the pound which further emphasized the need to increase exports. Yet by continued use of wartime controls to suppress imports and effective deployment of demobilized servicemen, the export drive was an outstanding success in world markets still depleted by the devastation of war. The 1950s seemed 'the golden years' of capital as economic growth between 1950 and 1964 increased twice as fast as between 1913 and 1950.[7] From 1953 there was a steady rise in real wages (see Table 3.1). Rationing, the symbol of post-war austerity, ended in 1954. Higher living standards were reflected in lifestyles: in 1956, only 8 per cent of households had refrigerators; by 1962, the figure was 33 per cent. By that year three-quarters of households had television. By 1964 nearly half of all houses were owner-occupied, and there were eight million cars on the road, four times the number in 1947. It was confidently asserted that capitalism had been 'reformed out of all recognition'.[8] The working class now had a greater stake in society.

There were, however, clouds on the horizon. The 1950s witnessed the emergence of the 'stop–go' cycle, of economic expansion reducing unemployment and increased spending sucking in imports, thus endangering the balance of payments and prompting government intervention to reduce demand. There were small but not insignificant rises in the rate of unemployment in 'stop' phases of the cycle (see Table 3.1). The extent of the relative decline in Britain's economic performance was apparent by the end of the 1950s: Britain's percentage share of world exports of manufactures declined from 25.5 to 16.5 over the decade while Germany's had increased from 7.3 to 19.3.[9]

These pressures shaped employers' strategies. Full employment enhanced workers' bargaining power, especially during labour shortages at the peak of the 'go' phase, product demand inhibited resistance to wage pressure, while increasing competition stiffened employer resistance. There was industrial concentration through mergers and an increasing trend towards conglomerates: in 1958 there were 16 large enterprises engaged in ten or more industrial groups; by 1963 the number had doubled to 32. In 1958 enterprises with 10,000 or more workers employed a quarter of workers in manufacturing.[10]

But most companies failed to transform their internal structures in ways which might have facilitated more efficient planning of production.[11] They remained reliant on relatively large numbers of skilled workers whose diversity and job control impeded standardization and whose day-to-day organization remained remote from senior management's concerns. According to one eminent academic, the 'vast majority of managers in British industry at every level' preferred 'to have as little as possible to do with labour relations' and were content to delegate such matters to the personnel department or departmental supervisor.[12] Although the numbers of personnel managers increased from around 5,000 in 1945 to 15,000 in the mid-1960s, they retained a lowly status within the managerial hierarchy.

72

Supervisors were usually promoted from the shop floor and, in the metal working trades for example, shared the craft culture of the labour force, often colluding in the maintenance of custom and practice.[13]

Employers' associations also served to protect companies from competitive inefficiencies through industry-wide wage negotiation. Forty-seven local associations were affiliated to the Engineering and Allied Employers' National Association (EEF); the National Federation of Building Trade Employers had 261. Such national bodies were linked in the Federation of British Industries (FBI), which represented the trade interests of manufacturing industry, and the British Employers' Confederation (BEC) which had the primary object of relaying employers' views on labour matters to government. Although a decision was taken to fuse the two bodies as early as 1946, it was only two decades later that a unified organization, the Confederation of British Industry, was established in 1965.[14]

The principal function of employers' associations was collective bargaining (itself a factor in restricting industrial relations expertise among managers in the workplace). The war saw the extension of the coverage of collective bargaining through national agreements. This occurred primarily through the establishment or revival of Joint Industrial Councils. Nationalization resulted in the growth of bargaining for clerical and professional employees, while statutory wage regulation was extended among the low paid under the Wages Council Act, 1945. Hugh Clegg reflected with satisfaction that, by the end of the war, 'most of the interstices of the British industrial relations system had been filled up by collective agreements or by statutory wage fixing bodies, and by organization on both sides'. By 1950, 80 per cent of Britain's 20.5 million employees were covered by joint negotiating machinery or statutory provisions.[15] There were alternative views on this trend – F. A. Hayek's *Road To Serfdom* was published in 1944, his *Constitution of Liberty*, with its influential critique of unions as labour monopolies, in 1960 – but they were a minority and their time had not yet come.

Employers were generally willing, though to varying degrees, to broadly accept the post-war settlement as a 'necessary evil'. Influential industrialists had actively organized support for the Beveridge Report and the welfare state. British employers did not seek systematically to break established trade unionism as did their counterparts in Japan and the USA in the 1940s and 1950s.[16] But outside the public sector, opposition to union recognition of white collar workers was common. Neither did employers seek to develop the corporatist coalition with labour and the state pursued in Germany and Sweden. The 'most formidable reactionary obstacle to such a partnership' in the engineering industry was the Engineering and Allied Employers' National Federation, claimed its future historian.[17] British employers vacillated between the strategic poles of frontal attack and corporatism, unable to extract the advantages of either, negotiating with the unions in a system of national wage bargaining and colluding informally with their employees in the workplace.[18]

Full employment and soft product markets undermined national agreements during economic upswings, with employers competing for labour through supplementary local bargaining. 'Wage drift' was reflected in the increasing proportion of supplementary payments as a percentage of earnings. By 1959 these payments accounted for 27 per cent of earnings in the metalworking and chemical industries and 14.5 per cent in food, drink and tobacco.[19] To some degree this represented the emergence of shop stewards as workplace bargainers while 'combine committees' linking shop stewards in the different plants of a company developed in the engineering and motor industries. These committees sought to raise and standardize wage rates across companies but federated employers were often constrained by nationally negotiated agreements. Lerner cites an example from the mid-1950s where an engineering company allowed managers in plants where shopfloor pressure was strongest to disaffiliate from the local employers' federations and conclude independent local agreements.[20] As competition sharpened and profit levels were eroded, 'from the late 1950s onwards, industrial relations became an issue which the senior managers could no longer ignore. How to regain control became a major concern, leading in many cases to the appointment of industrial relations specialists at Board level'. The conclusion of the pioneering productivity agreement at Esso's Fawley refinery in July 1960 symbolized the start of new management initiatives aimed at 'buying back' control from the shop floor.[21]

Even in the same industry, employers' responses to union strength varied enormously. A survey of engineering companies in the West Midlands during the post-war period, for example, found that management oscillated between vigorous attacks on union organization when they felt their prerogatives under threat and a willingness to accept shopfloor custom and practice, their specific response often dictated by the state of labour and product markets. In vehicles, employers displayed a range of policies: Vauxhall's sophisticated attempts at labour relations have been contrasted with Ford's more overtly antagonistic approach.[22]

Despite the spread of 'affluence', the class structure and patterns of inequality displayed considerable conformity to pre-war configurations. The distribution of personal income after tax between 1949 and 1964 remained stable, while the share of income between labour and property as a percentage of the gross national product increased by only 0.6 per cent between 1946–9 and 1960–63. Despite the welfare state, poverty stubbornly refused to be eradicated. One report suggested that in 1954, 12.3 per cent of the population lived in income tax units with incomes below the National Assistance Scale; in 1963 the estimate was 9.4 per cent. While the share of total wealth owned by the top 1 per cent declined significantly from 55 per cent in 1938 to 34.5 per cent in 1964, any redistribution was largely confined to the wealthy: the share of the top 20 per cent dropped only from 91.2

to 84.3 per cent. Inheritance remained a key element underpinning the concentration of wealth.[23] The ruling class continued to be linked through kinship, marriage, business, and educational background. Its nucleus contained entrepreneurs, internal capitalists, such as senior executives, and finance capitalists. Despite speculation about the 'managerial revolution' mistakenly held to separate ownership from control, this class retained strategic dominance over capital. 'The old boy network', centred on the leading public schools and Oxbridge, linked its business core with the key personnel of the judiciary, the civil service and armed forces.[24]

There were, however, important shifts in the occupational structure. Although the 1951 census revealed a workforce not very different from that of 1931, thereafter the position began to change significantly as older industries declined and the balance between manual and white-collar work tilted towards the latter. Thus between 1950 and 1964 total employment grew by 10 per cent while the number of manual workers remained static, declining as a proportion of the workforce from 64 to 53 per cent; clerical workers increased from 10.4 per cent to 13.2 per cent of the occupied population. While mining employment declined from 880,000 workers in 1948 to 629,000 in 1965, the distributive trades gained almost a million jobs, and banking and insurance increased by 220,000 during the same period; between 1951 and 1965, textiles and clothing lost almost half a million jobs.[25] Although the percentage of women workers dropped in the immediate post-war years, from 1948 onwards they constituted just over a third of the workforce, increasing slightly to 36 per cent in 1964. The impact of changes in the ethnic composition of the working class remained small: in 1951 there were only around 150,000 black and Asian immigrants.[26]

The state and industrial politics

Measured against the economic background, Labour's achievements were major and enduring. The Attlee administrations fulfilled the nationalization pledges contained in the 1945 manifesto, although the manifesto omitted a number of the industries, such as banking, as well as land, demanded by the 1944 Party Conference, and the structure of the private steel industry was left largely intact. Nationalization of coal and the railways represented the fulfilment of long-standing political commitments to the unions while a conventional socialist argument for bringing 'basic' industries under state control underpinned state ownership of water, gas and electricity. By 1951 some 20 per cent of industrial assets were in the nationalized sector. But they represented for the most part the less efficient sections of the economy, for which private owners had been generously compensated, and which functioned to subsidize the remaining private sector. Management structures eschewed worker participation let alone control. Though prominent union leaders were recruited to nationalized industries, their boards were predominantly staffed by directors from the former private enterprises, civil servants and retired military officers. No attempt was made to use the nationalized industries to exert leverage within the private sector whose owners opposed Labour's experiments in economic planning. Fundamentally, 'the major parameter imposed on the Labour government by private industry was Labour's own commitment to the private enterprise system'. A further conservative influence was continuity in state personnel, with a civil service neither equipped nor pressurized to set about modernizing the economy or constructing a 'developmental state'.[27]

Unions, too, remained ambivalent in their attitudes towards the state. A central, if at times exaggerated, theme of the post-war history of industrial relations has been their enduring commitment to 'voluntarism', a commitment rooted in the unions' historic compromise with nineteenth century liberalism. Voluntarism displayed three key features: the priority of collective bargaining over state regulation; the preference for voluntary, non-legally enforceable collective bargaining; and the autonomy of the parties as to their constitution, procedures and regulation of bargaining outcomes.[28] Through a long tradition of negative legislation, parliament had curbed judicial law making. Auxiliary legislation such as that covering wages councils and health and safety did not greatly detract from the central principle of legal abstention. The system had been bolstered after 1918 when new powers were delegated to the Ministry of Labour to promote collective bargaining. The Trades Disputes Act 1927 not only symbolized the anti-union bias of the Conservative government in the aftermath of the General Strike, but also the success of the Ministry of Labour in deflecting more vindictive reparations. There was little need for further intervention in the depression years, when mass unemployment permitted the smooth operation of the Ministry's strategy of 'home rule for industry and social control via moderate union leaders'.[29]

But if the state played only a limited legislative role – dramatically so in comparison with the USA or some European countries – its influence cannot be ignored.[30] The increase in state intervention during the Second World War, and the need for union support brought the movement's influence into the heart of government.[31] None the less, as Minister of Labour, TGWU General Secretary Ernest Bevin successfully resisted Treasury demands for statutory wage controls, instead relying on 'Order 1305' which outlawed strikes and established mechanisms for compulsory arbitration. The 1945–51 Labour government maintained this incursion into voluntarism without serious question by employers' organizations, union leaders or the Conservative opposition. However, retention of Order 1305 represented a transitional stage in post-war adjustment, and its continuance rested on the TUC's consent, a factor which made the Ministry of Labour more cautious in its application. On the other hand, speedy repeal of the Trade Disputes Act

1927 not only symbolized the Labour government's intimate relationship with the unions, but also the re-assertion of the voluntarist tradition.[32]

In practice, this restoration of the pre-1926 *status quo* had no immediate impact on industrial conflict due to the continuation of Order 1305. However, the Order only applied to strikes within the legal definition of a trade dispute: sympathy strikes, inter-union disputes and political stoppages all lay outwith its scope. Moreover the futility of mass prosecutions of strikers had been exposed during the war.[33] Davis Smith argues that the legal blocking of official strikes led to an increase in unofficial action, and the government reactivated the pre-war contingency plans for emergencies, deploying troops on a number of occasions and justifying its anti-strike policies as economic necessity.

Tripartite commitment to voluntarism influenced industrial policy after 1945. In relation to the nationalization programme, Geoffrey Goodman recalls in his chapter in this volume 'the historic negative' of miners' leader Will Lawther in response to Shinwell's attempts to involve the NUM in the management of the coal industry. Similar attitudes undermined Joint Production Committees (JPCs), which had been encouraged in the engineering industry during the war, as a potential mechanism for filling what Harold Wilson, President of the Board of Trade in the Attlee government, described as the 'vacuum in Socialist thought' concerning the relations between the government and private industry.[34] As Hinton has recently shown, engineering union activists had well developed plans for workers' involvement in the management of private industry, but these came to little in the face of employer hostility, rank and file apathy, Cold War anti-communism and government inertia. For the voluntarist proclivities of many union leaders articulated smoothly with a government commitment to the restoration of a depoliticized industrial relations.

Tomlinson concludes, perhaps with some exaggeration, that the 'sustained pursuit of JPCs as instruments ... of industrial democracy would have cut across this voluntarist tradition with incalculable consequences'.[35] But at the very heart of voluntarism lay free collective bargaining over wages. Although some ministers supported a national wages policy as a central element of socialist planning, they met determined opposition from Bevin and the Ministry of Labour, an opposition endorsed at the 1946 TUC by union leaders such as Arthur Deakin, Bevin's successor as TGWU General Secretary. Yet some trade unionists supported certain kinds of state intervention in wage determination. The demand was made at the 1946 Congress for a legally enforceable minimum wage by the NUVB. The seconder of the motion, Joe Scott of the AEU, argued that: 'The Trade Union Movement should determine what that minimum wage should be and ... take steps to have it enforced by law. We are now in a period of full employment, and there must be a new approach to the question of wages'. Given its violation of voluntarist principles and the opposition of General Council speakers who denounced

77

it as naive, the motion was rejected by a relatively narrow majority: 3,522,000 votes to 2,657,000.[36] This sort of policy was supported by many on the left. It held out the possibility of a unified focus on wages and a realistic wages floor that might have generalized economic aspirations across different groups of workers rather than the traditional reliance on sectional competition.

As economic problems and fear of inflation increased after 1947, the union stance on pay policy shifted. Deakin, a resolute opponent of wages policy in 1946 had changed his views by 1948, although he retained his antagonism to a legal minimum wage and was insistent that pay restraint be enforced by the unions, not imposed by government.[37] The government was able to secure the support of the TUC leadership for a voluntary policy of wage restraint in 1948 in exchange for commitments on retaining food subsidies, a policy unsuccessfully opposed by the Communist Party (CP) and its allies.[38] The new incomes policy had some temporary effect in checking the rise in real wages (see Table 3.1). It failed, however, to resolve Britain's underlying economic problems. Its success lay in its acceptance in practice for almost two years by Britain's trade unionists. Their capacity for self-sacrifice was however becoming exhausted. Devaluation and the Korean War ratcheted up prices. By the TUC Congress in September 1950 there was a small majority in favour of rejecting incomes policy and the following months witnessed the collapse of wage restraint.[39] One of the last acts of the Labour government was revocation of Order 1305, at the behest of the TUC General Council, whose leaders had become concerned at their own inability to control their members' propensity to strike illegally.[40] Nevertheless, it was replaced by Order 1376, affording the unions access to arbitration on a greatly restricted basis. Neither employers, government nor union leaders were yet ready to abandon completely the wartime framework.

The Conservative's desire to retreat from intervention and for reductions on subsidies for food and housing strengthened voluntarism and, in the context of full employment, decentralized collective bargaining as workers looked more to money wages rather than the social wage. Churchill hoped 'to work with the trade unions in a loyal and friendly spirit' while the TUC in its turn stated its intention of treating the new government on its merits. Favourable experience of wartime collaboration predisposed the Conservatives to make the maintenance of an open relationship with the unions a priority and Churchill ordered his Minister of Labour, Walter Monckton, 'to preserve industrial peace'.[41] By 1954 one authoritative account recorded that 'the right of direct approach to ministers or departments has been maintained intact, and is exemplified by the frequent meetings between the Chancellor of the Exchequer and the Economic Committee of the [TUC] General Council'. The TUC had made the transition to peacetime and Tory government with their voice in the councils of state secure. At the mid-point of Churchill's administration, it appeared that the Conservatives had consolidated the wartime intimacy between governments and unions and that this partnership would continue indefinitely.[42] As late as the 1980s, the TUC looked back nostalgically to the wonderful days of Walter Monckton.

However, the 1955 general election was announced in the middle of a newspaper strike and a national railway stoppage, the first national strike for over twenty years, was threatened. These clouds presaged a change of climate: 'The industrial problems which Walter Monckton had handled from 1951–5 without serious challenge from his government colleagues and from the Conservative Party became from this time a source of disagreement and debate'. Churchill's successors, Eden and then Macmillan, made determined attempts to reconcile two conflicting aims, 'the avoidance of serious industrial trouble' and restraining the rate of wage increases.[43] But as Nina Fishman shows in two detailed case studies of the 1957 shipbuilding and engineering strikes and the London busworkers' stoppage the following year, the government's competing policy imperatives precluded a clear strategy. After initially supporting the engineering employers' resistance to wage increases, the Cabinet, fearful of the impact of industrial unrest upon sterling, pressed for a settlement which left the unions victorious. However, the effect of the dispute was to encourage a firmer government policy on wages, embodied in its determination to defeat the busworkers the following year.

From 1957 onwards the necessity to align trade unionism to solutions to Britain's economic predicament moved up government agendas. There was serious discussion over the need for a policy of wage restraint and how best to achieve it. In 1958 Iain Macleod, the Minister of Labour, jettisoned the legislative provisions for arbitration as inflationary. A growing tendency inclined towards legislation to reduce union power but Macmillan's determination to maintain a conciliatory approach and explore the fringes of corporatism was reflected in the 1959 election manifesto. Significantly, the FBI, too, endorsed plans for closer involvement in state regulation of the economy.[44] By 1961, however, pressure on sterling prompted the introduction of a 'pay pause' followed by a 'guiding light' target of 2.5 per cent wage increases, both without consultation with the unions. The latter was seriously undermined by strikes, culminating in a 9 per cent increase to dockers in the face of a threatened stoppage.

The government based its calculations on the belief that an incomes policy could only succeed with union cooperation. However, the TUC rejected the Conservatives' overtures. Despite the convictions of many union leaders that a system for determining non-inflationary wage levels was required, the General Council refused to cooperate in the establishment of the National Incomes Commission (NIC) which Macmillan and his Chancellor, Selwyn Lloyd, hoped would provide the foundations of such a system. The government had little option but to fall back upon a less ambitious advisory committee, the National Economic Development Council (NEDC). The General Council was willing to nominate representatives, but only on condition that wages and other issues at the heart of collective bargaining should not be considered.[45] At the 1962 Congress, TUC General Secretary George Woodcock was scathing in his criticism of the NIC and wage restraint, but spoke supportively of the NEDC: 'in form we have got pretty much what we wanted and the possibilities are still there that it can become the kind of planning instrument that we want'. His views were echoed by Frank Cousins, the mover of a successful motion declaring 'complete opposition' to incomes policy but reaffirming support for economic planning.[46] Cousins was reluctant, however, to allow the NEDC to work too well. He recognized that it could be a vehicle for economic regeneration and was anxious that the Conservatives should not steal the initiative on planning from the Labour Party, whose programme differed little from Macmillan's *dirigiste* approach. Though Woodcock remained convinced that the TUC could exploit the NEDC, Cousins' ambivalence reflected the concerns of the majority of General Council members.[47]

It was under Macmillan's Conservative administration that the state began to traverse the terrain of tripartism which was to dominate industrial politics until 1979. But the unions' journey from Trafalgar Square to Whitehall was not a smooth one. By 1962 the tensions between greater influence in the corridors of power, the unions' cherished objective, and the price to be paid – restriction of what was for many the unions' fundamental purpose, free collective bargaining – were on display. Moreover, governments' quest for a wages policy was partially hindered by the Ministry of Labour for whom collective bargaining remained 'the best incomes policy there is'.[48]

The problem of control of wages under full employment was to be the central theme of industrial politics in the following decades. As John Kelly demonstrates in his chapter on the evolution of the politics and policy of Allan Flanders, a founding father of industrial relations as an academic discipline and an influential moulder of public policy, the reconciliation of the sectional demands of workers with 'the public interest' in the 'new social order' of the immediate post-war years became a central theme in his thought. Increasingly inflected by anti-communism, Flanders' version of right-wing social democracy informed his approach to industrial relations. His prescriptions for reform, such as a national incomes policy and the need for 'responsible' trade unionism were forged in the experiences of the late 1940s and 1950s.

An alternative legislative strategy for dealing with 'the trade union problem', in particular unofficial strikes, had been considered – and rejected – both by the Attlee government in 1950 and by the one-nation patrician, Monckton, in 1955.[49] However, Conservative lawyers returned to this theme in their 1958 pamphlet, *A Giant's Strength*, proposing radical changes to the law. Although its prescriptions were rejected by Macmillan, its publication marked renewed interest in the legal status of unions and their immunities. This issue was taken up by the courts, most notably in the 1964 case of

Rookes v. Barnard, which held that the threat of strike action in breach of contract grounded the obscure tort of 'civil intimidation' and lay outside the protection of the 1906 Act.[50] This threatened the legal basis of industrial action and added an important new twist to the growing perception of a crisis in industrial relations. The TUC was willing to support a Royal Commission in exchange for legislation to reverse the decision, a course rejected by the Conservative government which insisted that legislative change should await the outcome of the inquiry. The TUC's offer was taken up by the incoming Wilson administration which speedily restored union immunities in its Trades Disputes Act 1965 and established the Donovan Commission. Whilst the pace of change and state intervention intensified after 1964, Macmillan had reversed the attenuation of state intervention from 1950 and had begun to lay the first foundations of Britain's 'corporatist experiment'. The politicization of industrial relations was by 1964 already under way.

Trade union structure and politics

The increase in membership during and immediately after the war represented a significant step forward for the unions. Whereas union density had stood at 30.5 per cent in 1938, it had increased to 38 per cent in 1945 and 45 per cent by 1948. As Table 3.2 illustrates, the latter figure marked a plateau for the remaining years of the period, as density fluctuated by one or two percentage points around this mark. Union growth of almost three million members only kept pace with increases in the total workforce. Yet these aggregate figures conceal significant compositional shifts. While the membership of manual unions grew by only 0.6 per cent between 1948 and 1964, white collar unionism expanded by a third in the same period, particularly in the public sector where government encouraged recognition.[51]

The growth or decline of individual unions is illustrated in Table 3.3, which lists the ten largest TUC affiliates in 1945 and 1963 and their percentage change in membership between these years. It can be seen that some unions significantly increased their membership: NUPE almost trebled its 1945 membership of 82,500, while the ETU and NUDAW (later USDAW) more than doubled in size. The AEU and the big general unions registered significant increases, as did the Post Office Workers, while the NUM and NUR experienced absolute declines. This pattern was the outcome of a number of factors: the general context of full employment; the readmission of civil service unions following the repeal of the Trades Disputes Act 1927 (UPW); government support for union organization in the greatly enlarged public sector (NUPE); the changing industrial structure, in particular the decline of employment from the mid-1950s in mining and the railways (NUR and NUM); the greater willingness of employers to engage in collective bargaining and to tolerate the closed shop (AEU, ETU); willingness to recruit new groups of workers

(NUPE's total of 230,000 in 1963 included 130,000 women workers); mergers with other unions (notably the creation of USDAW, but the TGWU also absorbed nine smaller bodies during these years).[52]

There was little movement in or out of this 'top ten' – NUPE was the only newcomer (although focus on the largest unions obscures significant growth among white collar unions which was not to register in the upper reaches of the movement until later). Although the TUC Organization Committee held discussions in 1946 with a range of unions on 'trade union structure and closer unity', there were few results of any substance, other than the amalgamation of the National Union of Distributive and Allied Workers (NUDAW) with the Shop Assistants Union to form USDAW, although as with many post-war mergers, this represented a greater complication of the pattern of union structure as much as its simplification.[53] In 1945, 192 TUC affiliates had a total membership of 6,671,120; the ten largest organized 52.3 per cent of this figure. In 1963, there were still 175 separate unions affiliated, with a total membership of 8,325,790, although the share of the ten largest had increased to 61.7 per cent. When Woodcock sought a fundamental review of union structure in the early 1960s involving moves towards industrial unionism and the ultimate abolition of the general unions, his proposals came to nothing.[54] While there were real problems, the implications of the fragmented structure of British trade unionism for managerial and economic efficiency were overstated by contemporary observers: demarcation disputes were relatively rare outside shipbuilding and only accounted for about 2 per cent of recorded stoppages.[55] And from a union point of view, sectionalism could be constrained in the workplace by the development of joint shop stewards' committees and in the wider movement by informal links, federations and the TUC.

The politics of the General Council were dominated by the leaders of the 'big six' unions, whose membership by 1959 exceeded the total of the remaining 180 affiliates. The leaders of the 'big six' could exert enormous potential influence within both wings of the movement. According to NUPE's disillusioned General Secretary: 'They can decide the composition of Congress Standing Orders Committee, delegations at home and abroad, and who shall sit as trade union representatives on Government Boards, Committees and enquiries'. Moreover, the composition of the General Council was the product of a complex trade group structure, in which a number of unions were guaranteed a place by virtue of being the sole member of a group, and by horse trading for support among the others.[56]

However, the personalities, industrial characteristics and political complexion of their individual unions, meant that the large unions did not form a coherent grouping. In terms of internal organization, democracy and ethos, this period has been delineated as the epoch of professional trade unionism. This makes some sense as a broad characterization, centred on the *commandiste* TGWU where each layer of activists had their province and where ultimately bargaining was the preserve of the paid official. But, as the tensions within the TGWU itself aver, this model does less than justice to the rich, complex variations in the internalities and politics of the unions.[57] The TGWU, which remained the largest union through the 1950s and 1960s, was based on a coalition of industrial groups with internal power relations skewed in the direction of appointed full-time officials. Its sizeable, lay executive comprised representatives from the trade groups as well as the regions, with limited purchase on the national politics of the organization. The TGWU's devolved structure and big, biennial conference enhanced the central authority of the General Secretary, Deakin, conventionally viewed as lacking Bevin's statesmanlike qualities, but nevertheless dominant. In fact, a concerted examination of Deakin's record discloses his constant struggle to impose his conceptions of top-down democracy and right-wing politics. He proved capable of dealing with centrifugal currents but in a combative fashion which alienated many. Deakin lacked Bevin's feel for the need to orchestrate by conciliation. 'An awkward, intolerant man', he found it difficult to delegate or deploy patient persuasion.[58] He was a fervent Labour leadership loyalist and vocal anti-Communist, an attitude in part rooted in his identification with TGWU traditions, knowledge of the fragility of its cohesion, and his view of Communists as unpredictable fomenters of unofficial action. Although many members shared Deakin's views, the conduct of the union became more conflictual. Instances can be found in the case studies in this volume on unofficial militancy in the docks by Jim Phillips and on the London buses by Nina Fishman. Deakin's successor in 1955, Jock Tiffin, a TGWU traditionalist, died after only a year in office, to be replaced by the left-wing Frank Cousins. Change was constrained to a degree by the established bureaucracy appointed under Bevin and Deakin and by Cousins' own insecurities.

In the AEU, with its tradition of elected officials who shared a common craft culture, the dominant post was the presidency. Its incumbent from 1939 until 1954 was Jack Tanner, who had risen through the AEU's ranks with a commitment to rank and file militancy, underpinned by close cooperation with the influential CP caucus of 'constitutional militants' which organized inside the union's lay institutions as well as its full-time officer corps.[59] In 1948, after the Stalinist coup in Czechoslovakia, Tanner broke with his allies and shifted decisively to the right. The AEU's turn right continued under Bill Carron, President from 1957, a devout Roman Catholic and committed anti-Communist. The major figure in the rightwing faction in the AEU, Carron sought to informally circumscribe the democracy of the union and flouted its agreed policies at Labour Party conferences under 'Carron's Law'.[60]

The NUGMW was the other major general union, with a structure based on powerful regional organization. Officers were initially appointed by the regional councils before subsequent election (which no appointed official ever lost) and the union displayed a propensity towards nepotism: Tom

Williamson, the strongly right-wing General Secretary from 1946–61 was the nephew of the Liverpool District Secretary; his successor, Jack Cooper, was a nephew of Charles Dukes, General Secretary from 1934–46.[61] These leaders shared a common right-wing stance and were resolute supporters of the Labour leadership. Their anti-Communism was deep-rooted: the ban on Communists holding office remained in place. The left had some strength in the London district and the union eventually imposed sanctions on leaders of unofficial strikes; conference approval of disciplinary action by 289 votes to 36 was indicative of the leadership's dominance.[62]

The NUM was a very recent creation, representing the novel, fragile transformation of the miners' union from a federation of autonomous regional bodies into a national union which perforce allowed great autonomy to its regions.[63] Although the CP was strong in South Wales and Scotland, and its veteran member Arthur Horner was elected General Secretary in 1946, the balance of power in the union lay with the right-wing. The President from 1945, Will Lawther, had been a left-winger who had worked closely with Communists inside the union and was a close colleague of Horner. From 1948, Lawther became strongly rightwing, his anti-Communism underpinned by a knowledge of the CP's methods. Renewal of left influence had to await the 1960s. Political divisions did not undermine NUM support for the nationalized industry or collaboration with the Coal Board. The drastic programme of pit closures from 1958 did not put an end to such collaboration but reinforced the union's commitment to the return of a Labour government.[64]

The politics of the larger unions are examined in more detail by David Howell in his chapter. But we can briefly note the centre-left politics of the newly expanded USDAW; and the rightward drift in the declining NUR, as the leadership of Jim Figgins and Jim Campbell gave way to that of Sid Greene. The CP's electoral victories in the ETU during the war developed into the party's stranglehold on the union which endured until the removal of its leadership after the ballot-rigging trial of 1961 and its replacement by a new, rightwing elite. And there was the dramatic growth of NUPE under the leadership of the former miner, Bryn Roberts, its General Secretary from 1934 to 1962, an anti-Communist with a keen eye for the recruitment opportunities in the health service and local authorities.[65] A brave if broad summary, inevitably static and somewhat schematic, of the location of unions on the political continuum in the mid-1950s was essayed by Martin Harrison (see Table 3.4). Not all the large unions were affiliated to the TUC or the Labour Party. NALGO was a pacific white collar union, its rule book making no provision for strikes until 1961, and it relied on the arbitration provisions for much of our period. The issue of affiliation to the TUC was drawn out, and only agreed in 1964, after the experience of the 'pay pause' had stiffened members' attitudes and it had become apparent that the TUC was the only available route to influence government.[66]

The General Council reflected the differing traditions and policies of its affiliates. The resignation of Walter Citrine, the architect with Bevin of the drive towards greater union influence on the state, as General Secretary in 1946 to join the National Coal Board represented the loss of a very able leader. His successor, Vincent Tewson, lacked Citrine's tenacious determination to thrust the unions into the centres of state policy making. The unfriendly alliance between Citrine and Bevin on the TUC General Council, and later during Bevin's tenure at the Ministry of Labour, had been crucial in carving out a position of power and influence for the TUC in British political life. Before 1945, the General Council relied on an effective bond between the general secretaries of the TUC and TGWU. After the war, the limitations of the occupants of these offices, as well as the rapid loss of ten incumbent members, caused strains.[67] Tanner was viewed as a coming force and the two AEU representatives on the General Council were a possible alternative to the TGWU's four as a foil for a TUC general secretary. Having joined the General Council in 1943, Tanner was increasingly influenced by its high politics in the post-war period and had to guard his new position on the centre-right against his left flank.

Although the Miners' Federation had by long practice placed its general secretary on the General Council, the rightwing of the NUM ensured this privilege was not extended to the talented, experienced but – and in the new politics of the Cold War this was what mattered – CP member, Arthur Horner.[68] The NUM Vice-President, Jim Bowman, had some intellectual force and whilst he sat on the General Council, he combined personal ability with the NUM's numerical strength and prestige. But Bowman was recruited by the Coal Board in 1950. His successor, Ted Jones from North Wales, was considerably less formidable. Lawther retired in 1954, and was succeeded as NUM President and General Council representative by Ernest Jones, from Yorkshire, a right-wing Labour loyalist. Horner remained the miners' most capable national official but outside the TUC General Council.

Clegg noted the decline in TUC influence on the Attlee government. This in part reflected the changed conditions from wartime. Bevin's successor as Minister of Labour, George Isaacs, a former general secretary of the Operative Printers and member of the General Council, lacked his authority and ability to act as a bridge between government and unions. Clegg assessed the capabilities of right-wing leaders of the 1950s such as Williamson of the NUGMW, as no more than 'competent'. Other centrist leaders on the General Council had particular virtues. Lincoln Evans, for example, General Secretary of the Iron and Steel Trades Confederation, was intelligent and articulate; Joseph Hallsworth, General Secretary of the Shopworkers, possessed 'outstanding ability'.[69] But Evans left the trade union movement in 1953 to serve on the Iron and Steel Board; Hallsworth had already gone to the Coal Board to replace Citrine in 1947.

Tewson marked time as an increasingly ineffectual TUC General Secretary. His Assistant General Secretary, the more capable and enterprising George Woodcock, succeeded him in 1960. Woodcock was intellectually ambitious but less adroit politically. He proved incapable of founding an effective partnership with either of the two outstanding union leaders who had succeeded to office in the mid-1950s, Cousins and Carron. Though both were, in their own unions, able strategists, neither attempted to rehabilitate the General Council as a key political agency. Cousins retained an ambition to assume Bevin's mantle but he declined to take a leading role inside the General Council and its minority of left-wing members vainly waited for his approach to form an alliance.[70] Carron similarly refused to make common cause with other right-wing leaders on the Council, his circumspection perhaps due to the strong presence of left-wing activists in the AEU.

Consequently Woodcock lacked any consistent support for his vision of streamlining the unions, reconstituting the TUC as an effective instrument of intervention with the state. During his first year of office, Woodcock benefited from the presence on the Council of the NUM General Secretary, the thoughtful CPer, Will Paynter, whose views often coincided with his own. However, Paynter's brief tenure on the Council was brought to an end by concerted opposition from right-wing members and from within the NUM.[71] Relatively isolated, Woodcock's initiatives to reform the movement of which he was notionally chief administrator were unsuccessful. By 1964, with the exception of Carron and Cousins, the General Council lacked leaders of vision. Its members were either ageing veterans – Sir Tom O'Brien (Theatrical and Kine Employees), Harold Collison (Agricultural Workers) and John Newton (Tailor and Garment Workers) on the right, Ted Hill (Boilermakers) and Bob Willis (NGA) on the left – or comparatively younger bureaucrats – Alf Allen (USDAW), Cyril Plant (Inland Revenue Staff), Sid Greene (NUR), Jack Cooper (NUGMW), Sid Ford (NUM). The remainder lacked the motivation to participate in much beyond the affairs of their own unions and the routine business of the TUC.[72]

What all the union leaders – whether from the left or right – shared in practice was a powerful commitment to the Labour Party. In addition to the mechanisms of affiliation and sponsorship, trade union MPs occupied a variety of posts in the 1945–51 governments and strongly supported their achievements. Within the Party Conference the right-wing union leaders constituted a 'Praetorian Guard', armed with their block votes to defend the party leadership and support its policies. Although apparently enduring and monolithic, this axis was eventually destabilized by shifts in political dispositions within the unions in the later 1950s. As David Howell concludes in his chapter, the suppression of any adequate discussion of key economic issues – such as wages policy – which resulted from this stifling party regime left critical issues of social democratic strategy unresolved.

Cold War polarization after 1947 and the CP's left turn provided the basis for the Labour Party and union leaderships to attack British Stalinists and stigmatize left-wing opponents more widely. In his chapter, Richard Stevens first outlines the proliferation of overlapping networks of anti-Communist groups and their organizations in the unions, and the complex motivations of right- and left-wing opponents of Stalinism, before analysing the industrial structures of the CP and mapping its union influence. While the decline in membership from its war-time peak is well known, Stevens' demonstrates that the party successfully regrouped in the unions after 1956; what is remarkable is that Hungary and the Khrushchev revelations had such little long term impact on the party's industrial cadre. More significant to the party's future fortunes in the unions was the exposure of ballot-rigging in the ETU, which stimulated a fundamental review of industrial strategy.

Anti-Communism and the Cold War is also the central theme of Tony Carew's chapter which points up the pragmatism of the TUC leadership in its dealings with Communism. He demonstrates how the TUC's attitude to the World Federation of Trade Unions, which was increasingly under Russian domination, was shaped by its labourist attachment to the division of industrial and political spheres. Cold War pressures eventually ruptured relations between union centres with fundamentally conflicting conceptions of trade unionism. After its departure from the WFTU in 1949, the TUC played an important role in the establishment and development of the International Confederation of Free Trade Unions (ICFTU), yet it failed to avoid American accusations of being 'soft' on communism as it sought to demonstrate the practical benefits of free trade unionism rather than engage in strident ideological denunciations. As the Cold War slowly thawed, the TUC was willing to re-establish independent links with unions in the Soviet sphere. A similar pragmatism informed the TUC's activities in British territories where its emphasis was on building trade unionism from the base rather than abetting anti-colonial struggle.

A common theme in the history of this period is that many union and Labour Party activists were to the left of a timid and cautious leadership.[73] The TUC's 1944 report on post-war reconstruction, for example, had accepted the Labour leadership's approach to public ownership and agreed that the appointments to governing boards of nationalized industries should be on the basis of competence, efficiency and the public interest.[74] Yet amongst the ranks of activists there was a strand of thinking which held that, gradually educated by the experience of nationalization, union representatives would play a greater role in the regulation of the newly socialized industries. The TUC President at the 1946 Congress voiced the optimistic aspirations of a section of the movement for an extension of workers' influence:

It seems that the position of management and its relations with the conduct and control of industry will undergo profound modifications as the area of socialist enterprises widens, and as the representatives of the organised workers claim to exercise the right of participation in the conduct of the socialised enterprises.

That same year Congress agreed to remit to the General Council – 'which fully accept[ed] the spirit of the resolution' – a demand for 'workers' participation at all levels in the management of nationalized industries'. Calling for the nationalization of steel at the 1948 Labour Party Conference, the delegate from Salford North declaimed: 'Our resolution calls for workers' control of the industry. We want to see for once that the nationalization of an industry will give the workers real control, will give them a real say in the running of their industry and will take the burden of interest and profit off the back of the industry'.[75]

Yet the right-wing leadership of the General Council remained opposed to any moves in the direction of workers' self-management. The Cabinet's views on radical re-organization were reflected in a private note from Hugh Gaitskell to Herbert Morrison in 1949 defending 'the present set up in the socialised industries' in the light of the resolution passed by the TGWU conference (in a rare rejection of its General Secretary's views):

> The resolution carried against Deakin to the effect that TU representatives should be placed on the Boards with the right of members to recall such representatives ... is a more extreme example of syndicalist tendencies than anything yet put forward ... Even the NUM ... is becoming infected with the same critical and mistaken attitudes.[76]

Such currents among other unions – notably the NUR, UPW and the Chemical Workers – point to some disillusion with nationalization and to the significant minority reservoir of support which more radical schemes might have tapped. The position on the left was not helped by the role of the CP which, in industries where it had influence, notably mining, failed to put forward proposals for alternatives to the 1944 TUC Report on the disingenuous grounds that 'nationalization under capitalism was not socialism'. Even as his party turned left, Horner opposed strikes as a threat to the new arrangements, crusading for increased productivity into the 1950s.[77]

Trade unionists and labourism

However, the view that a right-wing Labour leadership simply held back or 'betrayed' a mass popular radicalism must be treated with caution. Recent revisionist historiography has sought to invert this now traditional critique and suggest that it was rather the apathy and conservatism of working-class electors which constrained Labour's radicalism.[78] There is much that is inadequate in this version of events: its mechanical division between activists and the 'people', its sustained failure to think historically and to specify whether popular apathy was greater or lesser compared with previous and succeeding decades, its unsubtle reading of sources, and its inability to address evidence which contradicts its central and unmodulated thesis – such as the 84 per cent turn-out in the 1950 election.[79]

Despite these flaws, this school has reminded us of the conditional nature of Labour's support among some sections of the working class. Labour's peak vote in 1951 with 48.8 per cent of the poll was remarkable after six years in government but masks the defection of 5 per cent of working-class male supporters between 1945 and 1950.[80] Labour's share of the vote declined in the two elections after 1951: to 46.4 per cent in 1955 and 43.9 per cent in 1959.[81] The third successive electoral defeat prompted critical reflection within the party and was analysed by the dominant revisionist tendency led by Gaitskell, with Tony Crosland as its main theorist, in terms which supported its own political agenda of abandoning public ownership and pursuing egalitarianism via the successful running of the mixed economy. Two publications in 1960 – Crosland's pamphlet *Can Labour Win?* and the book *Must Labour Lose?* by Mark Abrams, Richard Rose and Rita Hinden – were central to this analysis. Crosland argued that a shrinking, more affluent working class had eroded Labour's traditional base while the party's image had become identified with workers in cloth caps and unpopular issues such as nationalized industries and trade unions. Hinden drew 'The Lessons for Labour' from a survey conducted by Mark Abrams for the revisionist *Socialist Commentary* which she edited. She concluded that there was a need to remove 'the three major obstacles' revealed in the survey: Labour's identification as the party of the working class, its association with public ownership and its appearance of being divided. These dogmatic conclusions were based on a relatively small sample – 724 people, of whom only 255 considered themselves Labour supporters – and contrasted with Abrams' more tentative treatment.[82]

At the heart of these prognoses lay the *'embourgeoisement'* thesis, that more affluent consumption patterns led workers to acquire, in Crosland's words, 'a middle class psychology'.[83] The collapse of Conservative support in the early 1960s fatally undermined this argument. Labour won the 1964 election with 44.1 per cent (and went on to increase this share to 48.1 per cent in 1966); the 56 seats Labour gained in 1964 more than redressed its total losses of 52 seats in the 1951, 1955 and 1959 elections.[84] Data on Labour's vote among manual workers demonstrates continuing – if anything growing rather than diminishing – support between 1945 and 1964: it was 62 per cent in 1945, 63 per cent in 1951, 62 per cent in 1955, dipped to 57 per cent in 1959, but rose to 63 per cent in 1964. The ephemeral drop in 1959 had 'far more to do with changing politics than with the alleged change in the character of the working class'.[85] *The Times* description of Labour's 1959 manifesto summarized the lukewarm electoral appeal to its traditional constituents 'of a party with some misgivings about the few doctrinaire experiments to which it is committed and with a coherent programme of minor social reform ...'.[86]

More extensive surveys in the early 1960s confirmed the resilient sense of working-class identity. Runciman's study of manual workers conducted in 1961–3, suggested the continuing salience of class; that of Goldthorpe and his colleagues, conducted at the same time, demonstrated the enduring support for Labour even among Luton's archetypal affluent workers.[87] The links between class identity and party support were examined by Butler and Stokes in a study based on a large sample of over 2,000 people which began in 1963. Among working-class Labour voters they identified an overwhelming view of politics as the representation of their class interests. The researchers were sceptical of *embourgeoisement* theories. Even among the small numbers who changed their self-ascribed class following a move from publicly owned to private housing, there was no diminution in support for Labour. More significant was the weakening of class alignment with Labour among younger voters who had entered the electorate after 1945 and declining willingness to vote in mining and inner city constituencies. One possible source of such trends was held to be the weakening of Labour's projected identity as the party of the working class, suggesting that revisionist 'solutions' to this problem may instead have contributed to it.[88]

The strong and enduring association between union membership and support for Labour is also clear. Although the early studies in the Nuffield series on British general elections rarely address the issue, a survey of trade unionists before polling day, 1955, indicated that Labour's support stood at 59 per cent, compared with Conservatives, 25 per cent, Liberals and others, 2 per cent, and 'Don't knows', 14 per cent. A poll at the 1964 general election estimated Labour support among trade union members at 62.2 per cent. Butler and Stokes found that support for Labour at that election among families containing a union member amounted to 73 per cent (compared with 42 per cent in non-union families). Such figures provide no evidence that a decade of rising living standards had eroded Labour's union base; indeed they suggest the reverse. However, support for Labour was less strong among lower grade, non-manual (56 per cent) and supervisory non-manual union families (42 per cent) than among skilled manual (72 per cent) and unskilled manual union families (78 per cent). This was noteworthy and it indicated that the shifting composition of the workforce and changes in union structure held implications for Labour in the years to come.[89]

Moreover, if electoral support for Labour held up, despite fluctuations, we should not assume the character of that support, or of the party's grassroots organization, was unchanging. Individual membership is a strong measure of the party's organizational vitality. It had more than doubled between 1943 and 1945 to 487,000 in the latter year, and almost doubled again by 1950 to over 900,000, reaching a post-war peak of just over one million in 1952. It only marginally declined in the following years until a drop of 9 per cent in 1955.[90] As Mark Jenkins points out, this 'flood-tide' of members coincided with the Bevanite movement, while decline was paralleled by the triumph of

Gaitskell's right-wing, revisionist leadership. Similar patterns were reflected in the women's sections and Labour's youth and student movements.[91] Bevanism stimulated wide political discussion in the constituencies. Its 'Brains Trusts' of panels of speakers with audience participation were hugely popular in 1953–4, attended by hundreds, sometimes thousands, of members. Bevanite support within the unions at all levels was greater than sometimes supposed, but there was a failure to translate this into a cohesive movement able to challenge the entrenched right-wing leaderships whose votes guaranteed leadership policy at Party Conference. Bevan's personal ambiguity towards the unions as instruments of high politics and his instinctive respect for labourism's divide between industrial and parliamentary politics was disabling. His reliance on 'spontaneous union democracy' was over optimistic as his defeat by Gaitskell for Party Treasurer by a majority of two to one in 1954 demonstrated. Union support for Bevan in 1956 was as much a sign of an emerging compromise with the party leadership as a victory for the left.[92]

A change in mood had been detected during the 1955 election. One authoritative study reported that 'in most constituencies, union leaders and Labour agents agreed that, while the [electioneering] activity on the shopfloor followed the same pattern as in previous years, it was more belated and less enthusiastic ... the sense of urgency had gone'. In 1960, Harrison catalogued a depressing lack of political interest in many union branches.[93] A survey of 36 Constituency Labour Parties over the winter of 1962–3 found that 'active factionalism' existed in only three, although nine others had experienced recent intra-party disputes, stimulated by the rise of CND.[94] Only 12 per cent of union members in Butler and Stokes' sample attended an election meeting in 1964 (compared with 24 per cent of all electors in 1950); over 43 per cent did not discuss the campaign with their fellow workers; and less than 2 per cent had any recollection of a union representative approaching them to ask for their electoral support.[95]

As in the past, there were impediments to dialogue between activists and wider sections of the working class, and a failure to develop a vernacular political language which could engage with the changing concerns of trade unionists in the workplace and consumers in the community. Institutionally this was reflected in the lack of interest in the establishment of Labour Party factory branches (outside the West Midlands) which might have questioned the dichotomy of industry and politics.[96] The CP did, unevenly, endeavour to build party organizations in the workplace, as Richard Stevens shows in his chapter, but such efforts were circumscribed by the party's declining appeal. The Bevanite 'Brains Trusts' did essay a more participatory, if still limited, style of political education but they were confined largely within the existing ranks of constituency activists and were far from welcome in sections of Labour's establishment.[97]

In the context of political and cultural renewal, the absence of a vital, well-resourced scheme of labour movement education is important. In his chapter on workers' education, John McIlroy analyses its constricted and contested nature in these years, and the dashing of hopes for a mass education which might develop grassroots activists towards socialism. Both the political weaknesses of the unions and the reality of a minority tradition of political debate within them was exemplified by their reliance on two external bodies, the National Council of Labour Colleges (NCLC) and the Workers' Educational Association (WEA), to educate their members. A range of factors, not least minimal resources and the lack of practical enthusiasm of union leaders, ensured that the NCLC, which had evolved from Marxism, and the WEA, broadly in the Fabian tradition, had an impact only at the margins. When the TUC took an interest after the war, it was to concentrate its resources on the practicalities of collective bargaining, with the object of union education increasingly the training of shop stewards in orderly industrial relations. The decision, consummated in 1964, to establish a TUC scheme based on the take-over of the NCLC extended this approach. Union leaders expected the Labour Party to finance political education, but the party's initiatives were both protracted and unfruitful. The development of education in this period followed and reinforced the industrial/political fractures in the labour movement. It did little to redress its pallid internal culture or create a thinking, strategic, voluntary cadre, still less an informed, committed membership.

The opportunities for working-class renewal presented by the increased numbers of women and workers from the former British Empire entering the workforce also went largely disregarded and unrealized by the leaders of the labour movement. Issues of gender and ethnicity played only a small role on the formal agendas of industrial politics in comparison with their increasing salience in the years after 1964. In all probability these developments enhanced differentiation rather than expanding the movement's cultural and political vision. Historians of women's struggles in the unions during the post-war period have distinguished 'between roughly the first fifteen years 1945–60 when the militants made little impression on the traditional male domination of the unions ... and the next fifteen years when a trickle of small concessions became a flood'.[98] If gender divisions were long standing, Eric Hobsbawm pertinently characterizes the working-class racism which began to emerge in the 1950s after around half a century of slumber as a 'significant and unwelcome development'.[99]

In the twenty years after the war, women remained concentrated in low paid work, concentrated in the service sector, with more than a third working part-time. In this context, and in a climate where sexism was 'natural' and the 'marriage bar' still operated, union density of around 25 per cent through the period was significant, particularly as recruitment and representation of women workers by the unions continued to be neglected. Perhaps the most notable achievement in these 'barren fifteen years' when women were stereotyped as housewives working for 'pin money' and often treated as second-class trade unionists, was the attainment of equal pay in the public services. But there were other successes, legislative through enactment of the Office, Shops and Railway Premises Act 1963 and, by means of direct action, such as the recognition of USDAW by Woolworth's after a sustained campaign. The handful of prominent women leaders, Florence Hancock and Ellen McCullough of the TGWU, Anne Godwin of the Clerical Workers, Anne Loughlin of the Tailors and Garment Workers and Ethel Chipchase of the TSSA, were only the best known of the women activists who fought year after year for redress of inequality in union and TUC conferences and negotiating bodies. The uneven progress of this period was typified by the 1959 decision of the National Society of Metal Mechanics to admit women as 'half members'. But the publication in 1963 of the *TUC Charter for Women* heralded better times.[100]

Britain's new black workers encountered a range of responses from trade unionists at all levels, from welcome and support to grudging acceptance and racist discrimination. If many were accorded support – Bill Morris, later to become General Secretary of the TGWU, is only the best known of those who testify to this – hostility caught the eye and the headlines. At the extremes it was embodied in resolutions of shop stewards' committees, branches and regional bodies, and even in strikes to enforce the 'colour bar', against immigrant workers. The leadership of unions such as the TGWU which organized in industries such as passenger transport, which recruited large numbers of black workers, was far from impressive. Indeed unions sometimes took up positions which could exacerbate the difficulties of immigrant members. The NUR supported immigration controls from the mid-1950s, while Frank Cousins declared, 'We cannot afford that these people should be allowed unrestricted entry into this country'.[101]

Despite his lack of any noteworthy contribution towards the cause of anti-racism, Bill Carron sternly lectured black trade unionists on their ingratitude: 'It would be very acceptable to the rest of us if some small measure of appreciation and thanks were in evidence'.[102] While TUC Congresses applauded delegates opposing racism and explaining the excellent work members were doing to combat it, the General Council took few positive initiatives. As early as 1955 it explored immigration controls 'not based on colour' with the Ministry of Labour but automatically opposed any 'special measures' – even minimal anti-discrimination legislation – which might improve the position of black workers. The TUC supported the Labour Party's increasingly uncertain opposition to the landmark 1962 Act which introduced modern immigration controls. But the General Council remained opposed to formal initiatives to combat discrimination on the grounds that it was negligible and that even mild affirmative action would introduce divisions into a movement where none existed. In 1964 they reported to Congress, '... the General Council has no evidence that the trade unions provided special services for immigrants nor did they consider that they were necessary or desirable'.[103] Yet it was in these years that tensions which were to test working-class unity in succeeding decades developed, demonstrated most dramatically by the Notting Hill riots of 1958.

Workplace organization and strikes

A vigorous shop stewards' movement had been stimulated by the wartime conditions of the engineering industry.[104] The industry's expansion in the post-war years, in contrast to the numerically declining traditional union heartlands of coal, rail and textiles, meant it was increasingly considered by both academic and popular opinion as the epitome of industrial relations.[105] Despite its partiality, generalization from this view was later to inform public policy. Between 1947 and 1961 the number of AEU shop stewards increased from 19,000 to 31,000; the number of TGWU stewards was estimated at over 25,000 by 1956; in the NUGMW, there were about 14,000 stewards in 1961. By the latter year, Clegg and his colleagues estimated that there was a total of 90,000 workplace representatives throughout British industry, less than half the number – 'at least 200,000' – which the TUC had suggested the previous year; it seems likely that by the early 1960s the total lay somewhere between the two. It is probable that most of these representatives were in the metal-working industries: in 1947, of the ten unions whose rules required the appointment of stewards, only one did not organize in these industries, although other unions, notably in printing, mining and the railways, also possessed forms of workplace representation.[106]

We should not assume that there was a steady increase in the presence of stewards as a natural and spontaneous outcome of full employment and the inevitable growth of 'informality'. Some employers sought to victimize stewards after the war and by the late 1940s workplace organization was probably weaker than it been five years previously. In 1955 the TUC Congress was sufficiently concerned to pass a resolution, against the wishes of the General Council, condemning 'the systematic campaign' against union activists and 'victimization of shop stewards'. Following the national engineering strike in 1957 there were a number of attempts not to re-employ stewards.[107] By 1961, however, a survey of stewards showed a different picture. Only 19 per cent recalled cases of victimization in their workplace during the previous decade, while 94 per cent stated that management had not seriously hampered them in carrying out their own duties. Certainly workplace organization became more established after 1960: there was a rapid leap in the numbers of AEU stewards in 1960 and 1961, almost as great as the total increase during the previous twelve years.[108] Yet engineering was far from typical. Batstone later summarized the situation in the early 1960s: steward organization was limited, even in manufacturing, and was a rarity amongst white collar workers and in the service industries; even in its strongholds such as vehicles it was often fragile.[109]

Focusing on Clydeside, Alan McKinlay and Joseph Melling in their chapter point to the extremely varied conditions between engineering factories in the region and show the highly contested ways in which stewards established their authority before winning grudging acceptance from employers. In particular, they highlight how stewards represented the collective values of workgroups and rewove the fabric of authority relations in the workplace. The frontier of control was not uniformly or easily redrawn in the unions' favour and there was considerable variation in employer strategy. In vehicles effective workplace organization was only permanently established by the early 1960s, and remained vulnerable to counter-attack, as the victimization of seventeen stewards, including the convenor, at Ford Dagenham in 1962 demonstrated. For much of the period, stewards were embattled, digging in and entrenching their status.[110]

'Restrictive practices' related to strong workplace organization have almost certainly been exaggerated as a factor in Britain's economic decline in the 1950s.[111] But such practices must be understood in the context of the continuing insecurity of many groups of workers in the 'stop-go' economy and industrial restructuring. Strikes to resist redundancy increased from 7.3 per cent of recorded stoppages in 1946–52 to 10 per cent in 1953–9.[112] The growth of steward organization can at least in part be viewed as the continued operation of a mentality of insecurity in the age of full employment, the development by workers of 'protective practices', a defensive warrening of the workplace against managerial prerogatives. Nor was the construction of such defences confined to skilled workers, as had largely been the case in the past, but was increasingly developed autonomously by semi-skilled operatives in manufacturing industry.[113]

This was unevenly reflected in the rule books and constitutions of unions.[114] As early as the late 1940s, a detailed study of a London TGWU branch concluded that stewards had 'in practice become a new level in the structure' of the union, 'wedged firmly though unofficially between the rank and file member and the branch'. Multi-unionism within the metalworking industries fostered joint shop steward committees in the workplace, and, particularly in the case of vehicles, combine committees linking stewards' committees in individual plants.[115] Fear of such organizations outwith formal union structures was a matter of growing concern in the latter part of the 1950s. Lord Cameron's inquiry into Briggs Motor Bodies at Dagenham in 1957 revealed a joint shop stewards' committee with its own substantial funds, its own office and a monthly newspaper: 'a private union within a union, enjoying immediate and continuous touch with the men in the shop, answerable to no superiors and in no way officially or constitutionally linked with the union hierarchy'. Professor Jack's report on London airport the following year also discovered a well-organized, self-funded stewards' organisation.[116]

95

We should beware of generalizations from such cases as to a deep, structural fissure between workplace organization and official union structures during these years. In 1961 a quarter of stewards who responded to Clegg and his colleagues sat on higher union committees. Full-time officers were also sometimes involved in the establishment of steward organization.[117] Tensions certainly existed between stewards and officers but they should not obscure areas of cooperation, particularly where there was a shared political commitment. The contradictory elements in this relationship were symbolized at the 1960 TUC Congress when – in the face of contemporary media hostility to workplace unionism – the leadership felt obliged to place on record its appreciation of the voluntary work carried out by stewards. The mover of the resolution, Bill Carron, had a few weeks previously referred to stewards as 'werewolves'.[118] Some unions sought to exercise control over their stewards prior to this. The NUGMW responded to the unofficial strikes in its London region by not only revising its rules in 1951 to codify the steward's constitutional position, it also embarked on a training programme in industrial relations and work study for representatives. As John McIlroy demonstrates in his chapter, such moves prefigured the growing use of training to civilize and constrain stewards within the boundaries of responsible workplace bargaining.

The real tension between shop stewards' committees and official structures, and the involvement of stewards in grassroots struggles, led both the CP and the Trotskyists in the 1950s to focus on stewards as the potential basis for a rank and file movement.[119] But steward organization developed through a complex mixture of worker initiative and managerial accommodation. Some companies were opposed in principle to recognizing stewards. For many it depended more pragmatically on who the stewards were, what they did and how they lubricated or impeded managerial functions.[120] Stewards came under attack not only as 'irresponsible agitators' but also as susceptible to corruption: 'they can make a good thing for themselves in terms of creature comforts if not of hard cash'.[121] And the relationship between struggles over job control and political consciousness was considerably more complex than that suggested by claims that such disputes might lead to a 'questioning of the essential nature and purpose of production within a capitalist society'.[122] Far from it: the absence of such fundamental questioning remained a feature of most post-war factory organization. Even well-organized workplaces could display features of sectionalism more evocative of the middle of the nineteenth century than the age of television. For example, trade unionism in the London ship repair industry, with a strong network of stewards and an active CP workplace branch, was nevertheless based on a strict craft/labourer division: strikes were called by meetings of craftsmen and the labourers subsequently informed of the decision.[123]

Whilst recognizing the limited ambitions of 'factory consciousness', we should not overlook the significant role played by political activists. In her chapters, Nina Fishman points to the role of Communists in the engineering and busworkers' disputes, Jim Phillips to the Trotskyists and Communists in the docks, while Richard Stevens describes the attempts by CP militants to construct industry-wide solidarity in the motor industry. Many other stewards were Labour Party activists: Coventry provides only one well documented example of a situation where the local party enjoyed especially close links with shop steward organizations in the workplace.[124]

Much of the contemporary attention to stewards concerned not only the alleged Communist affiliations of their leaders but also their involvement in unofficial strikes. In 1959 the TUC General Council set up an inquiry into 'Disputes and Workplace Representation' and produced a report which recognized that a small minority of 'individualistic stewards' had engaged in 'needless strikes'. The inquiry was in part prompted by adverse press publicity – the American term 'wildcat strike' entered the vocabulary of the British media that same year.[125] As Geoffrey Goodman recalls in his memoir of a life as an industrial correspondent, coverage of union affairs was a critical feature of the political content of all newspapers in the 1940s and 1950s. In its treatment of the unions, the press was a more significant medium than radio or television and the function of the industrial correspondent was increasingly perceived as 'the strike reporter', relaying the industrial effects of the 'Communist conspiracy'.

The interpretation of strike data is problematic.[126] The official strike statistics exclude short, small-scale stoppages, as well as industrial action short of a stoppage. The very high incidence of strikes in coalmining distorts the total figures, particularly the number of strikes. For this reason, the data on strike activity described in Table 3.5 are presented to include and exclude mining. Durcan, McCarthy and Redman identified three main phases during this period: 'the postwar peace, 1946–52', 'the return of the strike, 1953–9', and from 1960 'the shopfloor movement', which extended to 1968.[127] In contrast to the sharply upward trend of strike activity in the later years of the war, the immediate post-war period was distinguished by relative industrial tranquillity. This trend was reversed in the latter part of 1953 and by 1959 stoppages outside mining had increased by 79 per cent on the former year's total. This increase was accompanied by renewed 'set piece' national strikes, commencing with a one-day national engineering strike in December 1953, which resulted in sharp rises in the number of working days lost.[128] 1960 marked a further turning point in the accelerating unrest from the late 1950s, being the first year that the total number of strikes outside mining exceeded 1000; by 1964 it was 1,466.

These figures take no account of inter-industry variations: a small group of industries was consistently strike-prone. Coalmining was the outstanding case, and piece work, insecurities caused by mechanization and rationalization combined with high demand for coal, generated grievances which frequently resulted in short strikes involving small groups of workers. But

97

we should note also that under nationalization the regional distribution of mining strikes continued to reflect pre-war regional concentrations, particularly in Scotland and South Wales.[129] Other strike-prone industries included docks (for reasons which Jim Phillips examines in more detail in his chapter), iron and steel, vehicles, engineering and shipbuilding.[130]

If strike activity was greater than is sometimes recalled, the explanation for its slow rise under conditions of increasing union membership and full employment in the 1950s remains unclear. But it may plausibly have involved a combination of factors: initially, support for the Labour government; a willingness to trade off wages for improved social services and food subsidies; then, a rise in real wages during the 1950s; the limited nature of workers' aspirations throughout this period related to generational experience; low rates of inflation; the greater competitive pressures upon employers; and the gradual, evolutionary, uneven establishment of workplace organization.[131]

The reasons for striking changed over these years. Only a small percentage of strikes were in support of wage increases. In the two decades after 1940 the trend in the reasons for striking was towards disputes over the effort bargain, working arrangements and the treatment of workers. This led one observer to conclude 'that these disputes all involve attempts to submit managerial discretion and authority to agreed – or failing that – customary rules'.[132] Such a trend is consistent with the gradual and uneven establishment of workplace controls. However, the percentage of strikes in support of wage increases show a steady increase from the mid-1950s – from 8.1 per cent in 1955, to 16.6 percent in 1960 and 21.4 percent in 1964.[133] This growing wage militancy was in line with the rising trend in real wages (see Table 3.1) and may reflect both the stiffening of managerial resolve in a more competitive market situation and the countervailing confidence of better established steward organization.

Reflections

Some labour historians have seen this period as a time of stagnation and lost opportunities. In his influential overview of British labour in the twentieth century published in 1978, Eric Hobsbawm located the halt of its forward march in the years 1948–53. In the following decades, labour's crisis was evidenced by decline in electoral support, the changing sociology of the working class, the growth of sectionalism and economistic militancy. For John Saville, 'the Labour government began to lose its nerve during the second half of 1947' and by 1951 'Labour socialism had arrived at a dead end'; the subsequent period he characterizes as 'the wasted years.[134] They may be characterized alternatively as constituting a period of qualitative advance followed by a period which combined elements of retreat, consolidation and, by 1964, forward progress. The years 1948–53 may be viewed as Labour's high point rather than its entry into a long decline, the years in which the welfare state, full employment and historically high levels of union density were consolidated.

The 1951 vote, the party's highest ever, was electorally the climax of labourism: Labour was robbed of office, for only the fractional vagaries of a system which awarded the Conservatives more seats for fewer votes kept Attlee from five more years in Downing Street. The ensuing period saw Labour's highest ever individual membership. Compared with 1945–51, CLP records and party histories suggest an increase in party activism in the early 1950s. 1955, a year of real electoral defeat, might seem a better benchmark from which to date what was to be only a temporary decline in the party's electoral fortunes. For in 1964 and 1966 under Wilson's stewardship they were to be restored, albeit briefly, to Attlee-like dimensions. Trade union membership continued to grow in absolute terms and by 1964 was almost a million higher than in 1948. It is more difficult to assess whether Labour's sense of mission was blunted compared with earlier periods. Certainly for many the defeat of Gaitskell and the revisionists over Clause 4 and the subsequent installation of Wilson, perceived, albeit erroneously, as a man of the left, meant that in 1964 there was a discernible sense that the labour movement was again moving forward, that the work of 1945–7 would be resumed.

The two post-war decades were far from years of unprecedented working-class decomposition or political defeat as any comparison with the 1920s and 1930s discloses.[135] The structural changes in the working class were surely as profound in the interwar as in the post-war years. The number of miners declined from their peak of 1.2 million in 1924 to 696,000 in 1946. Moreover, this decline was most acute in those mining regions such as Lancashire and Scotland which had been the 'front runners' in Labour's advance prior to the First World War.[136] Trade union membership slumped after 1921: that of the Miners' Federation, often conceived as the core of the labour movement, dropped from 948,000 in 1920 to 501,000 thirteen years later. The affiliated membership of the TUC dropped at a similarly precipitous rate: from an interwar peak 6.5 million to 3.4 million over the same period.[137]

The association between union density and support for Labour was far from straightforward. Labour consolidated its position in the 1930s, and increasingly became the party of the urban working class; yet it never won more than 38 per cent of the vote in general elections, compared with 44 per cent in 1964. The shift in the centre of Britain's industrial gravity during the interwar years from the North of England, Scotland and South Wales towards the newer industries of the Midlands and the South East posed a major problem for class *rassemblement* and for the mobilization of support for the party: 'Labour in the 1930s was the party of the old and decaying places, rather than the new and dynamic ones'.[138] It is generally accepted, on the basis of by-election results, that Labour would not have won the general election due to be called in 1940. Had it not been for the Second World War, 1926 industrially or 1929 or 1935 politically might have been regarded as the key turning point in Labour's forward march.

Nor is it evident that the 'traditional' working-class identity forged from the end of the nineteenth century, which found its political expression in labourism, was unproblematically positive. Its emphasis on occupational solidarity and class loyalty were important elements in support for trade unionism and the Labour Party; yet it could also embrace a deference to authority, a parochialism and narrowness of vision which circumscribed its political ambitions and restricted them industrially to collective bargaining and politically to a bureaucratic welfarism. Working-class culture – particularly youth culture – shifted after 1950, and developed, in however distorted a form, a new anti-authoritarian ethos, with which Labour's traditional discourse, based in the moral codes of non-conformity, found it difficult to engage.[139]

There were undoubtedly lost opportunities and failures of political will. Saville's comments on the Labour government faltering after 1947 are compelling. If there was a moment in this period for radical transformation it was probably 1944–5. That was the time to mobilize, nurture and institutionalize the real, if not to be exaggerated, desire for change; to ensure the planning and mobilization of the war economy was developed not displaced; to break down the barriers between the industrial and political spheres; to politicize the unions and extend industrial democracy. But this projection is abstract. A major, evenly balanced internal struggle would have been required to achieve it. Attlee, Morrison, Bevin, Dalton, Cripps, Deakin, Williamson and Lawther, for all their virtues, were not the men for such a project. The hour was economically unpropitious. Moreover, as Britain moved into the Cold War, planning on the model of the USSR which had influenced sections of the Labour Party became increasingly taboo. The yearning of many in the ranks of both the Labour Party and unions for more drastic social change produced no movement from below, for their radicalism was always circumscribed and took second place anyway to their loyalty to their leaders. There was little else on offer on the left. Those who looked beyond Labour encountered the violent oscillations of Stalinist policy between 1945–51: for the majority of dissidents, the CP was simply not a viable substitute. The best insertion point for any alternative history seems to be Labour winning the 1951 general election and hence availing itself of the new political space offered by the long boom to move towards more corporatist approaches. But if Labour could – and should – have won in 1951, the good times which were just around the corner have rarely acted to stimulate radical reform and its rigours.[140]

In reality, the best alternative to be had, the belated opposition to the limitations of the 1945 government, was Bevanism. Its predecessors in the 1945 parliament had essentially limited themselves to a speedier pursuit of more nationalizations.[141] The Bevanites have often had an unfair press. They were hemmed in by the block votes and 'trespassers will be prosecuted' placards of union leaders. But as the 1950s developed, the limitations of the contest between the revisionists and the left became more apparent. Both currents were paternalistic and ambivalent in different ways towards trade unionism. The former's strategy was based on an economic complacency concerning the success of the mixed economy. The policies of the latter focused particularly on international and defence issues and developed no fundamental critique of domestic policy; rather the task was to 'ensure the carrying out of policies already agreed upon', nationalize more industries, and to 'keep left'.[142]

Yet while hindsight inevitably shapes and colours such conclusions, by 1964 things looked different. Trade union popularity had fluctuated in the post-war years, but it had not declined as much as the TUC sometimes feared: in August 1964 a Gallup poll found that 70 per cent viewed trade unions as 'a good thing', only fractionally lower than a decade earlier.[143] Nevertheless the images of carworkers and dockers as the carriers of social disorder which increasingly figured in the press, and the stereotyping of trade unionists as purveyors of restrictive practices and pliant fodder for extremists in films such as I'm All Right Jack (1959) and The Angry Silence (1960), were finding political resonance within sections of the Conservative Party and the judiciary.

The changes in working-class culture and structure after 1950 were far-reaching. But they were not wholly antagonistic to labour's advance. More than Marxists have embraced a concept of the working class which extends beyond manual workers. The increasing willingness of white collar employees to embrace trade unionism, if in numbers inadequate to significantly increase density, was a positive development. The unions in general had achieved significant gains in the immediate post-war years and protected them in the ensuing period of Conservative dominance. The welfare state was established as a seemingly fixed element; there had been no erosion of government commitments to maintain full employment: both represented important gains for the working class. Nor had there been any serious counter-attack by employers and the state upon union organization which was sinking deep roots in the workplace. Union membership had increased beyond the 10 million mark for the first time in 1962 and seemed poised for new inroads into expanding sectors of the economy.

While the Tories had caught a mood of post-war weariness with austerity in 1951, thirteen years later it was the Conservatives, not Labour, who seemed jaded and incompetent. The be-tweeded Earl of Home's grouse-moor image, redolent of Britain's relative decline during the 'wasted years', was cruelly juxtaposed against a modernizing, Gannex-clad Harold Wilson who appeared able to dissolve the divisions between left and right in his party through the alchemy of the 'white heat of technology' and to offer the unions a new future via an influential role in his grandiose National Plan.

Table 3.1 Index of real wages and percentage unemployed in the United Kingdom, 1945–64

Year	Real wages [Jan. 1956 = 100]	Percentage unemployed
1945	87.9	0.4
1946	94.5	1.7
1947	97.4	1.3
1948	96.3	1.3
1949	96.5	1.4
1950	94.8	1.4
1951	93.8	1.1
1952	93.5	1.5
1953	95.0	1.5
1954	98.1	1.2
1955	100.4	1.0
1956	103.4	1.9
1957	104.6	1.3
1958	104.0	1.8
1959	106.6	2.0
1960	108.3	1.5
1961	109.2	1.4
1962	108.3	1.9
1963	110.2	2.2
1964	111.9	1.5

Sources: J. Cronin, *Industrial Conflict in Modern Britain* (1979), Table B.7, pp. 226-7; R. Taylor, *The Trade Union Question in British Politics* (Oxford, 1993), Table A5.1, p. 378.

Table 3.2 Aggregate union membership and density in the United Kingdom, 1945–64

	Union membership (000s)	Potential membership (000s)	Density level %	Density annual % change
1945	7,875	20,400	38.6	
1948	9,363	20,732	45.2	
1949	9,318	20,782	44.8	-0.9
1950	9,289	21,055	44.1	-1.6
1951	9,530	21,177	45.0	+2.0
1952	9,588	21,252	45.1	+0.2
1953	9,527	21,352	44.6	-1.1
1954	9,566	21,658	44.2	-0.9
1955	9,741	21,913	44.5	+0.7
1956	9,778	22,180	44.1	-0.9
1957	9,829	22,334	44.0	-0.2
1958	9,639	22,290	43.2	-1.8
1959	9,623	21,866	44.0	+1.9
1960	9,835	22,229	44.2	+0.5
1961	9,916	22,527	44.0	-0.5
1962	10,014	22,879	43.8	-0.5
1963	10,067	23,021	43.7	-0.2
1964	10,218	23,166	44.1	+0.9

Source: G.S. Bain and R. Price, 'Union growth: dimensions, determinants, and destiny', in G.S. Bain (ed.), *Industrial Relations in Britain* (Oxford, 1983), Table 1.1, p. 5.

Table 3.3 Ten largest TUC affiliates, 1945, 1963

1945			1963			1945–63
	Union	Membership		Union	Membership	% change
1	TGWU	815,675	1	TGWU	1,373,560	+68
2	AEU	635,884	2	AEU	980,639	+54
3	NUM	533,265	3	NUGMW	781,940	+64
4	NUGMW	475,463	4	NUM	501,643	-6
5	NUR	360,346	5	USDAW	354,701	+111
6	ASW	176,000	6	NUR	282,801	-22
7	NUDAW	168,328	7	ETU	271,912	+113
8	ETU	127,819	8	NUPE	230,000	+178
9	UPW	98,720	9	ASW	191,587	+9
10	NUAW	95,200	10	UPW	171,200	+73

Source: TUC, *Report*, 1946, 1964.

Table 3.4 Political classification of trade unions in the 1950s

Extreme left	Moderate left	Unreliable right	Consistent right
ETU	ASSET	ASW	TGWU
NUVB	AEU	UPW	NUM
CEU	USDAW	ASLEF	NUGMW
AUFW	NUFTO	NUDBTW	NUS
NSMM	PTU		BISATKA
USB	AESD		NUB
CWU	NUTGW		UTFWA
TWU	NUR		NUBSO
FBU			

Source: M. Harrison, *Trade Unions and the Labour Party since 1945* (1960), pp. 212–13; see also M. Jenkins, *Bevanism: Labour's high tide* (Nottingham, 1979), pp. 132–3.

Table 3.5 Trends in recorded strikes, 1946–64

Year	No. of strikes		No. of workers involved (000s)		No. of working days lost (000s)	
	Excl. mining	Incl. mining	Excl. mining	Incl. mining	Excl. mining	Incl. mining
1946	876	2,205	313	526	1,736	2,158
1947	668	1,721	315	623	1,521	2,433
1948	643	1,759	237	426	1,480	1,944
1949	552	1,426	186	434	1,053	1,807
1950	479	1,339	161	303	958	1,389
1951	661	1,719	244	379	1,344	1,694
1952	493	1,714	143	416	1,132	1,792
1953	439	1,746	1,206	1,374	1,791	2,184
1954	525	1,989	246	450	1,989	2,457
1955	636	2,419	317	671	2,669	3,781
1956	572	2,648	267	508	1,581	2,083
1957	635	2,859	1,094	1,359	7,898	8,412
1958	666	2,629	276	524	3,012	3,462
1959	786	2,093	454	646	4,907	5,270
1960	1,166	2,832	581	819	2,530	3,024
1961	1,228	2,686	530	779	2,309	3,046
1962	1,244	2,449	4,268	4,423	5,490	5,798
1963	1,081	2,068	440	593	1,429	1,755
1964	1,466	2,524	711	883	1,975	2,277

Source: J.W. Durcan, W.E.J. McCarthy and G.P. Redman, *Strikes in Post-War Britain* (1983), Table 6.1, p. 174.

Notes

1. K. Middlemas, *Politics in Industrial Society: the experience of the British system since 1911* (1979), p. 428.
2. J. Turner, 'Commentary' on D. Marquand, 'The decline of post-war consensus', in A. Gorst, L. Johnman and W.S. Lewis (eds), *Post-war Britain, 1945–64: themes and perspectives* (1989); N. Whiteside, 'The politics of the "social" and "industrial" wage, 1945–60', in H. Jones and M. Kandiah (eds), *The Myth of Consensus: new views on British history, 1945–64* (1996); see also the other essays in this collection by Jones and Kandiah.
3. Cf P. Addison, *The Road to 1945: British politics and the Second World War* (2nd edition, 1993), p. 279.
4. J. Hinton, *Labour and Socialism: a history of the British labour movement, 1867–1974* (1983), p. 179; E. Hobsbawm, 'The forward march of labour halted?' [1978], reprinted in M. Jacques and F. Mulhern (eds), *The Forward March of Labour Halted?* (1981).
5. C. Crouch, *The Politics of Industrial Relations* (1979), chs 1–4; A. Fox, *History and Heritage: the social origins of the British industrial relations system* (1985), pp. 368–73; R. Taylor, *The Trade Union Question in British Politics: government and unions since 1945* (Oxford, 1993), p. 265.
6. K. Jefferys, *The Attlee Government, 1945–51* (1992), pp. 15, 69; Hinton, *Labour and Socialism*, p. 169; J. Saville, *The Labour Movement in Britain* (1988), pp. 93–5; A. Glynn and J. Harrison, *The British Economic Disaster* (1980), p. 44; F. Carr, 'Cold War: the economy and foreign policy', in J. Fyrth (ed.), *Labour's High Noon: the government and the economy, 1945–51* (1993), pp. 140–1.
7. S. Pollard, *The Development of the British Economy 1914–50* (1962), pp. 361–2; M. Kidron, *Western Capitalism since the War* (1968), p. ix; P. Armstrong, A. Glynn and J. Harrison, *Capitalism since World War II: the making and breakup of the great boom* (1984), ch. 8.
8. A. Marwick, *British Society since 1945* (Harmondsworth, 1990 edition), p. 117; A. Halsey (ed.), *Trends in British Society since 1900* (1972); C.A.R. Crosland, *The Future of Socialism* (1956), p. 517.
9. P. Howlett, 'The "golden age", 1955–73', in P. Johnston (ed.), *Twentieth-Century Britain: economic, social and cultural change* (1994), pp. 328–9; B.W.E. Alford, *British Economic Performance, 1945–75* (1988), pp. 14–15.
10. J. Purcell and K. Sisson, 'Strategies and practice in the management of industrial relations', in G. Bain (ed.) *Industrial Relations in Britain* (1983), p. 97.
11. H. Gospel, *Markets, Firms and the Management of Labour in Modern Britain* (Cambridge, 1992), pp. 109–11; J. Melling, 'Managing the labour problem: the British worker question and the decline of manufacturing industry', *Labour History Review*, 57, 3, 1992.
12. A. Flanders, *The Fawley Productivity Agreements: a case study of management and collective bargaining* (1964), p. 251.
13. Gospel, *Markets*, pp. 132–3; A. McKinlay and J. Melling, 'The shop floor

politics of productivity: work, power and authority relations in British engineering, *c.*, 1945–57', in this volume.

14. H.A. Clegg, 'Employers', in A. Flanders and H. A. Clegg, *The Systems of Industrial Relations in Great Britain* (1954), pp. 213, 233; R.M. Grant and D. Marsh, *The Confederation of British Industry* (1977).

15. Clegg, 'Employers', pp. 199, 215; A. Flanders, 'Collective bargaining', in Flanders and Clegg, *System*, pp. 283, 285–6.

16. A. Fox, *History and Heritage: the social origins of the British industrial relations system* (1985), p. 367; Armstrong, Glynn and Harrison, *Capitalism*, pp. 190–2.

17. E. Wigham, *What's Wrong with the Unions?* (Harmondsworth, 1961), pp. 190–2; E. Wigham, *The Power to Manage: a history of the Engineering Employers' Federation* (1973).

18. Gospel, *Markets*, pp. 34–5.

19. S.W. Lerner and J. Marquand, 'Workshop bargaining, wage drift and productivity in the British engineering industry', *Manchester School of Economic and Social Studies*, 30, 1, 1962; L. A. Dicks-Mireaux and J. R. Shepherd, 'The wage structure and some implications for incomes policy', *Economic Review*, November 1964, p. 42.

20. S. Lerner and J. Bescoby, 'Shop steward committees in the British engineering industry', *British Journal of Industrial Relations*, 4, 1966, pp. 161–2; S. Lerner and J. Marquand, 'Regional variations in earnings, demand for labour and shop stewards' combine committees in the British engineering industry', *Manchester School of Economic and Social Studies*, 31, 3, 1963.

21. Purcell and Sisson, 'Strategies and practice', p. 101; Flanders, *The Fawley Productivity Agreements*; T. Cliff, *The Employers' Offensive: productivity deals and how to fight them* (1970).

22. P.K. Edwards and M. Terry, 'Conclusion: another way forward', in M. Terry and P.K. Edwards (eds), *Shopfloor Politics and Job Controls: the post-war engineering industry* (Oxford, 1988), p. 215; D. Lyddon, 'The car industry, 1945–79: shop stewards and workplace unionism', in C. Wrigley (ed.), *A History of Industrial Relations, 1940–79: industrial relations in a declining economy* (Cheltenham, 1996), pp. 193–8.

23. Royal Commission on the Distribution of Income and Wealth, *Report, no. 7* (1979), p. 76; B. Burkitt and D. Bowers, *Trade Unions and the Economy* (1979), p. 62; A. B. Atkinson, *Poverty in Britain and the Reform of Social Security* (Cambridge, 1969), p. 32; P. Townsend and B. Abel Smith, *The Poor and the Poorest* (1965); A. B. Atkinson and A. J. Harrison, *Distribution of Personal Wealth in Britain* (Cambridge, 1978), p. 218; J. Westergaard and H. Resler, *Class in a Capitalist Society: a study of contemporary Britain* (1975), pp. 113–14.

24. J. Scott, *The Upper Classes: property and privilege in Britain* (1982), pp. 114, 160; S. Aaronovitch, *The Ruling Class: a study of British finance capital* (1961); J.A.G. Griffith, *The Politics of the Judiciary* (1977), pp. 25–6.

25. J. Cronin, *Labour and Society in Britain, 1918–79* (1984), pp. 136, 147.

26. See the overviews by C. Wrigley, 'Women in the labour market and in the

unions' and K. Lunn, 'Complex encounters: trade unions, immigration and racism', in J. McIlroy, N. Fishman and A. Campbell, *British Trade Unions and Industrial Politics, vol. 2: the high tide of trade unionism* (Aldershot, 1999); C. Holmes, 'Immigration', in T. Gourvish and A. O'Day (eds), *Britain since 1945* (1991), p. 215.

27.   H. Mercer, 'The Labour governments of 1945–51 and private industry', in N. Tiratsoo (ed.), *The Attlee Years* (1991), p. 84; M. Cunningham, '"From the ground up?": the Labour governments and economic planning', in Fyrth, *Labour's High Noon*; P. Hennessy, *Never Again: Britain 1945–1951* (1992), pp. 379–81.

28.   A. Flanders, 'Collective bargaining: prescription for change' [1967] in A. Flanders, *Management and Unions: the theory and reform of industrial relations* (1970), p. 174; H.A. Clegg, *The Changing System of Industrial Relations in Britain* (Oxford, 1979), pp. 290ff.

29.   P. Davies and M. Freedland, *Labour Legislation and Public Policy* (Oxford, 1993), ch. 1; J. Saville, 'The Trades Disputes Act of 1906', *Historical Studies in Industrial Relations*, 1, 1996; R. Lowe, *Adjusting to Democracy: the role of the Ministry of Labour in British Politics, 1916–1939* (Oxford, 1986), pp. 105, 108, 130.

30.   O. Kahn-Freund, 'Legal framework' in Flanders and Clegg, *System of Industrial Relations*; cf K.D. Ewing, 'The state and industrial relations: "collective laisser-faire" revisited', *Historical Studies in Industrial Relations*, 5, 1998.

31.   D. Barnes and E. Reid, 'A new relationship: trade unions in the Second World War', in B, Pimlott and C. Cook (eds), *Trade Unions in British Politics: the first 250 years* (2nd edition, 1991).

32.   K.O. Morgan, *Labour in Power 1945–1951* (Oxford, 1984), p. 80; Davies and Freedland, *Labour Legislation*, pp. 87–95.

33.   J. Davis Smith, *The Attlee and Churchill Administrations and Industrial Unrest, 1945–1955* (1990), pp. 12–13.

34.   J. Hinton, *Shop Floor Citizens* (1994), p. 5.

35.   J. Tomlinson, 'Productivity, joint consultation and human relations in postwar Britain: the Attlee government and the workplace', in J. Melling and A. McKinlay (eds), *Management, Labour and Industrial Politics in Modern Europe: the quest for productivity growth during the twentieth century* (Cheltenham, 1996), p. 39.

36.   Taylor, *Trade Union Question*, pp. 47–9; TUC, *Report*, 1946, pp. 417–24.

37.   V. L. Allen, *Trade Union Leadership: based on a study of Arthur Deakin* (1957), pp. 125–32.

38.   N. Branson, *History of the Communist Party in Britain, 1941–1951* (1997), p. 183.

39.   H.A. Clegg, *A History of British Trade Unions since 1889, vol. 3: 1933–1951* (Oxford, 1994), pp. 352–404.

40.   N. Fishman, 'The demise of wartime social partnership: the unexpected revocation of Order 1305 and unintended consequences of Order 1376', unpublished paper, British Universities Industrial Relations Association

Conference, University of Keele, July 1998.

41. *The Times House of Commons 1951* (1951), p. 19; Lord Birkenhead, *Walter Monckton*, (1969), p. 276.

42. J.D.M. Bell, 'Trade Unions', in Flanders and Clegg, *System of Industrial Relations*, pp. 180–2.

43. D. Barnes and E. Reid, *Governments and Trade Unions: the British experience 1964–79* (1980), p. 25.

44. Clegg, *Changing System of Industrial Relations*, p. 314; A. Taylor, 'The Conservative Party and the trade unions', in McIlroy, Fishman and Campbell *British Trade Unions and Industrial Politics, vol. 2*; Barnes and Reid, *Governments and Trade Unions*, p. 34; P.A. Hall, *Governing the Economy: the politics of state intervention in Britain and France* (Cambridge, 1986),p. 86.

45. Barnes and Reid, *Governments and Trade Unions*, pp. 30–9.

46. TUC, *Report*, 1962, pp. 366–72.

47. G. Goodman, *The Awkward Warrior. Frank Cousins: his life and times* (1979), pp. 316, 326–32.

48. Barnes and Reid, *Governments and Trade Unions*, pp. 15, 30; Barnes and Reid, 'A new relationship', p. 153.

49. P. Maguire, 'Labour and the law: the politics of British industrial relations, 1945–79', in Wrigley, *History of British Industrial Relations*, pp. 48–9; Smith, *Attlee and Churchill Administrations*, p. 31.

50. Davies and Freedland, *Labour Legislation*, pp. 129–30, 243–4; K.W. Wedderburn, *The Worker and the Law* (Harmondsworth, 1986 edition), pp. 38–47; Griffith, *Politics of the Judiciary*, pp. 67–9.

51. G. Bain, *The Growth of White Collar Unionism* (Oxford, 1972), pp. 25–8, 183–8.

52. K. Coates and T. Topham, *Trade Unions in Britain* (Nottingham, 2nd edition, 1982), p. 59.

53. TUC, *Report*, 1946, p. 40; Clegg, *History, vol. 3*, p. 418.

54. R. Taylor, '"What are we here for?": George Woodcock and trade union reform', in McIlroy, Fishman and Campbell, *British Trade Unions, vol. 2*.

55. R. Hyman, *Industrial Relations: a Marxist introduction* (1975), pp. 58–60.

56. B. Roberts, *The Price of TUC Leadership* (1961), pp. 124, 137–9.

57. E. Heery and J. Kelly, 'Professional, participative and managerial unionism: an interpretation of change in trade unions', *Work, Employment and Society*, 8, 1, 1994; P. Smith, 'Change in British trade unions since 1945', *Work, Employment and Society*, 9, 1, 1995.

58. Allen, *Deakin*, pp. 249–59; J. Jones, *Union Man: the autobiography of Jack Jones* (1986), p. 132.

59. N. Fishman, *The British Communist Party and the Trade Unions, 1933–45* (Aldershot, 1995), pp. 77–80, 91–2.

60. R. and E. Frow, *Engineering Struggles: episodes in the story of the shop stewards' movement* (Manchester, 1982), pp. 260, 307, 439–40; G. Carlsson, 'The noble knight', in D. Widgery (ed.), *The Left in Britain, 1956–68* (Harmondsworth, 1976), pp. 183–4.

61. Clegg, *History, vol. 3*, pp. 304–5; T. Lane and K. Roberts, *Strike at Pilkingtons* (1971), pp. 49–54; H.A. Clegg, *General Union in a Changing Society* (Oxford, 1964), pp. 211–17.

62. Clegg, *History, vol. 3*, pp. 310–13; Clegg, *General Union*, pp. 174–8.

63. D. Howell, '"All or nowt": the politics of the MFGB', and H. Francis, 'Learning from bitter experience: the formation of the NUM', both in A. Campbell, N. Fishman and D. Howell (eds), *Miners, Unions and Politics 1910–47* (Aldershot, 1996).

64. V. L. Allen, *The Militancy of British Miners* (Shipley, 1981), pp. 62–5.

65. J. Lloyd, *Liberty and Light: the history of the EETPU* (1990) chs 15–21; B. Fryer and S. Williams, *A Century of Service: an illustrated history of the National Union of Public Employees, 1889–1993* (1993).

66. A. Spoor, *White Collar Union: sixty years of NALGO* (1967), chs 32, 33; D. Volker, 'NALGO's affiliation to the TUC', *British Journal of Industrial Relations*, 4, 1, 1966, p. 65.

67. V. L. Allen, *Trade Unions and Government* (1960), p. 288.

68. N. Fishman and H. Francis, *Arthur Horner: a political biography* (in preparation).

69. Clegg, *History, vol. 3*, p. 319; interview with Geoffrey Goodman by N. Fishman, June 1997.

70. Goodman, *Awkward Warrior*, p. 126; information from Geoffrey Goodman.

71. W. Paynter, *My Generation* (1972), pp. 145–6; interview with Geoffrey Goodman by Nina Fishman, June 1995.

72. Information from Geoffrey Goodman.

73. J. Mortimer, 'The Changing Mood of Working People', in Fyrth, *Labour's High Noon*, pp. 243–54; Hinton, *Labour and Socialism*, p. 168; R. Miliband, *Parliamentary Socialism: a study in the politics of Labour* (2nd edition, 1972), p. 277; B. Hindess, 'The decline of working class politics: a re-appraisal', in Pimlott and Cook, *Trade Unions in British Politics*, pp. 227–8.

74. TUC, *Report*, 1944, p. 400.

75. TUC, *Report*, 1946, pp. 10, 401; K. Coates and T. Topham (eds), *Workers' Control: a book of readings and witnesses for workers' control* (1970), p. 320.

76. R. Saville, 'Commanding heights: the nationalization programme', in Fyrth (ed.), *Labour's High Noon*, pp. 45, 59.

77. J. Schneer, *Labour's Conscience: the labour left, 1945–51* (1988), pp. 143–51; Coates and Topham, *Workers' Control*, pp. 299, 310–11.

78. S. Fielding, P. Thompson and N. Tiratsoo, *'England Arise!': the Labour Party and popular politics in 1940s Britain* (Manchester, 1995).

79. For a powerful critique of *England Arise!*, see J. Hinton, '1945 and the Apathy School', *History Workshop Journal*, 43, 1997.

80. J. Hinton, 'Women and the Labour vote, 1945–51', *Labour History Review*, 57, 3, 1992, p. 61.

81. F. W. S. Craig, *British Parliamentary Election Statistics, 1918–1970* (Chichester, 1971), pp. 16–17.

82. M. Abrams, R. Rose and R. Hinden, *Must Labour Lose?* (Harmondsworth,

1960), pp. 99–118, 9–10; Hindess, 'The decline of working class politics', pp. 229–30.

83. A. Crosland, *Can Labour Win?*, Fabian Tract 324, 1960, p. 12.

84. Craig, *Election Statistics*, pp. 18, 19, 54.

85. A. Heath, R. Jowett and J. Curtice, *How Britain Votes* (Oxford, 1985), pp. 29–30.

86. Quoted in D. Butler and R. Rose, *The British General Election of 1959* (1960), p. 50.

87. W.G. Runciman, *Relative Deprivation and Social Justice: a study of attitudes to social inequality in twentieth century England* (1966). pp. 137ff; J. H. Goldthorpe, D. Lockwood, F. Bechofer and J. Platt, *The Affluent Worker: political attitudes and behaviour* (Cambridge, 1968); Cronin, *Labour and Society in Britain*, pp. 169–72.

88. D. Butler and D. Stokes, *Political Change in Britain: forces shaping electoral choice* (1969), pp. 92, 101–4, 117–22.

89. M. Harrison, 'Trade Unions and the election', in D. E. Butler, *The British General Election of 1955* (1955, reprinted 1969), p. 213; D. E. Butler and A. King, *The British General Election of 1964* (1965), p. 296; Butler and Stokes, *Political Change in Britain*, pp. 155–6.

90. H. Pelling, *A Short History of the Labour Party* (2nd edition, 1965), p. 135.

91. M. Jenkins, *Bevanism: Labour's high tide* (Nottingham, 1979), pp. 118–25.

92. Ibid., pp. 171–2, 133–8; D. Howell, *British Social Democracy: a study in development and decay* (1976), pp. 185, 207.

93. Harrison, 'Trade unions and the election', p. 226; M. Harrison, *Trade Unions and the Labour Party since 1945* (1960), pp. 109–28.

94. E.G. Janosik, *Constituency Labour Parties in Britain* (New York, 1968), pp. 97–107.

95. Butler and Stokes, *Political Change in Britain*, pp. 161–3; Fielding, Thompson and Tiratsoo, *'England arise!'*, p. 199.

96. L. Minkin, *The Contentious Alliance: trade unions and the Labour Party* (Edinburgh, 1992 edition), p. 64.

97. Jenkins, *Bevanism*, pp. 171–3.

98. S. Lewenhak, *Women and Trade Unions: an outline history of women in the British trade union movement* (1977), pp. 206–7.

99. Hobsbawm, 'Forward march', p. 11.

100. Lewenhak, *Women and Trade Unions*, pp. 274–6; S. Boston, *Women Workers and the Trade Union Movement* (1980); Wrigley, 'Women in the labour market and in the unions'.

101. Quoted in K. Tompson, *Under Siege: racial violence in Britain today* (Harmondsworth, 1988), p. 72; J.A.G. Griffith et al., *Coloured Immigrants in Britain* (Oxford, 1960); R. Miles and A. Phizacklea, *White Man's Country: racism in Britain* (1984), pp. 32–3; J. McIlroy, 'Adrift in the rapids of racism: Syd Bidwell (1917–1997)', *Revolutionary History*, 7, 1, 1998, pp. 149–51.

102. Quoted in E. Rose, *Colour and Citizenship* (Oxford, 1969), p. 222.

103. TUC, *Report*, 1964, p. 282; R. Miles and A. Phizacklea, *The TUC, Black*

Workers and New Commonwealth Immigration, 1954–1973 (Warwick, 1977). See also Lunn, 'Complex encounters'.

104. R. Croucher, *Engineers at War, 1939–1945* (1982).

105. Clegg, *History, vol. 3*, p. 296.

106. A.I. Marsh, *Managers and Shop Stewards* (1963), p. 8; Clegg, *General Union*, p. 177; H.A. Clegg, A.J. Killick and R. Adams, *Trade Union Officers: a study of full-time officers, branch secretaries and shop stewards in British trade unions* (Oxford, 1961), p. 153; N. Barou, *British Trade Unions* (1947), pp. 64–5.

107. Croucher, *Engineers at War*, p. 344; Frow and Frow, *Engineering Struggles*, pp. 314ff, 341; R. Page Arnot, 'Class strategy', *Labour Monthly*, 39, 5, 1957, pp. 204–5.

108. Clegg, Killick and Adams, *Trade Union Officers*, p. 175; A.T. Marsh and E.E. Coker, 'Shop steward organization in Engineering', *British Journal of Industrial Relations*, 1, 2, 1963, Table 1, p. 177.

109. E. Batstone, *Working Order* (Oxford, 1984), p. 79.

110. Lyddon, 'The car industry, 1945–79', pp. 186–203; Frow and Frow, *Engineering Struggles*, pp. 275–312.

111. N. Tiratsoo and J. Tomlinson, 'Restrictive practices on the shopfloor in Britain, 1945–60: myth and reality', *Business History*, 36, 2, 1994.

112. J.W. Durcan, W.E.J. McCarthy and G.P. Redman, *Strikes in Post-War Britain: a study of stoppages of work due to industrial disputes, 1946–73* (1983), pp. 48, 80.

113. D. Lyddon, 'Workplace organization in the British car industry', *History Workshop*, 15, 1983; J. Belanger and S. Evans, 'Job controls and shop steward leadership among semi-skilled engineering workers', in Terry and Edwards, *Shopfloor Politics and Job Controls*.

114. J. F. B. Goodman and T. G. Whittingham, *Shop Stewards in British Industry* (1973 edition), ch. 3.

115. J. Goldstein, *The Government of British Trade Unions: a study of apathy and democratic processes in the Transport and General Workers' Union* (1952), p. 243; Lerner and Bescoby, 'Shop steward combine committees'.

116. *Report of a Court of Inquiry into the causes and circumstances of a Dispute at Briggs Motor Bodies ...* (Cmnd 131, 1957), p. 26; *Report of a court of Inquiry into the causes and circumstances of a dispute at London Airport ...* (Cmnd 608, 1958).

117. Clegg, Killick and Adams, *Trade Union Officers*, p. 168; M. Terry, 'The development of shop steward organization: Coventry Precision Tools 1945–1972', in Terry and Edwards, *Shopfloor Politics and Job Controls*, pp. 46–8, and J. Salmon, 'Wage strategy, redundancy and shop stewards in the Coventry motor industry', in Terry and Edwards, p. 203; Jones, *Union Man*, p. 133.

118. TUC, *Report*, 1960, pp. 356, 359.

119. P. Fryer, *The Battle for Socialism* (1959), pp. 163–7.

120. Terry and Edwards, *Shopfloor Politics and Job Controls, passim*; H.A. Turner, G. Clack and G. Roberts, *Labour Relations in the Motor Industry* (1967), p. 214

121. *Economist*, 15 February 1958, quoted in Fryer, *Battle for Socialism*.
122. H. Beynon, *Working for Ford* (Harmondsworth, 1973), p. 129.
123. Interview with Kevin Halpin, 11 November 1997, by J. McIlroy and A. Campbell. Halpin recalled that when drinking at lunchtime, craftsmen would go to the saloon bar, their unskilled 'mates' to the public bar.
124. N. Tiratsoo, *Reconstruction, Affluence and Labour Politics: Coventry, 1945–60* (1990), pp. 119–20. See also the references to a number of senior stewards who were political activists in the West Midland engineering industries in Edwards and Terry, *Shopfloor Politics and Job Control*.
125. TUC, *Report*, 1951, pp. 79–80; TUC, *Report*, 1960, pp. 124–30, 346–54; Wigham, *What's Wrong with the Unions*, p. 111.
126. Durcan et al., *Strikes in Post-War Britain*; R. Hyman, *Strikes* (1972); J. Cronin, *Industrial Conflict in Modern Britain* (1979).
127. Durcan et al., *Strikes*, chs 2–4.
128. Ibid,, p. 59.
129. R. Church and Q. Outram, *Strikes and Solidarity: coalfield conflict in Britain, 1896–1966* (Cambridge, 1998), ch. 12.
130. Durcan et al., *Strikes in Post-War Britain*, pp. 43, 78, 116.
131. J. Cronin, *Industrial Conflict in Modern Britain* (1979), pp. 138–41.
132. H.A. Turner, *The Trend of Strikes* (Leeds, 1963), pp. 18–19.
133. Calculated from Cronin, *Industrial Conflict in Modern Britain*, Table B.3, p. 213.
134. Hobsbawm, 'Forward march', p. 1; Saville, *Labour Movement in Britain*, pp. 115, 121ff.
135. D. Howell, 'When was "the forward march of labour"?', *Lfafur*, 5, 3, 1990.
136. B. Supple, *The History of the British Coal Industry, vol. 4, 1913–46: the political economy of decline* (Oxford, 1987), p. 21; R. Gregory, *The Miners and British Politics, 1906–1914* (Oxford, 1968).
137. H.A. Clegg, *A History of British Trade Unions since 1889, vol. 2: 1911–1933* (Oxford, 1987 edition), p. 570.
138. M. Savage, 'Urban politics and the rise of the Labour Party, 1919–1939', in L. Jamieson and H. Corr (eds), *State, Private Life and Political Change* (Basingstoke, 1990); M. Savage and A. Miles, *The Remaking of the British Working Class, 1840–1940* (1994), pp. 87–8.
139. Tiratsoo, *Reconstruction, Affluence and Labour Politics*, p. 117.
140. N. Whiteside, 'Industrial relations and social welfare, 1945–79', in Wrigley, *History of Industrial Relations*, pp. 113–14, 123–4; J. McIlroy, review of Wrigley, *History of British Industrial Relations*, in *Historical Studies in Industrial Relations*, 2, 1996.
141. D. Rubinstein, 'Socialism and the Labour Party: the Labour left and domestic policy, 1945–1950', in D.E. Martin and D. Rubinstein (eds), *Ideology and the Labour Movement* (1979); see also Schneer, *Labour's Conscience*, chs 4 and 6.
142. Jenkins, *Bevanism*, p. 289; Howell, *British Social Democracy*, pp. 186–200.
143. Taylor, *Trade Union Question*, Table A3.3, p. 371.

PART THREE

Case Studies, 1945–64

CHAPTER FOUR

'Shut Your Gob!':[1] Trade Unions and the Labour Party, 1945–64

David Howell

Wilf Cannon was a Reading railway man, an active member of the National Union of Railwaymen and of the Reading Labour Party. He has been portrayed as a fine example of the politically active trade unionist – 'a lean, vigorous, silver-haired patrician looking man, a good talker, a good listener and a discriminating reader, an intensely political animal'. One evening in 1944 he came straight from his work in the Great Western marshalling yard to a meeting of the NUR Reading (No. 1) Branch. Members discussed possible motions for the forthcoming Party Conference and he succeeded in gaining support for a resolution advocating specific extensions of public ownership. This subsequently became one of the Reading Party's two submissions to the Party Conference agenda. No doubt Wilf Cannon as a delegate to the Reading General Management Committee was an effective advocate for his union branch's proposal. This Reading resolution became a core element in the composite moved successfully at the national conference against the wishes of the Party's National Executive by the Reading Prospective Parliamentary Candidate, Ian Mikardo. The significance of this decision for the policy of the post-war Labour Government is debatable; it provides nevertheless a classic demonstration of the party-union relationship as exemplified at local level in the action of, often talented, activists. Within this scenario experiences at work led to a progressive – and often explicitly socialist – political agenda.[2]

The episode has a wider resonance through Wilf Cannon's employment. The National Union of Railwaymen often claimed to be a union that had made a distinctive contribution to the rise of the Labour Party. The union's principal predecessor, the Amalgamated Society of Railway Servants had moved the TUC resolution in 1899 that had led to the formation of the Labour Representation Committee (LRC). In rural areas and small towns, railway workers had played leading roles in the development of Labour's political organization. They had shown how their experience of a rule governed industry dominated by powerful, paternalistic and sometimes autocratic employers had produced firstly an effective trade unionism, and then often a political commitment. Railway workers sat on local councils, they became Labour Mayors. Eventually the senior NUR official, Jimmy Thomas, sat in two Labour cabinets. The fate of Thomas, the only trade union Member to defect in 1931 suggests that this political advance was not without its ambiguities. But in July 1945, it could truly seem a 'magnificent journey'.[3] Yet the imagery and the rhetoric did not offer adequate guidance to a complex reality. One assumption behind the formation of the LRC was that trade union affiliations could contribute not only organizational and financial resources, but also political unity. Solidarity developed at work and expressed in trade union organization could be extended to the ballot box. The electoral victory of 1945 could be characterized as a powerful vindication of that strategy: but this would be too simple an assessment.[4]

The pattern of union affiliation

The complexities can be approached through an appraisal of the affiliation of individual unions to the party. In the 1940s several smaller trade unions were not linked to the Labour Party, but almost all the larger ones were. They affiliated both through branches adhering to local parties and at national level. The rules governing affiliations had been the subject of revisions resulting from judicial intervention and legislative changes. Initially trade unions affiliated to the LRC, and from 1906 to the Labour Party, contributing out of their general funds on the basis of size of membership. This practice was challenged successfully in the courts by Walter Osborne, a member of the Railway Servants. His objective was to prevent the use of union funds for specific – and in his view unacceptable – political purposes; but the final judgement prohibited the use of union funds for all political objectives. The subsequent 1913 Act did not reverse the Osborne Judgement; instead it permitted unions to ballot their members for authority to create a separate political fund from which members could contract out. Unions, keen to maintain and strengthen their relationship with the Labour Party, balloted quickly and successfully. The resulting authorization did not require subsequent re-endorsement.

By 1945 many of those who had balloted to set up political funds were no longer union members. There was no good reason to believe that later generations would wish to withdraw the authority given in 1913, but there was in no sense a positive consent. Alongside active exponents of the party–union link such as Wilf Cannon, there were many for whom the relationship was simply one, perhaps relatively unimportant, aspect of union affairs. This sense of marginality is strengthened by the evidence that payment into the political fund was affected significantly by the legal procedure governing it. In 1927, following the General Strike, the Baldwin Government shifted the onus onto the would-be contributor. The need to contract in led to a serious decline in levy payers. Officials might deplore the low level of political commitment, but collection of the levy was heavily dependent on the zeal of local activists, and the development of an appropriate supportive branch culture. Such factors were obviously uneven in their incidence. In 1945, the overall proportion paying the levy across affiliated unions stood at 48 per cent. Major unions demonstrated significant divergences between their levels of TUC and Labour Party affiliation.[5] The figures for 1946 suggest that interpretations of the 1945 electoral success which emphasize the workplace as a source of political radicalism are problematic; see Table 4.1. Perhaps predictably the NUM showed the smallest gap between the two affiliations; circumstances of workplace and residence could combine to produce political conformity. The modest political affiliation for the Engineers in all probability indicates that craft union's low evaluation of political action. The NUR case demonstrates how even in a union where political issues were raised relatively frequently, over 40 per cent of members did not pay the political levy.

Table 4.1 Some trade union affiliations to the TUC and Labour Party, 1946

	TUC	Labour Party
Amalgamated Engineering Union	704,317	235,266
National Union of General and Municipal Workers	604,992	242,000
National Union of Mineworkers	533,265	414,557
National Union of Railwaymen	409,826	241,229
Transport and General Workers' Union	974,765	450,000

Sources: TUC Reports; *LPCR*, 1946

One early initative by the Attlee Government was to reverse the 1927 Act, and to reinstate contracting out. The impact can be seen in the sharp rise in trade union affiliations to the party indicated in Table 4.2. Political levy payers had shown a limited increase since 1943 and it is probable that the early record of the Attlee government would have maintained this modest improvement. But the sizeable increases apparent in the table were far from unique. They were paralleled by proportionate increases in medium-sized unions such as the Steelworkers.[6] Obviously the legislative change accounts

Table 4.2 Trade union affiliations to the Labour Party, 1946, 1947

	1946 Affiliation	1947 Affiliation
Amalgamated Engineering Union	235, 266	605, 843
National Union of General Municipal Workers	242, 000	400, 000
National Union of Mineworkers	414, 557	629, 559
National Union of Railwaymen	241, 299	289, 268*
Transport and General Workers' Union	450, 000	800, 000

Sources: *LPCR*, 1946, 1947.
* The NUR's 1948 Affiliation was 357, 343

for most of this expansion. In no sense could this be characterized as evidence of an active political commitment. Rather it was indicative of apathy, indifference and even ignorance. The level, and indeed the practice, of affiliation could be used to license claims about the party–union relationship that were credible for the active few, but they could slide easily into a convenient mythology that hid uncomfortable truths about political commitment and the making of the unions' political policies.

Affiliation levels could be arbitrary. Some unions attempted with painstaking exactitude to return the precise number of levy payers. Others produced a round figure which was maintained over several years. Thus the National Union of Agricultural Workers affiliated on a figure of 70,800 through the late 1940s as if the 1946 Act had made no difference. Affiliation could be increased for factional purposes. The two general unions showed significant increases between 1954 and 1955; the Transport Workers from 835,000 to 1,000,000 and the General and Municipal from 400,000 to 650,000. This was part of the trade union right's strategy for ensuring that the left stayed a minority within the Party Conference. Hugh Gaitskell, establishing himself as the most significant political ally of the trade union faction felt that the practice could be profitably extended:

> I think it would be a good thing if I went into this in greater detail, and visit some of the unions on our side and try and get them to increase affiliation. What we want, if we can get it, is a complete safeguard, certainly against the Engineers going wrong, and possibly the Miners ...[7]

As Gaitskell's comment indicated, many trade unions had clear political positions in the late 1940s and some were firmly on the right, most notably the general unions and the NUM. Others were perhaps less firmly on the left – the NUR and the Shopworkers. A few – for example the Engineers – were keenly contested territories. Such identities, together with those of internal union factions, were central to the unions' formulation of political policy. These outcomes in turn fed through the Party Conference and into the making of party policy. However, the character of the affiliated membership and the sometimes arbitrary levels of union affiliations produced a much less open process than that suggested by Wilf Cannon and the fate of the Reading resolution. In some unions, political questions were debated keenly; in others they were considered rarely. The pattern of decision making varied greatly. Sometimes the officials kept a tight control; elsewhere, as in the Engineers, dispersal of power and ambiguity over the location of responsibility could bring deadlock and chaos. Across the political spectrum and the diversity of union structures, participation in the making of political policy was extremely limited.[8]

One demonstration of the discrepancy between a union's position and members' views came in 1946 within the Communist Party (CP) influenced Electrical Trades Union. The wartime alliance with the Soviet Union had led to some unions, such as the Engineers, favouring CP affiliation to the Labour Party. In February 1946, the ETU's Executive Council agreed to submit a pro-affiliation resolution to that year's Labour Party Conference. However opposition from several branches encouraged two non-CP executive councillors to successfully seek a membership ballot on the issue. The ballot was restricted to political levy payers – only 28 per cent of the membership. The turnout was 45 per cent and the vote was over two to one against Communist affiliation. Only 6,603 members supported Executive policy; in 1946 TUC affiliation was over 133,000. The union membership had little sympathy with the ETU's political direction and culture, but a broadly pro-Soviet policy was followed by the union for the next fourteen years. This was not a simple matter of domination by a ruling faction. The leadership's robust industrial policies enjoyed widespread support and delegates to the annual conference sometimes blocked the most thorough pro-Soviet proposals. As elsewhere within the trade union movement, political debates within the ETU were between the few, but adversaries claimed the legitimacy of the many.[9]

The sponsored members

A similar gap between image and reality could be found in the trade union presence within the Parliamentary Labour Party (PLP). The 393 Labour Members returned in 1945 included 120 who were sponsored by trade unions and several more who had had trade union experience. The proportion was lower than in the previous election in November 1935, indicating the tendency of sponsored candidates to be concentrated in the safest seats. More surprisingly, the unions sponsored fewer candidates in 1945 than ten years earlier. Caution about the use of funds and scepticism as to Labour's likely advance meant that the trade union presence in the post-war PLP was unnecessarily restricted. Subsequently the trade union section retained much of its position, despite periodic concerns that sponsored candidates were scoring badly at selection conferences; see Table 4.3.

Table 4.3 Sponsored candidates and Members, 1945–59

	Sponsored candidates	Sponsored members	All Labour members	Percentage Sponsored members (%)
1945	124	120	393	30.5
1950	137	111	315	35.2
1951	136	105	295	36.6
1955	127	95	277	34.3
1959	129	92	258	35.6

Source: M. Harrison, *Trade Unions and the Labour Party since 1945* (1960), pp. 265, 267.

The rhetoric that this presence represented the organized working-class within the Parliamentary Party obscured the extent to which the trade union presence was dominated by specific occupations: see Table 4.4.

Table 4.4 Sponsorship of MPs: the predominant unions

	1945	1950	1951	1955	1959
NUM	34	37	36	34	31
TGWU	17	16	14	14	14
NUR	12	10	9	8	5
TSSA	9	7	7	5	5
NUGM	10	6	6	4	4
USDAW	8	8	9	9	9
AEU	4	8	8	6	8
Sub total	94	92	89	80	76
Total	120	111	108	95	92

Source: M. Harrison, *Trade Unions and the Labour Party since 1945* (1960), p. 267.

The sponsored members were drawn from a band of traditionally well unionized industries. The shifts in numbers reflect a variety of factors. Some unions failed to produce credible nominees; others, for example the Engineers, revived their interest in political initiatives.[10]

The trade union Members were almost wholly male. After the death of Ellen Wilkinson in 1947, no woman sat as a sponsored Member during this period. The occupational bases and cultures of the dominant unions ensured this pattern would continue and thereby helped to maintain the marginalization of women within the Parliamentary Party. The group were largely politically conformist. There were few critics of the parliamentary leadership; most were loyal and cautious backbenchers who had uneventful parliamentary careers. Tom O'Brien, who did not fall into this category, sketched the typical routine of the trade union backbencher in the early fifties:

> He breakfasts in his Bloomsbury hotel and arrives in time for the Tea Room to open at eleven and serve morning coffee. Then he reads the papers which are provided there free until one o'clock, when the Tea Room serves the one and ninepenny lunch. After lunch he does his constituency correspondence in the library, goes into the House to hear a part of Question time, and if there is a big debate, the first two speeches. Then he has high tea in the Tea Room at six o'clock, staying there until the policeman shouts 'Who goes home?'[11]

They were the loyalist ballast within the PLP who could be mobilized to resist the claims of intellectuals, fellow-travellers and other unreliables. When such loyalism meant that sponsored Members supported the party leadership against the policy of their sponsoring union, the latter made no attempt to intervene. There was no suggestion that the activities of sponsored Members could be influenced let alone determined by sponsoring bodies. In one sense such autonomy reflected the career choice made by trade unionists who entered parliament. They were now on the political wing of the labour movement. Discipline would come from the party and not from the union.

Unions in government

Several trade union Members were given office in the 1945 government. Many occupied junior ministerial positions or dominated the Whips' Office. Some became much more prominent. Aneurin Bevan was hardly typical of the trade union Members in career path, political view and style. Much more characteristic was another South Wales miner, James Griffiths. A former President of the 'Fed' and an ethical socialist, his years at the Ministry of National Insurance demonstrated humanity and competence.[12] If this record exemplified the practical wisdom of a trade unionist in a relatively familiar field, his subsequent time at the Colonial Office showed that his negotiating skills could be relevant to an unfamiliar agenda. A loyalist with a strong awareness of the Labour Party's diversity, Griffiths had a commitment to the compromises needed to maintain party unity.

The close ties between the Attlee administration and trade union loyalists were personified above all in two ministerial figures. The Chief Whip William Whiteley epitomized the culture of the Durham Miners' Association (DMA). He had worked briefly in the pit, but had then been employed by the DMA, initially as a clerk but later as a miner's agent. Elected to the Commons in 1922, he was readily identified as reliable and loyal.[13] His time as Chief Whip saw the realization of many of his political ambitions, most notably the public ownership of the coal industry. Whiteley's political strength was that he was an ordinary trade union administrator, charged with organizing the realization of a party's dreams. In contrast, Ernest Bevin's appeal was that he proclaimed how extraordinary someone from an impoverished background could be. He had not made the career choice typical of trade union Members. He was the architect of a major trade union and the dominant trade union figure of the 1930s. His political career and membership of the PLP were the consequence of the emergency of 1940. He retained a deep suspicion of career politicians as brittle and untrustworthy. Much of this contempt was focused on the left and on intellectuals – for Bevin the categories often merged – but his anathemas extended to include Herbert Morrison, a man of the robust right.[14]

Suspicion of politicians did not prevent Bevin from assuming the role

124

played by Arthur Henderson in the Cabinet crisis of 1931. He was the representative of trade union priorities in the post-war government, a symbol of the unions' status within the party. His preoccupation with foreign affairs and his deteriorating health meant that his detailed links with trade union leaders were limited; but his presence and style were both a symbol of trade union support, and a resource in the winning of that support for government policies. The style could be used to thoroughly vanquish criticism. In November 1946, around 120 Labour Members abstained on the King's Speech to express their concern about the direction of Bevin's foreign policy. His private response was that this was 'treachery'. His public riposte at the following year's Party Conference was to present a dramatic if implausible contrast between the standards of some politicians and those of decent trade unionists: '... I was stabbed in the back ... if you are to expect loyalty from Ministers, the Ministers – however much they may make mistakes – have a right to expect loyalty in return. I grew up in the trade unions, you see, and I have never been used to this kind of thing'.[15]

The rhetoric was at one with those political arts that Bevin affected to despise; but its force was acknowledged by one of those against whom it was directed:

> ... Bevin stands quite still waiting for the ovation to cease. It surges up from a thousand delegates on the floor and from the packed galleries to left and right ... Ernest Bevin wipes the sweat from his forehead. The papers shake in his hand, but the voice is as strong as ever, and soon rises to a hoarse roar of righteous indignation ... No man alive is so skilful at handling a working-class audience, mixing the brutal hammer blow with sentimental appeal ... He did not merely smash his critics; he pulverised them into applauding him.[16]

This anatomy of party culture identifies the environment within which party–union relationships developed during and after the Attlee government. Most trade union officials and sponsored Members took a highly positive view of the government's domestic programme. Full employment, welfare reforms and extensions of public ownership all ranked as major achievements. So did one negative decision: the government had acknowledged that wage determination was a matter for the unions. The Cripps Wage Bargain of 1948 was a triumph for the politics of persuasion, facilitated by a shared pride in the government's achievements.[17] By 1950, despite signs that the government's radicalism had lessened, the post-war settlement seemed complete. It should be defended not just against reaction from the right, but also against radical demands from the left that could have a destabilizing effect. Provided that the political and industrial leaders acted sagaciously, the settlement showed every sign of durability. Moreover there was a strong belief that the achievements were of major significance; perhaps they were the first steps towards a socialist society, or possibly the new dispensation offered a credible and acceptable alternative. The defensiveness, and sometimes

125

complacency, of many trade union leaders was understandable given the contrast with their pre-war experiences of depression and antagonistic employers. Moreover, their access to government expanded under the wartime coalition and was maintained subsequently by both the Attlee and Churchill governments. Their enhanced status was one more factor in the promotion of a conservatism that led to vigourous reprisals against critics.

The Cold War and Bevanism

These sentiments were given a harsher flavour due to international developments. The deepening of the Cold War left a thorough mark on trade union factionalism. Since the 1920s this had been influenced heavily by attitudes to the CP. Many trade unionists were hostile, but others were prepared to ally with Communists in the name of solidarity and perhaps socialism. The depth of antagonism had varied in response to specific controversies, but the factional battles had been presented as essentially domestic matters. There were squabbles over union offices, industrial strategy and political questions; but many who opposed the British CP, still claimed sympathy with the Soviet Union. From 1947, this limitation no longer obtained. British foreign policy, led by the most eminent trade unionist of his time, had identified the Soviet Union as a national enemy, and its regime as a tyranny. Factionalism within several unions was rapidly affected. Communists and those who allied with them ceased to be mere opponents; they became the agents – malign or naive – of a foreign power opposed both to British interests and to democratic socialism. The extent of the denunciation varied. The Transport Workers banned Communists from holding office; elsewhere trade union activists drew distinctions between Communists as industrial and political actors.[18] In the NUM, the Area structure and the entrenchment of Communists in some significant coalfields meant that some restraint was essential.[19] One crucial consequence was that issues were not always discussed on their merits. Criticism of established practices could be discredited by claiming that it was communist inspired. The defensiveness of the trade union right was strengthened.

The most obvious expression of this politics was a 'Praetorian Guard', an alliance of trade union leaders committed to the defence of the party leadership against its critics.[20] Its members brought contrasting styles to the task. Arthur Deakin of the Transport Workers and Will Lawther of the NUM combined appeals to loyalty with abuse and, sometimes defamation, of opponents.[21] Tom Williamson of the General and Municipal was a more circumspect loyalist who preferred understatement to confrontation.[22] All believed that the sizeable votes of their unions – totalling 1,881,465 at the 1951 Party Conference – should be used consistently to block the left. Initially the task met with few obstacles. Government achievements and Cold

War polarization combined to reduce and disorientate critics. When the conference debated the expulsion of the left MP Konni Zilliacus in 1949, Deakin responded to the claim that such a political matter was not the concern of a trade union:

> Our people are entitled through their trade union through its affiliation with the Labour Party, to express their views on these things which we think of importance to our Movement at this time ... The suggestion made that the trade union block vote is unfair, is a challenge to the democratic practices of the conference which we are not prepared to accept. It has been said too that as far as the trade unions are concerned the question can properly be posed whether or not we have a mandate. Our mandate is constantly to support the foreign policy of this government because we believe it to be right.[23]

From October 1951, with Labour's loss of office, such arguments became more vehement and more contested. The factional balance had been transformed six months before by the resignation of three ministers – Aneurin Bevan, Harold Wilson and John Freeman.

The periodic bitterness of those early years in opposition has been overshadowed perhaps by the disputes and secessions that followed the 1979 defeat. The controversies of the early 1950s included many issues – international policy, the party's future domestic strategy, preparations for an anticipated leadership vacancy and acceptable methods of party discipline. Sometimes the personal animosities disguised the fact that underlying differences were relatively small. Throughout the kaleidoscope of conference scenes, journalistic attacks, disciplinary initiatives and apparent armistices, the 'Praetorian Guard' maintained a fixed position. Their task was to safeguard the party leadership; they would ally with politicians who endorsed their tough stance, they would reject those who appeared to temporize and they would seek to discipline and ultimately expel any who failed their stringent loyalty test. As a result Hugh Gaitskell emerged as this group's favoured candidate for the leadership. Morrison was marginalized as too weak, and the incumbent Attlee was characterized as damagingly lax; the group were keen advocates of the expulsion of Bevan in March 1955.[24]

One justification for this stand was provided by a particular interpretation of '1931'. Lawther, during the acrimonious 1952 Conference, articulated the basic claim: 'Nobody can ever accuse the trade union section of running away from its obligations. In that dark period of 1931 it was the intellectuals that funked the issue'.[25] As an account of the past, this was partial and misleading; as a maxim for the 1950s, it ignored the obvious differences between the two situations – a Labour Cabinet under pressure from the economically orthodox, and a Labour Party in opposition genuinely uncertain about future policies. It also rejected the obvious divisions between the trade unions during the early 1950s. The right-wing bloc was the more stable, yet the NUR, USDAW and the Engineers could often be found acting with the left.

Such factional positions reflected the greater strength of the left in some unions, the traditions of particular unions on specific issues – for example, USDAW on armaments – and to a degree the preferences of prominent union officials.[26] Moreover, the insistence that it was the responsibility of trade unionists to stabilize the party ignored the extent to which critical party activists were often trade unionists who might take a sceptical view of trade union officials.

Bevan's campaign for the Party Treasurership from 1954 to 1956 can be seen as an attempt to undercut the claims of some officials to be representative of their members on political issues.[27] The flavour of the 1954 decision-making was noted by his opponent, Hugh Gaitskell:

> In the background of the AEU decision was a bit of high TU Politics. Arthur Deakin told me that he was being pressed by the AEU to vote for their nominee for the National Executive. He said he would make it quite plain to them that he would do that, but only if they nominated me for the Treasurership. This was not the only reason. At least three AEU MPs are strong supporters of mine, and worked very hard for me on the members of the AEU Executive. As for the miners, the vote was most satisfactory, being taken by the Conference as a whole, and giving me a two to one majority. This was largely due, I am sure, to Ernest Jones and Sam Watson, and perhaps to the fortunate chance that many of the others knew me as Minister of Fuel.[28]

Bevan's search for union votes remained within the same world of deals and factional competition. Many felt they had to respond to diverse considerations; voting for a left candidate was just one factor. Understandably many trade unionists felt that a united and effective party was more important than an ideological crusade. The NUR, in the early 1950s, often voted with the left. In 1954 the union nominated Bevan for the Treasurership but a year later different considerations applied:

> Our Executive Council feel that the decision having gone in Mr Gaitskell's favour, the best interests of the Labour Party are now served by accepting it and avoiding bitterness within the Party. The battle for the Treasurership took place in 1954. What useful purpose can be served in reviving it year after year?[29]

The decisive election of Gaitskell as party leader in December 1955, and his subsequent rapprochement with Bevan, ended this period of intense factionalism. The enmity left legacies that survived through into the Wilson governments; but, in crucial respects, developments in the second half of the 1950s began to suggest some potential for change in the party–union relationship.

Openings for change

The control exercised by the alliance between the party leadership and the 'Praetorian Guard' had been so firm that many commentators began to assume the normality of this pattern of domination. This assessment ignored the diversity of earlier relationships within the party, and neglected the degree to which the current pattern had been facilitated by specific national and international contexts. Developments in the late 1950s did not precipitate any rapid change but enough happened to indicate that the established pattern might not be fixed for ever. Those who had endorsed the established alliance faced new challenges; those who had felt marginalized became a little more optimistic.

One shift was provided by the revised character of Conservative government policy on industrial issues. Sir Walter Monckton's conciliatory approach at the Ministry of Labour had epitomized Conservative anxieties about the risk of any confrontation with the trade unions.[30] From late 1955, when Monckton was replaced by Iain Macleod, the departmental style became more robust within a broader context where ministers and many commentators were beginning to identify wage costs as a central problem for the British economy. Given the radical perspective provided by later Conservative administrations, the shift in policy was modest. This was very much an administration which accepted an agreed post-war economic and social settlement; but for contemporaries the change was significant and an appropriate response was a source of controversy within the TUC. The symbolic clash came in the spring of 1958 when a strike of London busmen became in effect a clash between Macleod for the government's pay policy and Frank Cousins, the recently elected General Secretary of the Transport Workers, and leading TUC critic of government policy. The strike ended effectively in a victory for the government. In critical respects, this episode was a pivotal moment in post-war industrial relations.[31] Some Conservatives began to raise the issue of trade union power and possible amendments to the law; some ministers could be tempted by the prospect that opposition to carefully selected strikes might be electorally popular. In contrast, the TUC and the Labour Party leadership did not readily produce an agreed and credible response to this shift.

The emergence of a leader of the Transport Workers as a critic of TUC caution and as the focus of Conservative anti-union feeling indicated the erosion of old certainties. Deakin's death in May 1955 had been followed by the succession of the heir-apparent, Jock Tiffin and, to the surprise of some, the consequent vacancy for the Assistant General Secretary had been filled by Cousins, in the union's terms, a man of the left. This choice by the Transport Workers' Executive acquired even more significance when Tiffin soon went on sick leave. By the end of the year he was dead; by May 1956, Cousins was head of the union.[32]

The significance of this transition acquired its own mythology. Critics could present this shift in the leadership of the Transport Workers as itself destructive of the 'Praetorian Guard', and thereby of the controlling alliance within the party. Obviously Cousins' arrival at the head of the union happened because of the unexpected death of Deakin's successor. But his election as General Secretary was precisely that, an endorsement by a very large majority in a ballot in which over 580,000 members participated. The critical and unexpected step had been Cousins' appointment as Assistant General Secretary by the Executive. This again seems to have been by an overwhelming margin given on grounds of competence but also perhaps with a feeling that Deakin's conservatism had neglected too many members' concerns, the union was stagnating and a new outlook was needed. Analysis of the shift from Deakin to Cousins has often carried an implication that Cousins as a sympathizer with the left did not represent his members' views, whereas Deakin did. Yet, even in the context of Cold War trade unionism, the latter's regime was notable for its authoritarianism.

In fact, the impact of Cousins' election as General Secretary on the political policies of the Transport Workers has often been exaggerated. The powers and influence of the union's chief official were significant – a fact made good use of by Cousins' predecessors, Bevin and Deakin.[33] Yet Cousins' leadership had to recognize the need for co-operation with senior figures who were products of the Bevin-Deakin era. This meant that any move to the left had to be cautious and had to be based on persuasion. On the other side of the ledger, the left's strength within the union had been marginalized during the early 1950s; in some sectors there were militant traditions on which a sympathetic general secretary could begin to develop a new policy. For three years under Cousins' leadership, the Transport Workers largely underwrote Gaitskell's leadership. The one formal exception was on education policy, an area where the union under Deakin had been comparatively radical.[34] Nevertheless Gaitskell felt concerned about the weakening of the trade union right. He reflected with caution on the style of the 1956 Party Conference: 'it is important that the group that runs the TUC and ultimately the Labour Party should be re-established, otherwise a very dangerous situation might emerge'.[35] This conference had seen the election of Bevan as Party Treasurer. The right had attempted to secure the election of George Brown of the Transport Workers; but a feeling that Bevan should be brought back into the leadership helped to ensure that the two general unions backed a loser, unlike the NUM who supported Bevan.[36]

Nevertheless some developments favoured the right. Except on the Treasurership, the NUM remained alongside the NUGMW as a firm supporter of the political leadership. The Engineers were still heavily factionalized but from 1956 the union's President, Bill Carron, ruthlessly pursued the maximization of support for the party leaders. Creative in his interpretation of the union rule book or when necessary in the evasion of the rules, he limited the left's influence in the AEU and consequently within the party.[37] A less Machiavellian shift to the right could be found in the politics of the National Union of Railwaymen. The union had often appeared firmly on the left under the leadership of Jim Figgins from 1948 to 1953, and remained left of centre on many issues under his successor, Jim Campbell. Such opinions indicated the often radical decisions of the Annual General Meeting: for example, the NUR was the only major union to oppose the document *Industry and Society* at the 1957 Party Conference on the ground that it marked a retreat from socialist principles.[38] Shortly afterwards, Campbell was killed in a road accident during a union visit to the Soviet Union; his successor Sid Greene was firmly on the right and gradually the union's political decisions shifted rightwards. The reasons for this were complex; but curiously this shift, unlike the Transport Workers' case, has been largely ignored as an alleged demonstration of officials' power. USDAW, with its complex factionalism and despite its socialist rhetoric, also showed a significant move to the right.[39] One factor facilitating these right-wing advances was the weakening of Communist influence in several unions following the revelations of the 20th Congress of the Communist Party of the Soviet Union, and the Soviet intervention in Hungary. Several influential trade unionists resigned from the CP. In the long run this meant that some talented ex-Communists strengthened the Labour left within some unions, but in the short-term the events of 1956 probably damaged some trade unions' left factions.[40]

These complex developments did not indicate that changes within the large unions were posing a major problem of control for the party leadership; yet they occasioned some anxiety which linked with ideological and social concerns. The leadership victory of Gaitskell in 1955 can be seen as the initial success of a distinctive ideological perspective. Earlier generations of Labour socialists on the right of the party – for example, Herbert Morrison – had believed that in some sense the Labour Party's commitment was to an incremental transformation of capitalism into a qualitatively distinctive alternative – socialism.[41] Gaitskell's 'revisionism' claimed that old-style capitalism had been transformed – or at least radically modified. A mixed economy characterized by full employment and effective welfare services would not be challenged by the Conservatives. The old vision of the shift from capitalism to socialism should be abandoned; rather socialists should be concerned with the greater realization of socialist values within the framework of a mixed economy. This broad position seemed compatible with much of the trade union right's characterization of their own experiences. Their enhanced status as officials, the apparent permanence of full employment, the behaviour of Conservative governments since 1951 – all suggested that the revisionist assessment was realistic.[42]

But this affinity was counteracted by other factors. One diagnosis of electoral defeat focused on the loss of much of that minority middle-class backing secured in 1945. The idea that the party should target these voters to ensure the capture of marginal seats shaded easily into the view that core working-class voters could be taken for granted and, by extension, into a judgement that too close an identification of the party with the unionized working-class could be electorally limiting. This tied to a second assessment that economic and social changes were eroding familiar identities; affluent workers were allegedly less class conscious and less responsive to the traditional symbols of the labour movement. This view was thoroughly ahistorical; the peak of working-class support for Labour had not been in the inter-war years when traditional class loyalties supposedly had greater resonance, nor in 1945 – but in 1950 and 1951.[43] Yet the acceptance of such an assessment, not least by the party leader, meant that the revisionist perspective could begin to raise difficult questions about the place of the unions within the party.

This scepticism was also fed by a concern about the alleged unpopularity of some trade union practices. Crossman noted in June 1959 that a row between the party leader and Cousins over nuclear disarmament might have electoral benefits: 'I have no doubt that electorally we are gaining from this. There is a printing strike to make us unpopular and the picture of Bevan and Gaitskell fighting Frank Cousins is something really useful to counteract it'.[44] Bevan in private seemed ready to attack not just Cousins, but the conventions that governed trade unions' contributions to party policy making:

> Nye ... burst out that trade unions have useful functions but were a poor place for making serious political decisions. He would rather get out than be told by the trade unions what to do in the Foreign Office. Anyway, the way union delegates voted at their conferences bore no relation to the way their members voted at the Elections.[45]

The basic ambiguity about the party–union relationship was not new. Ramsay MacDonald had reacted with hostility to trade union radicalism in the 1920s. Gaitskell's alleged claim before the 1959 election that he was 'determined to smash Cousins' indicated the changing quality of the party–union relationship.[46] Nevertheless the party leader seemed happy to to launch Labour's 1959 election campaign from the platform of the TUC. Symbolically this was a coming together of the labour movement, a public demonstration – and perhaps private reassurance – that the familiarities of post-war Labour politics persisted. Yet Gaitskell, with his eye on an electorate beyond the delegates, insisted that no leader of the party could be dictated to by the unions. The distancing was mutual. Several members of the General Council seemed uneasy about the injection of partisanship into their proceedings. After all, they had their special relationship with government.[47]

The party's third successive electoral defeat in October 1959 was followed by its most serious internal crisis since 1931. The renewed factional conflict proved in two respects more far-reaching than the controversies of the early 1950s. One critical development was ideological. Gaitskell abandoned the relatively conciliatory approach that had hitherto characterized his leadership and acted more as the leader of a revisionist faction. Explanations of Labour's defeat often included themes from the revisionist perspective. Recent economic and social changes were held to require changes in Labour priorities, strategy and culture; there were a few suggestions that such revisions might include even the party–union link. The criticisms of party practice and style became focused around the abortive attempt to reform Clause Four of the party constitution with its commitment to extensive public ownership. When Gaitskell raised this issue at the party's post-mortem conference, the preoccupation of a few became the project of the party leader.[48]

The result was a thorough rejection of the proposal. Replacement gave way to amplification and then simply to a Statement of Aims which would co-habit with the existing Clause Four. This denouement occurred because Gaitskell's strategy united against him the Labour left, sceptics who felt that the affair was strategically inept and traditionalists who saw themselves as on the right, but who remained attached to the view that the party was fundamentally, if cautiously, committed to the ending of capitalism. Trade unionists, both within the PLP and within many unions' policy-making bodies, were well represented amongst these categories. In part this reflected the trade union view that the party had to be above all an effective instrument; three election defeats followed by what many saw as a theological dispute suggested otherwise. Moreover several trade unions – for example the NUM – contained within their own rule books, statements of their objectives which were the equivalents of Clause Four. These were elements in these unions' political identities; such rule-governed and precedent-conscious bodies could not just ignore them.[49]

The revisionist retreat over Clause Four was also influenced by the advent of a second dispute over the unilateral renunciation of nuclear weapons. The party leadership felt that this was more familiar and manageable territory for a factional struggle. Gaitskell seems to have made this assessment along with an acknowledgment that his previous priority had been misconceived:

> On Clause 4 the PLP didn't care one way or the other, and the trade union leaders were tied by their own constitutional provisions, which pledged them to support a specifically socialist party. But here, on the defence issue, I have got the support of the trade union leaders, and the majority of the PLP. This is a much better issue on which to have it out.[50]

The official policy of opposition to unilateralism could utilize Cold War sentiments that linked to the trade union maxim that effective negotiation could only be from a position of strength. Traditionally the party's anti-militarist section had been subordinate to the political and trade union advocates of *realpolitik*. Yet there were warning signs that this crisis was not so containable. Prior to the election, the unbelievable had occurred at the

General and Municipal Workers' 1959 Congress when a unilateralist resolution had been carried. The vote was reversed decisively at a subsequent special Congress. But the affair suggested that the unilateralist cause might attract support from beyond the traditional left.[51]

The union conferences of 1960 indicated that the major unions previously associated with the Bevanite faction had moved towards unilateralism. The AEU, the NUR and USDAW all backed unilateralist resolutions; they joined the Transport Workers which had taken this position at its Biennial Delegate conference in 1959. This line-up signposted the decisions at the 1960 Party Conference where the official defence policy was rejected.[52] More was at stake than the minutiae of competing resolutions. The controversy could not be separated from the broader debates about party strategy and the character of Gaitskell's leadership. The rhetoric of the Cold War seemed no longer sufficient to guarantee a majority alliance between party leaders and right-wing trade union officials.

The immediate crisis was resolved twelve months later when the 1961 Party Conference shifted back to a multilateralist position. Whereas in 1960, the major unions had split four to two in favour of unilateralism, now the balance was five to one in the opposite direction. Only the Transport Workers maintained its unilateralist stance. Yet the shift of policy in the other major unions was typically shrouded in ambiguity. Both USDAW and the Engineers showed a preference for compromise and then moved further to back the party leadership. The NUR's 1961 Annual General Meeting endorsed neither unilateralism nor the official party policy; yet the union's Executive subsequently backed the party leadership, as did its delegation at the 1961 Party Conference. The earlier commitments to unilateralism had often been fragile; in each of these unions there were senior officials who were keen supporters of the party leadership. They were able to influence shifts that were often ambiguous in their actual language. The reversal was very much a case of old-style union politics; there was little evidence of the ideological crusade favoured by revisionist zealots.[53]

The 1961 triumph of the party leadership suggested a return to normality; their defeat the previous year could be presented as anomalous, and relationships down to 1964 seemed to endorse this judgement. Gaitskell reverted to a more consensual leadership style, and this pattern was strengthened following his unexpected death in January 1963. His sucessor, Harold Wilson, could capitalize when appropriate, on his Bevanite past, but above all he saw himself as a reconciler who viewed the revisionist agenda and style as counterproductive. One facet of the Wilson leadership in opposition was the cultivation of a closer relationship with Cousins culminating in the latter joining the 1964 Government. The concordat involved misunderstandings on both sides. Cousins regarded Wilson as more progressive than his predecessor, a widely held view in 1963–64; Wilson characterized Cousins as the heir to Ernest Bevin, not just in his trade union position, but also in his

134

potential for linking the trade union movement and a Labour government.[54]

The misunderstandings were not just a matter of personalities. Alongside the post-1961 accommodation, there remained tensions. There were some within the party who still felt that too close a connection with the style of a traditional working-class was an electoral handicap. This left its mark on Labour's 1964 campaign with its emphasis on classlessness and meritocracy. The immediate target was the Conservative Party, its traditionalism accentuated by the choice of Home as leader. But such anti-traditionalism could be turned also against the institutions of the labour movement. Equally the TUC in the early 1960s had responded positively to the Conservative Government's modernization agenda. This reflected the predisposition for insider bargaining of the TUC's new General Secretary, George Woodcock, but it also indicated a willingness to welcome any government which seemed to take consultation seriously.[55] This shift did not indicate any erosion of trade union officals' political commitment to Labour, but it indicated a strong sense of the TUC's own interests and of the priorities of many unions. A growth in white collar unionism, typically through organizations that were not affiliated to the Labour Party, was another symptom of divergence. The National Council of Labour, which had helped to integrate party and TUC policies in the 1930s, became increasingly ritualistic largely on account of trade union indifference. Whatever the rhetoric of cooperation in 1963 and 1964, it was clear that the TUC and its affiliated unions would not simply become transmission belts for the policies of a Labour Government.[56]

These differences mattered because the actions of subsequent Labour governments would impose pressures on the party–union relationship that were comparable with those of 1929–31. In the longer historical perspective, the Attlee years appear in this respect as exceptional, yet the party–union relationship as it existed for the first post-war decade was often seen by practitioners and analysts as typical. In fact, this regime helped to ensure that key problems were inadequately debated, despite the sound and fury of the recurrent factional feuds.

Wage restraint and modernization

One fundamental issue concerned the role of the unions in the economic policies of a Labour government and in particular over the question of wage determination. The traditional position that this was not an area for political intervention had been robustly asserted by Arthur Deakin at the 1947 Party Conference: 'The question of wages, and conditions of employment, are questions for the trade unions, and the sooner some of the people on the political side appreciate that and leave the job to the unions the better for production'.[57] In the radical optimism of the immediate post-war years, such heresies were not restricted to 'the political side'. Some left-inclined unions were prepared to advocate a national wages policy as one element in a planned economy. In early 1948 these roles were reversed. The Labour Government produced a White Paper – the *Statement on Personal Incomes, Costs and Prices* – which tied increases in wages to improved production. The TUC supported the strategy; the majority was composed largely of those who had previously opposed a wages policy; the critics were drawn largely from the enthusiasts for socialist planning. The latter opposed what they characterized as a policy of wage restraint. The former insisted that the Labour government must be supported. Sam Watson's position epitomized the loyalist outlook: 'If I were confronted with the defeat of the Government or the reduction of wages, then I would advocate a reduction of wages to save the Labour Government'.[58] The policy was also underpinned by the politics of the Cold War. The critics included the Communists within the trade unions. It was easier for the majority to appeal to political prejudices than to address the complex substantive question. The eventual rejection of the policy at the 1950 TUC reflected concern over the disparate treatment of wages and profits, and the expanding gulf between the sentiments of loyalist trade union officials, and the expectations of their members.

This episode was followed by a renewed trade union insistence that the determination of wages was not a political issue. The demarcation line was defended by many on both right and left, by Deakin and then by Cousins. However the indication of a lack of economic competitiveness in the late 1950s produced some cautious and limited reassessment by some within the political leadership. The Conservative government had become increasingly preoccupied by the problem of inflation in a fully-employed economy, an agenda which led easily to pressure for trade union restraint. Similarly by 1958, Gaitskell was canvassing the prospect of a counter-inflationary policy in the context of Labour's public expenditure proposals. But the political leadership encountered a mixture of trade union caution and hostility. Prior to the 1964 election, it seemed that there had been a considerable shift in party and trade union attitudes.[59] The increasingly obvious difficulties of the British economy, the Conservative government's shift towards intervention, the Selwyn Lloyd 'pay pause' and Labour's increasing use of the rhetoric of planning – all suggested that the socialist agenda of a planned economy might be revived. The brittleness of the apparent change was indicated in pre-election interventions by Cousins. At the 1958 Party Conference he dismissed any idea that the election of a Labour goverment could affect of itself the behaviour of trade unions: 'we do not change our views on the entitlement of the workers by the transference of Government from one Party to another'.[60] Five years later, at both the TUC and the Party Conference, his hope that a Labour administration might plan the economy so that 'a planned growth of wages' was feasible lived uneasily alongside a tough presentation of the realities of wage bargaining:

There is nobody here who can say what a level of wages is for an individual worker or the comparison between two groups of workers or the relative importance of a collective group of workers to the community. We do not determine them here, we determine them over board room tables, we determine them sitting opposite the employers; and we shall continue to do that until such time as the system changes to ensure that we do get a better rate of return for the labour that we put in ...[61]

Any hope that Labour planning would permit a revision of such bargaining practices was soon extinguished after October 1964, as incomes policy soon became simply wage restraint and then freeze backed by statutory powers. This experience above all damaged the party–union relationship. Beneath the increasingly acerbic exchanges lay fundamental questions of social-democratic and trade union strategy within a mixed economy. They had barely been raised in the years of opposition.

The experiences of workers in the publicly-owned industries provides a similar range of unresolved problems which led to difficulties after 1964. The initial response of unions in the newly nationalized industries were on balance positive. For example, the political differences within the NUM did not prevent generally close cooperation between union officials and Coal Board managers. The rhetoric of cooperation was not always found in the workplace; the industry's level of unofficial strikes was high, but most involved few miners and were of brief duration. The industry's relationships were influenced by the post-war shortage of coal which ensured a high demand for labour and buoyant wage levels. But reductions in industrial and domestic demand brought a serious decline in the industry's fortunes from 1957. The initial response within the NUM was largely one of resignation. The number employed in the industry fell and the miners slid down the earnings league. The concentration of closures in particular regions – South Wales, the North East, Scotland – threatened the vitality of labour institutions in some of its heartlands. Yet most miners took comfort from the fact that the decline was occurring under a Conservative government. They reasoned that a Labour goverment should promote a revival in the industry's fortunes.[62]

Such optimism might have been dented by an examination of the experiences of railway workers under the Attlee government. Public ownership had coincided with a deteriorating market situation as road competition revived after the artificial constraints of the wartime economy. The industry required major new investment, yet the government seemed to show little interest in its predicament. Management responded to its economic problems with strong resistance to wage demands. This, together with the railway workers' experience in an often obsolescent industry, led to unofficial strikes and go-slows in the summer of 1949. Gaitskell's assessment was critical of the principal trade union:

There can be no doubt that the NUR by their attitude are going to do an immense amount of harm to the government indeed to the whole cause of nationalization. Maybe it is [the fault of] the Railway Executive as well, though with a heavy deficit on their first year it is not so easy to blame them.[63]

One response within the NUR was to advocate reform of the structure of the publicly owned industries so as to permit some involvement by the workers. Conditions within the industry, where railway workers were frequently required to show initiative within a rule-governed industry, no doubt gave particular credibility to this reaction.[64] However this stress on industrial democracy produced hostility from most other public sector unions. This was underpinned once again by the images of the Cold War. The NUR's leader in the first years of public ownership, Jim Figgins, was widely seen as close to the CP. The image ignored the complexity of policy-making within the union and the industrial experiences that had generated strong demands for workers' participation. The currency within which debates were conducted both within the unions and the Labour Party meant that one significant experience of public ownership was marginalized.

The problems of the railway industry were not addressed effectively by the belated Modernization Plan of 1955. Road competition in both the passenger and freight sectors was increasingly severe, and the subsequent new investment in layouts, signalling and new forms of motive power was often carried through without adequate awareness of its likely impact. Closures had been regular but limited in the 1950s. Conservative concern with national modernization led to the Beeching Report of 1963 which proposed a drastic surgery of the railway network. The rail unions too had their expectations of a Labour Government.[65]

Workers in both industries found that the change of government made very little difference. Most of the Beeching proposals were implemented and the pit closure programme became more severe. In the coal industry these experiences bred a disillusion and then a militancy which led eventually to the radicalization of the NUM. The unofficial strikes of 1969–70 and the national stoppages of 1972 and 1974 were a response not just to the disappointments of the Wilson years, but also to the complacencies of the earlier years in opposition. The trajectory of the NUR was different. The drive to change working practices produced some unofficial actions but the union machinery was consolidated under the control of the right. NUR debates still included socialist rhetoric but officials argued with some effect that the industry's generally low wages could be remedied only through some kind of incomes policy. Thus the NUR remained sympathetic to the Wilson government's policies in this field after many unions had withdrawn their backing.[66] The experiences of public sector workers produced contrasting political outcomes as the government implemented rationalization lubricated with the rhetoric of modernization. Once again the years in opposition had produced no serious discussion – this time of the place of public sector unions in a modernization strategy.

The shortcomings of the 1964 government eroded confidence in the effectiveness of a social democratic response to problems of economic and social obsolescence. The result was arguably an enhancing of the credibility of the radical right. The root of this failure is located often in the meeting of three senior ministers – Wilson, James Callaghan and George Brown – on 17 October 1964. Their decision not to devalue the pound is typically presented as the effective marginalization of the government's progressive agenda. Much debate has focused on whether these key figures could plausibly have made a different decision, and whether an alternative choice could have allowed a significantly changed outcome.[67] Yet some of the key problems facing the government were independent of any decision on the parity of the pound. The contribution of trade unions within a social democratic strategy of modernization raises basic issues concerning incomes and planning and the extent and organization of the public sector. These problems had barely been discussed in opposition, an absence which helped to deepen the crisis after 1964.

Conclusions

The reasons for this failure may be complex. Some concern the impact of the post-war settlement on relationships within the party and the unions. A prevailing belief that the settlement was economically viable and would not be challenged politically led to complacency. The polarities of the Cold War helped to produce a factionalism in which an alliance between party leaders and the trade union right seemed permanent. The weakening of this alliance from the mid-1950s produced anxieties on the right, and then in 1960 a crisis. But the apparent reassertion of the old order hid the extent to which the organizational predictability of the decade after 1945 could not be restored. The pattern of control had been associated with a culture in which disturbing questions could not be raised easily. The folk memory of '1931' placed a high premium on solidarity.

A more radical claim would be that the failure should be attributed to the distinctive structures of the Labour Party and their complex system of affiliations. From such a vantage point, the political networks within which Wilf Cannon operated, produced a brake on, rather than an engine for, radical change. Such a response can offer its own narrative for the understanding of twentieth-century British politics. Thus David Marquand has emphasized the alternative of a Progressive agenda that was marginalized because of a conjuncture of circumstances during and after the First World War.[68] This counterfactual involves a Progressive Liberalism re-negotiating the pre-1914 alliance between itself and organized labour to the latter's advantage, but without the consequent dominance by a Labour Party that Marquand indicts as defensive and intellectually cautious. Rather the outcome would have been a British New Deal Coalition, with a broader electoral base than that of the Labour Party and with a greater capacity for programmatic renewal.

This argument points us to major historiographical controversies about the character of the British left across the twentieth century which have acquired an immediate practical significance with the contemporary discussions between Labour ministers and the Liberal Democrat leadership. These can be interpreted as an attempt to redress a historical accident – the supersession of a Progressive Alliance by a trade union centred, and thereby limited, Labour Party. From this standpoint, 1945–64 becomes just one instalment in a melancholy sequence of underachievement and recrimination. However, such a thesis raises serious problems. The feasability or otherwise of the counterfactual is clearly central; so is the claim that there were endemic limitations to the progressive potential of the Labour Party. The argument can degenerate into an ahistorical assertion of the inevitable failings of 'labourism', an assessment which ironically provides a meeting place for both Marxist and Progressive Liberal critics.

In contrast, this analysis has emphasized the singularity of the party–union relationship during this period and has suggested its specific contribution to the failings of the Wilson government. If the years after 1964 were 'the Strange Death of Social Democratic England', then at least some of the roots of this lay in an earlier social democratic triumph.[69]

Notes

1. The comment was made by Sir Will Lawther, the President of the NUM and leading figure of the trade union right, in response to a heckler at the 1952 Labour Party Conference (*Labour Party Conference Report*, hereafter *LPCR*, 1952, p. 79.)
2. For this episode, with the characterization of Wilf Cannon, see I. Mikardo, *Back-Bencher* (1988), pp. 72, 74–9; for an influential discussion, see R. McKenzie, *British Political Parties* (1967), pp. 507–9. The debate is in *LPCR*, 1944, pp. 160–8.
3. The phrase is from F. Williams, *Magnificent Journey* (1945).
4. For a discussion of aspects of this political development, see D. Howell, *Respectable Radicals: studies in the politics of railway trade unionism* (Aldershot, 1999), chs 4–7.
5. For analysis, see M. Harrison, *Trade Unions and the Labour Party since 1945* (1960), ch. 1; L. Minkin, *The Contentious Alliance* (Edinburgh, 1991), pp. 61, 64–5.
6. The percentage of members paying the political levy in the Steelworkers

changed from 41.1 per cent to 88.7 per cent between the first and second quarters of 1947; see Harrison, *Trade Unions and the Labour Party*, p. 37.

7.   Diary entry for 14 October 1954, in P.M. Williams (ed.), *The Diary of Hugh Gaitskell, 1945–1956* (1983), p. 341. See also the entry for 9 November 1954 at p. 345, reporting a comment of the TUC General Secretary Sir Vincent Tewson: 'the best way to get the unions to pay up was to make it clear to them that the Labour Party would help in their internal troubles with the Communists – in other words, that the Labour Party machine would be put into operation in favour of the Labour Party and against Communist candidates at Union elections'.

8.   For analyses of this diversity, see Harrison, *Trade Unions and the Labour Party*, ch. 4; L. Minkin, *The Labour Party Conference* (Manchester, 1980), pp. 90–131, and chs 6 and 7.

9.   See J. Lloyd, *Light and Liberty: a history of the EEPTU* (1996), pp. 336–7; see more broadly chs 16–20 for controversies within that union from 1945 to the unseating of the Communist leadership in 1960–61. For a summary of the union's procedures and politics, see Minkin, *Labour Party Conference*, pp. 111–13.

10.   For the AEU, see I. Richter, *Political Purpose in Trade Unions* (1973).

11.   The portrait is in J. Morgan (ed.), *The Backbench Diaries of Richard Crossman* (1981), entry for 9 March 1953, at p. 209. Tom O'Brien was General Secretary of the National Association of Theatrical and Kine Employees (1932–70), a member of the TUC General Council (1940–70), and a Labour MP (1945–59). Crossman referred to him as 'an Irish rogue of the highest quality' (p. 142, entry for 26 September 1952).

12.   For a comparison of Bevan and Griffiths, see K.O. Morgan, *The Red Dragon and the Red Flag* (Aberystwyth, 1989). For an illuminating study of the making of Aneurin Bevan, see D. Smith, *Aneurin Bevan and the World of South Wales* (Cardiff, 1993).

13.   Attlee's retrospective view of Whiteley can be found in the entry in *Dictionary of National Biography, 1951–1960* (Oxford, 1971). The Durham Miners' political style was also articulated by Sam Watson, a leading figure on the party's National Executive for most of the period.

14.   The major biographical study of Bevin is the three-volume work by Alan Bullock; but see also P. Weiler, *Ernest Bevin* (Manchester, 1993).

15.   *LPCR*, 1947, p. 179.

16.   Richard Crossman in the *Sunday Pictorial*, 1 June 1947, cited in J. Schneer, *Labour's Conscience: the Labour left, 1945–1951* (1988), p. 63.

17.   For discussion of wages policy under the Attlee govenment, see S.H. Beer, *Modern British Politics* (1969), ch. 7; L. Panitch, *Social Democracy and Industrial Militancy* (Cambridge, 1976).

18.   For the Transport Workers' policy, see V.L. Allen, *Trade Union Leadership: based on a study of Arthur Deakin* (1957), ch. 17; see also the chapter by Richard Stevens in this volume.

19.   The Communist Party was well represented amongst the full-time officials in two coalfields, Scotland and South Wales, and from 1946–68, the General

Secretaryship was held successively by two Communists, Arthur Horner and Will Paynter.

20. See R. McKenzie, *British Political Parties* (Second edition, 1967), Epilogue, p. 597. This was first published in 1963 and refers to 'a few leading trade unionists who were prepared to act, in effect, as a kind of "Praetorian Guard"'.

21. For Lawther, see the entry by John Saville in J. Bellamy and J. Saville (eds), *Dictionary of Labour Biography*, vol. 7, (1984), pp. 140–4.

22. Tom Williamson was General Secretary of the National Union of General and Municipal Workers (1946–61) and sat on the TUC General Council (1947–62); he was also a Labour MP (1945–8). For a contemporary analysis of the union, see H. Clegg, *General Union* (Oxford, 1954).

23. *LPCR*, 1949, p. 125.

24. See the material in Williams, *Diary of Hugh Gaitskell*, ch. 7.

25. *LPCR*, 1952, p. 89.

26. For example, Walter Padley, President of USDAW, had been a member of the ILP until the 1940s.

27. Bevan had written to a member of the Ebbw Vale Party in June 1954: 'There seems no other way of challenging the ascendancy of the two general unions. Unless that ascendancy is challenged, there will be no hope at all for a progressive movement within the party' (Aneurin Bevan to R. Evans, Jennie Lee Papers, cited in P. Hollis, *Jennie Lee: a life*, Oxford, 1997, p. 184).

28. Diary entry for Summer and Autumn 1954, in Williams, *Diary of Hugh Gaitskell*, p. 335. In particular Gaitskell was close to the AEU-sponsored Leeds Member, Charles Pannell. Jones and Watson were leaders of the Yorkshire and Durham Miners respectively.

29. *Railway Review*, 7 October 1955.

30. For one case study, see J. Phillips, 'The post-war political consensus and industrial unrest in the docks', *Twentieth Century British History*, 6, 3, 1995, pp. 302–19.

31. See R. Shepherd, *Iain Macleod* (1994), chs 6 and 7; G. Goodman, *The Awkward Warrior: Frank Cousins, his life and times* (1979), chs 12 and 13; the circumstances of the strike are analysed in the essay by Nina Fishman in this volume.

32. See Goodman, *Awkward Warrior*, ch. 9.

33. The decision-making procedures within the union are examined in Minkin, *Labour Party Conference*, pp. 93–7 and 166–8; the influence of Cousins and the complexities of the union's procedures are apparent in Goodman, *Awkward Warrior*, chs 9–20.

34. See *LPCR*, 1953, p. 174, for Deakin's view, and *LPCR*, 1958, pp. 100–1, for TGWU concern about Labour Party policy on private educaton.

35. Diary entry, 9 October 1956, in Williams, *Diary of Hugh Gaitskell*, p. 616.

36. Bevan received 3,029,000 votes, George Brown of the TGWU, 2,755,000, Charles Pannell of the AEU, 2,644,000, and David Rhydderch of the Clerical and Administrative Workers, 42,000 (*LPCR*, 1956, p. 98). For a breakdown of the voting, see Harrison, *Trade Unions and the Labour Party*, pp. 316–17.

37. See Minkin, *Labour Party Conference*, ch. 7.

38. *LPCR*, 1957, pp. 131–2.
39. Walter Padley, the President, was a former Bevanite and strongly anti-communist, who used traditional socialist rhetoric in support of increasingly cautious decisions. The General Secretary, Alan Birch, was close to Gaitskell. USDAW had supported *Industry and Society* at the 1957 Party Conference, a position many activists regarded as at odds with union policy. For Birch's support for the document, see *LPCR*, 1957, p. 141.
40. See the chapter by Richard Stevens in this volume for further discussion of the Communist Party's influence in the unions after 1956.
41. The difference is captured in Samuel Beer's conception of the 'Socialist Generation'; see Beer, *Modern British Politics,* chs 5 and 6.
42. The classical presentation of this revisionist analysis was C.A.R. Crosland, *The Future of Socialism,* (1956).
43. The principal expressions of this view came after the 1959 defeat; see, for example, P. Abrams and R. Rose, *Must Labour Lose?* (Harmondsworth, 1960). However the New Left from 1956 had begun to consider questions of social and economic change without reaching revisionist conclusions; see M. Kenny, *The First New Left: British intellectuals after Stalin* (1995), ch. 2.
44. Diary entry for 24 June 1959, in Morgan, *Back Bench Diaries of Richard Crossman,* p. 764.
45. Diary entry for 23 June 23 1959, p. 759.
46. Diary entry for 13 August 13 1959, p. 770. Gaitskell could be dismissive of Cousins' abilities – 'profoundly ignorant of the real issues either on the economic or the political side' (Diary entry for 9 October 1956, Williams, *Diary of Hugh Gaitskell,* p. 615).
47. *TUC Report*, 1959, pp. 456–61. The ambiguities in the TUC leadership are apparent in the Crossman Diary entry for 15 September 1959, in Morgan, *Back Bench Diaries of Richard Crossman,* pp. 774–7.
48. See *LPCR*, 1959, pp. 110–13, for Gaitskell's proposal; see also P. Williams, *Hugh Gaitskell: a political biography* (1979), ch. 21; B. Brivati, *Hugh Gaitskell* (1996), ch. 14; D. Jay, *Change and Fortune* (1980), pp. 271–8.
49. For example, the NUM's objectives included 'to join in with other organizations for the purpose of and with the view to the complete abolition of Capitalism'.
50. The quote can be found in R. Winstone (ed.), *Tony Benn – Years of Hope: diaries, papers and letters, 1940–1962* (1994), p. 344, diary entry for 1 October 1960; for the complex pre-conference manoeuvres, see Williams, *Gaitskell,* ch. 22.
51. The NUGMW vote was 150 to 126 for unilateralism; at the recall Congress, this was reversed by 194 to 139; see Minkin, *Labour Party Conference*, p. 100; see also Harrison, *Trade Unions and the Labour Party*, p. 151.
52. For the debate, see *LPCR*, 1960, pp. 176–242.
53. Details of union reversals can be found in F. Parkin, *Middle Class Radicalism* (Manchester, 1968), pp. 124–32; note also K. Hindle and P. Williams, 'Scarborough and Blackpool: an analysis of some votes at the Labour Party

Conferences of 1960 and 1961', *Political Quarterly*, 33, 3, 1962.

54. For the relationship between Wilson and Cousins, see Goodman, *Awkward Warrior*, chs 19 and 20; for Wilson's political strategy in 1963–64, see B. Pimlott, *Harold Wilson* (1992), chs 13 and 14.

55. For Woodcock's views, see R. Taylor, '"What are we here for?" George Woodcock and trade union reform', in J. McIlroy, N. Fishman and A. Campbell (eds.), *British Trade Unions and Industrial Politics, vol. 2: the high tide of trade unionism, 1964–79* (Aldershot, 1999).

56. See Minkin, *Contentious Alliance*, pp. 109–10.

57. *LPCR*, 1947, p. 144.

58. *Daily Herald*, 24 February 1948.

59. See Williams, *Gaitskell*, pp. 464–5.

60. *LPCR*, 1958, p. 166.

61. *LPCR*, 1963, p. 198; see Panitch, *Social Democracy*, ch. 2, for the broader picture.

62. For early relationships between the Attlee government and the NUM at both national and area levels, see a series of diary entries by Hugh Gaitskell during his time as the reponsible minister, in Williams, *Diary of Hugh Gaitskell*; for developments in one major, right-wing coalfield down to 1964, see A. Taylor, *The Politics of the Yorkshire Miners* (1984), ch. 1.

63. Diary entry for 28 June 1949, in Williams, *Diary of Hugh Gaitskell*, p. 116. For the strikes of 1949, see Howell, *Respectable Radicals*, ch. 9.

64. For Figgins' criticism of public ownership management, see *LPCR*, 1949, pp. 127–9.

65. Labour relations in the industry are analysed in T. R. Gourvish, *British Railways, 1945–1973: a business history* (Cambridge 1986); P. S. Bagwell, *The Railwaymen, Volume 2: the Beeching era and after* (1982), ch. 4.

66. These developments in the politics of the NUR are noted in Minkin, *Labour Party Conference*, pp. 110–11; in contrast, the beginnings of the NUM's move to the left are noted at pp. 103–4.

67. See Pimlott, *Wilson*, pp. 349–54.

68. D. Marquand, *The Progressive Dilemma*, (1991), especially ch. 1.

69. The characterization is by Alasdair MacIntyre; see his piece with that title in the *Listener*, 4 July 1968; reprinted in D. Widgery (ed.), *The Left in Britain, 1956–1968* (Harmondsworth, 1976), pp. 234–40.

CHAPTER FIVE

The Trades Union Congress in the International Labour Movement

Anthony Carew

As the second largest national trade union centre in the non-Communist world, the Trades Union Congress (TUC) was a major force in international labour circles in the years after the War. More than any other central organization, the TUC played a leading role in the evolution of the international labour movement. It was pivotal in the short-lived attempt in these years to unify the world movement within the World Federation of Trade Unions (WFTU) formed in Paris in October 1945. It led the 1949 walk-out from the WFTU and then largely coordinated the preparatory work leading to the formation of the rival International Confederation of Free Trade Unions (ICFTU) later that year. And in the late 1960s, with the ICFTU failing to live up to the expectations of its principal backers, seemingly unable to provide a platform for effective trade union coordination in Europe, and unsympathetic to making common cause with Communist labour bodies, the TUC took the first steps that would later lead to the founding of the European Trade Union Confederation (ETUC) with its narrower geographical focus but more inclusive membership.

Various factors contributed to the TUC having a leading role in international affairs. Its numerical strength and the financial contribution that it was prepared to make to international bodies, at times outstripping in per capita terms that of other big national centres, guaranteed it a seat at the top table. Beyond that, it enjoyed considerable esteem, especially among northern European and (notwithstanding the legacy of colonialism) many Commonwealth trade union centres. Generally the TUC took it for granted that its leading role was justified because of its long experience. In its own internal reports and memoranda it would distinguish between the 'mature', 'developed', 'stable' and 'experienced' national centres, among which it was paramount, and the rest – more recently established, possibly financially insecure or organizationally unstable, perhaps as a result of internal conflicts or their dependence on political parties – whose role was to follow and be guided by bodies like the TUC.

In these years, two broad issues dominated TUC international policy: the relationship with Communist organizations and work with trade unions in developing countries. Consideration of these brings into focus two sets of relationships of great importance in TUC international work – the first with the secretariat of the ICFTU and the second with the leadership of the American Federation of Labour – Congress of Industrial Organizations (AFL-CIO), the West's largest trade union centre and the TUC's chief rival for leadership of the international labour movement.[1]

The experience of membership of the WFTU

The TUC's postwar relations with Communist organizations were profoundly influenced by the formative experience of affiliation to the WFTU which, in the late 1940s, came to be increasingly dominated by Communists and fellow travellers. Walter Citrine led the TUC into the WFTU against a background of considerable rank and file and international pressure for a continuation of the wartime alliance of the Soviet, American and British trade unions. From the start there were misgivings within the General Council and Citrine, who was to become WFTU President, warned the founding congress not to get sidetracked into politics, otherwise widely differing aspirations would divide them.[2] Their job, he said, was to build an international geared to practical day-to-day trade union work and the pursuit of tangible gains for members of the unions. The original intention was to establish an international structure that would embrace all elements of the trade union movement. But recognizing the possibility of disagreement over the plan to integrate into the WFTU the autonomous International Trade Secretariats (ITS) which organized unions in particular trades and industries, the TUC made clear from the outset that a satisfactory settlement on this key issue was a condition of its continued membership. It had thereby left itself an avenue of retreat should its misgivings be realized.

From the earliest days the TUC was concerned about the administration of the WFTU and unhappy with the choice of Louis Saillant as General Secretary.[3] Saillant combined his WFTU work with the secretaryship of the French Confédération Générale du Travail (CGT). Though lacking international trade union experience, he enjoyed the backing of the Soviet All Union Central Council of Trade Unions (AUCCTU) and indeed had arrived at the founding conference of the Federation from Moscow with the Soviet delegation. The TUC regarded him as irresponsible. He was a poor administrator, frequently absent from his office, and was also apt to proclaim policy on sensitive matters without authorization. Under his direction, the secretariat also contained many staff appointed on the basis of political patronage.[4]

However, the most important concern of the TUC was that from 1946 literature emanating from WFTU headquarters offered a partisan view of the world with plentiful criticism of the western nations but no equivalent treatment of the Soviet bloc. The official in charge of publications was a Russian and all important releases had to be translated into Russian first before being rendered into the other official languages. May Day messages of a contentious nature were issued without full consultation with the Executive Board. In addition, WFTU delegations abroad were used as a vehicle for Communist members to engage in pro-Soviet propaganda and to identify the Federation with Communist unions in the places they visited. Such intrusion of factional politics in the work of the important 1947 mission to Japan left the members unable to concur on what they had actually seen. After a year of wrangling no agreed report could be issued.[5]

When Arthur Deakin succeeded Citrine as President in 1946 he was already suspicious of the Soviet tendency to dominate the organization but still believed he could act as a restraining influence.[6] The TUC view was that no effort should be spared to make the WFTU succeed. Not until 1947 were open criticisms made of its administration, the factor bringing them to the fore being the announcement of the offer of Marshall Aid in June. In October the Cominform laid down a firm line against Marshall Aid and a month later the secretary of the AUCCTU announced that it would press for the WFTU to become a militant instrument of this line, demanding in particular the removal of 'weak and reformist leaders'. This was an obvious reference to Deakin.[7] There was no WFTU policy on Marshall Aid, but Communist factional control of the Federation's *Bulletin* enabled it to be used overwhelmingly as a vehicle for denouncing the proposal along with those trade union centres that were thought likely to support it. This attack on the reformist leaders of the WFTU was sustained over several months from the end of 1947 during which Saillant and the AUCCTU blocked any formal discussion of the Marshall proposal inside the WFTU.[8]

After making every effort to arrange for such a discussion within the Federation, the TUC bowed to European trade union pressure and took the initiative in convening in March 1948 a European Recovery Plan Conference outside the WFTU structure. The aim of the conference was to declare support for Marshall Aid in time to influence American Congressional debate. Some of the participants, notably the American Federation of Labour (AFL) which was not a member of the WFTU, envisaged this conference as the launch pad for a proposed new trade union international to rival the WFTU. But that was not the TUC's intention, and for a year following this conference the British trade union leadership resisted all pressures to establish a breakaway organization. In particular, and contrary to the claims of Communists, there was no conspiring with the unaffiliated AFL to bring about a schism.[9]

Although the WFTU's future prospects were not bright, the TUC leadership believed they had to persevere with it. It was necessary at least to demonstrate to their own membership that they had sincerely tried to make it succeed. The TUC was well aware that a split might eventually be unavoidable, and in that case, if it were to carry with it other centres, it would need to be seen to have behaved in a thoroughly constitutional manner. If there were to be a split, it was firm in the view that it would have to be on a trade union issue such as relations with the ITS, rather than over a political disagreement such as that regarding Marshall Aid. In July 1948 Deakin was still publicly hopeful that a settlement on the crucial issue of WFTU links with the ITS could be reached and he had taken a firm line with the International Transport Workers Federation (ITF), warning them that he would disaffiliate the Transport and General Workers' Union (TGWU) if the ITF did not go into the WFTU.

However, by September 1948 three years of talks over the ITS issue had not led to a compromise between the Secretariats and the AUCCTU representatives on the WFTU negotiating team. Failure to integrate the ITS meant that the WFTU would be bereft of the means to operate industrially and would remain little more than a 'political' international. This did not accord with the TUC's interest in practical trade union work.

At the TUC congress that month a motion in the name of the Bakers and Tobacco Workers urged resistance to efforts to destroy the unity of the WFTU. In refusing a General Council request to withdraw the motion, the movers misjudged their strength and the mood of congress and gave Deakin the opportunity to go on the offensive. He painted a damning picture of the Federation and maintained that there had been little or no agreement within it. Most of his energy as President had been directed simply at preserving the organization as a going concern and he now considered that he was wasting his time. The WFTU, Deakin declared, was rapidly becoming nothing more than another instrument for the furthering of Soviet policy. His speech earned a rousing ovation and the motion was overwhelmingly defeated.[10]

Buoyed by the support of congress, the General Council now proposed that the WFTU suspend activities while its principal affiliates attempted to find a *modus vivendi*. The AUCCTU rejected this suggestion and the long anticipated split took place at the Executive Board in January 1949 following stalemate on whether or not to recommend suspension to the next WFTU congress. In justifying its withdrawal, the TUC pointed to the way ideological differences had undermined goodwill, preventing compromise within the organization.[11] The pressures of the Cold War had exacerbated fundamental differences between organizations for whom trade unionism meant quite different things. This was the essence of the message that TUC Chairman, Herbert Bullock, brought to the founding conference of the ICFTU ten months later when he warned the gathering against trying to embrace irreconcilable objectives and aims and confusing industrial with political objectives.[12]

The ICFTU and the issue of links with Communist organizations

The TUC was as prominent in launching the ICFTU as it had been in setting up the WFTU. Its General Secretary, Vincent Tewson acted as the secretary

148

to the preparatory committee, while the TUC hosted the founding conference and supplied secretarial services until the new international was able to function independently. Although some accounts suggest that the ICFTU was largely the creature of the American trade unions, the TUC had just as big an influence in defining its aims and organizational structure. Indeed the AFL was later to complain over the dogged way in which the British had fought to exert influence in the preparatory committee.[13] At the heart of ICFTU philosophy was the concept of 'free' trade unionism – unions free from political or employer domination and free to represent the interests of their membership. It was strongly anti-Communist, indeed unwaveringly against all forms of totalitarianism. An important part of the story of the TUC's membership of the ICFTU over the next twenty-five years concerns the way in which it gradually manoeuvred to extricate itself from what it came to regard as the Confederation's excessively inflexible stance on contacts with Communist organizations.

There was always a strand in ICFTU thinking that the relative advantages of free trade unionism over the Communist variety would be reflected in the tangible benefits it secured for its members. Many, including the mainstream TUC leadership, believed that the battle against Communism would be won through this demonstration effect. On this point the Americans in the AFL disagreed. They believed in the need to wage a more direct, ideological struggle against Communism.

The AFL had never forgiven the TUC for joining the 'Communist' WFTU, and in the years ahead would regularly complain that the TUC was soft on Communism. A pillar of the TUC right such as Arthur Deakin would be accused of behaving like a 'Bevanite'. And the Americans spoke of Vincent Tewson's 'appeasement' when, in the course of his presidential address to the 1953 ICFTU congress, he warned against sabotaging by word or deed the possibility of negotiations between East and West. The point was that the congress followed only a matter of weeks after the Berlin uprising, and the AFL believed the speech should have been used to denounce the action of the Soviet government in suppressing this. Between two leaderships which prided themselves on their anti-Communism, there was a measurable difference in the degree of animosity shown towards their ideological opponents. And while the TUC and AFL had the longest established fraternal links of any national trade union centres, their relationship was far from warm. Barely concealed anti-Americanism was widespread among members of the TUC General Council. For its part the AFL interpreted this as an expression of the TUC's sense of superiority.[14]

The issue of contacts with the dissident Communist unions in Yugoslavia was a bone of contention within the ICFTU almost from the moment that their trade union centre was expelled from the WFTU in April 1950. The following year the TUC was, along with other ICFTU affiliates, represented at their congress and this caused friction with the AFL in the ICFTU Executive Board. Tewson, as ICFTU President, used his position to prevent a vote on an American motion denouncing the lack of free trade unions in Yugoslavia. He argued the pragmatic case for maintaining a line of contact to the Yugoslavs, whereas the AFL suspected that the TUC was involved in preliminary manoeuvres to secure their affiliation to the ICFTU.[15] Partly as a result of this episode, the AFL boycotted the ICFTU for the next twelve months.

This was the first instance of ICFTU affiliates dealing bilaterally with a Communist centre. For many years, the Yugoslav trade union confederation was the only Communist organization with which the TUC would have any truck. Contacts with the WFTU itself were naturally out of the question, and it would be some years before the TUC considered bilateral contacts with individual national union centres that were affiliated to the WFTU. After Stalin's death the AUCCTU launched a vigorous campaign in 1954 to woo western unions and invited the TUC to its congress. This was promptly rejected. But in the following years, in what came to be seen as a 'charm offensive', invitations were regularly received from other Eastern European union centres. To counter this, the ICFTU congress adopted a policy of rejecting all such overtures, and the TUC adapted the policy by issuing a statement, *The TUC and Communism*, which warned affiliates against study visits to the Soviet bloc since they risked providing their hosts with a propaganda coup.[16]

However, the TUC had no power to block such contacts when undertaken by its own affiliates, and East–West visits involving individual British unions began to take place with increasing frequency. During the 1950s, Communist-backed motions in favour of contacts with the WFTU or national centres in Communist countries were also picking up increasing support at the TUC annual congress, though in the end they were always defeated. The AFL-CIO were alarmed by this trend and called for a more vigorous anti-Communist line within the ICFTU, but nothing practical could be done to enforce the Confederation's policy.[17]

The TUC line was to support cultural and scientific exchanges with Communist countries. At the same time it wanted to avoid giving any recognition to state-controlled unions. But Tewson insisted that national centres must be free to apply the ICFTU policy flexibly in light of their own circumstances. In the TUC's case, he recognized the difficulty of reconciling its 'no contacts' stance with its desire for government-level negotiations to end the Cold War. And in defence of the actions of TUC affiliates who had sent delegations to Soviet countries, he rationalized that some of them did engage in tough talking with their hosts on the defects of their socio-political system and their trade union record. Others, he pointed out, sought to nullify the dangerous effects of rank and file exchanges by providing leadership by officials whose job was to chaperon the party and ensure that the more inexperienced members were not manipulated or deceived by the Communists.[18] Where the TUC was prepared to draw a line with its affiliates was over any attempt to establish *multilateral* relations with Communist unions that might lead to a permanent organization. Thus the TUC intervened and threatened the ETU with disciplinary proceedings when in 1956–7 it attempted to convene an international conference of electrical workers regardless of whether they were affiliated to the ICFTU or WFTU.[19]

The problem of enforcing ICFTU policy persisted in the late 1950s and 1960s and other national centres began to experience similar difficulties in preventing contacts with the East. Some affiliates such as the Austrians and Finns visited the Soviet bloc in an attempt to demonstrate their neutrality. African centres travelled the same road in support of their countries' search for economic aid. From the late 1950s the German DGB, which was worried about the gap between policy and practice on this question, began to press the ICFTU for clearer guidelines. Could a distinction be made between informal study visits and formal representation at a congress? Was it meaningful to distinguish between contacts with, on the one hand, the Yugoslavs and on the other the rest of eastern Europe? The AFL-CIO warned of the dangers of seeking to legitimize visits in this way, but no refinement of the existing, unenforceable ICFTU policy was forthcoming.[20] The blanket line continued to be that all contacts with the Communists should be avoided.

With George Woodcock as General Secretary from 1960, signs of TUC restlessness under this policy increased. In 1961 the Soviet AUCCTU invited the TUC to the British Trade Fair in Moscow. The invitation was eventually turned down, but this time only after much deliberation.[21] The following year, in successfully opposing a congress motion that called for negotiations between the ICFTU and the WFTU, Woodcock phrased his argument in such a way as to suggest that the TUC stood above the contest between these two internationals. 'I make no qualitative judgement about the two', he said:

> But it is the fact that they are completely incompatible. The time may come when we are all grown up, when systems modify themselves…when we might find a basis for the common action and understanding which I agree is the basis of trade union unity.[22]

In 1963 the Yugoslav trade unions proposed the idea of an international conference to discuss economic development. The TUC were still wary of involvement in multilateral events of this nature and declined to participate, arguing that a more productive route would be to develop bilateral contacts.[23] But a clear indication that bilateral contacts extending beyond those with Yugoslavia were now becoming acceptable to the TUC came in 1964 when a congress motion calling for exchanges of study groups or trade union delegations between *all* countries was remitted to the General Council. It subsequently declined to give blanket approval to all visits, but considered the motion to be in accord with existing policy which took into account 'the broadening of attitudes in recent years'.[24]

In the context of the partial test ban treaty of 1963 and a modest easing in the arms race, the tendency to ignore the ICFTU policy increased. In private Woodcock conceded that the TUC would ultimately be prepared to exchange trade union visits with any trade union organization, be it in Spain or the USSR, provided that their meetings were devoid of political content, avoided matters of war and peace and confined themselves to practical trade union questions. In practice he also indicated that he did not subscribe to TUC orthodoxy about how the split with the WFTU had come about, with all responsibility levelled at the Communists.[25]

When the printing trades ITS, the International Graphical Federation (IGF) accepted into membership the French CGT bookworkers' union in 1965 without first requiring it to leave the WFTU fold, the ICFTU severed relations with the wayward ITS. With British printing unions prominent among the membership of the IGF and John Bonfield of the National Graphical Association (NGA) its President, the TUC backed the Federation and declined to support the ICFTU measure. Woodcock complained that the Confederation was introducing politics into a situation that was simply a product of industrial developments. The IGF, he insisted, was merely trying to strengthen its organization in the face of the internationalization of publishing and printing by the employers. He later reported to the TUC International Committee that there had been little response to his efforts to secure a discussion of the case on its merits. As a consequence the ICFTU suffered from the rigidity of its own decisions.[26]

Reflecting on the significance of this development in the ICFTU, the TUC International Committee noted that the attitudes that had brought the ICFTU into existence had produced the unfortunate result that its activities had mainly been directed by political considerations. But given that the AFL-CIO seemed to be edging towards withdrawal from the Confederation precisely because it felt the political battle against the Communists was not being waged strongly enough, the International Committee expressed guarded hope that the departure of the Americans might permit some reversal of the present policy. Without the Americans it might at least be possible to develop an informal relationship with the trade union movements of the Communist countries.[27]

A sign that the TUC leadership were thinking in terms of a more independent policy line came at the 1965 annual congress. Faced with a motion critical of the ICFTU and calling for a redefinition of 'free' unionism and a 're-evaluation of international trade union unity', Woodcock stressed that he was not antagonistic to the intention of the motion but argued:

> Unless there is common purpose, it is better sometimes not to have organizational unity and to work at a much lower level, to select the kind of things which you

can talk about … rather than to force yourself into a structure where … you can have a rush job and then it breaks up. On the TUC we are thinking at the moment rather more in terms of diversity than increasing unity.[28]

The future direction seemed to lie in a more modest range of international interests being pursued through more than one organization.

The gradual drift away from the ICFTU line was confirmed in 1966 when the TUC accepted for the first time an AUCCTU invitation to send a delegation to the Soviet Union. By now, with *detente* on the rise, there was extensive traffic between national union centres in East and West Europe and the TUC were simply joining the crowd. Woodcock defended this visit, arguing that a mere exchange of views or visits did not constitute a threat to free trade unionism. The TUC could not conceive of a world where nations and trade unions were indefinitely lined up against each other. A start had to be made somewhere, if for no other reason than to recognize the existence of the other side. He believed the TUC had something to teach and other things to learn from the Soviets. Such contacts did not constitute an organic link, and matters discussed were carefully circumscribed with political questions excluded. And, however constrained the Soviet trade unions were, it had to be accepted that they were responsible for the day-to-day protection of workers' interests.[29]

When in 1969 the AFL-CIO finally withdrew from the ICFTU, one of its underlying reasons for doing so was deep disillusionment at the behaviour of organizations such as the TUC in defying ICFTU policy on contacts with unions that were not 'free' in the accepted sense of the term and whose countries had a suspect record on human rights. The AFL-CIO's action now had two major consequences as far as the TUC was concerned. One was to remove from the ICFTU debate the most forceful opponent of contacts with Communist organizations. The other was to weaken the ICFTU so much that it became wholly inadequate to the global tasks that it had set itself. From this point the TUC set off in the direction it had initially contemplated in 1965 – a less ambitious international policy pursued through various institutional channels, with most emphasis now placed on European regional organization.

The TUC in developing countries

During the years of TUC affiliation to the WFTU, little practical trade union work had been attempted, the Federation's focus being on international political developments in the early Cold War. The TUC's interests overseas concentrated on British colonial and ex-colonial territories where it placed heavy reliance on labour officers in the colonial civil service who were often former trade unionists appointed on its recommendation. It was the TUC's belief that such people were responsible for some of the most practical and lasting work in encouraging the growth of trade unionism and industrial relations structures. In matters of colonial trade unionism the TUC also enjoyed ready access to government in Whitehall through its membership of the Colonial Labour Advisory Committee and the Colonial Economic Development Council.[30]

From 1949, however, the TUC began to place more emphasis on direct work abroad among colonial labour movements. In the first instance most attention was focused on British territories in the West Indies. In that year the TUC also convened the first annual Commonwealth Trade Union Conference in Geneva, timed to coincide with the International Labour Conference of the ILO. These meetings were chaired by a senior member of the TUC International Committee and for the most part discussed practical trade union topics chosen by the TUC. The format was intentionally informal, the belief being that to formalize it would be counter-productive, signalling that the TUC was organizing a caucus within the ICFTU. Initially the conferences were attended by representatives of the old white Commonwealth, but by the mid-1950s participation regularly involved 30–40 delegates from perhaps 15 territories – about one half of the Commonwealth countries having trade union movements. The numbers involved were to grow further in the 1960s. These gatherings were regarded as a valuable means of maintaining contact between people sharing certain values and approaches to labour questions.

In 1950 the TUC instituted a policy of providing all British colonial trade union centres with basic office equipment and a library of union literature. By the mid-1950s, over 30 centres had been equipped in this way. Correspondence courses to train colonial union officials were instituted by the TUC in 1952. Training and education in Britain was provided for a small number of more senior officials, a TUC-financed Colonial Scholar spending six months in Britain every year, with a number of others visiting on shorter TUC-sponsored study visits. From 1955 the TUC also published a monthly paper *Trade Union News for Overseas*.

As a leading affiliate of the ICFTU, the TUC played a key role in the development of its policies and programmes in British territories. The ICFTU's first forays in Africa were two missions, in 1951 and 1952 respectively, led by Fred Dalley, a retired Assistant Secretary of the Railway Clerks' Association and G.H. Bagnall, former General Secretary of the Dyers and Bleachers' Union. Two of the first three ICFTU field representatives in Africa were British, approved by the TUC. Congress played a full part in shaping the ICFTU's policy on national independence in 1952, and throughout most of the 1950s the TUC was comfortable with ICFTU work in this area which complemented its own activities. However, the British did not rely on the ICFTU, which was a new organization only beginning to cut its teeth. The TUC regarded itself as having more understanding of this field, and, both within and outside the confines of the ICFTU, the particular emphasis of its approach was to stress the practicalities of developing stable trade unionism at the base.[31]

For the British, the establishment of sound trade union structure and practice took priority over steps towards colonial independence. They preached the message that national independence was not the answer to all problems. It was important to focus on the intermediate stages before self-government during which the patient building of trade union structures and industrial relations practices was essential. It was an axiom of the TUC that you could not run a newly independent country if you could not run a union branch. This emphasis on the incremental, organic development of trade unionism at the base was not always well received by impatient nationalists, but the TUC was unwavering in its approach. The aim was not to create a trade union movement that would supply muscle for nationalist political movements but to enable concrete benefits to be won for workers in the here and now. The TUC was therefore very concerned that whereas there had been a relatively strong growth of trade union membership in some territories, there was often no comparable growth in the machinery for negotiation and consultation. Consequently considerable efforts were expended within the Colonial Labour Advisory Committee and in dealings with the Overseas Employers' Federation in nurturing the institutions of industrial relations.[32] On numerous occasions the TUC sought a solution to particular industrial relations disputes in colonial territories through its contacts with the Overseas Employers' Federation in London.

In 1954 Congress introduced a levy of twopence per member for a Colonial Development Fund which would finance an expanded programme of assistance to unions in British dependencies. By the mid-1950s the colonial division of the TUC's International Department claimed to have built up a body of knowledge on the trade union and industrial relations situation in thirty-five territories and was therefore in a position to offer advice to local unions. It was also keen to assist in organizing and training activities.[33] To a certain extent the TUC became a research and advice centre at the service of emerging trade union bodies abroad. In the latter part of the 1950s it was particularly concerned about the tendency for essential service legislation in colonial territories to be excessively restrictive regarding trade union activities and the right to strike. In this situation the TUC undertook a detailed examination of all legislation prior to making representations to the Colonial Office.[34]

Beyond acting as a general resource for developing unions, the TUC provided assistance in other ways. Under the ILO constitution, dependent territories were allowed to attend its conferences with observer status, but in situations where no such colonial delegation was sent, the TUC would frequently add to its own delegation trade union representatives from dependent territories who had a particular interest in items on the ILO agenda. The

British were ever keen to cultivate a role at the ILO for unions from dependencies and the concurrent annual Commonwealth Trade Union Conference provided a focus for such encouragement.

Assistance was also commonly provided by sending trade union advisers on visits of varying duration to help with practical problems on the spot. Thus in 1954 Len Murray was despatched to Trinidad to help the Seamen and Dockers' Union in negotiations and subsequently to assemble a case for arbitration. Will Lawther was sent to Northern Rhodesia for two months in 1957 to work with the African Mine Workers' Union. Jim Young, a former General Secretary of the Association of Engineering and Shipbuilding Draughtsmen (AESD), spent several lengthy periods in Aden in the late 1950s and early 1960s working with the Aden TUC to help resolve its difficulties with the colonial administration. Various TUC representatives spent extensive periods in British Guiana in the 1950s and 1960s working to strengthen the unions. An official was also loaned to the trade union centre in Fiji to assist with an organizing drive. There were numerous such instances of direct TUC aid, always at the request of the overseas organization.

With a modest budget, rarely more than £10,000, the TUC would also give financial assistance in needy situations – to help employ a full-time general secretary for a few months, to cover the cost of office rent or a duplicator, or to help with the purchase of a motorcycle or a car for a union organizer. These donations usually amounted to no more than a few hundred pounds, and hardly ever as much as the £3,000 granted to the British Guiana trade unions in 1954–5 to help them in their bitter battle with Cheddi Jagan's political movement.[35]

The TUC's stance on colonialism was to defend the record of the British government against generalized external attacks – arguing that since the War Britain had moved beyond colonialism – while using their influence with government to follow up any detailed criticism from trade unions in dependencies.[36] It intervened with the Colonial Office in the course of a number of bitter nationalist struggles, seeking the release of trade unionists detained for alleged terrorist activities in Kenya, Cyprus (where it was frequently vilified by the leadership of the Cyprus Confederation of Labour on whose behalf it was interceding), and Aden, where it also paid the cost of an Appeal Court case brought on behalf of the imprisoned leaders of the Aden TUC.

However, as nationalist and anti-colonial sentiment increased in the 1950s and 1960s, the tendency of the TUC to advise trade unionists in dependent territories that dramatic economic and social change could not come about overnight and that they had to learn to walk before they could run, often led to criticism of the British in international gatherings. Increasingly the TUC found itself challenged, not only by trade unionists from developing countries, but also by the Americans and ICFTU officialdom.

African unions and relations with the AFL-CIO and ICFTU

Serious differences between the TUC on the one hand, and the AFL-CIO and the ICFTU on the other, over the best way to develop trade unionism in Africa emerged in the latter part of the 1950s, as the movement for national independence gained pace. With the establishment of an Organizing Department in 1956 and an increase in the budget for this activity, the ICFTU began to plan for a more prominent role in trade union developmental work in Africa. The AFL-CIO, which had identified itself as a strong supporter of anti-colonialism, also impressed on the Confederation the importance of moving more swiftly in Africa. For the Americans, the urgent need for trade union organization arose from their fear that the continent might soon fall to Communism. However, the AFL-CIO lacked confidence in the ICFTU as a bulwark against Communism and was also keen to launch its own independent programme of activities in Africa.

An AFL-CIO representative had toured East Africa early in 1957 and was widely rumoured to have offered financial assistance to the Tanganyika trade unions. Subsequently the AFL-CIO agreed a $50,000 programme to train African union leaders in the United States, and in autumn 1957 their representative returned to East Africa to select candidates for training. This American interference in British colonial territories caused deep resentment in the TUC and nearly sparked off a diplomatic incident when the Colonial Office seriously considered expelling the representative.[37]

A settlement to the problem of independent activities by the AFL-CIO was negotiated at a meeting of American, British and German union leaders with ICFTU officials during the AFL-CIO convention in Atlantic City in December. The Americans agreed to cease independent activities in favour of ICFTU programmes. In particular the ICFTU would take over responsibility for training African trade union leaders at a centre to be established in Africa. However, the TUC refused to underpin the Atlantic City accord by agreeing that all its activities in Africa would also be conducted under the aegis of the ICFTU and with its overseas representatives carrying ICFTU credentials. The TUC position was that it had a special responsibility for trade union work in British dependencies, and that, with decades of experience of such activities, it was in a position to give practical help which others could not. Vincent Tewson argued that the TUC had no 'independent programmes' of the type operated by the AFL-CIO and only responded to specific requests for assistance from individual territories.[38]

In a strained atmosphere, the TUC's Colonial Advisory Committee met ICFTU General Secretary J.H. Oldenbroek and Director of Organization Charles Millard in February 1958 to thrash out this matter.[39] The ICFTU officials insisted that the Confederation should be responsible for all international projects. They also claimed that the British overestimated their popularity in Africa and the desire of the colonial unions to receive help from the TUC. But senior members of the General Council were adamant that British dependencies in Africa were primarily the TUC's responsibility. Bill Carron of the Amalgamated Engineering Union (AEU) argued that the ICFTU must not interfere in this relationship. And while the TUC were willing to keep the Confederation informed of their projects in Africa, Frank Cousins of the TGWU insisted that no procedure for consultation must be allowed to hold up the urgent task of rendering assistance in the continent.[40]

The ICFTU were forced to accept this arrangement, though warning that it might give the AFL-CIO an excuse for resuming independent activities. In the eyes of the Confederation, the TUC were seeking to apply double standards, and their refusal to surrender autonomy in Africa would eventually rob the Confederation of any meaning or importance.[41]

The TUC also had misgivings about the new African training centre which was an integral part of the Atlantic City settlement. The ICFTU proposed to locate this in the Ugandan capital of Kampala, but Vincent Tewson believed that the African movement would be better served by having itinerant instructors who would conduct courses on the spot in different territories. The TUC feared that the college would become a centre for political propaganda promoting Pan-Africanism. Also, with the AFL-CIO having a stake in the college, it would establish a base for Americans 'prancing around in Africa'. Because it was a product of the Atlantic City accord, the TUC found it difficult to oppose the Kampala College project, but their acceptance of it was no more than grudging.[42]

Still dissatisfied with the pace of trade union development in Africa, and judging the continent to be at a dangerous turning point politically, in February 1959 the AFL-CIO offered to make available to the ICFTU the assistance of one or two black American union representatives who would be prepared to spend several months in Africa. Diplomatically, the ICFTU side-stepped the offer, but the TUC were now greatly exercised, not only about the prospect of an increasing American presence in Africa but also the spread of ICFTU projects. In a series of meetings of the TUC International and Colonial Advisory Committees in 1959 and in position papers adopted by them, the TUC's growing differences with the Americans and the ICFTU secretariat were now highlighted.[43]

The basic difference was that the TUC emphasized the importance of building unionism up from the base – concentrating on establishing branch organization, the effective control of finances, developing industrial relations machinery and servicing members. In contrast, the ICFTU and the AFL-CIO focused their energy on supporting national trade union centres. The TUC recognized that the task of creating African trade union solidarity would take decades whereas the AFL-CIO believed that the future of African trade unionism and politics was likely to be decided in a much shorter time frame. This divergence reflected the political emphasis of the Americans and the ICFTU whose aim was to preempt the WFTU establishing a bridgehead in Africa. In so doing they were securing the affiliation of national labour movements as bastions of anti-Communism. The TUC, on the other hand, considered that Communism was not the real threat in Africa. Indeed, more dangerous was the prospect of national union centres falling under the domination of governments and nationalist political movements as had already happened in Ghana. This led the TUC to complain of the 'fundamental unsoundness of the AFL-CIO approach to the problem of trade union organization'.[44]

The TUC warned against the danger of national centres being artificially stimulated by outside financing and thereby acquiring a false status that was not justified either by a dues-paying membership or viable union structure at the base. National centres created in this way in Sierra Leone, Nigeria, Uganda, Nyasaland and Northern Rhodesia were, the TUC claimed, ineffective while the Ghana TUC and the Kenya Federation of Labour (KFL), both having benefited from extensive assistance from the ICFTU and the AFL-CIO, were outstanding examples of undemocratic and manipulated organizations. The KFL had for years evaded its obligation to pay dues to the ICFTU, and organizations like this, the British claimed, did not deserve to belong to the Confederation. Within the TUC, the KFL General Secretary Tom Mboya was widely regarded as an archetypal nationalist politician masquerading as a trade union leader. Their claim was that a form of 'licensed corruption' set in when *real* African union leaders were unable to compete with artificially created ones whose strength derived from outside financing.

Beyond this, the TUC complained of the 'black racialism' at the core of the rapidly spreading Pan-African movement which had nothing to offer trade unionism. The AFL-CIO and the ICFTU had both given indirect support to this by continuing to make negative attacks on African colonialism. Yet the TUC believed it was wrong to suggest that the colonial governments were the enemy of the trade unions. The TUC defended their record in this field. There were no British dependencies whose workers were not legally free to organize, and frequently the recognition of trade unions was stimulated by British firms and employers' associations in search of a body with which to negotiate. Only where the Colonial Office had ceased to have influence, as in Ghana, were trade union freedoms at risk. Overall the TUC complained that the Americans and the ICFTU were insufficiently frank in pointing out to African trade unionists that their real problem was their lack of unity, leadership and financial integrity.

The TUC accepted that there was more work to be done on behalf of African trade unionism than could be undertaken by the TUC, AFL-CIO and ICFTU put together. The tasks would necessarily have to be shared. What was needed, therefore, was agreement on basic principles of trade union work and a division of spheres of influence. The British obviously felt they should take the lead role in their dependent territories, with the Americans and other mature national centres collaborating elsewhere under the auspices of the ICFTU. Under such an arrangement, the TUC envisaged the ICFTU operating essentially as a 'clearing house' for African requests for assistance, rather than having a direct role in organizing.[45]

Throughout 1959 the TUC sought to arrange a top level meeting with the AFL-CIO and ICFTU to agree such an approach, but without success. The AFL-CIO leadership had other fish to fry and were busy manoeuvring to replace the top leadership of the ICFTU with people more malleable than Oldenbroek and Millard.

The 1960s: deteriorating relations with the ICFTU

Until their disagreement over policy in Africa, the TUC had enjoyed very good relations with the ICFTU. Vincent Tewson had probably played a bigger role in the Confederation than any other national union leader during the 1950s and he had developed a close understanding with General Secretary Oldenbroek. Both men retired in 1960 after which TUC commitment to the ICFTU declined steadily under Tewson's successor George Woodcock. This trend had its roots in General Council disenchantment with ICFTU policy in Africa. But now the critique widened, influenced by Woodcock's perception of ICFTU inefficiency under its new General Secretary, Omer Becu.[46] Quite simply, Woodcock regarded the Confederation as an organization that squandered money on ill thought-out projects, not least of which was the recent decision to erect at considerable expense a permanent building to house the Kampala College.[47]

From the outset he was opposed to the Confederation's heavy dependence on voluntary financial contributions by affiliates which furnished three-quarters of its income. Large numbers of poor affiliates accounting for about a quarter of total membership were unable to afford more than a fraction of standard fees, income from which was barely enough to sustain the cost of headquarters administration. To finance its wider programme in the field, the ICFTU therefore relied on the half-dozen largest centres subscribing to an International Solidarity Fund (ISF) on a triennial basis. The TUC had initially been the largest benefactor, contributing over $1.4 million between 1958 and 1960, a third of the total sum collected.[48]

The Solidarity Fund was controlled by a committee independent of the regular ICFTU governing structures, with the result that there was no overall budgeting exercise in the Confederation and no considered, long-term planning of projects. Tewson had been the original chair of the ISF Committee during which period TUC criticisms of spending decisions had been muted. But Woodcock was less attached to the ICFTU than his predecessor. He was much more critical of the Secretariat for its lack of rigour in costing and monitoring activities funded by the ISF and also for what he saw as the lazy assumption that funds would always materialise from *ad hoc* appeals to cover costs that had already been incurred.[49] Much of his criticism focused specifically on assistance to Africa which received nearly a third of all ICFTU spending. The beneficiaries were the national centres rather than the local unions, and he argued that this top-down approach to organizing was unlikely to produce independent unions capable of being sustained by a dues-paying membership. Woodcock strongly condemned policies which resulted in trade union leaders such as Mboya becoming 'permanent pensioners of the ICFTU'.[50]

In the face of this, the TUC declined to contribute further to the ISF when it was asked for a donation of $2 million for the period 1961–4. Attending his first ICFTU Executive Board meeting in December 1960, Woodcock gave the impression that the TUC had only just learned of the $2m figure, though in actual fact Tewson had been party to the original decision to set the target. However, Woodcock well understood the mood of the TUC General Council and made it clear that there was no chance of their agreeing to it. The TUC now withdrew from membership of the ISF Committee.[51]

Over the next three years Woodcock engaged in a sustained critique of the ICFTU, gradually extending his range of targets. Misgivings about the reliance on unpredictable, one-off donations for what needed to be a long-term development programme widened into general criticism of the ICFTU leadership and its methods, the lack of coherence in its policies and operations, and the tendency to engage in ambitious work for which it had little competence. The weakness of the Secretariat, the absence of a powerful finance and general purposes committee to give the organization direction, an overlarge Executive Board with membership too diverse to make firm decisions, and the consequent absence of clear, long-term strategy and purpose were the subject of repeated interventions by Woodcock at Executive Board meetings in the first half of the 1960s.

The TUC position gradually won the support of other affiliates and in 1964 an accommodation was reached, with the TUC agreeing to contribute to the ISF on a scaled-down but regular annual basis over an indefinite period. All this was conditional on other affiliates also being prepared to facilitate the more effective long-term planning and financing of projects. It meant that the ICFTU would have to operate with smaller funds, but Woodcock contended that some past expenditure had corrupted and even prevented the growth of trade unions. He maintained that the need to work within a tighter budget would be a useful discipline for the Confederation. As a comparatively inexperienced organization, it needed to understand that it was not capable of dealing with all the problems of trade unionism in every part of the world.[52]

At this point the AFL-CIO began to join in the attack on the ICFTU in a way that was even more damaging than the TUC's criticism. The ICFTU's African policy that the Americans had strongly backed was clearly failing.

Pan-Africanism had taken a hold and many of the national centres that the ICFTU had helped were now turning against it and had been subordinated to the government in an increasing number of one-party states. The AFL-CIO saw its future role in Africa being better served by a recently created African-American Labor Centre which, like the American Institute for Free Labour Development in Latin America, had been launched with generous US government funding. It cut back drastically on its contributions to the ISF and by 1965 it seemed that the Americans might soon pull out of the Confederation.

With the ICFTU close to paralysis as a result of uncertainty over its future, and activities in developing countries curtailed for lack of funds, the TUC began to reflect on deeper problems associated with the Confederation – indeed the fundamental problems of making any international organization work. An important factor was the TUC's perception of a lack of goodwill, especially between western and third world centres. Woodcock suggested that the range of ICFTU affiliates was too wide to provide the basis of a compact organization able to address itself effectively to trade union questions.[53] This had a bearing on finance and policy.

Given the diverse interests of unions from countries at different levels of economic development, it was difficult if not impossible to construct within the Confederation a system of dues payment and voting that did not give offence to one or another section of the membership. Woodcock complained that within the Executive Board it was impossible to question spending proposals, even mildly, without it being inferred that the intention was to stand in the way of progress:

> The fundamental deficiency of the ICFTU was that it provided no machinery for compromise since the discussion in the Executive Board served only to stimulate antagonism if any measure of restraint were proposed on trade union grounds.[54]

Returning to the theme of the ICFTU as an over-ambitious body, the TUC believed that the Confederation should attempt less in developing countries, where three-quarters of expenditure was directed, while at the same time devolving more responsibility for field programmes to the ITS and the mature national centres.

The TUC also held the view that more decentralization of activity was necessary within the ICFTU, with greater initiative left to its regional structures. These, it felt, were better equipped to develop a unanimity of purpose among unions within a more limited geographical framework.[55] This linked in with another important TUC theme that was beginning to find expression: the ICFTU ought to focus more on international matters that had a bearing on the domestic concerns of the larger affiliates in America, Britain and Germany, whose role hitherto had been restricted to giving aid to the poorer centres. In future it wanted these larger centres to derive benefits from ICFTU membership and not simply be seen as distributors of largesse. In following such a course, the Confederation would necessarily have to emphasize more the role of its American hemispheric and European regional structures. At the TUC's annual congress in 1965 Woodcock had already floated the idea of strengthening the European Regional Organization. All of this implied a moderation of the earlier ambitious global project for free trade union development, with the ICFTU reduced to playing a consultative and coordinating role.

The TUC was therefore looking for radical reform of the ICFTU or, it judged, the Confederation would have to be abandoned. Yet there were few grounds for optimism that change would come about, and the TUC International Committee minuted:

> If the question arose of starting afresh the TUC – taking experience as a starting point – would perhaps not be in favour of establishing an organization such as the ICFTU with its present functions, nor disposed to accept that the somewhat heterogenous political attitudes of major ICFTU affiliates provide a satisfactory basis for common and large-scale trade union operations directed towards developing countries.[56]

Three years later, these doubts about the ICFTU's future viability were realized when the AFL-CIO finally disaffiliated. It left the Confederation in financial crisis and confirmed the TUC in its belief that the immediate way forward was to concentrate its international effort in a European regional grouping.

Conclusion

The TUC's post-war international policy was characterized by pragmatism and an emphasis on the promotion of practical trade unionism. Committed initially to building a global movement, experience of the inner workings of both WFTU and ICFTU had taught it to be cautious about what could be achieved at this level. Over time its approach became, if not less altruistic, at least more calculating and more inward looking as it focused on international activities in a European context that were considered more likely to produce tangible benefits for British trade unions.

The post-war period began with the TUC affiliated to the WFTU, hoping that it would succeed as a genuine trade union international, but wary over the possibility that fundamental ideological differences would undermine unity. Such differences arose over the Marshall Plan, and from late 1947 Communist factional influence in the organization, which had existed from the outset, destroyed any remaining goodwill. Equally the AUCCTU's determination to bring the autonomous ITS under the disciplinary control of the WFTU killed off all hope that the movement might operate effectively on basic industrial issues. On balance the TUC had every justification for pulling out.

Yet it was the practical side of the TUC that caused it to differ with the AFL-CIO in the ICFTU over the question of contacts with Communist organizations. By the mid-1960s the TUC was well on the way to turning full circle as it moved gradually to restoring the link with the Eastern bloc unions whose policies in the late 1940s had caused it to abandon the WFTU. Anti-Communists to a man though they were, the TUC's leading spokesmen in international affairs in the 1950s and 1960s – Deakin, Tewson, Alfred Roberts, Charles Geddes, Tom Yates and Fred Hayday – recognized that an ideological crusade against Communism must not obstruct, or become a substitute for, the regular practice of trade unionism. All of them had to contend with Communists among the membership of their own unions and had learned to be nimble in their handling of domestic union politics. One manifestation of this was their acceptance of the need for flexibility in applying the policy of 'no contacts' with Communist organizations abroad.

At first the TUC approach was to support the spirit of the ICFTU policy, advising affiliates against liaison with Communist groups in other countries, while recognizing that individual unions could not be disciplined on this matter. Over a decade and a half, and especially under the influence of the Soviet 'charm offensive' from 1954 and the slight softening of the face of Communism under Khrushchev, the TUC's approach became more agnostic and they were increasingly prepared to condone their affiliates' breaches of ICFTU policy. As calls for rapprochement with Eastern bloc trade unions grew louder, and with the General Council and International Committee more left wing in membership from the 1960s, *ostcontact* came to be seen, not so much as something to condone but as a strategy to be embraced and pursued with vigour.

In assistance to colonial and ex-colonial union movements, the TUC demonstrated in the clearest manner its own distinct approach to international affairs. It stressed the importance of the routine, unspectacular side of trade union activity: building solid foundations of membership at the base; sound financial structures rooted in the regular habit of dues payment; education and training for practical leadership; the creation of basic industrial relations structures and the importance of negotiating and, where necessary, compromising in the interests of achieving tangible if piecemeal gains. Indeed the TUC was accused by some (including Americans who shared their basic approach to economic trade unionism) of failing to recognize that this seemingly unhurried 'British' approach to building African unions gradually over an extended time frame failed to take into account that here was a continent in turmoil, whose people, engaged in struggles for independence, were already on the move. In such situations the need was, perhaps, to organize workers speedily by building the movement from the top down. Yet the TUC would not compromise on this point and it became a major factor in its loss of confidence in the ICFTU in the early 1960s.

The bruising internal fight for a more rationally organized ICFTU that Woodcock waged from 1960 to 1964 was justified and was beginning to pay dividends with beneficial changes that might have led to a more productive phase of work. However, at that point the AFL-CIO began to cut its losses as far as the ICFTU was concerned and thereby deprived the Confederation of vital financial resources.

The TUC's gradual shift to a more independent approach to international affairs using a variety of institutional channels that was first hinted at by Woodcock in 1965 was probably a sensible accommodation to outside changes. The ICFTU was in a parlous state following the AFL-CIO withdrawal, and the means to turn it around were beyond the capacity of a single centre such as the TUC. The British leadership did make a genuine effort to keep the Americans in the ICFTU fold, but once they had gone their own way it was necessary to re-focus priorities. European level trade union organization, with a more flexible approach to Communist union organization, was now accepted as the main priority.

Notes

I wish to acknowledge generous financial assistance from the Lipman-Miliband Trust and the British Academy which enabled me to undertake the research for this project.

1. The AFL-CIO was formed in 1955 out of a merger between the American Federation of Labor (AFL) and the Congress of Industrial Organizations (CIO). Until 1955 it was the AFL which had the greatest immediate influence on the events described below.
2. George Meany Memorial Archives, Silver Spring, Maryland, Irving Brown Papers, 29 (6), Lincoln Evans to David Dubinsky, 19 January 1949.
3. State Historical Society of Wisconsin, Madison, Germer Collection, 25, Adolph Germer Diary, 27 January 1947; Tamiment Institute, New York, Elmer Cope Collection, 19 (4), Deakin to Saillant, 16 March 1948. Almost the entire meeting of the WFTU Executive Board in May 1948 was taken up with TUC criticisms of the inefficiency and political partisanship of Saillant and his Secretariat.
4. Elmer Cope Collection, 19 (4), Elmer Cope to Philip Murray, 20 March 1948.
5. Meany Memorial Archives, Michael Ross Papers, 1 (25), Tarasov to Saillant, 6 July, 1948; Townsend to Saillant, 25 August 1948.
6. V. L. Allen, *Trade Union Leadership*, (1957), p. 290.
7. *Bolshevik*, 15 November 1947; *Trud*, 16 November 1947.
8. *WFTU Information Bulletin*, 15 December 1947, 15, 31 January, 15, 29 February, 1948; A. Carew, 'The schism within the WFTU', *International Review*

of Social History, 29, 3, 1984, pp. 303 *et seq.*

9.   Ibid., pp. 319–20, 327–8.

10.   TUC, *Report*, 1948, pp. 447–49.

11.   TUC *Why We Have Left the WFTU*, 1949; International Institute for Social History, Amsterdam, ICFTU Archives, Tewson speech in 'International trade unionism: report of the preparatory international trade union conference', Geneva, 25–26 June 1949 .

12.   H.L. Bullock, opening address to the Free World Labour Conference, London, 28 November, 1949.

13.   Hoover Institute, Stanford, Lovestone Collection, L 307 (ICFTU 1952), Notes on International Committee Meeting of AFL, 18 June 1952.

14.   A. Carew, 'Conflict within the ICFTU: anti-Communism and anti-colonialism in the 1950s', *International Review of Social History*, 41, 1996, pp. 153–4.

15.   ICFTU Archives, ICFTU Executive Board, Minutes, November 1951.

16.   TUC, *Report*, 1955, p. 208.

17.   ICFTU Executive Board, Minutes, November 1956.

18.   ICFTU Executive Board, Minutes, October 1955.

19.   TUC, *Report*, 1957, pp. 206–8.

20.   ICFTU Executive Board, Minutes, June 1959.

21.   TUC, *Report*, 1961, p. 223.

22.   TUC, *Report*, 1962, p. 393.

23.   TUC, *Report*, 1963, p. 228.

24.   TUC, *Report*, 1964, p. 256.

25.   Canadian National Archives, Ottawa, Canadian Labour Congress Papers, Reel H 193, file 4, Kalmen Kaplansky to Claude Jodoin, 25 February, 1964.

26.   ICFTU Executive Board, Minutes, March 1965; Modern Record Centre, Warwick, TUC Archives, TUC International Committee, Minutes, 15 December 1965.

27.   TUC International Committee, Minutes, 25 May 1965.

28.   TUC, *Report*, 1965, p. 521.

29.   ICFTU Executive Board, Minutes, October 1967.

30.   'Trades unions in developing countries', TUC International Committee, 26 July, 1966.

31.   TUC, *Report*, 1952, p. 177.

32.   TUC, *Report*, 1954, pp. 227–8.

33.   TUC, *Report*, 1956, p. 215.

34.   TUC, *Report*, 1958, pp. 236–7.

35.   TUC, *Report*, 1956, pp. 223–4.

36.   Interview with Stefan Nedzynsky, Geneva, November 1995. Transcript in author's possession.

37.   Carew, 'Conflict within the ICFTU', pp. 169–70.

38.   Colonial Advisory Committee, Minutes, 5 February 1958.

39.   Oldenbroek was Dutch and had worked for the NVV and then the International Federation of Trade Unions and the International Transport Workers Federation of which he became General Secretary in succession to Edo

Fimmen. Millard had formerly been Canadian Director of the United Steelworkers of America.

40. Colonial Advisory Committee, Minutes, 5 February 1958.

41. Ibid., Minutes, 2 April, 16 July, 1958; A. Carew, 'Charles Millard, a Canadian in the international labour movement: a case study of the ICFTU 1955–61', *Labour/Le Travail*, 37, Spring 1996, pp. 138–40.

42. TUC International Committee, Minutes, 22 July 1958; TUC Archives, 292 919.66/2, ICFTU 1958–60, Notes by Walter Hood, 29 April 1958.

43. 'Reassessment of situation in British Africa', Colonial Advisory Committee, 4 February 1959; Joint Meeting, Colonial Advisory Committee and International Committee, Minutes, 17 February 1959; 'The Conception of Pan-Africanism and other influences affecting trade union organization in Africa', Joint Meeting, Colonial Advisory Committee and International Committee, 9 March, 1959; International Committee, Minutes, 21 April, 1959; 'The trade union situation in British dependencies in Africa', 'Assistance to unions in British dependencies in Africa', Joint Meeting, International Committee and Colonial Advisory Committee, 14 May 1959 and Minutes; 'The situation in British Africa with reference to the activities of the ICFTU and AFL-CIO', Joint Meeting, International Committee and Colonial Advisory Committee, 10 June 1959.

44. Joint Meeting, International Committee and Colonial Advisory Committee, Minutes, 9 March 1959.

45. 'Reassessment of the situation in British Africa' (amended), Colonial Advisory Committee, 14 May 1959.

46. Omer Becu was Belgian and had been General Secretary of the International Merchant Marine Officers' Association and then the International Federation of Transport Workers in succession to Oldenbroek.

47. TUC International Committee, Minutes, 20 December 1960.

48. TUC International Committee, Minutes, 24 October 1961.

49. TUC International Committee, Minutes, 21 November 1961.

50. TUC International Committee, Minutes, 27 February 1962.

51. ICFTU Executive Board, Minutes, November–December 1960; TUC International Committee, Minutes, 20 December 1960. Under Tewson's general secretaryship, Woodcock, as his assistant, was often kept in the dark about developments and it is possible that there had been no discussion between the two men over the ICFTU plan to request a contribution of this size. Given the lack of enthusiasm of the General Council for the ICFTU at this time, it is questionable whether Tewson himself could have secured agreement on the contribution had he remained in post.

52. ICFTU Executive Board, Minutes, March 1963.

53. TUC International Committee, Minutes, 15 July 1965.

54. TUC International Committee, Minutes, 22 March 1966.

55. TUC International Committee, Minutes, 15 July 1965.

56. TUC International Committee, Minutes, 26 July 1966.

CHAPTER SIX

Cold War Politics: Communism and Anti-Communism in the Trade Unions

Richard Stevens

The British Communist Party (CP) was formed in 1920. In line with its Marxist-Leninist philosophy, the CP placed great emphasis on the importance of the class struggle at the point of production. As mass working-class organizations, trade unions were seen as vital instruments in that struggle. Therefore, the CP sought to influence their policies and tactics. Such activity came naturally to many of the CP's foundation members, who were experienced trade unionists. So, too, were many of the CP's opponents, who tried from its inception to contain Communist influence in the unions. Henceforward, Communist and anti-Communist activity became a significant feature of the internal politics of trade unionism. Indeed, in many respects 'Cold War' politics and antagonism existed in the unions from 1920 onwards, although without doubt it intensified greatly during the late 1940s and early 1950s. This was due not only to the deterioration of international relations, but also to the rapid extension of CP influence from 1941 onwards. Communist influence before the war had to a large extent been contained by its opponents, particularly at a national level. That said, it is true that the CP had been making considerable progress, especially at 'grass roots' levels, from the mid-1930s onwards. It is unlikely that the wartime expansion would have been as significant as it was without this important 'foundation' work. Wartime conditions did, however, help the CP to expand quickly to its highest ever membership of 56,000 in late 1942. Membership subsequently declined, but the CP's influence in a number of unions remained strong.[1]

In spite of its wartime expansion, the number of Communists in the unions was never great. There were 34,810 members in unions in March 1944 and 31,731 in March 1945 (approximately 0.42 per cent and 0.39 per cent respectively of the total union membership), and numbers declined during the next few years (see Table 6.1).[2] However, a constant source of concern for anti-Communists was that CP influence seemed to be far out of proportion to its actual membership. This raises another important point: it should be emphasized that the struggle for influence, although it was conducted at various levels in the unions, was usually confined to a very small section of the membership – the activists and full-time officers – and to a handful of interested parties outside the unions. For the mass of trade unionists, and indeed, most activists, the Cold War and factional in-fighting was only rarely of interest, let alone a stimulus to participation. Nevertheless, although the conflict was limited to a small minority, it was a key minority for the unions as they could not function effectively without their active members. It is important that the struggle is not seen, despite the rhetoric of the CP, purely in terms of a 'bureaucratic', 'right-wing', 'leadership' versus a 'militant', 'left-wing', 'rank and file'. Certainly, many on the left at the time viewed it in those terms. Yet, while 'right-of-centre' social democrats dominated the movement as a whole, Communism and anti-Communism often cut across full-time leadership and lay activist or rank and file divisions. Furthermore, the divisions were not always clear-cut, even to many of the participants. Truly dogmatic Cold War 'warriors' were a minority of a minority: there was frequently a great deal of tolerance and practical co-operation at all levels in the movement.

We have emphasized that economic struggles at the workplace were central to Communist thinking. Communist influence in the unions was primarily built on such struggles and the willingness of CP members to take on leadership roles and risk victimization. This explains the resilience of the CP in the unions during the sharpest phase of the Cold War from 1948 to 1953. Certainly, the Cold War badly damaged the position of the CP in the unions. What is more surprising, perhaps, is that it did not damage it to a greater extent. The importance of concentrating on economic issues is perhaps best illustrated by the failure of the CP to prevent the departure of the Trades Union Congress (TUC) from the World Federation of Trade Unions, compared with the overturning of TUC General Council policy on wage restraint in 1950, though this was not solely due to Communist agitation. Nevertheless, Communists could claim with justification some credit for this. In terms of influencing Labour's foreign policy, the Communists were invariably unsuccessful until the late 1950s, when the CP peace campaigns fed into the wider upsurge of interest in nuclear disarmament. However, the CP was slow to appreciate the change of mood towards unilateral disarmament during 1959–60.[3]

Communists were on more solid ground when they concentrated on grass roots economic issues. Their incessant demands for higher wages, shorter hours, and better conditions, found a sympathetic response in conditions of full employment. It also earned them notoriety. Communist shop floor activists were often model trade unionists. They attended branch meetings, recruited non-unionists, organized shop stewards', works and combine committees, and generally embedded themselves in union structures. This enabled them to ride out the most bitter phase of the Cold War. There were, of course, major setbacks: new or continuing bans of varying kinds in the Transport and General Workers' Union (TGWU), Clerical and Administrative Workers' Union (CAWU), National Union of General and Municipal Workers (NUGMW), National Union of Boot and Shoe Operatives (NUBSO), National Society of Painters (NSP), the London, Glasgow and other smaller Trades Councils; purges in the civil service and Middlesex Education Authority; defeats in various union elections; and falling membership.[4] But many Communists remained in the positions that they had come to occupy in the 1930s and 1940s. Most Communist strongholds remained just that, and their position was in some respects strengthened by the advent of a Tory Government in 1951.

Structures and attitudes of anti-Communism

The changing international situation, especially during 1947–49, had enabled committed anti-Communists to attack Communist influence at all levels in the unions. In the late 1940s these activities were bolstered by the now hostile attitude of the previously sympathetic Will Lawther of the Miners, and the growing detachment of Jack Tanner of the Engineers. However, as indicated above, the late 1940s marked an intensification of Cold War hostility in the unions, not the beginning of it. For committed anti-Communists, the battle against CP influence continued from the inter-war period, and was uninterrupted by the wartime rapprochement. Thus the TUC continued to monitor Communist activity throughout the war. This included producing detailed lists of Communists in various unions, and the close scrutiny of trades councils' activities. The removal in 1943 of the 'black circular' of 1934 – which banned Communists and fascists from attending trades councils – was undertaken reluctantly, and owed much to the pressure of widespread Russophile feeling. Labour Party officials attempted to maintain all proscriptions. Anti-Communists in individual unions tried to contain CP influence by various means. In the Electrical Trades Union (ETU), for example, there was an attempt in 1943 to bar Communists from holding office. In the Musicians' Union disciplinary measures were taken against leading Communists in 1944.[5]

The late 1940s and early 1950s brought an intensification of anti-Communist activity and a proliferation of anti-Communist groups. Their principal aims were to reduce the numbers of Communists holding office, and prevent unions from adopting CP policies. Anti-Communism was multi-layered, with both formal and informal structures, albeit chiefly the latter. Formal structures included the Defence of Democracy Trust, publishing *Freedom First*. This was formed in 1948 by some leading union officials, including TUC General Council members, notably George Chester and Lincoln Evans. It was, in theory, disbanded the same year, yet *Freedom First* was still being issued as late as December 1951.[6] The Association of Catholic Trade Unionists (ACTU) developed a national structure during the second half of the 1940s. ACTU was not an avowedly anti-Communist organization. However, given both the antipathy of committed Catholics to Communism and the prominence of various individual Catholic anti-Communists, it seems reasonable to assume otherwise.[7] Indeed, Catholic activists provided significant opposition locally and nationally to Communists in several unions, including above all the Amalgamated Engineering Union (AEU), but also the Union of Shop, Distributive and Allied Workers (USDAW), ETU, the Tobacco Workers, Foundry Workers, Civil Servants, Teachers, and Railwaymen. A considerable Catholic presence was also to be found among the chief supporters of two major anti-Communist groups formed in the 1950s. The first, Common Cause, was launched officially in 1952. Several of the Defence of Democracy Trust's leading figures resurfaced in Common Cause, such as Tom O'Brien, Labour MP and General Secretary of the Theatrical and Kine Employees. Common Cause made much of 'exposing' Communists standing in various union elections. In 1956 Industrial Research and Information Services (IRIS) was launched. In many ways very similar to Common Cause, IRIS concentrated in particular on the AEU. This was partly because several of its major figures were members of that union, and partly because of the strength of the CP in the AEU. IRIS also paid great attention to union elections.[8]

In individual unions, various anti-Communist groups developed organized structures. These included in the late 1940s the 'Progressive Labour Group' in USDAW, the 'Club' in the AEU, and the 'Conference Campaign Committee' in the Civil Service Clerical Association. Less organized groups – or those with only a sporadic existence – were formed in the Cinematic Technicians, the Supervisory Staffs and Executives, and the CAWU. Others emerged in the NSP in 1960, and the Scottish Miners in 1964. Apart from issuing general denunciations of Communism, these groups often circulated lists of 'approved' candidates in elections. There were also numerous individual activists.[9]

The TUC remained deeply involved in anti-Communist activity. In this respect, its public pronouncements of 1948, 1949 and 1955 and its monitoring of trades councils were but the 'tip of the iceberg'. Many of the full-time personnel at the TUC had, for years, been cultivating networks of like-minded contacts at all levels within the labour movement, designed primarily to contain Communist influence. Victor Feather was a central figure. He devoted a great deal of effort to combating the perceived threat. He was not alone. Other leading anti-Communists in the TUC included the General Secretary, Vincent Tewson, Albert Carthy of the International Department, Herbert Tracey and T. N. Shane of the Publicity Department, Edgar Harries, Ray Boyfield and W. Widden of the Organization Department, along with a host of lesser officials, concentrated particularly but not exclusively in those departments. Their attitudes were unaltered by the changing international

171

climate of the Cold War. Rather, the changed conditions gave them greater opportunity for anti-Communist offensives. This included establishing links with a variety of groups external to the labour movement, such as personnel in the Home and Foreign Offices, the Information Research Department (IRD), and the Ministry of Labour. There were also links with American embassy officials and trade unionists, and other contacts, such as a certain F. J. Brown of Chelsea, who headed an organization entitled 'Industrial and General Information'. During the mid-1950s Brown supplied the TUC with information gleaned from CP documents. He also supplied a detailed commentary on the 24th Congress of the CP in 1956, including unpublished, apparently verbatim quotes.[10]

There were other interest groups and individuals involved, not necessarily directly connected to the trade union movement. These included numerous local and national newspapers and journals, many employers, anti-Communist pressure groups of various sorts, Labour MPs such as H.W. Butler and Woodrow Wyatt, Conservative MPs such as Aidan Crawley, the Economic League, the Conservative trade union movement, the International Confederation of Free Trade Unions, various clergymen, Moral Rearmament, the short-lived 'Democratic Association of Trade Unionists' in Manchester, and others. It also included state security services, particularly MI5 and the Special Branch. A 'classic' case of 'infiltration' is that of Harry Newton, who penetrated the Yorkshire Communist and labour movement from the mid-1950s until his death in 1983. The charge of 'outside interference', so often levelled at the CP, could equally be applied to the anti-Communist movement. Participation in the battle for influence in the unions was not confined to trade unionists alone.[11]

Nevertheless, trade unionists remained the key players. It should be noted though, that anti-Communist attitudes among trade unionists were rarely monolithic. Indeed, in practice, few anti-Communists were as one-dimensional as such prominent protagonists as Vic Feather, or Arthur Deakin of the TGWU. With hindsight it is apparent that any 'red threat' was exaggerated, sometimes intentionally. Yet to many committed anti-Communists the threat was perceived as all too genuine. Deakin undoubtedly used anti-Communism as a tool to retain control of dissident elements in his union, but he does appear to have believed that there was a real danger. Feather, too, remained very energetic in combating Communism. One of his colleagues at the TUC, Len Murray, described Feather as 'very effective, very knowledgeable. [He] shared some of the qualities of the CP (from [his] own ILP background) – perseverance, attention to detail'. However, he also added that 'I always thought that Victor Feather took them too seriously, in the sense of spending too much of his time on them'.[12]

Beyond the obsessive antipathy of the Deakins and Feathers, lay a wide range of attitudes. These were frequently complex and variable, depending on the issue concerned and the prevailing conditions. Indeed, often antipathy to the CP was subject to emotional and irrational swings. Yet anti-Communism was not necessarily a 'knee-jerk' reaction to perceived Communist strength, nor was it limited to right-wingers. There were a variety of left-wing anti-Stalinists. Some of these consisted of Trotskyist groups such as the forerunners of the International Socialists and the Socialist Labour League. These groups formed small pockets of influence in various parts of the country, but remained a minor force during this period despite a boost following 1956. There was a much larger number of non-Marxist left-wingers who also actively opposed the CP, albeit often on a irregular basis, as their attitudes were rarely dogmatic. Sometimes such opposition was due to antipathy towards the Soviet Union and totalitarianism, but it could also be derived from a dislike of British CP methods and sectarianism, or a mixture of both. This included leading figures such as Bob Willis of the London Compositors and Bryn Roberts of the Public Employees, as well as many rank and file trade unionists and Labour Party members. Such anti-Communism consisted of a desire to contain CP influence, but one which usually stopped short of proscriptions. Their generally democratic beliefs precluded this. There were also many anti-Communists who were prepared in practice to tolerate and cooperate with Communists. Such people conducted a limited or restrained form of anti-Communism, which was applied flexibly according to needs and circumstances. For example, the ex-Communist leader of the Furniture Workers, Alf Tomkins, became actively anti-CP, yet his working relationships with Communist full-time officials in the union were usually harmonious. At a lower level, several TGWU full-time officers – left- and right-wingers – were prepared to ignore their union's ban on Communists holding office as shop stewards and branch officials.[13]

Communist Party organization and policies

Most anti-Communist organizations and networks were well-established by the early 1950's. So, too, were the CP's organizational structures. During 1945 there had been a shift in emphasis from workplace-based CP branches, to local branches based on municipal and parliamentary divisions. However, workplace organization remained important, and in practice many branches continued to function. These included branches at Duples and De Havilland in North West London, Austin in Birmingham, and Players in Nottingham. Sometimes, such organization was boosted by strikes in which Communists played leading roles. Indeed, in 1950 the emphasis on area branches was altered in an attempt to reinvigorate workplace organization: 'the factory Branches are *the most important* [sic] basic organizations of the Party'.[14] Alongside these branches were the advisory committees. These consisted of CP members in each union or, occasionally, industry. The bulk of the major and many of the minor unions were covered, including some such as the NUBSO and the NUGMW, in which Communists had been barred from holding office since the late 1920s. The advisory committees played an important role in coordinating activity, exchanging information, organizing for elections, and transmitting policy from the Party Centre. Where possible, district and local advisory committees functioned as well. Circulating more general, and sometimes specific, guidelines and economic information was the CP's Industrial Department and the National Industrial Organizer – from 1951 until 1965 Peter Kerrigan. The Industrial Department worked closely with the party's Organization Department and Economic Committee. These bodies organized occasional industrial and factory branch conferences, weekend schools, and produced a steady stream of literature relating to industrial issues. Such literature was aimed both at CP and non-CP readerships. The former consisted mainly of policy guidelines such as 'Needs of the Hour' (which was produced annually and sent to party cadres) and factual information concerning the industry in question. The latter consisted largely of leaflets and pamphlets, and articles in the *Daily Worker* relating to a particular industry. Invariably these were accompanied by intensive distribution and sales campaigns.[15]

However, in practice the CP's organizational structures sometimes were looser than they were portrayed. Some workplace branches functioned only erratically, or confined themselves purely to economic or union affairs. They had the potential disadvantage of consisting of members from several different unions, which could hinder coordinated action. Organization was sometimes very small-scale: a mere three members was required to constitute a branch, and progress could be painfully slow. Indeed, in London, despite intensive campaigns such as the 'Edgware Road Project' during 1952–5, there was a decline in the numbers both of workplace branches and the membership thereof throughout the 1950s. (See Table 6.2.) Some advisory committees met irregularly, or concentrated on elections to the detriment of policies. The Industrial Department did not give consistent attention to various industries: in 1963 it was admitted that 'it is several years since the party published a policy statement on the building industry', and more damagingly, it did not control its members in the ETU.[16] In addition, the roles played by these bodies carried with them the potential charge of 'outside interference'. Nevertheless, no other political party or group matched this level of politico-industrial organization, and documents relating to AEU elections in the London area during 1959–60 bear testimony both to the efficiency of the CP's 'machine' and the energy that was put into such campaigns.[17] To an extent, Communist organization helped to offset the party's lack of numbers.

The much-lamented 'apathy' of union members did perhaps play a part in allowing the extension or continuation of Communist influence, but not necessarily in the sense that informed the arguments of contempo-

174

rary anti-Communists. Rather, apathy aided and hindered both sides. Indeed, many former CP activists felt that widespread apathy benefited the right- rather than the left-wing, and that the avowed Communist aim of drawing in as many people as possible into activity was constantly frustrated by this.[18] Conversely, the high turnout in the second ballot for the 1956 AEU presidential election supported claims that Communists benefited from low polls.[19] Anti-Communist complaints about apathy were fuelled by frustration that the CP's influence belied its sparse membership. The Central Office of Information commented in 1948 that the maximum proportion of Communists to total union membership was about 1 in 190, yet the estimated proportion among TUC delegates was 1 in 13. Indeed, the actual numbers were absolutely small and constituted a tiny percentage of union memberships: in the Fire Brigades Union (FBU) in 1955, just 71 (approximately 0.35 per cent of the membership); the AEU, 3,250 (0.38 per cent); the National Union of Mineworkers (NUM), 1,672 (0.24 per cent); and the ETU, 831 (0.37 per cent). However, CP influence and numerical strength varied greatly between different industries and unions, and the two were not necessarily inter-locking. Nevertheless, its sympathizers and 'fellow-travellers' were of great importance to the CP. Such people were vital for the party, given its own lack of numbers, but their support often was conditional and variable.[20]

Some of the hostility towards Communism subsided with the Cold War 'thaw' after 1953. This helped Communists to maintain their sphere of activities. On the other hand, given good organization and a few energetic individuals, they were capable of expansion even at the height of the Cold War. More usually, progress was achieved by painstaking effort and attention to detail over a lengthy period. This characterized the extension of Communist influence in the Yorkshire coalfield. Here, a sustained campaign was launched in 1953 to turn the crucial Yorkshire Area of the NUM from a right-wing to a left-wing stance. Such a transition carried the possibility of radical changes in the entire labour movement. Concentration on the important Doncaster district and an early breakthrough, centring on the Armthorpe strike of 1955, marked progress, as did the election of Communists to official positions between 1959 and 1966. However, it was not until the late 1960s that Yorkshire could be viewed as a consistently left-wing area. The extension of CP influence had involved a lot of hard work and taken a long time.[21] Conversely, influence could decline due to a variety of factors not necessarily linked to active anti-Communism, including disillusion, migration, deaths, retirements, redundancies or even exhaustion among key figures. CP activists also continued to be hampered by association with a foreign country. This was fully recognized by CP members themselves. For instance, at a meeting of industrial cadres in 1953 the North West London Area Secretary, Max Egelnick, recorded the comment: 'Once many Lab workers come up against our policy cannot argue against us. But have reserve about are we agent foreign power [sic]'.[22] Such attitudes among many active trade unionists continued to act as a barrier to CP expansion.

Retreat and recovery: the impact of 1956 in the unions

Despite the hostility and setbacks generated by the onset of the Cold War, many Communists still by the mid-1950s held established and significant positions in considerable sections of British trade unionism. That position was again threatened by the repercussions of the events in the Soviet bloc during 1956. Between the spring of 1956 and the beginning of 1958, CP membership fell from nearly 34,000 to under 25,000. This was often seen as an exodus of the 'intellectuals'. Yet the composition of the CP was heavily weighted towards industrial and manual workers, so the losses must have included large numbers of these members as well as professionals and white collar workers. However, an internal assessment during 1957–8 claimed that losses consisted of a quarter of white collar workers, but only an eighth of industrial workers. It was noted, though, that the overall proportion of members in unions had declined.[23]

Certainly a number of leading trade unionists left during 1956–7: Lawrence Daly, Bert Wynn, Willie Allan, Alex Moffat and Jim Hammond among miners; Brian Behan among builders; George Smith of the woodworkers; John Horner, Jack Grahl, Bob Bagley and Leo Keely of the FBU; Frank Chapple and Les Cannon of the ETU; and many lesser figures in a range of unions.[24] In addition, the CP lost its dominance of the FBU, and eventually lost control of the ETU. The CP's position was also damaged in other unions where it had a powerful presence such as, for example, the Foundry Workers. Consequently, Communist input at the 1957 and 1958 Trades Union Congresses was much more subdued than that of previous years.[25] Without doubt, the events of 1956 were very damaging indeed for the CP in the unions. However, the extent to which the party managed to cling on and to recover a large part of its position in spite of these losses is of considerable significance. This is all the more surprising given that 1956 gave anti-Communists ideal opportunities to go onto the offensive. Yet, in numerical terms, the CP had recovered by 1962 much of the position of 1955–6. (See Table 6.1) Most members continued to be as active as before in the unions, with many holding leading positions. In most unions where it had been a major force before 1956, it remained at least a considerable force, albeit with some exceptions.

There were a number of reasons for the recovery. Many of those who left during 1956–7 were already discontented, and were likely to have left at some point.[26] There was the general discipline of the CP, and its organizational structures. Most of these remained intact – although again there were exceptions, particularly in the FBU, where initially the CP lost all its leading members and between 52 and 61 of its 1955 membership of 71.[27] More fundamentally, Communists continued to wage economic struggles, continued to risk victimization, and continued to do the boring jobs necessary for the basic functioning of unions. In short, they continued in many cases to win respect for their industrial and workplace activities, if not necessarily for their politics. This had always been the key to Communist influence in the unions.[28] Moreover, it is not apparent that most rank and file union members cared greatly about the revelations concerning Stalin, nor more than fleetingly about the events in Hungary. In the longer term, the majority were perhaps more concerned with the daily round of wages and conditions. 1956 principally affected union activists rather than the mass membership.[29]

The events of 1956 sparked a wide-ranging controversy within the CP. While many members left because they were unhappy with the extent and openness of debate, for those who remained, these discussions helped them to come to terms with the situation.[30] These internal debates eventually had a significant effect on the CP's industrial policy and tactics. However, other events, such as the ETU affair, Ford's strike at Dagenham of 1962, and indeed even peace campaigns, were necessary for this fully to come about. In the meantime, there was understandable retrenchment; intensification of the siege-mentality, which was compounded by the campaign against the Communist leadership of the ETU; and reliance on tried and trusted ways of working in the unions. This was demonstrated by the renewed campaign in 1958–9 to strengthen factory branch organization, which had been hit particularly badly in London. (See Table 6.2) In the short-term, these methods helped to stabilize the situation.[31]

Many of those who left the CP remained very close to it. Some, of course, dropped out of activity, and some became hostile to the party. Nevertheless, many continued to cooperate closely with it on a wide range of issues. For example, the Secretary of the Derbyshire NUM, Bert Wynn, resigned from the party although his brothers and sisters all remained members. Wynn was fully capable of independent action after 1956 – not all of it pleasing to the CP – but his conduct as a miners' leader in many respects was very similar to when he had been a Communist, and his relations with former comrades in the East Midlands were generally amicable.[32] The London bus workers' leader, Bill Jones, is another example of a former member remaining close to the CP. Indeed, his 'defection' may even have been an asset, since it meant that he was elected to the Executive of the TGWU in 1957. The other leading Communist among the bus workers, Bert Papworth, did not leave the CP, and several former members at the Dalston bus garage quickly rejoined and re-established the workplace branch. Overall, the party's position among bus workers had recovered sufficiently for it to play an active role in the 1958 London bus strike. At other levels in the movement there were many examples of individuals leaving, but remaining friendly and cooperating with

Communists. This applied, for instance, to Leo Keely of the FBU. Indeed, if one looks at the stance of the FBU at the TUC before and after Hungary, there is not a great deal of difference. The FBU continued to support militant, left-wing policies, even if its line was no longer always that of the CP. Furthermore, Bob Bagley of the FBU soon rejoined, as did Alex Moffat of the Scottish NUM.[33]

The effects of 1956 were very patchy. In some organizations the CP lost its leading position only briefly, and recovered rapidly. In many cases its position – whether leading or not – was barely affected. This included, for example, the Nottingham and Mansfield Trades Councils, where Communists remained the leading force in the former, and a secondary force in the latter, while in both Suez produced a more vociferous response than Hungary. There was also little change in the Nottinghamshire NUM. Despite the presence of Les Ellis as an Area official, the CP was not particularly strong in the Nottinghamshire coalfield. 1956 reinforced the well-organized, anti-Communist Area leadership's periodic condemnations of party activists. Yet, a handful of Communists continued to be elected to the Area Council. Ellis was followed as an official by the Communists Bill Baker and Joe Whelan. The main CP pit branches remained intact. Such an outcome, however, was not necessarily the same in other coalfields. In terms of membership alone there were considerable variations. Thus, among NUM members between 1955 and 1957 the number of Communists in the Northumberland and Durham Areas dropped by two-fifths; in Kent it remained the same; in Lancashire it rose by nearly a third. Such variations were not limited to the mining industry.[34]

Sometimes there was a slow but steady advance. In the Association of Engineering and Shipbuilding Draughtsmen (AESD), for instance, the CP continued to extend its influence. In Birmingham, the leading Communist on the AEU Divisional Committee, Dick Etheridge, was elected the deputy delegate to the National Committee during 1955–7, then a full delegate during 1958–61. In 1957 the Divisional Committee passed three resolutions in line with, and none opposed to, CP policy; there was nothing regarding Hungary. In the West Midlands motor industry the CP factory branches at Longbridge, Norton, Lucas, and Tractor and Transmission in Birmingham, and Standard, Coventry, remained intact, as did the positions of leading Communists Dick Etheridge, George Jelf, Harold Marsh, Derek Robinson and Jim Crump in Birmingham, and Peter Nicholas and Bill Warman in Coventry. A major reason for this resilience was the role played by Communists in the strikes against redundancies during 1956–7. Indeed, Communist activity in the motor industry continued to expand, based partly on the attention paid by the party to the development of automation. The major and widely sold policy statement, *Men and Motors*, was produced in 1959. A Combine Committee was quickly established following the formation of the British Motor Corporation. National conferences were held of the CP-led rank and file organization, the Motor and Ancillary Industries Shop Stewards, and of the CP motor industry group.[35]

Elsewhere in the West Midlands, the repercussions in Birmingham Trades Council – one of the largest in the country – demonstrated a situation where the CP recovered rapidly in spite of fierce opposition. Since the war a powerful Communist element had dominated the Council, despite the close attentions of the TUC. In 1956 the sixteen-strong Executive included seven Communists, plus sympathizers. The anti-Communists on the Trades Council, though vociferous, were poorly organized. That was changed by 1956. Although the CP did not lose any leading members on the Council, the full-time Secretary, Harry Baker, moved from previously quite close co-operation with Communists to become dogmatically anti-Communist. Baker started liaising closely with Boyfield and Feather of the TUC. The backlash following Hungary reduced the Communists on the Executive to three in January 1957, although they clawed back two seats the following year. During 1957–60 there was bitter infighting as the Communists sought to regain ground. The situation was confused by personal animosities and the re-emergence of a small Trotskyist faction. Nevertheless, although the CP was not as dominant as before 1956, it had recovered much of its position by 1959–60.[36]

The repercussions of 1956 produced different effects on the leading Communist bastions in the AEU: the Sheffield, Manchester and North London Districts. The Manchester District Committee (DC), along with the neighbouring Stockport and Ashton DCs, had established 'broad left' organizations in the late 1940s and experienced no real challenge following 1956. Indeed, the election of the Communists Edmund Frow and John Tocher to the AEU National Committee from the Division remained unaffected.[37] Communist dominance of the North London DC continued, although there were electoral defeats in the Division. Indeed, North London and two neighbouring Districts were censured in 1958, due to their attempts to circumvent the new (non-Communist) Divisional Organizer, Tom Chapman.[38] The Sheffield DC, which had attracted interest from the Economic League for many years, experienced perhaps the most concerted challenge. Indeed, Communists occupied all significant offices, and dominated the DC. There were sixteen CP factory branches in Sheffield, and Communists occupied leading roles in many shop stewards' committees.[39] The Sheffield DC frequently was in conflict with the AEU Executive. In the Division as a whole, the Sheffield District was supported by the Chesterfield District, which also had a strong CP element.[40]

A significant feature of the campaign to dislodge the Communists in Sheffield (as it was in North London) was that it was led by the local and much of the national press, along with IRIS, various employers, and publications such as the *Catholic Herald*. The campaign centred on trying to defeat the Communist AEU District President, Herbert Howarth, and this was eventually achieved at the end of 1957. It was a serious blow, and caused much concern both locally and nationally, with Kerrigan taking a direct interest.[41] However, the Communists regrouped rapidly, and were successful in the other District and Divisional elections. Fundamentally, Communist influence among the shop stewards proved resilient. Furthermore, the left-wing majority on the DC ensured that the new President, Ted Law, was unable significantly to influence the political stance of the District: it continued to function, to all intents and purposes, as it had done prior to his election. This situation was sustained despite the attentions of the press, and (sometimes public) interventions and disciplinary sanctions by the national leadership.[42]

Law was replaced in 1961 by George Caborn, a member of the CP's National Executive. Communist strength in the Sheffield District was based on the shop stewards, and was built primarily on economic struggles. Bill Moore, himself a CP member, attributed the resilience of Communists in the Sheffield AEU to their shop floor activities: 'They were never afraid to take up any issue, and they were never willing to compromise, unless it produced the main part of what they were aiming for'.[43] Of course, not all Communist shop stewards maintained such high standards; yet the strongholds in the factories were not significantly dented by 1956. Despite a concerted effort led primarily by 'outside bodies' and supported by a right-wing Executive, the CP's standing proved enduring.

Communist influence, such as it was, also remained intact in the Tobacco Workers' Union (TWU) – a small union of some 20,000 members. However, the debates within the TWU Executive following the invasion of Hungary are illustrative of the range and complexity of opinions concerning Communism. They arose from a proposal to ban Communists from holding office. The TWU generally adopted left-wing policies and its General Secretary, Percy Belcher, was widely regarded as a fellow traveller. Yet, in 1955 there were a mere twenty-one Communists – although four of these were full-time officials – in membership. Nevertheless, there was a significant anti-Communist element, and the move to ban Communists from office after 1956 was the third attempt in eight years. The lay Executive, which contained no Communists, was evenly split on the subject. An avowed anti-Communist 'of no particular political opinion' praised the qualities of a Communist TWU District Organizer, and voted against the proposal. He was joined by a Labour municipal candidate, whose voting record was very erratic. The right-of-centre National Organizer also opposed the motion, stating that the officials concerned had been known Communists when appointed. Belcher vehemently opposed the proposal, but belied his fellow traveller tag by protesting vigorously to the Soviet Embassy after the invasion of Hungary. The President, Doug Bowry, initially supported the motion and then opposed it at the next meeting. Others denied that the TWU was Communist-influenced, and argued that democracy, freedom and the unity of the Union would be harmed by a ban. Proponents of the motion argued the exact opposite: the TWU was indeed responsive to CP pressures, and Communism was alien and evil. This was often expressed in emotive terms: 'You have got to think of the future, the future of our children ... The right thing is not the way of Communism'. The proposal was eventually defeated, but the key point was that neither the Executive nor the union was split on straightforward left-right or even necessarily ideological grounds. A survey of the general voting patterns in the TWU further emphasizes the complexity of division. It is likely that such mixed attitudes were very widespread in all unions.[44]

Conclusions

The post-war move away from workplace to area branches did not mean a diminution of the CP's interest in the unions. Nor did it mean the demise of all workplace branches. However, with the onset of the Cold War, the deterioration of Communist workplace organization may have undermined some of the CP's resistance to attacks in the unions. Certainly, in terms of numbers the CP's losses often were much greater during the ten years 1945–55 than in the following period. (See Table 6.1) Nevertheless, the CP proved remarkably resilient, and most of the structures underpinning Cold War politics were in place by the early 1950s. These structures were used to varying degrees of effectiveness by the participants, who remained a small but important minority of trade unionists plus a number of external groups.

The extent of the effectiveness of anti-Communist groups such as Common Cause, Moral Rearmament and IRIS, and of individuals such as Woodrow Wyatt, is difficult to quantify. While they may have affected some elections and periodically stirred up anti-Communist sentiments, on several occasions their activities produced a significant backlash from non-Communists who resented such 'outside interference' and the right-wing connections of the perpetrators.[45] Nevertheless, Cold War antagonism continued with varying intensity throughout the 1950s and early 1960s. It was given renewed edge by the events of 1956. These gave anti-Communists new opportunities for offensives, while they temporarily demoralized many Communists.

The CP's immediate response to these developments was one of regroupment and retrenchment. In many cases this helped Communists in various unions to recover quite quickly, although there were, of course, severe losses. There were also further setbacks, particularly electoral defeats. Probably the most damaging of these was in May 1960, when two Communists – Alex Moffat of Scotland and Les Ellis of Nottinghamshire – stood for the Presidency of the NUM. CP policy for union elections generally was to have just one Communist standing, or alternatively, to support a sympathetic left-winger. In the event, the leading Communist candidate, Moffat, was narrowly defeated by an orthodox Labour candidate, Sid Ford. This breakdown of discipline resulted in many recriminations, as Scottish Communists in particular blamed their Nottinghamshire counterparts for Moffat's defeat. This probably was an erroneous assumption, as it seems that Ellis's decision to stand was not supported by his comrades in the area, and it is unlikely that his candidature seriously damaged the unanimity of the left-wing vote. However, the defeat was all the more galling because Ford was a clerical worker at the NUM headquarters, rather than a miner. Moreover, the CP had earlier that same year successfully supported a left-wing, non-Communist candidate, Alwyn Machen, but he had unfortunately died before taking office.[46] In 1962 the defeat of a strike at Ford's Dagenham plant, led to the disarray of the CP factory branch, and demonstrated the detachment of its leadership from ordinary workers in the plant.[47] Undoubtedly the most serious setback of the period took place in the ETU, the repercussions of which were felt much more widely. The defeat of the Communist leadership of the ETU arising from its ballot-rigging activities was nothing short of a disaster. It was further compounded by the banning of Communists from holding office in the Union in 1964.[48]

These defeats helped to push forward the level and extent of internal debate about methods of working in the unions. The result was a decisive move towards Broad Left strategies. It was symbolized by the appointment of Bert Ramelson as National Industrial Organizer. It was not a wholly new initiative, but from the mid-1960s onwards it was applied with new vigour. This, coupled with the recovery of membership, and a still potent capacity for organization, underpinned the continuing influence of the CP, and the continuing antipathy of its active opponents.

Table 6.1 Communist union membership in various industries, 1945–62

	1945	1955	1957[a]	1960[b]	1962
Building	1,409	2,055	1,379	1,707	2,065
Clerical	1,486	1,668	1,224	1,197	1,525
Clothing	n.a.	691	596	507	590
Distribution	1,223	860	660	682	777
Engineering	13,578	4,721	2,504	3,905	4,786
Iron & steel	1,152	526	165	276	323
Mining	2,864	1,683	1,109	1,724	1,695
Printing	n.a.	457	362	534	445
Teachers & professional	1,633	1,585	1,032	1,109	1,294
Postal	n.a.	131	117	200	259
Textiles	733	286	166	248	265
Transport	4,354	1,803	996	1,518	1,710
Foundries	n.a.	178	46	124	130
Housewives[c]	5,677	6,256	3,741	5,353	6,325
Total registered membership	45,285	32,681	18,266	25,772	30,129
Total membership in unions	31,731	18,509	n.a.	n.a.	17,928

Sources: NMLH, CP/CENT/ORG/19/1–2, CP Organization Department membership analysis, 1944–62.
Notes:
a Figures for Midlands, Scottish and Sussex districts are unavailable for 1957.
b figures for Hampshire and Dorset district are unavailable for 1960.
c In addition to 'housewives', the other main sections of non-union members were students, self-employed and retired people.

Table 6.2 Workplace organization in the London District of the CP, 1952–8

	Number of workplace branches and groups	Membership of such branches and groups	Total district membership	Percentage of members in workplace organizations
June 1952	196	1,605	n/a	n/a
Aug. 1953	170	1,437	9,819[a]	14.6
July 1954	145	1,183	n/a	n/a
Feb. 1955	152	1,251	8,255	15.2
April 1956	150	1,241	8,234[b]	15.0
March 1957	125	862	7,225	11.9
Nov. 1958	105	716	6,248	11.5

Sources: NMLH, CP/CENT/ORG/19/5 and CP/LON/MEMB/1/6, CP London District membership and factory organization analyses, 1952–9.
Notes:
a. Figure given is for June 1953.
b. The number of workplace branches/groups includes those listed by the CP which had less than three members.

Notes

I wish to thank the editors for their advice, particularly Alan Campbell and John McIlroy for drawing my attention to a number of sources; Dave Turner for the Parsons and Hudson theses (see note 24); all correspondents and interviewees for their co-operation, and particularly Fred Westacott and Bill Moore for their hospitality and access to their documents.

1. N. Fishman, *The British Communist Party and the Trade Unions, 1933–45* (Aldershot, 1995), particularly chs 5–6, 8, 12; N. Branson, *History of the Communist Party of Great Britain, 1941–51* (1997), pp. 26–37, 252.
2. National Museum of Labour History, Manchester (hereafter NMLH), CP Archives, CP/CENT/ORG/19/1, CP Organization Department, membership analysis, 1944–59; D. and G. Butler, *British Political Facts, 1900–1985* (6th edition, 1986), p. 372.
3. TUC *Reports*, 1948–50, 1959–60; Labour Party Annual Conference *Reports*, 1959–60; W. Thompson, *The Good Old Cause: British Communism, 1920–91* (1992), pp. 116–18.
4. Modern Records Centre, University of Warwick (hereafter MRC), MSS 292/79C/24, Chesterfield Trades Council file, 1925–60; 292/79N/22, Nottingham Trades Council file, 1925–60; MSS 126/T&G/1/1/27, TGWU National Executive Committee minutes, 1949; CP Archive, London, unclassified, now in NMLH, CP Papers relating to London Trades Council, 1950–53; TUC Library, London, Harvester Microform, now in University of North London, TUC Trades Councils Joint Consultative Committee minutes, 1950–53; Scottish TUC *Annual Reports*, 1951–53; TUC *Reports*, 1948–53; Branson, *History of the CPGB*, pp.160–71, 177–8, 183–7. S. Parsons, 'British Communist Party school teachers in the 1940s and 1950s', *Science and Society*, 61, 1, 1997, p. 48; W. Roy, *The Teachers' Union* (1968), pp. 107–11, 122–5; A. Fox, *A History of the National Union of Boot and Shoe Operatives, 1874–1957* (Oxford, 1958), pp. 466–71; H. A. Clegg, *General Union* (Oxford, 1954), pp. 118–21, 340; interviews with Fred Westacott, Chesterfield, 12 August 1991, Bas Barker, Chesterfield, 9 December 1991, and Derek Robinson, Birmingham, 1 December 1997, tapes in author's possession; correspondence with Noreen Branson, 3 June 1996.
5. MRC, MSS 292/770/4–5, TUC files on Communism, 1936–50.
6. Public Records Office, London (hereafter PRO), FO.1110/98–99, Information Research Department (IRD) files, 1948; MRC, MSS 292/770/5–6, 292/777.5/1, TUC files on Communism, 1944–62; R. Ramsay, 'The clandestine caucus', *Lobster*, June 1996, p.7.
7. For example, Bill Carron, President of the AEU 1956–67, claimed in an interview published in the *Daily Mail*, 27 February 1962, that 'I have always asked for Divine guidance', in union affairs. Carron did not, however, associate with ACTU. For a discussion of Catholic trade unionism, see J.E. Keating, 'Roman Catholics, Christian Democracy and the British labour move-

ment, 1910–60', unpublished PhD thesis, University of Manchester, 1992, particularly ch. 9.

8. MRC, MSS 292/770.2/3, 6; 292B/759/6, 9, TUC files on Communism, 1952–70; Ramsay, 'Caucus', pp. 7–11, 25; J.D. Edelstein and M. Warner, *Comparative Union Democracy* (1975), pp. 281–4; I. Richter, *Political Purpose in Trade Unions* (1973), pp. 144–5, 160–1.

9. The 'Club' in the AEU may have been first formed in 1943 or 1944 (MRC, MSS 292/770/5–7; 292/770.2/3, 6; 292/777.5/1; 292B/759/6, 9, 11, TUC files on Communism, 1944–70); interviews with Frances Dean, Salford, 19 May 1997, Laurie Nickolay, Nottingham, 31 January and 23 February 1997, Edmund and Ruth Frow, Salford, 9 April 1997, tapes in author's possession; correspondence with Ron Halverson, 7 December 1997; Ramsay, 'Caucus', pp. 7, 11; E. Roberts, *Strike Back* (Orpington, 1994), pp. 122–36; E. Wigham, *What's Wrong With The Unions?* (Harmondsworth, 1961), pp. 127–8; Edelstein and Warner, *Union Democracy*, p. 247.

10. MRC, MSS 292/770/4–7; 292/770.2/3, 5–6; 292/777.5/1; 292B/759/6–14, TUC files on Communism, 1936–70. See also the trades councils files (MSS 292/79/A–Y), and R. Stevens, 'Containing radicalism: the TUC organization department and trades councils, 1928–53', *Labour History Review* (hereafter *LHR*), 62, 1, 1997, pp. 5–21; PRO, FO.1110/11, 32, 98–99, 213, 261, IRD files, 1948–49; A. Carew, *Labour under the Marshall Plan* (Manchester, 1987), pp. 127–30. For the IRD, see also W.S. Lucas and C.J. Morris, 'A very British crusade: the IRD and the beginning of the Cold War', in R.J. Aldrich (ed.), *British Intelligence, Strategy and the Cold War*, 1992, pp. 85–110.

11. MRC, MSS 292/770/4–7; 292/770.2/5; 292/777.5/1; 292B/759/7–8, TUC files on Communism, 1936–66; A. J. Taylor, 'The Conservative trade union movement, 1952–61, *LHR*, 57, 1, 1992, pp. 21–8; A. Crawley, *The Hidden Face of British Communism* (1962); W. Wyatt, *The Peril In Our Midst* (1956); Ramsay, 'Caucus', p. 25; S. Milne, *The Enemy Within* (1994), pp. 283–4; interview with Martin Ashworth, Sheffield, 8 July 1997.

12. Correspondence with Lord Murray, 5 August 1997. For many of Feather's activities, see the TUC files at MRC listed in note 8; see also, PRO, FO.1110/261, IRD file, 1949. Deakin is discussed in some detail by V. L. Allen, *Trade Union Leadership: based on a study of Arthur Deakin* (1957), particularly pp. 270–88.

13. MRC, MSS 292/770/5–6, TUC files, 1944–57; H. Reid, *The Furniture Makers* (Oxford, 1986), pp. 169–71; correspondence with Jack Moss, 16 October 1997, and Jack Jones, 1 June 1997; interviews with George Bromley, Leicester, 24 June 1992, and Harry Thompson, Leicester, 17 March 1992.

14. NMLH, CP/CENT/EC/02/1, CP Executive Committee (EC) minutes 14–15 October 1950; CP/LON/BRA/1/4, 8, North West London Area (NWLA) CP industrial papers, 1945–52, and Hendon Borough CP papers, 1949; CP/LON/BRA/2/2, 4, Duples CP factory branch papers, c.1948–c.1952, and NWLA CP factory branch and industrial papers, 1949–59; interviews with Derek Robinson, 1 December 1997, and Len Squires, Nottingham, 23 October 1991;

R.A. Leeson, *Strike: a live history* (1973), pp. 192–5.

15. *Reports* of the CP EC to the 18th–29th Congresses, 1945–65; *Reports* of the 18th–29th CP Congresses; *Memorandum of the [CP] EC on Party Organization*, March 1945; *Report of the [CP] Organization Commission to the EC*, September 1946; NMLH, CP/CENT/IND/1/1–3, CP Industrial Department factory and industrial papers, reports and leaflets, 1950–69; CP/CENT/IND/10/4–5, 7–8, CP Industrial Department papers relating to building 1945–48, agriculture c.1953–c.1963, CP National Industrial Conferences 1946–47, 'A Militant Wages Policy', 1962; CP/CENT/IND/Unclassified, CP 'Needs of the Hour', 1963–64, 1969, Bert Ramelson Papers, 1952–65; CP/IND/MATT/4/4–6, George Matthews Papers, 1949–56; CP/IND/HANN/7/5, Wal Hannington Papers, 1942–58; CP/LON/ADVI/12/4, London District CP Labour Movement Committee reports, 1957–59; CP/LON/BRA/1/4 and 3/9, NWLA CP industrial papers, 1945–52, and NWLA CP factory branch and industrial papers, 1952–59; CP/LON/IND/1/3, London District CP industrial papers, 1949–65; F. Westacott, Chesterfield, 'East Midlands District [CP] Bulletin', 1946–49, 1953, 1954, 1956–64; MRC, MSS 202/CP/40–42, 52, 57, 60, 62, 66, Dick Etheridge Papers, 1943–66.

16. NMLH, CP/CENT/IND/Unclassified, Ramelson Papers, 1952–65; CP/CENT/ORG/19/5, London District CP membership reports and analysis, 1952–59; CP/LON/BRA/2/4; 3/9; 4/1, NWLA CP factory papers, 1949–59, 'Edgware Road Project' 1952–55; CP/LON/MEMB/1/6, London District CP membership file, 1953–56; B. Moore, Sheffield, Papers relating to CP campaign in Yorkshire woollen textile industry, 1950–55; correspondence with Reuben Falber, 7 June 1997, and Stan Davison, 25 June 1997; interviews with Fred Westacott, Chesterfield, 11 February 1997 and Derek Robinson, 1 December 1997.

17. NMLH, CP/LON/IND/1/4, 7, CP papers relating to AEU elections, 1959–61.

18. Correspondence with George Matthews, 23 May 1997, Reuben Falber, 7 June 1997, Noreen Branson, 3 June 1996, Stan Davison, 25 June 1997, Jack Moss, 16 October 1997, George Barnsby, 1 January 1998.

19. MRC, 292/770.2/3, *Common Cause Bulletin*, July 1956. However, it is notable that a survey of three AEU Nottingham branches from the late 1940s to the mid-1960s reveals no set pattern (Nottinghamshire Archives Office, hereafter NAO, DDTU/16/3/2–5, 16/4/1–3, 16/8/2–8, AEU Nottingham Numbers 1, 5 and 11 Branches minutes, 1945–69, 1953–67, 1945–68 respectively). See also, for example, Edelstein and Warner, *Union Democracy*, pp. 274–9, regarding the AEU, and J. Goldstein, *The Government of British Trade Unions* (1952), particularly chs 1, 4, 7, 10, 14–19, regarding the TGWU.

20. PRO, FO.1110/32, IRD file, 1948; NMLH, CP/CENT/ORG/19/1–2, 5, CP membership analysis, 1944–62; D. and G. Butler, *Political Facts*, p. 367. Note the comments by Wigham, *What's Wrong With The Unions?*, p. 129.

21. F. Watters, *Being Frank* (Barnsley, 1992), pp. 13–27, 35–40; J. Kane, *No Wonder We Were Rebels* (Doncaster, 1994), pp. 42–64, 83, 88–90, 93; Edelstein and Warner, *Union Democracy*, ch. 8; P. Kahn, 'An interview with

Frank Watters', *Bulletin of the Society for the Study of Labour History* (hereafter *BSSLH*), 43, Autumn 1981, pp. 57–61; interviews with Frank Watters, Barnsley, 6 May 1997, Martin Ashworth, 8 July 1997, Fred Westacott, Chesterfield, 17 December 1996, and Bill Moore, Sheffield, 3 February and 6 May 1997.

22.   NMLH, CP/LON/BRA/3/9, NWLA CP cadres meeting, hand-written notes, 12 January 1953.

23.   *Reports* of the 25th and 26th CP Congresses, 1957 and 1959; NMLH, CP/CENT/ORG/19/01, CP Organization Department, 'Notes on Examination of 1957/8 Industrial Analysis compared with 1955/6'. See also, S. R. Parsons, '1956 and the Communist Party of Great Britain', *BSSLH*, Vol. 47, Autumn, 1983, pp. 9–10, and his unpublished MA thesis, 'Crisis in the British Communist Party: the impact of the events of 1956 on the membership, with particular reference to trade unionists', University of Warwick, 1981; and K. J. Hudson, 'The double blow: 1956 and the Communist Party of Great Britain', unpublished PhD thesis, University of London, 1992.

24.   Parsons, thesis, pp. 136–41, and '1956', pp. 9–10; L. Daly, 'The Fife Socialist League', in D. Widgery, *The Left in Britain, 1956–68* (Harmondsworth, 1976), pp. 86–9; C. Thornton and W. Thompson, 'Scottish Communists, 1956–57', *Science and Society*, 61, 1, 1997, pp. 68–93; Watters, *Being Frank*, pp. 17–18; O. Cannon and J.R.L. Anderson, *The Road from Wigan Pier: a biography of Les Cannon* (1973), pp. 129–30; Edelstein and Warner, *Union Democracy*, pp. 246–8; Thompson, *Good Old Cause*, pp. 101, 105; H. Pelling, *The British Communist Party: a historical profile* (2nd edition, 1975), p. 174; interview with Leo Keely, Nottingham, 19 May 1992.

25.   TUC *Reports*, 1954–58; H. J. Fyrth and H. Collins, *The Foundry Workers: a trade union history* (Manchester, 1959), pp. 310–17; Amalgamated Union of Foundry Workers, *Annual Reports*, 1956–57.

26.   Parsons, thesis, pp. 137, 141.

27.   NMLH, CP/CENT/ORG/19/1–2, CP membership analysis, 1944–62.

28.   This assessment is based on opinions expressed in some 80–90 interviews and correspondence conducted by the author with both Communist and non-Communist former activists between 1991 and 1997.

29.   See R. Stevens, 'Trades Councils in the East Midlands, 1929–51: trade unionism and politics in a "traditionally moderate" area', unpublished PhD thesis, University of Nottingham, 1995, ch. 2, for a discussion of factors underpinning high levels of activism, and the importance of political commitment therein.

30.   *Report* of the 25th CP Congress, 1957. However, Willie Thompson is highly critical, and Kate Hudson has stated that 'the real tragedy of 1956, was that it was a wasted opportunity' for internal change (Thompson, *Good Old Cause*, pp. 99–113; Hudson, thesis, p. 8).

31.   *Report* of 26th CP Congress, 1959; NMLH, CP/CENT/IND/1/2, CP papers relating to factory organization, 1958; correspondence with Ken Gill, 25 August 1997.

32.   Interviews with Fred Westacott, 11 February 1997, Bill Moore, 3 February

1997, Martin Ashworth, 8 July 1997, Frank Watters, 6 May 1997, and Barry Johnson, 15 May 1997, Nottingham; telephone conversation with Ida Hackett, Mansfield, 20 August 1997; F. Westacott, Chesterfield, East Midlands District [CP] Bulletin, 1956–64. See, however, the comments of Watters in *Being Frank*, pp. 17–19, and in Kahn, 'Frank Watters', pp. 58–60; see also, Kahn's 'An interview With Tom Mullaney', *BSSLH*, 44, Spring 1982, p. 54, and V.L. Allen, *The Militancy of British Miners*, 1981, pp. 6, 119, 126–7.

33. Correspondence with Jack Jones, 1 June 1997; NMLH, CP/CENT/IND/Unclassified, Bill Jones Papers, c.1947–68; TUC *Reports*, 1955–9; interview with Leo Keely, 19 May 1992; Parsons, thesis, pp. 134–6, 140–1; Leeson, *Strike*, pp. 190–2. Ken Fuller, on the other hand, claims that Communist influence among London busworkers was declining throughout the 1950s (K. Fuller, *Radical Aristocrats: London busworkers from the 1880s to the 1980s*, 1985, pp. 221–2).

34. MRC, MSS 292/79N/22, Nottingham Trades Council (NTC) file, 1955–60; 292/79M/10, Mansfield Trades Council (MTC) file, 1955–60; Nottingham Local Studies Library, NTC *Annual Reports*, 1955–59; Mansfield Unemployed Workers Centre, MTC Minutes, 1956–57, MTC *Annual Reports*, 1955–58; interviews with Harry Loach, Nottingham, 19 March 1991, John Hose, Nottingham, 3 June 1991, Fred Harris, Nottingham, 24 June 1991, Lionel Jacobs, Nottingham, 12 July 1991, Ida Hackett, Mansfield, 14 November 1991, Fred Westacott, 12 August 1991 and 16 March 1993, Barry Johnson, Chesterfield, 16 March 1993 and 15 May 1997, Frank Ellis, Hucknall, 5 August 1991 and 13 October 1997, Alan Griffin, Clipstone, 16 December 1991, Bernard Savage, Blidworth, 9 and 17 June 1992; correspondence with Don Devine, 14 March 1993; *Nottingham Evening Post*, 6 March 1964; *Sheffield Telegraph*, 17 November 1958; NMLH, CP/CENT/IND/Unclassified, Ramelson Papers, 1956–73; CP/CENT/ORG/19/1–2, CP membership analysis, 1944–62; F. Westacott, Chesterfield, Fred Westacott Papers, 1948–70.

35. MRC, MSS 202/A/1/2/3–4, AEU Number 16 Divisional Committee minutes, 1955–59; 202/CP/40–41, 60, 62, 66, Etheridge Papers, 1947–63; NMLH, CP/CENT/IND/Unclassified, Ramelson Papers, 1959–60; CP/LON/IND/1/3, London District CP papers relating to the motor industry, 1956–57; AEU National Committee *Reports*, 1955–62; *Men and Motors*, 1959; correspondence with Lorna Warman, 1 August 1997, Ken Gill, 25 August 1997, and George Jelf, 4 February 1998; interview with Derek Robinson, 1 December 1997; G. Wootton, 'Parties in union government: the AESD', *Political Studies*, 9, 2, 1961, pp. 141–56; Leeson, *Strike*, pp. 196–204.

36. MRC, MSS 292/79B/36–8, Birmingham Trades Council files, 1944–60; 202/5/30–31, Etheridge Papers, 1953–59; Birmingham Trades Council *Annual Report*, 1953–54; correspondence with Bill Alexander, 30 June, 2, 11 July 1997; interviews with Frank Watters, 6 May 1997, and Derek Robinson, 1 December 1997.

37. AEU National Committee *Reports*, 1955–61; interview with Edmund and Ruth Frow, 9 April 1997; 'Interview with Bob Wright', *Marxism Today*, Sep-

tember 1978.

38. NMLH, CP/IND/HANN/7/4, Hannington Papers, 1958; MRC, 292/770.2/6, *IRIS Newsletter*, 31 May 1957.

39. B. Moore, Sheffield, AEU Sheffield DC minutes, 1945–57. It was claimed that there were 15 Communists and fellow-travellers against 10 non-Communists on the 25-member DC at the end of 1956; and at the end of 1957, 18 to 7 (*Daily Telegraph*, 30 December 1957). Interviews with Bill Moore, Sheffield, 17 June 1996 and 3 February 1997; *Sheffield Star*, 4 March 1952.

40. B. Moore, Sheffield, AEU Sheffield DC minutes, 1945–61; AEU Number 13 Divisional Committee minutes, 1955–61; AEU National Committee *Reports*, 1955–62; interviews with Bas Barker, 9 December 1991, Bill Moore, 3 February 1997, and Fred Westacott, 11 February 1997.

41. NMLH, CP/CENT/IND/Unclassified, Ramelson Papers, letter, Kerrigan to Ramelson, 17 December 1957; B. Moore, Sheffield, AEU Sheffield DC minutes 1956–7; interview with Bill Moore, 3 February 1997; *Sheffield Star*, 5–6 April, 6–17 December 1957; *Sheffield Telegraph*, 14 September and 12 October 1956; *Daily Worker*, 13 December 1957; *Daily Mail*, 6 April 1957; *Daily Express*, 6 April 1957; *Sunday Dispatch*, 7 April 1957.

42. *Catholic Herald*, 31 December 1957; *Daily Telegraph*, 30 December 1957, 27 October, 17 November 1958, 1 October 1963; *Daily Worker*, 16–31 December 1957, 12 March, 20–2 November 1958; *Empire News*, 5 January 1958; *Sheffield Star*, 24–31 December 1957, 17 January, 5 February, 10 March, 14 April, 29 May, 22–6 September, 27–8 October, 7–17 November 1958, 13 March 1959, 13 June 1960; *Sheffield Telegraph*, 18 January and 17 November 1958; B. Moore, Sheffield, AEU Sheffield DC minutes, 1957–62; AEU Number 13 Divisional Committee minutes, 1957–62; AEU National Committee *Reports* 1958–62; NMLH, CP/CENT/IND/Unclassified, Ramelson Papers, 1957–63.

43. Interview with Bill Moore, 3 February 1997. See also the comment by a Coventry CP activist: 'To be effective, trade unionism, which is the workers' basic weapon in their struggle, must be militant, immediate and democratic' ('The convenor', *New Left Review*, 48, March–April 1968, p. 29).

44. NMLH, CP/CENT/ORG/19/1, CP membership analysis, 1944–59; Nottingham University Library, Tw1/1/1–128, TWU Nottingham DC minutes, 1948, 1952; Tw1/2/1–57, TWU Nottingham Numbers 1–3, 5–6 Branches, and Shop Stewards minutes, 1948; Tw1/7/1–98, TWU EC minutes, reports, correspondence, and miscellaneous papers, 1941–9; Tw1/14/15–19 and Tw1/15/4–8, TWU EC minutes, 1955–6 and 1957–8; Tw6/19/4/1–19, TWU District Organizers' Meetings minutes, 1950; TWU *Annual Reports*, 1946, 1949–51; TWU Annual Delegate Meeting *Reports*, 1948–9, 1956; TUC, *Reports*, 1945–56; *Nottingham Journal*, 14, 21 September 1950; interview with Len Squires, 23 October 1991.

45. MRC, 292/770.2/3, 5–6; 292/777.5/1; 292B/759/6, 9, TUC files on Communism, 1927–70; B. Moore, Sheffield, AEU Sheffield DC minutes, 1956–62; NAO, DDTU/16/4/1–2, AEU Nottingham Number 5 Branch minutes, 1956–

64; TUC, *Report*, 1960, pp. 485–6, 509.

46. Allen, *British Miners*, p. 119; Edelstein and Warner, *Union Democracy*, pp. 220, 226–7; interviews with Frank Ellis, 13 October 1997, Fred Westacott, Chesterfield, 28 October 1997 and Frank Watters, 6 May 1997; correspondence with Frank Ellis, 15 April 1998, and Frank Watters, 7 May 1998; telephone conversation with Fred Westacott, 5 April 1998.

47. H. Beynon, *Working For Ford* (Harmondsworth, 2nd edition, 1984), pp. 60–72, 82–3; Thompson, *Good Old Cause*, p. 128; interviews with Laurie Nickolay, 23 February 1997, and Vernon Mock, Nottingham, 31 January 1997, tape in author's possession.

48. NMLH, CP/CENT/IND/1/5, CP Industrial Department file relating to the ETU, 1943–61; J. Lloyd, *Light and Liberty: the history of the Electrical, Electronic, Telecommunication and Plumbing Union* (1990), chs 18–21; Cannon and Anderson, *Wigan Pier*, pp. 129–263; Thompson, *Good Old Cause*, pp. 125–8. See also, C.H. Rolph, *All Those In Favour?* (1962), and R. Bean, 'Militancy, policy formation and membership opposition in the Electrical Trades Union, 1945–61', *Political Quarterly*, 36, 1965, pp. 181–90.

CHAPTER SEVEN

Social Democracy and Anti-Communism: Allan Flanders and British Industrial Relations in the Early Post-war Period

John Kelly

In June 1968 the Royal Commission on Trade Unions and Employers' Associations (the Donovan Commission) published its famous report advocating the voluntary reform of collective bargaining. The major problems identified in the report – wage drift, 'restrictive practices' and unofficial strikes – were said to require far-reaching changes in the organization and policies of both management and unions.[1] The Commissioners sat for three years and received over 450 submissions. But according to Lord McCarthy, Allan Flanders' essay *Collective Bargaining: prescription for change* was 'the only written evidence that made a significant impact on their thinking'.[2] As well as influencing the Donovan Commission, Flanders also worked for several public agencies that played a central role in the design, implementation and evaluation of state industrial relations policies in the 1960s, notably the National Board for Prices and Incomes (NBPI) and the Commission on Industrial Relations (CIR). Indeed Flanders' rise to prominence as an academic was largely the result of his policy-oriented writings of the 1960s, many of which were brought together in the influential and widely read collection *Management and Unions* (1970).[3]

Hugh Clegg's Introduction to *Management and Unions* conveys the impression that many of Flanders' insights into British industrial relations emerged from his study of the Fawley refinery: 'Nearly all these essays explore the wider implications of the Fawley study for theory and for reform'.[4] In fact I shall argue that the main features of Flanders' industrial relations views were actually formed over twenty years earlier. The main themes of the 1964 *Fawley Productivity Agreements* were all set out in the chapter subheadings of Flanders' 1941 pamphlet *The Battle for Production*: 'Payment by results', 'Increased earnings and inflation', 'The responsibility of management', 'Workshop autocracy' and 'The folly of excessive overtime'. Moreover his appraisal of British industrial relations was heavily influenced by his political philosophy, a highly distinctive variety of anti-Marxist, anti-Communist, ethical socialism. That Flanders was a long-standing political activist is clear from just two facts: from 1933 until 1949 he was the leading intellectual force in the tiny Socialist Vanguard Group, whilst from 1942 until 1973 he was variously editor and joint editor of *Socialist Commentary*, the principal voice of right-wing social democracy in Britain in the post-war period.[5] The final argument of the chapter is that Flanders' role in the construction of industrial relations as a field of study in the 1940s and 1950s was inextricably bound up with his own contribution to, and participation in, the social democratic struggle against Communism. In the face of Communist-backed unofficial strikes and wage militancy from the late 1940s onwards, Flanders asserted the case for 'responsible' collective bargaining and wage restraint with strikes as a weapon of last resort. As Hyman observed in the mid-1970s, the problems of order and stability therefore loomed large in this influential approach to the subject.[6]

The chapter begins by tracing the origins and implications of Flanders' work, locating it in the political context of the earlier part of this century. The first section describes the Internationaler Sozialistischer Kampfbund (ISK), the political organization in which Flanders acquired his world outlook. Section 2 examines Flanders' political writings in the 1930s to establish the continuing influence of the ISK over his thinking. Section 3 explores the shifts in his political views during the Second World War and the Cold War, and Section 4 traces the consequences for his ideas about unions and industrial relations.

Flanders' political formation: the Internationaler Sozialistischer Kampfbund (ISK)[7]

Flanders was born in 1910, the only child of a shop manager, and attended a grammar school until the age of sixteen. After leaving school in 1926, he became involved in the rationalist and free-thinking circles in London. It was at one of their meetings in 1928 that he encountered Gerard Kumleben, a recruiting agent for the German socialist organization the ISK.[8] After a short period of activity in the British section, Flanders was persuaded by Kumleben to spend the next three years at the 'Walkemuhle', the group's cadre training school in Germany.[9] He began there in July 1929 and joined the ISK in December 1930 during an intensive three-year education in politics, economics and philosophy (as well as other subjects, such as the use of firearms!). He returned to Britain in 1933 as effective head of the British section of the ISK. The group's main activity was the publication of a regular journal, edited by Flanders, initially (and grandiosely) called the *Vanguard* (January 1934–April 1936) before its name was altered first to *Socialist Vanguard* (June 1936 –June 1940) then to the bland *Commentary* (July 1940–October 1941) before ending up as the more familiar *Socialist Commentary* (from October 1941).

The ISK began life as a faction of the German Social Democratic Party in

1918 but was expelled in December 1925. A month later the group transformed itself into an independent political organization. It began illegal underground work in 1933 and survived until 1946, when it was dissolved by its German leadership, then anxious to return to the Social Democrats. The British section lingered on for another few years before being wound up in 1949. The ISK was a tiny organization, even by the standards of the political left. At its peak in the early 1930s, total membership in Germany was no more than about 300 people with a periphery of around a thousand sympathizers.[10] In Britain its highest recorded membership figure (achieved in 1949) was just 26![11] One reason for taking such an organization seriously is that its members continued to exert a significant influence in the labour movement even after the group's demise. For instance in 1959 at the famous Bad Godesborg congress of the German Social Democrats, the party agreed to a radical revision of its programme, purging it of all traces of Marxism. The commission which drafted the new programme was chaired by Willi Eichler, leader of the ISK from 1927 until its dissolution.[12]

Like other small sects, the ISK was dominated by the charismatic figure of its founder, the German philosopher Leonard Nelson. It is to Nelson's own world view that we must turn in order to shed light on Flanders' political development.[13] Nelson was an ethical socialist, part of a current of left-wing opinion which took issue with Marxist historical materialism.[14] According to Nelson, Marxists were committed to the view that the material interests of the working-class would inevitably lead its members to develop a revolutionary class consciousness and to participate in the struggle for socialism.[15] Both the existence of the class struggle and its successful conclusion were for Marxists the inevitable products of the capitalist system of production. The ultimate goal of revolutionary struggle was the abolition of private ownership in the means of production and its supersession by state or collective ownership, as in the Soviet Union.

Nelson disagreed profoundly with this rather bastardized version of Marxist theory. Material interest alone, he thought, was insufficient to overcome the problem of free-riding. An additional source of motivation had to be present to help workers bear the costs of political struggle, and Nelson believed he had found it in the ethical commitment to a just society. How did workers acquire this conviction, if not through their direct experience of exploitation? For Nelson, it was through reason and debate that people would be brought to see the case for socialism. This commitment to reason meant that Nelson was deeply hostile to any form of dogmatism and part of the ISK's developing critique of the world Communist movement focused on the growth of what it saw as a rigid orthodoxy, with the associated tendency to label dissent as counter-revolutionary treason (as in the Moscow Trials of 1936–9).[16] Despite their emphasis on reason and discussion, Nelson and his followers were deeply hostile to democracy: 'Democracy is not the great arena from which the best men come forth as victors. It is the fool's stage on which the most crafty or best-paid chatterbox gets the better of the nobility of character which relies only upon the goodness of the cause'.[17] The leaders of the ISK were never elected but 'emerged' out of informal discussion amongst the party elite.[18]

In terms of party programme, the ISK was heavily involved in the struggle against Nazism, but if its anti-fascism was conventional on the left, its economic programme definitely was not and departed radically from current orthodoxy. Marxist political economy held that the root of labour's exploitation by capital lay in the private ownership of the means of production. Consequently the essence of socialist economic policy was to expropriate the capitalist class and replace private with public ownership. The structure of the Soviet economy convinced many socialists that the most appropriate instrument of public ownership was the state. By contrast, Nelson and the ISK were heavily influenced by the writings of a German economist, Franz Oppenheimer, who took a very different view.[19] For Oppenheimer it was not private ownership *per se*, but monopoly, that generated inequality, and the break up of monopoly ownership was, therefore, a key part of the ISK programme. It would be some years before the full implications of this line of argument would be worked through, at first in a critique of the USSR as an unjust system of state monopoly power, and later in relation to the nationalization proposals of social democrats in the capitalist democracies.

In broad terms the ISK can therefore be characterized as anti-Marxist (because of its ethical distaste for materialist philosophy), anti-Soviet (because the USSR represented another form of monopoly power), anti-Communist (because Communist parties were Marxist and pro-Soviet), but also anti-social democrat (because social democracy was regarded as insufficiently committed to revolutionary struggle against capitalism). The caveat 'in broad terms' is important for a number of reasons. Despite the hostility to historical materialism, the publications of the ISK routinely deployed Marxist categories, such as exploitation, revolution and class struggle and it would therefore be misleading to describe the group as anti-Marxist *tout court*. Again, whilst the group was highly critical of the policies of the world's Communist parties, its own organization shared the elite and centralised character of the Leninist vanguard party (whilst lacking the internal democracy). It is perhaps worth adding, in less serious vein, that the ISK maintained very strict controls over recruitment and over the behaviour of its members. Potential recruits had to serve six months' probationary membership and their application had to be supported in writing by at least two existing members. They also had to agree to become vegetarians and to undertake a mandatory visit to an abattoir to drive home the evils of eating meat! Alcohol was strictly forbidden and marital and sexual relations amongst members were discouraged as distractions from the revolutionary cause.[20] The stringent, puritanical character of these rules (many of which were relaxed over the 1930s and 1940s) goes some way to explaining why the ISK recruited so few people.

195

Flanders and the British Section of the ISK in the 1930s

We know that Flanders spent three years being trained in the ISK school in Germany, but once he returned to Britain in 1933 did he remain faithful to the 'teachings' of Nelson? One way of addressing this question is to scrutinise the journal published by the British section of the ISK (or the MSI, Militant Socialist International, to use the British acronym). Flanders was both editor of the group's journal, which began in 1934 as a quarterly and from June 1936 went monthly, as well as a prolific contributor. From January 1934 until the outbreak of war in September 1939, he wrote a total of thirty-six articles and reviews, as well as five articles for the ISK's German-language journal *Sozialistische Warte* and an MSI pamphlet on the Churches' support for fascism.[21] Many of the core themes of the ISK recur in Flanders' writings in this period. There is first of all the hostility to both social democracy and Communism, though given the smaller size and influence of the British Communist Party (CP) compared to its German counterpart before 1933, it was social democracy that bore the brunt of Flanders' attacks.[22] As late as September 1937, at the height of agitation for a Popular Front of all left and progressive forces to combat fascism, he wrote that it was 'futile' to try and transform the Labour Party into a vehicle for socialism.[23] By contrast hostility to the CP and to the Soviet Union was muted. Writing about the 1937 busmen's strike, controversially timed to coincide with the Coronation of King George VI, Flanders was at pains to downplay the idea of its being a Communist conspiracy despite the fact that it was led by CP members.[24]

Given the pervasive influence of social democracy and the weakness of the British section of the ISK, it is not surprising to find that Flanders was an ardent advocate of trade union militancy. For instance, in August 1938 he criticized the idea that unions should tackle unemployment by working for a Labour government. On the contrary he argued, unions should go on strike and force the government to act.[25] In May 1939 he argued that May Day should be the occasion for stoppages not a day of rest.[26] And he complained bitterly (in 1937) about the union leaderships' policy of industrial peace 'which had been steadily ruining British trade unionism'.[27] Finally, Flanders also adhered to the anti-democratic sentiments of the ISK. Writing about events in the USSR, he complained about the state terror, but attributed the problems of the Soviet regime to a surfeit of democracy, not a deficit![28] What is also interesting in the light of Flanders' later evolution is how little he wrote about industrial relations throughout the whole of the 1930s. It was the big issues of international politics – war, peace and fascism – that dominated his work at this time.

From revolutionary socialism to right-wing social democracy

During the early 1940s the Socialist Vanguard Group (the name was officially adopted in June 1941) radically transformed itself into a small, though significant component of the right wing of the British labour movement through its journal, *Socialist Commentary*, and latterly through the 'think tank' Socialist Union founded in 1951.[29] Its leading members, including Flanders, became active in the hitherto despised Labour Party and in the Fabian Society and the group found itself increasingly in opposition to the 'traditional' Labour left. Flanders' political outlook shifted in two phases, spanning less than ten years, from revolutionary socialism to right-wing social democracy. The first phase was triggered by the outbreak of the Second World War, whilst the second was stimulated by the onset of the Cold War and the consequent intensification of the ongoing struggle between social democracy and Communism. How exactly did these dramatic changes come about? Why did they happen? And what were the implications for Flanders' thinking about industrial relations?

Into the orbit of social democracy

It was the émigré leadership of the ISK under Willi Eichler that began to create more cordial relations with the social democratic movement from which the group had been expelled sixteen years earlier. In the wake of the Nazi-Soviet pact and 'under the influence of indigenous Labour Socialism', Eichler, then resident in Britain, entered negotiations with the German Social Democratic Executive in exile and in March 1941, along with three other organizations, created the Union of German Socialist Organizations in Britain (UGSOB). Just four years later Eichler completed his return to the social democratic fold, taking the UGSOB (including the ISK) back into the Social Democratic Party.[30] Flanders and the SVG quickly followed the same trajectory, and the group's 'National Letter' of February 1941 called on its members to affiliate to local Labour Parties, where practicable.[31] In February 1942 Flanders became Secretary of the Sheffield Branch of the Fabian Society and in August of that year lectured at the Fabian Summer School. By March 1945 he had been elected to the Fabian's Socialist Propaganda Committee and to the International Committee, serving on both bodies until 1946. [32] Through these committees he met with many of the leading figures of the contemporary labour movement, including Denis Healey (Labour Party International Secretary from January 1946 and the man who recommended Flanders for work with the British Control Commission in Germany), Jim Callaghan, Richard Crossman, James Griffiths and Rita Hinden (Head of the Fabian Colonial Research Bureau from 1940 until 1950 when she joined *Socialist Commentary* as a full-time editor).[33]

·What drove the growing rapprochement with social democracy was the

197

way in which international events were understood by members of the British group and the conclusions they drew from them. First came the trial in 1939 of the last remaining ISK activists in Germany. Although the ISK had been relatively well-equipped for the transition to illegal, underground work after 1933 because of its disciplined character and small-cell structure, its ranks had none the less been seriously depleted by Nazi terror, and the trial signalled the end of the ISK in Germany, at least for the foreseeable future.[34] When the Nazi-Soviet Pact was signed in August of the same year, it was branded a 'betrayal' which meant that the USSR must now 'forfeit any claim to working class loyalty'.[35] From this point on the anti-Sovietism of both the ISK and the SVG became markedly more pronounced. But so too did its sense of isolation in a hostile world.[36] Although the tiny British section of the ISK could publish a monthly journal with a circulation of nearly 2,000 and could attract up to 100 people to public meetings, it had signally failed to build up its organization or to make any impact on the political scene when compared with its main left-wing rival, the CP.[37] If the outbreak of war represented a crisis for the capitalist democracies it also brought to a head the emerging problems of a tiny leftist sect operating in a profoundly hostile environment.

Because of its German parentage and the ravages of the Gestapo, the SVG had more reason than most to adopt a policy of wholehearted prosecution of the war against Nazi Germany.[38] One practical consequence of this position was that the SVG soon became involved in the heated debates about the wartime economy. When Keynes published his highly influential pamphlet *How To Pay For the War* in January 1940, the ensuing debate saw Flanders make his first significant intervention into British political life and begin to develop the ideas that would come to fruition almost thirty years later in the Donovan Report. Starting with two 1941 pamphlets *Wage Policy in Wartime* and *The Battle for Production*, written whilst he was employed as a draughtsman in Sheffield, Flanders further developed his thinking in the 1943 book *Monopoly is the Enemy*, published shortly before he took up his three-year appointment at the TUC Research Department in December 1943.[39] He wrote very little during the next four years, partly no doubt because of the constraints of being a TUC employee.

From capitalist economy to the 'new social order'

The key to understanding the first stage of the political reorientation of Flanders and the SVG is the idea of a 'new social order' that was neither classical capitalism nor state socialism.[40] One of the main inferences drawn from this thesis was that under the new order the purposes of trade unionism must undergo radical change.[41] Two features of the wartime economy were thought to be indicative of this far-reaching change in the character of contemporary capitalism. The first was the emergence of an exceptionally tight labour market as the armed forces expanded from just under half a million people in 1939 to almost 3.4 millions by July 1941. Unemployment thus fell rapidly over the same period from 1.3 million to 198,000: 'By the summer of 1941 the long-predicted shortage of all labour, not just skilled, occurred'.[42] This state of virtually full employment meant that trade unions suddenly found themselves in a very powerful bargaining position. The second key feature of the wartime economy was the creation of state planning machinery, not only in the field of production, but in wage setting, dispute resolution and labour markets. As early as November 1940 Flanders used for the first time the notion of 'planned capitalism' to delineate contemporary developments and distinguish them from the pre-war economy.[43] By 1943 he was talking of a 'new order' defined as 'freedom and welfare for all' and comprising *inter alia* policies of full employment and a welfare state.[44]

These ideas in themselves were not new and had been in currency for some time. Milne-Bailey, the Head of Research at the TUC until his premature death in 1935, had written an influential book on *Trade Unions and the State* in which he foresaw an inexorable growth in the role and influence of unions within the planning machinery of modern capitalism.[45] Flanders would certainly have encountered Milne-Bailey's ideas once he began work at the TUC in December 1943. Moreover, as an active participant in the wide-ranging debates about postwar reconstruction (Flanders helped to draft the TUC's famous 1944 *Interim Report on Postwar Reconstruction*), he came into contact with influential advocates of planning such as G.D.H. Cole, Evan Durbin and Joan Robinson, all of whom had accepted invitations to join the TUC's Economic Committee in 1943.[46] By 1948, three years into the Attlee government, he was claiming that the society being created by social democracy was new on several major counts. Nationalization had ended the capitalist monopoly of ownership; poverty had been eradicated by the welfare state; and trade union power had ended the inferior status of the worker in industry.[47] The result, he observed a few years later, was that 'Exploitation in this crude [Marxist] sense no longer exists in Britain'.[48]

The Cold War against Communism: from new social order to ethical socialism

Despite being trained in a tradition of ethical socialism, Flanders made surprisingly little use of its principles in his early writings. Most of the early to mid-1940s editorials in *Socialist Commentary* were concerned with post-war reconstruction, a reflection of the actual politics of the period as well as of Flanders' own role at the TUC. Only after the onset of the Cold War in 1946 did he begin to recuperate these principles and rework them into a more or less coherent anti-Communist philosophy. In the first instance it was the Nazi-Soviet pact of August 1939 which gave new impetus to the traditional anti-Communism of the SVG. A few months later, following a radio broadcast by TUC General Secretary Walter Citrine on the 'problem of Communist disruption', Flanders wrote that whilst internal freedom of criticism in the trade union movement was valuable,

> this does not mean that the Labour Movement must tolerate organized penetration by those who are concerned ... with exploiting it for their own purposes ... the objects of Communist policy are purely disruptive, and what is more they threaten the existence of a free Labour Movement.[49]

Throughout the early 1940s the CP was routinely described in vitriolic terms: it was a 'poisonous growth within the labour movement'; it was 'unscrupulous'; it displayed 'an arrant disregard for the true purposes of trade unionism'; and was 'no more than a propaganda agency for Soviet Russia'. In 1943 and again in 1946, when the CP renewed its campaign for affiliation to the Labour Party, Flanders wrote passionately of the necessity to reject its overtures.[50]

The onset and progress of the Cold War further intensified Flanders' anti-Communism and lent it a new sense of urgency. The key events began with Churchill's 'iron curtain' speech in March 1946, followed a year later by US President Truman's declaration that America would lend military aid to 'victims of Soviet aggression' (the so-called Truman Doctrine). June 1947 saw the announcement of the Marshall Plan for European economic recovery within the framework of capitalism and liberal democracy and in September the Soviet Union created the Communist Information Bureau (or Cominform) to fight the Plan.[51] These developments would have had an unusual immediacy for Flanders because from summer 1946 until early 1948, he was literally working on the front line of the Cold War, as a political liaison officer in Germany. His job there was to help revive the social democrats (SPD), then under the virulent anti-Communist leadership of Kurt Schumacher; to help contain the resurgent German Communists (the KPD); and to resist the pressures for Socialist–Communist unity that were proving increasingly attractive to the left-wing of the SPD.[52]

The nature of working-class unity had become a live issue in the trade union world through the creation of the World Federation of Trade Unions (WFTU) in September–October 1945. The WFTU posed an acute dilemma for those, such as Flanders, committed to labour movement unity but without the Communists. On the one hand it embraced trade union movements from fifty-six countries, and the Presidency was held first by the TUC General Secretary Walter Citrine and subsequently by the anti-Communist head of the TGWU, Arthur Deakin. On the other hand, the WFTU included the state-controlled Soviet trade union movement and its General Secretary was the French pro-Communist Louis Saillant. Moreover the American AFL refused to have any connection with the organization and indeed worked ceaselessly to destroy it.[53] Though Citrine 'did not fully share the enthusiasm for the new organization which was displayed by most of the other delegations', he went along with its creation in the interests of unity. Flanders wholeheartedly approved of this cautious attitude, insisting as late as February 1948 that the TUC should stay in if at all possible and walk out only if necessary.[54]

But the growing influence and assertiveness of the Communist movement increasingly alarmed social democrats everywhere. In the immediate aftermath of the Second World War Communist political and industrial influence in Western Europe reached its zenith. Most parties scored their highest ever share of the vote and Communists held ministries in eight European governments.[55]

Even more alarming for Flanders were the events of February 1948 when the large and electorally successful Czechoslovakian CP successfully launched a revolutionary seizure of power and ousted its opponents. Described by anti-Communists everywhere as a *coup d'état*, the Czech events convinced many social democrats that peaceful co-existence and cooperation between Communism and social democracy was simply impossible. For Flanders the immediate lesson was that Prime Minister Attlee was fully justified in announcing (on 15 March 1948) that Communists would be banned from sensitive positions in the civil service and he urged the Labour Party to follow Attlee's example (which it duly did).[56] Within the trade union movement, the SVG's most senior official was George Green, an Assistant Secretary in the Civil Service Clerical Association. Green was already dispensing behind-the-scenes advice and support to the anti-Communist caucus, the Conference Campaign Committee.[57] Nevertheless, Flanders was always adamant that repression of the CP was not a sufficient strategy for its eradication. During the anti-Communist hysteria that gathered pace throughout 1949 and 1950, fuelled by unofficial dock strikes at home and the outbreak of the Korean War abroad, his position was not that it was wrong in principle to outlaw the British CP, but that a ban would be ineffective and was therefore inadvisable (a view also adopted by Hugh Clegg).[58] He always maintained that Communists thrived in the unions because workers had real grievances, which he said Communists cynically exploited because current union leaders were failing to undermine the attractions of Marxist dogma by counterpoising a coherent philosophy of ethical, democratic socialism.

In November 1947, for instance, as the Cominform stepped up its attacks on social democracy, Flanders asserted that the only viable response was 'clarification ... of what democratic socialism stands for' and its elaboration into 'a coherent and dynamic philosophy'.[59] It was to help in the creation of such a philosophy that Flanders and his colleagues took the decision in December 1949 to liquidate the SVG the following month (whilst preserving its journal *Socialist Commentary*) and create a new organization, the Socialist Union. One of Flanders' long standing associates, Jay Blumler, summed up the philosophy of Socialist Union as follows:

the essence of socialism was to be located, neither in certain institutional arrangements (such as public ownership), nor in some strategic tenet (like the class struggle), but in an unremitting effort to advance the ideals of freedom, equality and fellowship.[60]

And one commentator later observed,

During the high-tide of Bevanism, *Socialist Commentary* willingly served as a focus for the political and strategic thinking of the Right ... Socialist Union ... provided a major contribution to the growing philosophical justification for decent, moderate, parliamentary socialism.[61]

The international pressure to elaborate an anti-Communist philosophy coincided with a more parochial event, namely the entry of Rita Hinden into the SVG circle in 1945. Head of the Fabian Colonial Research Bureau since 1940, she quickly rose to become a member of the *Socialist Commentary* editorial committee in October 1947 and full-time editor in 1950.[62] A follower of the ethical socialist, R.H. Tawney, she extolled values of 'equality, freedom and ... fellowship' that were almost identical with those of Nelson and his supporters in the SVG, and she and Flanders developed a close working relationship that lasted almost twenty-five years.[63] In broad outline, the ideas of a new social order and its ethical implications stayed with Flanders for the rest of his life and informed his more detailed assessments of the key issues in industrial relations, to which we now turn.

Flanders' early industrial relations thought

Trade union purpose

One major consequence of the belief in a 'new social order' was that from socialists and trade unionists it 'demands a radically different approach to industry and society'.[64] Under the combined conditions of full employment and wartime mobilization Flanders soon came to reject the doctrine that the purpose of unions was to improve wages and conditions wherever possible. This, he loftily observed in his 1941 pamphlet *Wage Policy in Wartime*, was an 'old, rigid view of the class struggle', notwithstanding the fact that it had been the view of the SVG until very recently.[65] The pamphlet was apparently very influential and attracted comments from Citrine and Woodcock at the TUC as well as correspondence from the economists Joan Robinson and Michal Kalecki.[66]

What then was the overarching purpose of trade unions? In the early years of the Second World War the SVG in general and Flanders in particular focused on union involvement in, and contributions towards, macro-economic policy, very much in line with Flanders' own job at the TUC.[67] It was not until 1948 that he recuperated the ethical vision of a 'just society' in order to rethink the purpose of trade unionism. Wage demands were a major part of their activity, but even they reflected a 'desire for self-respect' as well as 'resentment against arbitrary or contemptuous treatment' and a 'conception of human dignity ... the claim to be treated as an equal'.[68] Following the creation of Socialist Union in 1951, this ethical strand in Flanders' thinking acquired even greater weight. With the 'ending of classical exploitation' and the worst excesses of poverty, he argued it was now time for the socialist movement to turn its attention away from simple material gain towards loftier ideals.

In practice this tendency to downplay the importance of material gain in trade union purpose would eventually open the way to one highly significant practical consequence. It would allow Flanders to defend state incomes policies by arguing that the short-term costs of pay restraint were easily outweighed by the advantages of 'union voice' in company and state policy making.

Collective bargaining as an inflationary wage–price spiral

The views of Flanders and the SVG on collective bargaining were quite rudimentary until about 1940–1. Insofar as wage claims represented the striving for social justice, then it was axiomatic that such manifestations of class struggle should receive unswerving support from socialists.[69] As early as 1940, in response to Keynes' pamphlet on paying for the war, Flanders had argued that wartime mobilization was rapidly leading to labour shortages. This dramatic and rapid shift from the mass unemployment of the 1930s meant that wage bargaining would soon lead to price inflation as manufacturers transformed the higher costs of labour into higher prices for customers. Flanders was normally careful to note that this danger, though real enough, was just that: one possible response by manufacturers though by no means the only one. For instance, some prices were subject to market restraints or administrative controls and he also noted that it was often feasible to offset higher costs with greater output.[70]

In the late 1940s Flanders began to integrate his ethical socialist principles into his analyses of industrial relations. He thus came to regard wage bargaining not only as an inflationary process, but as a competitive one, in which shortsighted union leaders vied with each other to drive up money wages without regard for any broader interest. Throughout the late 1940s it is the vitriolic language rather than the arguments that most clearly conveys his new attitude. References abound to 'narrow materialism' (1948), 'the wages scramble' (1949), 'the wages free for all' (1950), 'unrestrained collective bargaining' (1950) and 'wages anarchy' (1951).[71] If the language is redolent of the neo-liberal right, the meaning was certainly very different, at least in the 1940s. Flanders was here articulating a long-standing strain of socialist thought, impatient with the trade union concentration on wages and conditions, whilst waiting expectantly for signs of a more highly developed political class consciousness (for Marxists) or a concern for higher values and aspirations (for ethical socialists).

The implication of this emerging critique of wage bargaining was a rapidly growing sympathy for a national policy of wage restraint. Flanders' view was also a response to the political and economic situation of February 1948, when the Labour Government had suddenly announced a tough incomes policy based on zero wage increases unless there were rises in productivity. Despite the absence of consultation, the TUC's key leaders – the General Secretary Victor Tewson, Arthur Deakin (TGWU), Lincoln Evans (ISTC), Will Lawther (NUM) and Tom Williamson (GMWU) – had successfully recommended the government's policy to a Special TUC Conference in March 1948.[72] Left-wing critics, led by the CP, mobilized two million votes against the wage freeze (there were 5.4 million in favour). The incomes policy debate thus became tangled up with questions of loyalty to the Labour government and Cold War antagonism to the Communist movement.[73]

The wage–price spiral and monopoly

In thinking about the causes of the wage–price spiral Flanders returned to the economic training he had received in Germany and in particular to Franz Oppenheimer's critique of monopoly. Flanders had argued from 1941 that price inflation was not an automatic product of 'unregulated wage bargaining' because there were other possible outcomes. By 1943 he had arrived at the view that wage bargaining in monopoly firms was best understood as a process of collusion between powerful employers and strong trade unions. The former sought to protect their profits and the latter their wages, and both were able to achieve these aims through collective bargaining in which they gained at the expense of the firm's customers.[74] Flanders was also influenced in his thinking by the contemporary Marxist economist, Michal Kalecki, describing himself as 'a great admirer of his work'.[75] What he took from Kalecki was the idea that the distribution of national income was influenced by the degree of monopoly prevailing in different sectors of the economy and that consequently one could alter the former by adjusting the latter.[76] It is this line of argument which explains why the SVG published a pamphlet in 1943 under the provocative title *Monopoly is the Enemy*.

The consequences of this view were far-reaching. If the barrier to socialist progress was monopoly *per se* then Soviet-style state monopoly was no more defensible on socialist grounds than the private monopolies prevalent under capitalism. The anti-monopoly analysis thus both derived from, and reinforced the burgeoning anti-Sovietism of the SVG. From 1941 the political system of the USSR was being referred to as a type of 'totalitarian rule', a quintessentially liberal category which served to assimilate the radically disparate societies and economies of the Soviet Union and Nazi Germany.[77] Moreover, if both private *and* public monopolies had baleful consequences then it also followed that the form of property ownership, whether public or private, was a secondary matter from the standpoint of economic policy. Flanders thus became increasingly impatient with, and indeed hostile to, the Labour left for its equation of socialist advance with widespread nationalization, a position he caustically described as 'conservative militancy'.[78]

By the onset of the Cold War, however, the language of monopoly had largely disappeared from the pages of *Socialist Commentary*. The threat of the monopolists had given way to the twin dangers of international Communism and economic stagnation. More specifically Flanders now began to attack what he took to be a dogmatic attachment to state ownership as the panacea for economic and social problems, a position that conjoined Soviet Communism and traditional Labour leftism. The Labour left was also attacked for confusing means and ends: nationalization for Flanders and the Labour right was simply one means amongst many for achieving the ethical socialist goals of fellowship and equality.[79] This downgrading of the ownership question chimed in well with the thinking of right-wing social democrats in the Labour Party, many of whom looked with increasing favour on the notions of diverse patterns of ownership and of public regulation as alternatives to the traditional socialist policy of nationalization.[80] Speaking at the dissolution of Socialist Union in June 1959 Flanders argued that its greatest achievement was to have broken 'the identification of nationalization with socialism'.[81]

Collective bargaining and the public interest

If collective bargaining was a collusive process, then at whose expense did unions and employers achieve their gains? Flanders' answer to this question varied over the years, but in the first instance he identified consumers and unorganized (and presumably low paid) workers as the victims of high prices.[82] In other words he still thought in terms of the familiar class categories of producers, consumers and employers. By 1948 he had adopted the supra-class category of the 'public interest' as a third party with a legitimate interest in the outcomes of wage bargaining. In an editorial commentary on the Labour government's 1948 incomes policy Flanders argued that it was the duty of government to protect the public against the inflationary consequences of bargaining under full employment.[83] Indeed, so long as there was full employment, Flanders believed there had to be a 'permanent' national incomes policy. This was not to say that he opposed 'free collective bargaining', but rather that he wanted the process of bargaining to be subject to a much greater degree of state regulation than in the past.[84] In 1950, as Labour's incomes policy was falling apart in the face of rank and file union pressure, Flanders, an academic at Nuffield College, Oxford since October

1949, published a controversial Fabian pamphlet on wage policy. Apart from arguing for the creation of a permanent National Wage Board (see below), he also deepened his attack on 'free collective bargaining'. Economic evidence, he now argued, showed that bargaining had no long-term impact on profits and had failed to alter the distribution of national income between the social classes (i.e. between profits, rent and interest as compared with wages and salaries). Paradoxically therefore, free collective bargaining, traditionally defended by the more militant wing of the trade union movement, was a conservative social process, whilst state incomes policy, normally opposed by the union left, was, he believed, potentially far more radical.[85]

The strike as a social problem

Flanders' criticisms of collective bargaining went hand in hand with growing distaste for the strike weapon. Eager in the 1930s to advocate its use for political purposes, he became an increasingly strident critic, although he never abandoned the notion that workers should have the right to withdraw their labour.[86] In the first phase of his rethinking around the 'new social order' he wrote practically nothing about the subject, despite the fact that strike frequency and days lost due to strikes had risen almost continually between 1938 and 1944. Paradoxically he only took up the issue after a five-year decline in industrial action, from 1945 to 1950. By the late 1940s it was not the incidence of strikes *per se* that had become a public issue, but rather their unofficial character and their control by rank and file militants, some of whom not surprisingly were Communists.[87]

Flanders was reluctant at first to join in the chorus of condemnation of the wave of unofficial strikes that repeatedly closed Britain's ports in the late 1940s, arguing that poor union leadership often lay at the root of such action.[88] The remedy therefore lay in improving the quality of leadership, rather than in outlawing such action or stigmatizing strike organizers as Communist troublemakers. In 1950 Flanders argued that in the context of 'the new social order' of full employment, national incomes policy and the welfare state, the justification for 'guerilla warfare on the wages front had disappeared'.[89] But the persistence of unofficial strikes in industries such as docks, road haulage and the gas industry gradually shifted his views. In March 1951 he railed against the 'industrial anarchy' of broken agreements and rank and file defiance of union leaderships and condemned the 'despotic use of the strike weapon'.[90] Under conditions of full employment, he argued, it was imperative that unions exercised 'restraint' and 'responsibility', a position shared by a wide spectrum of contemporary political opinion from Churchill on the Conservative right through to Gaitskell and Morrison on the Labour right.[91]

The following year saw the launch of *Socialism: a new statement of principles*, the first publication from the newly created Socialist Union, an educational and research body set up in 1951 after the dissolution of the SVG. In line with its remit to rethink socialist principles in 'the new era', the booklet objected to strikes on grounds of ethical principles:

> what socialists want are civilised methods for resolving conflicts; power alone must not be the arbiter ... Strike action ... is not an end in itself. On the contrary, the unions have consistently tried to avoid it through agreed and peaceful methods of settling disputes. The concept of advancing towards our ideal society through hatred and schism has already, at least in this country, been discarded.[92]

Flanders had now arrived at a position of deep antagonism towards strike action and a preference for reason and dialogue as instruments of social change.[93] In one sense, this emphasis can be understood as part of the heritage of the ISK. Nelson was a firm rationalist but at the same time he always retained that part of his classical Marxist training which stressed the irreconcilable conflicts of interest between labour and capital, and the necessity of revolutionary force to crush the inevitable opposition of the old ruling class. It was that critical component of revolutionary Marxism which Flanders had now decisively rejected.

Industrial relations policy

By the late 1940s Flanders had become a convinced advocate of a permanent state incomes policy as a way of regulating the process of collective bargaining. He was a firm supporter of the February 1948 incomes policy, notwithstanding the significant minority opposition within the trade union movement at the time of its promulgation and the unions' rejection of the policy after just two years.[94] He believed free wage bargaining tended to be inflationary and thereby damaged the public interest without bringing any real or enduring wage gains to workers; the unofficial strikes sometimes used to back up wage claims often threatened the authority of collective agreements and of the union leaders who had signed them; and he thought the strike weapon itself was both a primitive method of resolving class conflicts and a potent means for reproducing class hatred. In his 1950 pamphlet he proposed the creation of a National Wages Board with four main responsibilities: the registration of collective agreements; the supervision of the Wages Councils; arbitration; and the conduct of enquiries into wage structures.[95] What is remarkable is how closely this set of tasks overlaps with those of the National Board for Prices and Incomes, created fifteen years later, which was also given powers to monitor and vet wage settlements and to conduct enquiries.[96]

In general, Flanders was at pains to emphasize that he did not regard state incomes policy merely as a method of wage restraint but looked upon it as a policy for aligning wage growth with increases in production.[97] On the other hand he was highly impatient with those whose attitude to any form of pay policy was 'No thanks'. In 1950, with the collapse of Labour's incomes policy, Flanders wrote of the 'need to minimise wage increases' or else to justify them by reference to productivity rises.[98] The theme of linking pay and productivity was a long standing one in Flanders' thought. As early as 1941 he had criticized the TUC opposition to government pay policy, arguing it was not sufficient merely to be negative: one had to have an alternative policy that could address the issue of inflation instead of simply trying to ignore it or pretend it was someone else's responsibility. At that time he had proposed to maintain free collective bargaining but establish Control Councils that would recommend efficiency improvements in order to dampen down any inflationary consequences.[99]

One might have thought Flanders would therefore be highly sympathetic to the Joint Production Committees (JPCs) that emerged from about 1941 in order to facilitate shop steward and worker involvement alongside management in raising output and efficiency. In fact he was very lukewarm about them, in part because of their perceived Communist provenance.[100] His main objection, however, was that they originated in the larger firms at a time when Flanders was deeply embroiled in his short-lived crusade against monopolies. Instead of being struck by the capacity of JPCs to raise the participation and status of workers in industry he was more alarmed at their potential for consolidating the economic and political influence of the despised monopolies.[101]

Some years later, when his anti-monopoly sentiments were no longer so all-consuming, Flanders actually came to regret the rapid post-war demise of the JPCs. In the context of Britain's export drive of the late 1940s he came to regard workplace institutions as potentially significant means of raising productivity.[102] At a highly select and influential Fabian gathering in 1950, the Problems Ahead conference series, he had begun to argue for the valuable role played by shop stewards in negotiating earnings rises linked to measured productivity improvements, involving the use of payment by results and motion study.[103] By 1952 his thinking about the fundamental importance of raising productivity through 'responsible participation' had crystallized:

> Economic survival is today a very real problem for this country ... higher productivity is needed, demanding a difficult readjustment in our thinking. In the past socialists were concerned mainly with the redistribution of income ... In the new situation since 1945 they have been compelled to preach the need for greater output and better utilisation of manpower. It has demanded a major effort to make the realities understood in the movement, and to secure the shift in outlook required from the worker at the bench or in the shop ... The leadership has had to wage a battle against the conservative elements in the ranks.[104]

By the same token it was essential that such 'responsible participation' did not hinder management's ability to manage. As he wrote in 1956, twelve years before Donovan: 'The problem is to share managerial responsibility without abandoning it'.[105]

One solution to this conundrum that attracted widespread support in the 1950s was joint consultation, particularly in the nationalized industries. For a while Flanders believed that consultation could reinforce cooperation between unions and management and serve as a practical form of industrial democracy, giving workers a real say in workplace decisions.[106] Only in the 1960s did he come to regard collective bargaining as the sole channel of worker representation.

The reference to leadership in the statement quoted above reflected Nelson's anti-democratic ideas on the subject. The British section of the ISK had complained throughout the 1930s about the poor quality of leadership in the British labour movement. But the poverty complained about was lack of revolutionary fervour and commitment.[107] Once Flanders and the SVG had developed the notion of a 'new social order', the references to leadership took on an entirely new inflection. In his 1948 monograph on trade unions (precursor to the successful textbook first issued in 1952) he observed that the demands of productive efficiency called for 'good management and responsible trade union cooperation'.[108] In similar vein he contrasted the need for 'responsible and responsive union leadership' with the 'irresponsibility' of certain activists.[109] And a few years later he suggested that a viable incomes policy required 'the traditional if indefinable qualities of British statesmanship – common sense, fair play and a willingness to compromise ...'.[110]

Summary and conclusions

By the early 1950s Flanders was well placed to influence the worlds of both socialist politics and industrial relations. He had built up an extensive network of both political and union contacts, through his work for the TUC and the Fabian Society and because of his key role in *Socialist Commentary*. He shared an ideological affinity with the increasingly influential Gaitskellite wing of the Labour Party and with leading trade union anti-Communists such as Sam Watson of the Durham NUM.[111] He had acquired a reputation as a rigorous, analytical thinker and an anti-Marxist through his writings on socialist philosophy and more concretely on wages policy. And he had worked out the main lines of an overall approach to industrial relations reform that would become very familiar in the 1960s but which were fairly novel in the previous decade: national incomes policy, based on consent; worker participation in decisions at work to improve economic performance and increase the status and dignity of the worker; union-management cooperation to raise output and productivity; workplace negotiation by responsible shop stewards. His plans envisioned

> a world without class conflict in which fully unionised workers cooperated with
> enlightened owners to manage the economy rationally, a world in which labour
> worked not out of 'force of hunger' but 'as an obligation to the State', while the
> State in turn accepted 'an obligation to them'.[112]

The statement actually refers to the ideas of wartime Minister of Labour
Ernest Bevin. But with only a few minor alterations it would serve as a reasonably accurate summary of Flanders' world view as of the late 1940s, first
elaborated in the light of wartime economic planning but then reworked and
refined in the crucible of Cold War anti-Communism.

The key to understanding his outlook is the anti-Marxist motif of the 'new
social order', an economic system that was neither classical capitalism nor
state socialism. According to this notion, capitalist power had been eroded
by nationalization and state planning whilst the perennial labour market
weakness and vulnerability of workers had been practically removed by full
employment and state welfare. Unions had, as a consequence, obtained new
rights in the corridors of state power and within firms, but in Flanders' judgement they had simultaneously acquired new responsibilities, chief among
which was to play a constructive role in handling the problems thrown up by
the new society. By around 1950 he had identified these as inflation, unofficial strikes and poor productivity and had come to label them as the chief
threats to orderly industrial relations and to socialist progress. From this
diagnosis flowed the major issues for academic research and for policy debate: how to secure a workable policy of wage restraint? How to ensure the
quality of trade union leadership, at all levels, that would act responsibly
and adhere to agreements? How to organize cooperation between workers
and employers to boost output and productivity without undermining the
independence of unions as bargaining agents? It was this same agenda of
problems and issues that Flanders would lay out almost twenty years later in
his memorable evidence to the Donovan Commission.

Yet for all its apparent coherence and rigour, Flanders' appraisal of the
strengths and weaknesses of British industrial relations was fatally flawed
by a series of contradictions, many of which would only work themselves
out and become clear in the deepening economic crisis of the 1960s and
1970s. As an ethical socialist he was convinced that workers were increasingly concerned about dignity and status at work. Yet his own empirical
study of productivity bargaining at Fawley underlined the continuing salience of money and power. As a committed voluntarist, he believed in 'free
collective bargaining'. Yet he became increasingly alarmed at what he took
to be its economic consequences. As an anti-Marxist, he had rejected the
concepts of exploitation and domination as no longer relevant for understanding 'the new social order', but then found himself unable satisfactorily

to explain worker resistance to the productivity agreements and incomes policies that were supposedly in their interests. As a Nelsonian anti-democrat, he hankered after the tough, centralized style of union leadership epitomized by Bevin and Citrine in the 1940s, but as a social scientist he readily acknowledged, and to some degree welcomed, the devolution of power to the shop floor which radically undermined such dreams.[113]

Flanders' major contribution to industrial relations in Britain was to assist in the creation of a field of study firmly imprinted with the political and economic priorities of right-wing social democracy and strongly oriented to the solution of policy problems.[114] There was certainly no inevitability about this achievement or about the subsequent evolution of the field because in principle the study of industrial relations could have developed in two quite different ways. Flanders' faith in reason, and in the prospect of reasonable people designing workable institutions, could both have been discarded. His tempered assessment of the 'Communist threat' could have been replaced by a more strident antagonism to the Left. Those intellectual moves would have taken industrial relations perilously close to the neo-liberal agenda that persisted, even if it did not quite prevail, in the Tory party of the 1950s and which revolved around the issue of how to curb trade union power.[115] Its best known academic exponent from the late 1950s was Ben Roberts, interestingly and ironically, a former comrade of Flanders from the SVG of the 1940s.[116] The other line of development for the field would have taken it in a radical, even a Marxist direction, revolving around issues of shop steward rights and power, problems of waging class struggle in the context of right-wing union leaderships and the broader issue of anti-Communist hegemony within the labour movement. These kinds of ideas were also the preserve of small groups, in and around the CP, in the world of trade union education and on the non-Communist left represented by G.D.H. Cole. In his review of Socialist Union's *Twentieth Century Socialism* Cole unerringly captured the political trajectory of Flanders and his associates when he remarked that they had 'thrown away socialism in a panic against totalitarianism'.[117]

Notes

1. *Royal Commission on Trade Unions and Employers' Associations 1965–1968*, (Cmnd 3623, 1968).
2. *Guardian*, 4 October 1973.
3. A. Flanders, *Management and Unions: the theory and reform of industrial relations* (1970).
4. H. Clegg, 'Introduction', in A. Flanders, *Management and Unions* (1970), p. 7 and see also A. Flanders, *The Fawley Productivity Agreements* (1964).
5. See Roy Jenkins' comment to this effect in R. Jenkins, *A Life At The Centre* (1991), p. 197.

6. R. Hyman, *Industrial Relations: a Marxist introduction* (1975), p. 11. There has been relatively little written about Flanders. M. Poole, *Theories of Trade Unionism* (1981) covers the 1960s academic writings, but makes no reference to the political writings. A. Fox, 'Collective bargaining, Flanders, and the Webbs', *British Journal of Industrial Relations*, 13, 2, 1975, pp. 151–74, is an excellent critique of Flanders' understanding of collective bargaining. B. Ahlstrand, *The Quest for Productivity: a case study of Fawley after Flanders* (Cambridge, 1990) is a very insightful appraisal of the failure of productivity bargaining. C. Rowley, 'Flanders, Allan David (1910–1973)' in M. Poole and M. Warner (eds), *The IEBM Handbook of Human Resource Management* (London, 1998) is a useful, though short, essay. Flanders also attracted attention from the Marxist left in the early 1970s: see T. Cliff, *The Employers' Offensive: productivity deals and how to fight them* (1970), Ch. 9, and P. Sedgwick, 'On Flander's field. Social democracy – R.I.P.', *Idiot International*, 7, July 1970, pp. 9–10.

7. For the history, organization and policies of the ISK see W. Link, *Die Geschichte der Internationalen Jugendbendes und des Internationalen Sozialistischen Kampfbundes* (Meisenheim am Glan, Germany, 1964); Militant Socialist International, *The Militant Socialist International: its aim, methods and constitution* (1935); Militant Socialist International, *Leonard Nelson: philosopher, politician, educationalist* (1939); L. Nelson, *Politics and Education* (1928); L. Nelson, *The Better Security. Being the heresies of a revolutionary revisionist* (Manchester, 1928).

8. Details of Flanders' early life are rather scarce but some material can be found in the following: H. Clegg, 'Flanders, Allan David', *Dictionary of National Biography 1971–1980* (Oxford, 1984); M. Saran, *Never Give Up. Memoirs* (London, 1976); M. Saran, 'In the thirties', *Socialist Commentary*, 37, 12, 1973, pp. 4–5; A. Flanders, 'Constant adventure', in H. Becker *et al.* (eds), *Erziehung Und Politik: Minna Specht zu ihrem 80. Geburtstag* (Frankfurt, 1960); Modern Records Centre, University of Warwick (hereafter MRC), Socialist Vanguard Group Papers (hereafter SVG), MSS 173, Box 18, Letter (n.d.).

9. For details of the School see Link, *Die Geschichte* and Saran, *Never Give Up*.

10. Link, *Die Geschichte*. According to one source the IJB initially had members in the three main German left parties, the SPD, the USPD and the Communist Party (KPD) (Saran, *Never Give Up*, p. 47).

11. MRC, SVG Papers, MSS 173, Box 4, Future of the Group – extended executive discussion, 29 May 1949.

12. A. Glees, *Exile Politics During the Second World War: the German social democrats in Britain* (Oxford, 1982), p. 242; S. Miller and H. Potthoff, *A History of German Social Democracy. From 1848 to the Present* (Leamington Spa, 1986), pp. 173–5. Another example is Mary Saran, a leading member of the British section of the ISK, who was appointed editor of the journal of the Socialist International shortly after its revival in 1951: see Saran, *Never Give Up*, p. 124.

13. G.K. [G. Kumleben], 'Notes to the International League of Youth', in Nelson, *Politics and Education*, p. 243.

14. On ethical socialism see L. Kolakowski, *Main Currents of Marxism: its origins, growth and dissolution. Volume 2: The golden age* (Oxford, 1978), pp. 240–54.

15. See Nelson, *Politics and Education* and *The Better Security* as well as Link, *Die Geschichte* for the material in the ensuing paragraphs.

16. See for instance A. Flanders, 'Communism and free criticism', *Vanguard*, 1, 6, 1935, pp. 137–45 and 'Dangerous tactics', *Socialist Vanguard*, 2, 10, 1937, pp. 221–5.

17. Nelson, *Politics and Education*, p. 48.

18. See for instance MSI, *Leonard Nelson*, p. 11; MSI, *The Militant Socialist International*. Although Nelson frequently cited Lenin's ideas on vanguard party organization to support his views, not even Lenin carried his contempt for 'bourgeois democracy' inside the ranks of the workers' party.

19. Link, *Die Geschichte*, pp. 22–7; MSI, *The Militant Socialist International*.

20. MRC, SVG Papers, MSS 173, Box 2, General conditions of membership and National Letter (May 1941).

21. The German articles were all written between 1935 and 1939. The pamphlet referred to was A. Flanders, *The Churches and Their Politics* (1938).

22. See for instance 'Socialism and the Labour Party', *Vanguard*, 1, 3, 1934, pp. 59–67; 'Election lessons', *Vanguard*, 1, 9, 1936, pp. 222–7; 'The Public Order Bill', *Socialist Vanguard*, 2, 7, 1936, pp. 145–50; 'Unity on the left', *Socialist Vanguard*, 2, 9, 1937, pp. 202–6; Editorials: 'The new union', *Socialist Vanguard*, 4, 5, 1938, p. 66 and 'In the shadow of war', *Socialist Vanguard*, 5, 8, 1939, p. 115. Editorials were written jointly by Flanders and a succession of collaborators over the period 1937 to 1973 and I have therefore taken them as expressing Flanders' own views.

23. 'Bureaucracy and democracy in the Labour Party', *Socialist Vanguard*, 3, 4, 1937, p. 75.

24. A. Flanders, 'The struggle of the London busmen', *Socialist Vanguard*, 3, 1, 1937. In similar vein Flanders' objection to the left unity initiative of 1937 embracing the Socialist League (then affiliated to the Labour Party), the CP and the Independent Labour Party was not based on suspicion of the CP but on deep distrust of the 'reformist' Labour Party and of any initiative which might strengthen it: see Flanders, 'Unity on the left'. G. Foote, *The Labour Party's Political Thought: a history* (1985) goes so far as to say that 'the hallmark of *Socialist Commentary* was its anti-Communism' (p. 203). Anti-Communism was certainly prominent in the pages of the journal, but so too was its advocacy of wage restraint, productivity growth and labour-management cooperation (see below). On the Soviet union see Flanders, 'Dangerous tactics'; 'Rome-Berlin axis', *Socialist Vanguard*, 3, 2, 1937, pp. 28–32; 'Strengthen the peace alliance', *Socialist Vanguard*, 4, 5, 1938, pp. 67–70; Editorial, 'Russia's outstretched hand', *Socialist Vanguard*, 5, 6, 1939, pp. 81–2.

25. Editorial, 'Resolutions without resolution', *Socialist Vanguard*, 4, 8, 1938,

p. 115.

26. Editorial, 'May first or Empire day?', *Socialist Vanguard*, 5, 5, 1939, p. 66.

27. 'The struggle of the London busmen', p. 1. For other expressions of union militancy see 'Labour's path to peace – or war', *Vanguard*, 1, 4, 1934, pp. 92–101; 'The cost of peace betrayal', *Socialist Vanguard*, 2, 11, 1937, p. 249; Editorials, 'Boycott Japan', *Socialist Vanguard*, 4, 3, 1938, p. 33 and 'Wage claims rejected', *Socialist Vanguard*, 5, 1, 1939, p. 5.

28. Flanders, 'Communism and free criticism', pp. 143–4.

29. MRC, SVG Papers, MSS 173, Box 2, National Letter, June 24th, 1941.

30. A. Glees, 'The SPD in emigration and resistance', in R. Fletcher (ed.), *Bernstein to Brandt: a short history of German social democracy* (1987); H. Grebing, *The History of the German Labour Movement* (1969), pp. 144–50; Miller and Pothoff, *A History of German Social Democracy*, pp. 138–9, 142; MRC, SVG Papers, MSS 173, Box 4, Statement on the future of the SVG as a brief outline by the Executive Committee.

31. MRC, SVG Papers, MSS 173, Box 2, National Letter, May 1941.

32. MRC, SVG Papers, MSS 173, Box 2, National Letter, 12 February 1942; BLPES, Fabian Society papers, File E 123/6; *Fabian Society Reports*, Years ending 1944, 1945, 1946. In 1939 control of the Fabian Society passed into the hands of G.D.H. and Margaret Cole. Their eagerness to use it as a vehicle for the development of a democratic socialist philosophy meant that the Society was a very congenial political home for Flanders: see A.W. Wright, *G.D.H. Cole and Socialist Democracy* (Oxford, 1979), pp. 226–8.

33. D. Healey, *The Time of My Life* (1990), p. 88.

34. Link, *Die Geschichte*, pp. 173–6, 224–31; MRC, SVG Papers, MSS 173, Box 1, Abbreviated Report concerning the development of the MSI (for our English comrades); L.J. Edinger, *German Exile Politics: the social democratic executive committee in the Nazi era* (Berkeley, California, 1956), p. 70; Grebing, *History of the German Labour Movement*, p. 144.

35. Editorial, 'The people must pay', *Socialist Vanguard*, 5, 9, 1939, p. 130 and see also Editorial, 'The Russian riddle', *Socialist Vanguard*, 5, 11, 1939, pp. 161–3.

36. See for instance Militant Socialist International, *Russia and the Comintern* (1942).

37. On the ISK in Britain see MRC, SVG Papers, MSS 173, Box 2, National Letter, 8 May 1942, for attendances at meetings; Box 18, Quarterly Report, Third Quarter 1937 for *Socialist Vanguard* circulation and Half Yearly Report November 1943–May 1944 for membership. The ISK's political activity did not include contesting any kind of election. On the threat posed by the CP see SVG Papers, MSS 173, Box 18, Report on Work in England, 22/6/42. British CP membership rose dramatically from 2,574 in June 1931 to 18,000 by September 1939: see N. Fishman, *The British Communist Party and the Trade Unions, 1933–45* (Aldershot, 1995), p. 345.

38. Editorial, 'Our attitude', *Socialist Vanguard*, 5, 10, 1939, pp. 145–7. This stance had in fact been argued for as early as April 1938: see Editorial, 'British policy in flux', *Socialist Vanguard*, 4, 4, 1938, pp. 49–50. The SVG contin-

ued to function throughout the war because leading members, such as Flanders, were in reserved occupations and therefore ineligible for conscription. Although some of the Group's German members were interned in 1940 they were soon released (Saran, *Never Give Up*, pp. 88–9).

39. Editorials, 'Stand four square against high prices', *Socialist Vanguard*, 6, 1, 1940, pp. 1–3 and 'How to pay for the war', *Socialist Vanguard*, 6, 4, 1940, pp. 56–7; A. Flanders, 'Wage policy in war-time', *Socialist Vanguard*, 6, 2, 1940, pp. 24–6; *Wage Policy in Wartime* (1941); *The Battle for Production* (1941); A. Flanders *et al.*, (eds), *Monopoly Is The Enemy* (1943).

40. See A. Flanders, 'Planned capitalism. Opposition or compromise?', *Commentary*, 10, 1940, pp. 1–3.

41. A. Flanders, *British Trade Unionism* (1948), p. 57.

42. C. Wrigley, 'The Second World War and state intervention in industrial relations, 1939–45', in C. Wrigley (ed.), *A History of British Industrial Relations, 1939–1979* (Cheltenham, 1996), pp. 12–15.

43. Flanders, 'Planned capitalism'.

44. A. Flanders, 'A system of public control', in Flanders, *Monopoly Is The Enemy*.

45. W. Milne-Bailey, *Trade Unions and the State* (1934), especially chs 28 and 30. Flanders had also come across the WEA pamphlet *Trade Unionism and the New Social Order* (1942) written by Joe Roper, a WEA tutor in Sheffield whom he knew. It was Roper's pamphlet that drew the distinction between the union as 'vested interest' and 'sword of justice', first used by Flanders in his 1948 monograph *British Trade Unionism*.

46. H. A. Clegg, *A History of British Trade Unions Since 1889 Vol. 111 1934–1951* (Oxford, 1994), p. 271; MRC, TUC Archive, MSS 292, File 806.9/2, Document 11 November 1943 and File 807.12/1; MRC, Flanders' Papers, MSS 65, Box 19, Letter from George Woodcock to Mary Saran, 19 February 1975.

47. Flanders, *British Trade Unionism*, pp. 57–60.

48. Socialist Union, *Socialism: a new statement of principles* (London, 1952), p. 28.

49. Editorial, 'How to deal with disruption', *Socialist Vanguard*, 6, 5, 1940, p. 73.

50. Editorials, 'Anti-war slogans won't do', *Socialist Vanguard*, 5, 12, 1939, p. 177; 'The case against affiliation', *Socialist Commentary*, 8, 11, 1943, p. 5; 'The Communists and unity', *Socialist Commentary*, 9, 2, 1943, p. 225; MRC, SVG Papers, MSS 173, Box 2, The future of British socialism, p. 6; Editorial, 'Labour and the Communists', *Socialist Commentary*, 10, 17, 1946, pp. 338–41.

51. On the Cold War and the labour movement see A. Carew, *Labour Under the Marshall Plan: the politics of productivity and the marketing of management science* (Manchester, 1987); R. Hyman, 'Praetorians and proletarians: unions and industrial relations', in J. Fyrth (ed.), *Labour's High Noon: the government and the economy 1945–51* (1993); D. MacShane, *International Labour and the Origins of the Cold War* (Oxford, 1992); A.S. Milward, *The*

Reconstruction of Western Europe, 1945–51 (1984), Chap. 11; P. Weiler, *British Labor and the Cold War* (Stanford, 1988).

52.   On Flanders' own role see MRC, Flanders' Papers, MSS 65, Box 19, A. Flanders, 'Personal Notes', Unpublished MSS, 1947. On the role of the British Control Commission more generally see N. Annan, *Changing Enemies: the defeat and regeneration of Germany* (1995); B. Marshall, *The Origins of Post-War German Politics* (1988); and I. Turner (ed.), *Reconstruction in Post-War Germany: British occupation policy and the Western zones 1945–55* (Oxford, 1989). On the rise of the KPD and the unity campaigns see P. Major, *The Death of the KPD: Communism and anti-Communism in West Germany, 1945–1956* (Oxford, 1998), pp. 37–53 and 196. KPD membership in the Western zones of Germany leapt from 75,000 in October 1945 to 324,00 by May 1947. The SPD and the KPD did merge in the Russian zone on 22 April 1946 to create the Socialist Unity Party. Needless to say the ISK leader Willi Eichler denounced 'any sort of cooperation whatsoever with the KPD' (p. 44).

53.   On the WFTU see A. Carew, 'The schism within the World Federation of Trade Unions: government and trade-union diplomacy', *International Review of Social History*, 29, 3, 1984, pp. 297–335; Carew, *Labour Under the Marshall Plan*, ch. 5; Weiler, *British Labor and the Cold War*, ch. 3; MacShane, *International Labour*.

54.   Editorial, 'World trade union unity', *Socialist Commentary*, 10, 3, 1945, p. 46. A. Flanders, 'Future of the W.F.T.U,', *Socialist Commentary*, 12, 2, 1948, pp. 27–9.

55.   K. von Beyme, *Political Parties in Western Democracies* (Aldershot, 1985), pp. 102–3; I. Inozemtsev et al., *The International Working Class Movement: problems of history and theory. Volume 6: the working class movement in the developed capitalist countries after the Second World War (1945–1979)* (Moscow, 1987), p. 36. For the British CP's influence in the unions see Fishman, *The British Communist Party and the Trade Unions* and E. Wigham, *What's Wrong With the Unions?* (Harmondsworth, 1961), pp. 125–8.

56.   On the Czech events see M. Myant, *Socialism and Democracy in Czechoslovakia 1945–1948* (Cambridge, 1981), Chs 8 and 9. For Flanders' response to the events see Editorial, 'The lessons of Czechoslovakia', *Socialist Commentary*, 12, 7, 1948, pp. 145–7. Although the scale of anti-Communist purges in Britain was dwarfed by events in the USA, both civil servants and lecturers felt the force of it: see A.J. Davies, *To Build A New Jerusalem: the labour movement from the 1880s to the 1990s* (1992), p. 177; R. Fieldhouse, *Adult Education and the Cold War: liberal values under siege 1946–51* (Leeds, 1985), Chs 3 and 4. According to Fieldhouse several Communist tutors were barred from working in British colonies by Colonial Secretary Arthur Creech-Jones, a close colleague of Rita Hinden, and by his successor, Jim Griffiths, a founder member of Socialist Union.

57.   E. Wigham, *From Humble Petition to Militant Action: a history of the Civil and Public Services Association 1903–1978* (1980), p. 106; MRC, SVG Papers, MSS 173, Future of the Group.

58.   Editorials, 'Why this industrial unrest?', *Socialist Commentary*, 13, 7, 1949, pp. 156–8; 'The strike issue', *Socialist Commentary*, 15, 3, 1951, pp. 49–51 and 'Collective security', *Socialist Commentary*, 14, 8, 1950, pp. 180–1. *Socialist Commentary* adopted an equally pragmatic position on the outlawing of the German Communist party in 1956 and on the proposed ban on the Australian CP in 1950: see M. Saran, 'Communists banned', *Socialist Commentary*, 20, 10, 1956, p. 26; Anon, 'Australia's anti-Communist Bill', *Socialist Commentary*, 14, 6, 1950, pp. 124–5. The global scale of the Cold War is clear from the wide range of countries (twenty three in all) that banned local Communist parties between 1940 and the late 1950: see W.S. Sworakowski (ed.), *World Communism: a handbook 1918–1965* (Stanford, California, 1973). For Clegg's view see H. A. Clegg, *General Union: a study of the National Union of General and Municipal Workers* (Oxford, 1954), p. 121. On the anti-Communism of the period see K.O. Morgan, *Labour in Power 1945–1951* (Oxford, 1984), pp. 435–8 and P. Coleman, *The Liberal Conspiracy: the Congress for Cultural Freedom and the struggle for the mind of postwar Europe* (New York, 1989). The growing anti-Communism of *Socialist Commentary* was matched (from about 1949) by an escalating pro-Americanism. In 1952 for instance its editors proudly extolled British links with, and dependence on, the USA, describing the latter as a bulwark of democracy and economic freedom and a vital part of the world struggle against Communism, particularly in the underdeveloped world (as it was then known): see for instance the Editorials 'Uncle Sam', *Socialist Commentary*, 16, 4, 1952, pp. 73–5 and 'Month after Morecambe', *Socialist Commentary*, 16, 11, 1952, pp. 241–3. On the Korean events as civil and revolutionary war, not invasion, see J. Halliday and B. Cumings, *Korea: the unknown war* (Harmondsworth, 1988), ch. 2. The political positions of *Socialist Commentary* have led some writers to suggest it was funded by the US Central Intelligence Agency, as was the case with *Encounter* magazine and a propaganda body called the Congress for Cultural Freedom (CCF). There is no evidence for this claim and it seems more likely that the two journals were simply part of the same anti-Communist milieu and therefore attracted the same set of contributors to their pages and their conferences, people such as Crosland, Gaitskell, Healey, Hinden, Jenkins and W. Arthur Lewis. On the alleged CIA connection, see R. Ramsay, *The Clandestine Caucus: anti-socialist campaigns and operations in the British labour movement since the war* (Hull, 1995); L. Walsh and R. Fletcher, *CIA Infiltration of the Labour Movement* (1982). On the business interests which funded British social democracy see B. Brivati, *Hugh Gaitskell* (1996), ch. 16. The SVG was financed by literature sales and donations from members: see MRC, SVG Papers, MSS 173, Box 2, Financial Statement: report on financial position at 5/4/46; Interview with Rene Saran, London, 22 May 1997; and P. Stephenson, 'The future of Socialist Commentary', *Socialist Commentary*, 42, 12, 1978, p. 1.

59.   See for instance the Editorials 'Labour and the Communists' and 'Our purpose', *Socialist Commentary*, 12, 1, 1947, pp. 1–2 and A. Flanders,

'Cominformity', *Socialist Commentary*, 12, 2, 1947, p. 29.

60. J. Blumler, 'In appreciation of Rita Hinden', *Socialist Commentary*, 36, 1, 1972, p. 19; see also N. Ellison, *Egalitarian Thought and Labour Politics: retreating visions* (1994), pp. 115–25; S. Haseler, *The Gaitskellites: revisionism in the British Labour Party* (1969), pp. 77–80.

61. Haseler, *The Gaitskellites*, p. 80. In 1952 Flanders and Hinden created an organization called Friends of Socialist Commentary. Its Treasurer until 1955 was Hugh Gaitskell, a close associate of Hinden's, who used his right-wing union connections to secure 1,500 bulk sales each month: see P.M. Williams, *Hugh Gaitskell: a political biography* (1979), p. 320; K.O. Morgan, *Labour People: leaders and lieutenants, Hardie to Kinnock* (Oxford, 1992), p. 242.

62. MRC, SVG Papers, MSS 173, Executive Committee Minutes 7/8 December 1945; *Socialist Commentary*, 12, 1, 1947.

63. A. Flanders, 'Hinden, Rita', in J.M. Bellamy and J. Saville (eds), *Dictionary of Labour Biography. Vol. II* (1974), p. 181; see also Morgan, *Labour People*, pp. 239–45. On the ethical socialism of the Socialist Union see the exceptionally thorough article by L. Black, 'Social democracy as a way of life: fellowship and the Socialist Union, 1951–59', *Twentieth Century British History*, 10, 1, 1999.

64. Flanders, *British Trade Unionism*, p. 57.

65. Flanders, *Wage Policy in Wartime*, p. 6.

66. MRC, SVG Papers, MSS 173, Box 2, National Letter (Sept 24th/41); MRC, Allan Flanders' Papers, MSS 65, Box 19, Letter from George Woodcock to Mary Saran, 19 February 1975. Woodcock stated that the ideas in the pamphlet helped Flanders to obtain a research post at the TUC in December 1943.

67. For example Flanders, 'Wage policy in war-time'; *The Battle For Production*; 'The production committee experiment', *Socialist Commentary*, 9, 3, 1943, pp. 45–51; Editorial, 'Labour's policy – truce or struggle?', *Socialist Commentary*, 8, 1, 1942, pp. 2–6. Much of the wartime planning machinery had been created or inspired by the ex-TGWU leader turned Minister of Labour, Ernest Bevin: see A. Bullock, *The Life and Times of Ernest Bevin. Vol. 2: Minister of Labour 1940–1945* (1967), p. 97.

68. Flanders, *British Trade Unionism*, pp. 56–7.

69. See for instance Flanders, 'The cost of peace betrayal'.

70. Flanders, *Wage Policy in Wartime*, pp. 16–17; 'A system of public control', pp. 16–17; 'The politics of full employment', *Socialist Commentary*, 9, 12, 1944, pp. 228–32; Editorial, 'How to pay for the war'. Flanders was very influenced by Joan Robinson's exposition of the inflationary consequences of wage bargaining under full employment: see *The Times*, 22–23 January 1943. Information from interview with Professor Ben Roberts, London, 9 October 1997.

71. Flanders, *British Trade Unionism*, p. 61; MRC, SVG Papers, MSS 173, Box 4, Wages policy, p. 1; *A Policy For Wages*, p. 30; Editorials, 'Limits of wage restraint', *Socialist Commentary*, 14, 5, 1950, p. 111. and 'The strike issue', p. 50.

72. G.A. Dorfman, *Wage Politics in Britain, 1945-1967* (Ames, Iowa, 1973), ch 4.

73. Dorfman, *Wage Politics*, pp. 65-7; L. Minkin, *The Contentious Alliance: trade unions and the Labour Party* (Edinburgh, 1992), p. 80.

74. Flanders, 'A system of public control'; see also MRC, Allan Flanders' Papers, MSS 65, Box 19, The Alternative to Monopoly Capitalism – a system of public control. That Britain's monopoly capitalists were highly conservative and resistant both to state intervention and increased union influence, as Flanders said, now seems clear: see L. Johnman, 'The Labour Party and industrial policy', in N. Tiratsoo (ed.), *The Attlee Years* (1991).

75. A. Flanders, 'Full employment and monopoly', *Fabian Quarterly*, 40, 1944, p. 24.

76. Ibid. Similar ideas about monopoly were fairly widespread at the time and were held amongst others by G.D.H. Cole: see Wright, *G.D.H. Cole*, pp. 203-4.

77. A. Flanders, 'Stalin's Russia and the crisis in socialism', *Commentary*, 16, 1941, p. 5. See also MSI, *Russia and the Comintern*; Editorials, 'Britain and the Big Two'; 'Russia and the West', *Socialist Commentary*, 11, 8, 1946, pp. 478-81; 'After the Moscow conference', *Socialist Commentary*, 11, 11, 1947, pp. 622-4.

78. Editorial, 'Militancy for what?', *Socialist Commentary*, 16, 5, 1952, pp. 97-9.

79. A. Flanders, 'Realistic proposals for reconstruction', *Socialist Commentary*, 8, 2, 1942, pp. 14-20; 'A system of public control'; 'Marxian and modern economics', *Socialist Commentary*, 8, 8, 1943, pp. 20-3; MRC, SVG Papers, MSS 173, Box 2, The Future of British Socialism; Editorial, 'The production drive', *Socialist Commentary*, 11, 1, 1946, pp. 314-17.

80. See N. Thompson, *Political Economy and the Labour Party* (1996), ch. 9 and 10, and S. Brooke, 'Revisionists and fundamentalists: the Labour Party and economic policy during the Second World War', *Historical Journal*, 32, 1, 1989, pp. 157-75 who argues that Hugh Dalton and Douglas Jay had begun to downgrade the value of nationalization from the late 1930s. It was this growing rapprochement between the ideas of an erstwhile revolutionary group and of social democracy that were reflected in Herbert Morrison's decision to write a Foreword to the SVG's 1943 pamphlet *Monopoly is the Enemy*. It is also worth noting that left wing socialists such as G.D.H. Cole were also coming to look with growing favour on diverse ways of regulating large corporations: see Wright, *G.D.H. Cole*, pp. 116-22.

81. MRC, SVG Papers, MSS 173, Box 13, Socialist Union AGM Minutes 13 June 1959, p. 2. On the critical distinction between ends and means see for instance the Editorials, 'First step or last?', *Socialist Commentary*, 17, 10, 1953, pp. 217-19 and 'Left or right?', *Socialist Commentary*, 18, 6, 1954, pp. 141-3.

82. Flanders, *Wage Policy in Wartime*, p. 18; 'A system of public control', pp. 16-17; *The Alternative to Monopoly Capitalism*, p. 6.

83. Editorial, 'Wages, prices and profits', *Socialist Commentary*, 12, 6, 1948, p.

122.

84. Ibid., p. 121.

85. *A Policy For Wages*, pp. 6–7. The Oxford lectureship in industrial relations had been created at the suggestion of G.D.H. Cole, who had then recommended Flanders for the job: M. Cole, *The Life of G.D.H. Cole* (London, 1971), p. 270 and interview with Annemarie Flanders, Kenilworth, 14 June 1997.

86. See notes 25, 26 and 27 above for the 1930s. In defence of the right to strike see *British Trade Unionism*, p. 41.

87. E. Screpanti, 'Long cycles in strike activity: an empirical investigation', *British Journal of Industrial Relations*, 25, 1, 1987, pp. 99–124. On unofficial strikes in the early post-war period see A. Hutt, *British Trade Unionism: a short history* (1975), ch. 12.

88. Editorial, 'Why this industrial unrest?'.

89. *A Policy For Wages*, pp. 11, 23.

90. Editorial, 'The strike issue'.

91. Socialist Union, *Twentieth Century Socialism: the economy of tomorrow* (Harmondsworth, 1956), p. 72.

92. Socialist Union, *Socialism*, pp. 43–4. On the subject of strikes, the Group Personnel Director of the British Motor Corporation wrote to the head of trade union education at Oxford University in 1963 congratulating him on their shop steward training programme which, he said, had contributed to a significant reduction in strikes at BMC's car plants. Flanders had been involved in union education at Oxford since 1949. See J. McIlroy, 'Trade union education for a change', in B. Simon (ed.), *The Search For Enlightenment: the working class and adult education in the twentieth century* (1990).

93. In 1954 he wrote of a recent wave of strikes that 'reason had succumbed to fist shaking': Editorial, 'Labour unrest', *Socialist Commentary*, 18, 2, 1954, pp. 29–31.

94. See *A Policy For Wages*, p. 3; 'Collective bargaining', in A. Flanders and H. A. Clegg (eds), *The System of Industrial Relations in Great Britain* (Oxford 1954), pp. 308–9; 'Wage movements and wage policy'.

95. *A Policy For Wages*, p. 20.

96. D. Barnes and E. Reid, *Governments and Trade Unions: the British experience 1964–79* (London, 1980), pp. 58–60.

97. 'Wages policy and full employment in Britain', *Oxford University Institute of Statistics Bulletin*, 12, 1950, 225–42.

98. *A Policy For Wages*, p. 30.

99. *Wage Policy in Wartime*, p. 17.

100. Editorial, 'Communists and the production drive', *Socialist Commentary*, 32, 1941, pp. 3–4.

101. 'A system of public control', pp. 16–17; 'The production committee experiment'.

102. *British Trade Unionism*, pp. 45–6.

103. BLPES, Fabian Society Papers, File G50/2, Manpower, Incentives and Industrial Democracy; File G50/3, Industrial Relations. On shop steward

training and workplace bargaining see the Editorials, 'The right to be consulted', *Socialist Commentary*, 15, 7, 1951, pp. 151–2 and 'The problem of apathy', *Socialist Commentary*, 16, 9, 1952, pp. 195–6. The attendance list for the conference was a roll-call of established and rising Labour figures and included Austen Albu (who had worked with Flanders in Germany), G.D.H. Cole, Tony Crosland, Richard Crossman, Roy Jenkins, Ian Mikardo, Harold Wilson and Michael Young.

104. Socialist Union, *Socialism*, p. 53.
105. Socialist Union, *Twentieth Century Socialism*, p. 109.
106. See, for instance, the Editorial, 'Human relations in industry', *Socialist Commentary*, 18, 9, 1954, pp. 237–40. On the debates about joint consultation at the time, see H.A. Clegg, *Industrial Democracy and Nationalization* (Oxford, 1951) and H.A. Clegg and T.E. Chester, 'Joint consultation', in Flanders and Clegg, *The System of Industrial Relations*.
107. See for instance Flanders, 'Democracy and bureaucracy in the Labour Party'.
108. *British Trade Unionism*, p. 59. The later book was *Trade Unions* (1952) and went through seven editions.
109. Ibid., pp. 25–6.
110. Flanders, 'Wages policy and full employment', p. 237.
111. On Watson's role see D. Howell, *British Social Democracy: a study in development and decay* (2nd edition, 1980), p. 208, and Minkin, *The Contentious Alliance*, pp. 93–4. It is also important to note that right-wing social democrats were by no means agreed on all major issues, not least in the sphere of industrial relations. The most famous social democrat intellectual of the period, Anthony Crosland, believed the dangers of inflation to have been exaggerated and was therefore an opponent of state incomes policies: see C.A.R. Crosland, *The Future of Socialism* (1956), p. 461.
112. P. Weiler, *Ernest Bevin* (Manchester, 1993), p. 136.
113. These observations are elaborated and explored more fully in my monograph *Social Democracy and Anti–Communism: Allan Flanders and the development of British industrial relations* (in preparation).
114. He was not alone in this endeavour of course and worked closely for many years with Hugh Clegg, a figure almost as anti-Communist as Flanders: see H.A. Clegg, *Autobiography*, unpublished MSS, p. 36.
115. See P. Maguire, 'Labour and the law: the politics of British industrial relations, 1945–79', in Wrigley, *A History of British Industrial Relations*.
116. See J. Gennard, 'Ben Roberts: an appreciation', *British Journal of Industrial Relations*, 24, 1, 1986, pp. 3–23.
117. See for instance the textbook by Communist historian Allen Hutt, *British Trade Unionism: a short history* (1941 and five subsequent editions). For Cole's quote see Wright, *G.D.H. Cole*, p. 131.

CHAPTER EIGHT

The Shop Floor Politics of Productivity: Work, Power and Authority Relations in British Engineering, c.1945–57

Alan McKinlay and Joseph Melling

Our perception of the shop steward in the British engineering industry continues to be refracted through the prism of the 1970s, the decade in which shop floor organization reached its zenith. There is little doubt that the engineering industry occupied a pivotal place in British industrial relations during the post-war years, though we still lack a detailed analysis of workplace relations in the two decades that followed 1945. Here we suggest that the polarization of formal and informal bargaining recorded by the Donovan Commission was symptomatic of the radical transformation of shop floor industrial relations that unfolded after 1945. Further, the national engineering dispute of 1957 was a watershed in the development of shop steward organization. Before that struggle, shop floor bargaining was not only restricted to individual plants but even to the concerns of particular departments. From 1957 we can detect the emergence of a more strategic approach by engineering shop stewards and a more assertive presence in national union politics. We suggest that the origins of this transformation are to be found in the labour process, the construction of different 'productivity' questions in the engineering industry, and the rising tensions over authority which were embodied in a growing challenge to the position of the foreman in the workplace.

The terrain on which engineering firms and engineering workers contested these issues was formed by the pressures of product and labour markets that prevailed in the two decades after 1945. Skill shortages persisted throughout the period as employers showed little inclination to change radically the established technologies of production or uproot the craft skills that continued to flourish in the workplace. At the same time, however, the leading engineering plants sought to tighten their control over the production process and to renegotiate the effort bargain away from the permissive practices which metal workers had secured in the war years. This process accelerated as competitive and political pressures mounted from the Conservatives' return to office in 1951. In response the Amalgamated Engineering Union (AEU) and its members sought to police entrance to the trade and the formal agreements and factory customs which regulated the pace of work flows and individual effort bargains. The tempo of these engagements quickened through the 1950s. From 1957 the politics of production shifted as job controls were increasingly linked to productivity bargaining. Factory-level bargaining became ever more dominated by contests to establish rules which specified the nature of work tasks, workloads and the protocols of workplace industrial relations. Employers sought to consolidate their position in the bureaucratization of work rules by developing human relations management whilst the stewards became acutely aware of the need to grasp and master the technical language now being deployed in discussions of 'productivity'.

If the struggles around rules in the workplace were the dominant theme in the industrial relations between 1945–57, a more brutal contest continued between employers and shop stewards centring on the lay delegate's right to participate in shop floor bargaining. We shall focus particularly on Clydeside where hard-line firms determined to maintain managerial prerogative unchecked challenged the stewards' representational rights; in response the stewards mounted direct confrontations with the power of the supervisors and gradually acquired a more strategic understanding of their power and authority in the workplace.

The micro-politics of engineering productivity

The starting point for an analysis of the engineering industry is the assumption that the workplace forms a space in which power is exercised and authority is socially constructed. We follow Michael Burawoy in viewing production as a locus for the creation of meanings and ideologies as well as the manufacture of goods and services.[1] We differ from Burawoy, however, in allocating to workers an autonomous and dynamic role in shaping the social world of the factory. For Burawoy, piecework systems which tie individual effort to reward inevitably undermine solidarity and individualize shop floor work. So profound is this individualization that workers become enmeshed in social relations in which their only freedom is *inside* the piecework system, in, for instance, finding ways to beat the times for specific jobs. This highly circumscribed freedom is profoundly corrosive of the very possibility of shop floor solidarity. Piecework systems, we contend, offer only the possibility, rather than the certainty, of imprisoning workers within an output regime that removes their capacity to imagine alternatives or construct collective defences.[2] The consent which workers offer is contingent rather than unconditional and unchangeable. The formation of collective organizations and the experience of bargaining which accompany such activities enable workers to think and act strategically, fostering and furthering collective cultures which provide the means to contest managerial definitions of productivity. British engineering workers devised their own notions of

223

which clocks they wanted to beat and which tactics they might use to achieve this.

The boundary between 'formal' and 'informal' organization validated in the Donovan era is an analytical convenience rather than a reflection of the objective realities of workshop life. Indeed, while the powerful Engineering Employers' Federation (EEF) was broadly sympathetic to the Donovan Commission's analysis and offered a qualified acceptance of its recommendations, it forcefully rejected the sharp distinction between 'formal' and 'informal' systems of industrial relations.

> The Federation's main objections to this diagnosis is the dramatic nature of the antithesis which is made between the formal and informal systems. Engineering employers are certainly not under the illusion that industry-wide agreements 'regulate pay' ... the arrangements for collective bargaining over wages nationally and domestically are complementary, not conflicting.[3]

Ironically, Tom Lupton's ethnographic studies of Manchester engineering works are an important source for Burawoy's thesis that the erosion of solidarity, the construction of game-playing individuals is an inevitable consequence of piecework. But in Lupton's original description of the timing of piecework in the early 1960s the emphasis is quite the reverse: that the pricing of a job was a *public* spectacle in which each worker was personally involved in the negotiations between ratefixer and skilled operative under scrutiny.

> In a very real sense, every worker in the shop was a participant in every argument over allowed times, and if it appeared on any single occasion that the ratefixer was trying to drive too hard a bargain with one worker, others would often leave their work for a few moments to join in the argument ... the system of rate-fixing, in a situation in which every worker might be called on to do any job, encouraged the worker's interest in what his colleagues were doing, and in the quality of his relationship with [the ratefixer], who represented management in the all-important process of fixing allowed times.[4]

Following Lupton's classic shop floor studies, we can derive two key features of factory bargaining which were transparent in the engineering struggles of the period 1945–65. The first is the collective participation of workers in representing their interests when it was perceived that common norms of workshop practice were involved. Here lay the essence of the shop steward's function as the representative of the workplace in which individual workers were occasionally compelled to assume the role of articulating the common good. In such situations there could be no fixed distinction between the formal role of the shop steward and the informal representation of common interests on the shop floor. Collective scrutiny, sanctions and discipline were vital to the dynamics of everyday bargaining. Formal union

224

procedures were invoked only if and when implicit codes of consent were violated and the normal strictures had failed to restore the *status quo*. Members of the engineering union were equally prepared to defend the accredited shop steward and the transient lay representative when their authority was questioned by management.

A second and related feature of the incident noted in Lupton's study is the scope offered for collective piecework bargaining under flexible batch production as workers strove to construct comprehensive prices and to secure mutual safeguards. Such collective tactics appear very different from the routinized, individualized tasks of the mass production shop floor where management's ability to 'manufacture consent' may indeed have been much greater in the multitude of plants making general engineering products in this period. Whilst engineering firms sought to use piecework to regulate effort and limit supervision costs, the co-existence of piecework and highly decentralized forms of workshop administration defined the shop floor as the key arena for conflict between capital and labour in the two decades after 1945.

Significantly, the dynamics of making and breaking consensus on the shop floor revolved around the figure of the trade foreman who continued to embody the traditional hierarchy of authority which capitalist enterprises had developed in the eighteenth and nineteenth centuries. Personally responsible for ensuring that a working consensus was reached on the shop floor by negotiating craft customs and peculiar precedents, the foreman could enforce standards by individual indulgences and the toleration of informal restrictions imposed by workgroups. The border between formal and informal bargaining was a shifting frontier rather than a fixed position and even the introduction of formalized rate-fixing regimes left the foreman with considerable latitude in setting the price of variable work. The pressure from both rationalizing management and articulate unionists to shore up their positions in the campaigns of the post-war years, restricted the trade supervisor's room to manoeuvre between managerial and shop floor pressures. The scope for tactical collusion remained but the tensions mounted steadily until the eruptions of 1955–6 exposed the degree to which the fragile consensus of the post-war era had been shattered.

How does our assessment compare with the established literature on the engineering industry and the strike of 1957 which has emanated from industrial relations specialists and labour historians? The first point to note is the continuing paucity of detailed research on the industry during the period, as well as the resilience of the institutionalist perspective on post-war workplace bargaining which followed the Donovan assessment of British industrial disorders. In this view, the 1957 national engineering dispute was a watershed in the structure and substance of collective bargaining. 'The employers' challenge', Clegg concluded, was 'a conflict of principle ... [rather] than ... a mere argument over a matter of shillings and pence in a boom year'.[5] More than a decade of tight control over wage rates stimulated shop-floor bargaining which in turn placed the authority of front-line management under novel pressures. By 1957 the pressure from below could no longer be contained by engineering's formal bargaining procedures. The war of attrition on the shop floor also meshed with the gradual emergence of a new generation of engineering workers with no experience of the inter-war depression and little sympathy for the craft conservatism of the engineering union. The 1957 national engineering dispute was, as Clegg argued, not simply over wage rates and earnings but symptomatic of a crisis of authority inside British engineering factories.

Strategy, control and resistance, 1945–57

The foreman is the representative of management who is constantly in contact with employees and who is at the same time constantly observed by them. Every opportunity should be taken to strengthen his position in the eyes of the employees.[6]

We still know too little about the dynamics of workplace trade unionism and employer organization during the Second World War to comment with much confidence about the nature of shop floor bargaining during the 1940s.[7] It is clear, however, that factory trade unionism and shop steward organization were extremely varied in scope, depth, and resilience. The immediate post-1945 period saw a marked deterioration in the engineering union's lay infrastructure. On Clydeside, local AEU officials bemoaned the complete collapse of steward organization even in some large factories, 'the half organized state' of most workshops, and, even where stewards remained in place, 'deplored the lack of understanding of Trade Unionism ... never any meetings or discussion'.[8]

During the Second World War engineering employers were often compelled by rank and file campaigns and by the Ministry of Labour to recognize shop stewards. Even then engineering firms organized in the regional Associations and national Federation consistently refused to reach any settlement with the unions which would alter the post-war balance of power in specific factories or the industry as a whole. The employers' readiness to make tactical concessions was matched by their determination not to cede any lasting influence to the shop stewards over the boundaries of skilled work, entrance to the trade, or the organization of production. The employers' strategy was largely successful and the governance of collective bargaining remained relatively untouched by wartime gains in union organization.

The humiliating terms of settlement imposed on the engineering unions after the seminal dispute of 1922 remained the foundation stone of collective bargaining after 1945: management's unilateral right to alter work processes

226

and payment systems remained the cornerstone of employer ideology, unchanged from the late nineteenth century. Equally, despite major membership gains, the AEU emerged from the war with only fragile shop steward organization and volatile union membership established in most engineering works.

Workplace relations remained highly personalized and specific to particular plants. Shop stewards reached a delicate balance of understanding with individual managers rather than formalized agreement. By definition, such personalized bargaining regimes were fluid, always a temporary truce, never a final settlement. The inherent difficulties of maintaining the delicate fabric of shop floor diplomacy contributed to the high levels of turnover among shop stewards in their first year in office. We have little hard demographic evidence about mid-century shop stewards. Broadly, engineering shop stewards tended to be elected in their mid-thirties and have a tenure of between seven and fourteen years.[9]

> The steward has to learn the art of representation with little (sometimes no) formal guidance and often without the steadying influence of an informed 'electorate' ... much of his work is on day-to-day matters not brooking delay. He receives complaints and is expected to rectify many grievances for which there may be little foundation in fact; seeking to get the full facts may lead the member concerned to ask 'Whose side are you on?' and rivals to denounce him as a boss's man.[10]

The diary of Colin Ferguson, a patternmaker in Babcock and Wilcox, Renfrew, noted that impromptu shop meetings of up to 110 employees were convened by word of mouth for lunch times to discuss virtually any question affecting the pay and conditions of any union member. Although the stewards were experienced representatives they were manifestly *delegates* from the shop floor with a clear and specific mandate.[11] This was the daily paradox which defined the limits of the shop steward's bargaining authority: the steward represented his immediate constituents whilst seeking to maintain a personal understanding with those who managed him and with his fellow-workers. Such a personalized nexus of relations between front-line managers and stewards tended to have two consequences in the years leading up to the 1957 struggle. On the one hand, flexible tactics tended to confirm departmental identities rather than generate factory-wide strategies under a convenor. The steward's growing stature, on the other hand, contributed to the erosion of the foreman's authority within the workplace as the piecemeal development of more cohesive union bargaining practices moved issues such as the constitution of bonus *systems* rather than specific prices beyond the direct control of the individual trade supervisor.

The nature and content of the foreman's role formed the other pole of authority that drew the employers and unions into conflict. Trade supervisors

227

were, like shop stewards, also identified with particular departments and their authority hedged and buttressed by personal loyalties and obligations. The foreman's role in the distribution of jobs and earnings opportunities was counterbalanced by their participation in a technical process and work practices which emphasized their common identity with the engineers they governed.[12] Metalworking foremen almost invariably came from a background working with the tools of their craft and drew much of their legitimate authority from this 'experience' rather than their formal managerial power. Several firms recognized the strategic value of using supervisors who possessed formal technical qualifications rather than a wealth of practical experience. What the employer lost in the personal respect given to the time-served man, they could gain in the readiness of technical supervisors to use their expertise in the service of increased output. This was particularly true if the individual was promoted while relatively young rather than by reference to some shared, if implicit, notion of seniority. For the employers, this was one way of insulating the supervisor from the obligations of past membership of the craft community: the collectivist culture of the workshop would be alien to the technically-trained foreman and would not cloud his judgement in the search for enhanced efficiency.

Nor were such cultural engagements confined to the engineering trades. The Foundry Workers' union contested the promotion of an individual who had returned from the forces and served in the Planning and Progress Department, drawing a distinction between 'managerial' responsibilities and those of practical supervision. Acknowledging that the man 'may have studied foundry theory and practice', they noted:

> This certainly may qualify him for some managerial post, particularly with reference to the Planning Department, but we hardly think it qualifies him to be the immediate supervisor of practical foundrymen. He has certainly been a very fortunate young man in having had the opportunities presented to him ...[13]

The sting in the tail of this ambiguous tribute to the promoted man was aimed at someone who had refused to join his fellow apprentices in joining the union a decade before. Nor was the opposition of the trade unionists reserved only for those who possessed the technical qualifications to challenge the tacit knowledge of the craft worker. To promote a young man to chargehand before his trade training was complete conflicted with norms of seniority and experience and flouted the convention that only individuals deeply embedded in the expectations of specific trades could supervise those tradesmen.

The EEF endorsed their member firm's position by insisting that this 'type of lad' stood out 'as a natural leader of his fellows' who would be able to handle the concerns of his peers more easily than 'a foreman or someone in a more responsible position'.[14] Here the industrialists were shrewdly

228

appealing to the qualities of leadership, ability and egalitarian exchange, a rhetoric that the union found difficult to oppose. Privately, however, the EEF cautioned their member firm that as they were unlikely to succeed in puncturing the traditional route to foremanship – of apprenticeship followed by long experience as a journeyman – they should seek pragmatic compromise without conceding the principle of union influence in managerial selection. The union was satisfied: it had seen off an attempt to install a management representative inside the workgroup structure. Key principles of the craft community remained intact: only tradesmen could supervise other tradesmen; craft supervisors always owed a double allegiance both to management and to the workgroup.

The wider political theatre in which these relations were conducted was defined by the refusal of the engineering firms to engage in any corporatist strategy which would have brought them closer to organized labour and the state. The EEF combined public gestures of qualified support for the periodic initiatives by the Attlee governments to promote productivity with a determined opposition to any initiatives to increase workers' participation in production planning. Engineering firms in Clydeside and Belfast were amongst the most ruthless opponents of shop floor representation, resurrecting the enquiry note system to screen out militants and develop a regional black list.[15] A number of firms were willing to combine this with efforts to impose new forms of supervisory planning and work setting on the shop floor.[16] Yet the attempts to isolate shop stewards who had been prominent in the struggles of the 1940s continued.[17] Such moves reflect an unyielding and unimaginative approach to labour relations which was only partially offset by the efforts of leading light engineering firms such as Hoovers to devise a welfarist personnel strategy. Most engineering firms were content to defend the 'right to manage' by invoking the industry's formal bargaining procedures, whilst restricting the activities of shop steward committees by denying stewards the most basic facilities and ignoring the claims of convenors for recognition of their status. Despite some measure of tactical flexibility, engineering employers remained resistant to any moves to incorporate stewards into the framework of factory bargaining throughout the 1950s. Before 1960, for example, 'convenor' was a title whose ambiguous formal status was routinely and publicly signified by quotation marks.[18] As the Scottish Engineering Employers' Association (SEEA) warned their member, Vactric, few local firms recognized full-time convenors and those that had often regretted their mistake: 'concede to him the right, of which he would probably take full advantage, to roam the factory at will attending to (and probably fermenting) labour problems arising in departments in which shop stewards would be constrained by Procedure'.[19]

The slow emergence of inter-union shop steward committees during the mid-1950s was a problematic development for companies, the more discerning of which recognized that obstructing the work of shop stewards – from discriminatory task allocation to outright victimization – merely ensured that the office was increasingly invested with added moral authority.[20] In the airframe sector, the EEF supported local employers' efforts to adapt and reinterpret a 1945 agreement covering the timing of work, whilst also acknowledging the importance of reaching a consensus 'at floor level' on domestic procedure.[21] By fostering good relations with stewards through developing *limited* departmental bargaining procedures and ensuring departmental representation, employers hoped to dampen the demand for overarching factory bargaining. As the Federation pointed out to its Scottish constituents, conducting a guerilla war against stewards would seldom eliminate the unions' presence completely and was likely to destabilize sectional truces:

> Sometimes difficulties have arisen from the appointment of too few Shop Stewards. The situation can, in some circumstances, be embarrassing to the management, particularly if it means that the stewards have a roving commission and can intervene in questions or Departments or Sections other than those in which they are employed. This may work out satisfactorily as long as the Shop Steward concerned is a good Shop Steward and is helpful in keeping the peace. If such a man leaves, however, his successor may be one of the objectionable type of Shop Steward and the Employer then wants to curb the roving commission which has been created by precedent. This is not an easy thing to do.[22]

This strategy of grudging accommodation was widely adopted, even in the hard-line district of west Scotland during the mid-1950s as firms recognized the drawbacks of their long-standing policy of victimization.[23] Such encounters were part of the employers' drive both to accept stewards yet isolate those leading resistance to alterations to production or payment systems. Where relationships between stewards and supervisors frayed beyond repair, front-line management were urged to find ways of eroding the steward's authority but not to exile him from the factory. This was a significant reversal of the Clyde employers' decade-long policy of rooting out union activists and causing maximum disruption to workplace union organization.

The final element of the employers' strategy was the maintenance of good understandings with union officials who shared their anxiety to avoid procedural friction. Even where a shop steward was identified as 'troublesome', the EEF no longer endorsed even discreet victimization if it jeopardized relations with full-time officials who would necessarily become aware of discrimination if the procedure was triggered:

> The opposition to this comes at the moment from one particular source, that is a Mr. Finch, the shop steward who is advising the workers generally not to have it at any price. I would suggest that if Mr. Finch does not like the scheme he could so easily leave the works and work on a scheme that he does like ... [If] we said: 'If you go on like this, we think you had better leave', I have a feeling that we might very

quickly, unless it was ventilated in the sense in which we are discussing it, get it back as a case of a victimisation of a shop steward ... We do not want a position like that to arise. Consultation means meeting the case from both sides ...[24]

Engineering firms did not move towards a strategy of incorporation of stewards in the decisions reached by management until the mid-1960s, but there was a departure from the astringent politics of stonewalling which had marked the 1940s. Increasingly, employers pursued a more variegated strategy of containment by playing on the boundary between the formal and informal systems of industrial relations from the factory floor to the negotiating chamber.[25]

By the 1950s industrial relations was increasingly conceived as a war of manoeuvre in which tactical versatility on the shop floor was critical for the employer. As the Scottish engineering masters advised the national Federation, leadership, tact and patience were as important as ingenuity: 'To be able to make a troublesome shop steward look ridiculous in the eyes of his followers is an achievement well worth very considerable thought and effort'.[26] That such small-scale jousts for authority were considered worthy of serious forethought rather than the subject for sporting comment signifies that the workplace had become the key arena of collective bargaining. For the employers, the shop floor had superseded the negotiating chamber as the front-line in industrial politics.

Power and authority on the shop floor

it is not quite so difficult to restrict the facilities afforded to the shop stewards to carry out their duties, particularly where they are under the control of a foreman who is a good disciplinarian.[27]

Debates about the origins and nature of British industrial decline and the role of labour relations in national economic performance continue to divide academics as well as political propagandists, though there is little disagreement that the language of British politics was punctuated by the refrain of 'the productivity question' in the decades 1945–65.[28] The debates on productivity and work organization that erupted again in the mid-1950s focused on the prevalence of demarcation lines and 'restrictive practices' which capped efficiency and hindered labour flexibility. After scouring industry for examples of restrictive practices, and contrary to their public rhetoric, employer organizations and the Conservative government privately admitted their disappointment at how rare and inconsequential job controls actually were outside the shipbuilding sector.[29] While we do not deny that this was part of the drive to demonize the British worker, there is no doubt that struggles over the effort bargain and work organization were prevalent

231

during these years and remained an unremarkable feature of shop floor life. As we have seen, 'informal' work group controls and bargaining were all-pervasive but only sporadically impinged on formal union procedures and collective agreements.

This duality in shop floor life was a product of the historical adaptation of the craft-based division of labour that dominated mid-century manufacturing. Equally, the interplay between the formal and the informal worlds of production was becoming ever more strained during the 1950s. The task of maintaining a viable fiction between the formal procedure and the informal accommodation on the shop floor fell to the industrial supervisor. As one exchange between senior managers noted, 'custom and practice' regulated work organization to such a degree that foremen 'have to skate around them', and 'so it does not become apparent' to the boardroom.[30] Custom and practice also set clear, if intangible limits to supervisory discretion and power. While it was accepted on the shop floor that the foreman had the right to discipline a worker by holding him on the poorly paid or dirty jobs that were customarily rotated around the workforce, any supervisor who used such power to penalize a shop steward would isolate himself as *unambiguously* a member of management. The consequence was the withering of any scope for a reciprocal exchange of 'gifts' between the foreman and his shop workers, such as flexibility in the working of overtime during particularly busy periods.[31]

The importance of mutual 'indulgences', of various kinds of allowances to ease production was, then, clearly understood by senior management. Underlying this tacit connivance in what employers' leaders were quick on other occasions to denounce as restrictive practices lay a perception of market advantage. Skilled workers could continue to claim their 'traditional' areas of work because their employers did not perceive any great cost advantage in deskilling or dislodging customs and practices which were the *ceteris paribus* of competition. As the Chairman of John Brown Engineering told his fellow industrialists, 'I think what many of us are liable to do is simply to give way and put a skilled man on the job because the skilled man does not cost us more than a semi-skilled man'.[32]

Pragmatism rather than conservatism was, similarly, at the root of the employers' reluctance to move towards more precise rate fixing. Heavy engineering was dominated by production runs which defied standardization and precise time and rate fixing. When criticized for an *ad hoc* system of 'gift payments' paid *after* the completion of work, the production manager of a Scottish engineering works, explained that:

> most of the jobs going through the shops are large jobs involving thousands of hours, and in some cases every man in the shop could be employed at one time or another on the job. It was not uncommon for jobs to go into the shop with a time allowance of 38,000 hours. For these reasons the firm had not made a practice of issuing times.[33]

In the absence of effective managerial bureaucracies capable of delivering a viable alternative to craft administration before the 1970s, engineering firms were unable to reform the traditional hierarchy of supervisory control. Nor could engineering firms deliver to the foreman the kind of power resources to shift the foundations of his authority from craft experience to management expertise. Shop floor administration owed little to impersonal rules and much to highly personalized processes of control.[34] In the post-war years employers were finding that merely reciting the mantra of managerial prerogatives did not provide them with an intellectual resource for overhauling this personalized form of production control. In parallel, workers increasingly eroded the supervisor's discretionary power by elaborating both the formal *and* customary rules that governed the shop floor. Before 1957 engineering shop stewards directed much of their energies to removing the most obvious inequities in piecework payment systems which had developed during the depression. These campaigns included attacks on the pernicious practice of carrying forward negative – but not credit – balances on bonus earnings from week to week, as well as the arbitrary exercise of foreman's power in the exclusion of individuals and small groups from piecework regimes. Employers were ready to sacrifice the authority of particular foremen to defuse moves to generalize a complaint from one department to the factory as a whole. Expediency could totally undermine the supervisor's position making his position unsustainable. On being discharged for falsifying bonus lines, two Kincaids, Greenock, fitters immediately had themselves elected as shop stewards. Management rescinded the discharge rather than risk accusation of victimization. This climb-down was 'broadcast throughout the works' and resulted in the foreman's ultimatum that he would resign unless the errant fitters were transferred.[35] Whilst this settlement restored the foreman's authority it also betrayed its limits: supervisory authority was defined in relation to both the person and the office of shop steward.

Skirmishes over payment systems encompassed a complicated world of workplace politics which ensured that piecework bargaining 'manufactured' at least as much conflict as consent in British engineering. So complex were the payment systems that decoding the terms of the effort bargain became almost a mystic art. To alter one piece-work price offered management no more than a temporary respite before comparability claims were lodged in other departments. To buy off the threat of a small sectional strike by offering individual merit awards would simply trigger claims by engineers with similar skills and experience: 'we shall certainly not be left long in peace by the men', despaired one firm in 1955.[36]

In this situation the shop stewards were seeking that minimum transparency which would bind the collectivity of the workers behind shared notions of effort and output. One important element in post-war collective bargaining was the growing readiness of non-skilled workers to devise their own workplace bargaining agendas rather than following that of the skilled grades. The fact that some of these employees were female gave a further edge to the tensions implicit within the masculine world of craft prerogatives. The existence of Transport and General Workers' shop stewards alongside AEU representatives was one indication of the growing diversity of workplace bargaining in these years. There was also the uncomfortable fact for both management and union that workers might abandon a shop where they could not chase piecework prices. For skilled engineers particularly, exit was an attractive alternative to voice. During low level forms of industrial action, shop stewards appear to have been undisturbed by a sharp rise in labour turnover. Indeed, any loss of skilled labour simply strengthened the steward's hand in workplace negotiations. Faced with a solid embargo on overtime or bonus working – a low cost tactic for bonus workers – and a steady loss of skilled labour, procedural bargaining offered the employer little chance of timely settlement. Engineering firms usually responded pragmatically to this leverage by conceding improved bonus payments for specific tasks whilst maintaining the general outlines of the piecework system. As attempts to renegotiate the industry's national wage structure dragged on to stalemate, firms simply acquiesced to wage drift as earnings were pushed up by a cycle of piecemeal concessions.

The rising pressure from below was characterized by sectionalism and limited engagements on the factory floor. Departmental identities were so powerful at the Rolls-Royce plant at Hillington in the decade after 1945 that the AEU convenor despaired of ever forging a factory-wide platform for negotiations. The Hillington shop stewards, particularly a group of leading Communists, emphasized the need to build a disciplined, hierarchical organization to sustain a coordinated strategy to overcome fragmentation. As small-scale disputes flared across the industry, departmental stewards were held accountable by the plant's convener for failing to control their constituents. The limits of their authority were quickly illustrated by a TGWU steward who commented that on many occasions their members simply decided 'they had a grouse', at which point they 'stop work and start talking amongst themselves. Quite often the Stewards know nothing about it'.[37]

An even more spectacular example of the Hillington shop stewards' weakness at plant-level came in 1951: a small department simply ignored the stewards' ban on piecework, forcing the departmental delegate to resign because his authority was fatally compromised. The incident ignited a flash of resentment against the skilled tradesmen who continued at their benches in the offending department and the wave of bitterness carried a mass of women protestors into the department, throwing pennies and 'screaming "Judas"' at the men working their machines. The women's action shocked the Hillington management who summoned the police to restore order. The union convenor was equally appalled: the outbreak of a 'near riot' by a 'mob' of women had compromised his masculine authority in the eyes of both management and

234

workers. The convenor commented in his own diary that the events had represented 'a real blow for the factory committee, ... a failure that Management will seek to exploit'.[38] The rapidity with which a critical distance could open up between shop stewards pursuing a factory strategy and shop floor workers wedded to sectionalism was a recurring feature of the early 1950s.

Small-scale wages disputes escalated in the mid-1950s as employers defended the continued salience of an increasingly anachronistic wage structure. By 1956 regional employers' organizations were reduced to helpless onlookers, unable to check wage drift. By 1956 the Clyde Employers' Association could only implore its member firms to report 'domestic adjustments' in bonuses so that pay levels could be tracked, not so that they could be controlled.[39] Control over wages and workload was the central feature of the intense shop floor conflict of the mid-1950s. The resolution of these issues raised profound questions, however, about the control of work as the employers sought to push up output whilst the unions defended their position by a network of entrenched customs and practices. The most visible custom in this case was the practice of redistributing tasks via the foreman or even the shop steward to any individual who was short of work. An acute general shortage of work in 1955 enabled and compelled management to reassert their control over the allocation of production. Yet the costs of an open ideological engagement between the right to manage and the collectivity of the engineering workers were also apparent to the employers who recognized this fundamental clash of principles.

This contest between managerial and trade prerogatives was vividly exemplified in Clydeside's 'Bonus Joe' dispute of 1956, which involved a man who refused to participate in the informal custom of worksharing even though he had benefited in the past from the practice and redundancies were imminent. After collective pressure from his workmates failed to persuade him, he faced escalating sanctions from his union and was eventually stripped of his union card. Given that 'Bonus Joe' worked in a *de facto* closed shop, the shop stewards demanded his dismissal. When his employer stood out against the threat of strike action, the regional engineering association reluctantly agreed to back them against the union. As their representatives noted in conference:

> This bristles with difficulties, because the moment you begin to discuss it you come up against the prerogative of management and what you like to do in the interests of your members. We take no exception when you say that you have the interests of your members at heart, which is what you are there for; but when those interests clash with Management's conception of their managerial responsibilities, you get an explosive situation.[40]

The question of wages and the management of output could easily ignite a fundamental clash over the politics of production in these conditions.

Even more seriously, such conflicts could damage the whole fabric of authority relations in the workplace and rupture the traditional hierarchy of management in the engineering shops. The procedures of conciliation could themselves be thrown into disrepute if the union officials failed to retain their control over shop floor activists as the failure of national bargaining corroded the confidence of their members in the AEU's capacity to deliver equitable outcomes through formal procedure.[41] The gap between the failings of the formal governance process and the comparative success of shop floor bargaining widened through the early 1950s. While the industry's archaic national wage structure remained frozen in dispute, shop steward pressure loosened rates within existing systems and skewed piecework rates in their members' favour. Determined shop stewards could prise wage drift of four per cent per annum, irrespective of productivity.[42] Although productivity bargaining notionally linked effort to reward, many advances were a response to labour market and workplace pressure, a process that fragmented rather than consolidated the standards of input and output expected of the workforce. The growing divergence of formal and informal bargaining practices also undermined the legitimacy of union executives.[43] This disenchantment with the official leadership was expressed by the convenor of Remington Rand, Paisley, when justifying the tactic of brief but effective wildcat strikes:

> If the Shop Stewards had abandoned all questions to 'procedure' their factory would now be a low paid 'sweat' shop and probably non-union. It is not part of the EC's responsibility to 'rubber-stamp' a report from the Employers without reference to the Shop Stewards.[44]

The national dispute of 1957 was the culmination of this crisis of established forms of authority not only on the shop floor but also in the negotiating chamber.

The most serious casualty of this collapse was the trade supervisor, who now had to deal with the growing self-confidence and aggression of shop stewards. Industrialists had striven for decades to isolate the staff employees from the shop floor and to ensure that their relations with the salaried grades remained 'domestic' and highly personalized rather than collective and general. This solid front had been dented by the EEF's acceptance of representations from unionized draughtsmen, clerical, scientific and technical employees in discussions on working hours in 1946, but even then the foremen remained unrepresented and the manual unions were unable to make the case for the staff grades.[45] Relations between the salaried and waged employees were embittered by the 1957 engineering dispute as staff employees were barracked for remaining at work.[46] Flouting supervisory authority became endemic, particularly among younger workers whilst foremen's control over the working day was relaxed as labour market pressures

236

again raised the stakes if scarce skilled men walked off the job.[47] When one recently recruited young workman publicly humiliated his foreman and was dismissed, the threat of a strike by the whole workforce forced his rapid reinstatement with compensation for loss of earnings.[48]

The employers belatedly registered the threat to their own position entailed by the destruction of the supervisor's authority, as well as the renewed campaigns by manual and staff unions to recruit the engineering foremen into their ranks. The Employers' Federation urged its member firms to integrate the supervisor more explicitly into management. Supervisors should figure in negotiations with the manual unions 'principally as a public demonstration that he was not simply an intermediary between the shop floor and management but an integral part of the management hierarchy'. Just as the Scottish employers had stressed the symbolic value of publicly humiliating the shop steward, so the Federation deployed the new language of human relations when advising its members that 'the psychological effect of seeing top management in contact and collaboration with the foreman on the shop floor cannot be over-emphasised'.[49] The deepening ambiguities of the supervisor's position and the growing formality of the shop steward's role after 1957 are noted in contemporary academic studies of their relative responsibilities in collective bargaining.[50]

Nor was it lost on the shop stewards. Formal acceptance of the shop steward was simply the platform for winning recognition in the workplace, a process that necessarily involved challenging the authority of the foreman. Recognition was not an event registered in formal agreements but won, secured and extended through small-scale conflicts on the factory floor. In factories such as the Caterpillar plant in Scotland, shop stewards only wrung recognition from a reluctant management by systematically undermining the foreman's position with an orchestrated campaign mobilized to isolate and humiliate individual supervisors. This process of harassment was logged in the stewards' cabin diary in which different hand-writing records incessant pressure until they gleefully note that they have a recalcitrant foreman 'on the run' like 'a headless chicken'.[51] Order could only be restored and maintained by dealing with the shop steward. The point was clearly demonstrated: foremen could not choose which stewards to negotiate with or on which issues. Supervisory authority no longer turned merely on balancing management directives against the observation of workplace norms but also on the recognition of the shop steward's legitimate role in the determination of how that balance should be struck.

Conclusion

The period 1945–57 witnessed a revolution in the nature of workplace industrial relations in British engineering. To understand the development of industrial relations in this period, we have drawn on a notion of the politics of production that emphasizes the collective values of the workforce as much as the institutional procedures of the principal organizations concerned. Rather than following the institutionalist account offered by the Donovan Commission in simply allocating these terms to the shop floor and the negotiating chamber, we suggest that it was the interplay between these arenas which was decisive in shaping the crisis of authority which dominated mid-century manufacturing. Above all, the boundary between the formal and the informal is the product of specific historical circumstances and is not an immutable feature of the British system of industrial relations.

Authority relations in British engineering were peculiarly personalized given the characteristic role of the trade foreman in relation to craft knowledge and traditional hierarchies of command inherited from earlier decades. The paradox remained that one of the most complex and diverse sectors of British industry with the most bewildering range of localized customs also possessed one of the most formalized, centralized and authoritarian procedures for settling industrial disputes. In the decade after 1945, engineering employers continued to withstand the formalization of the shop steward's role whilst shop stewards dedicated themselves to building their constituencies in particular departments with a fairly narrow agenda of interests. The public emphasis on productivity masked a complicated reality in which various local bargains were reached on bonuses and output which reflected the balance of power on the shop floor and in local labour markets as much as any reshaping of the effort bargain. The formal structures of industrial relations grew increasingly remote from and unresponsive to the demands of the shop floor. It was the failure of formal collective bargaining, particularly the widening gulf between national minimum wage rates and actual earnings, which provided the political space for the shop stewards to alter dramatically the politics of production.

The vacuum in formal collective bargaining was filled by the increasing importance of the workplace as the key level of industrial politics. This became evident in the conflicts that swept the workshops when the employers sought to reassert their control over production regimes in the early and mid-1950s. Before the 1957 national dispute, shop stewards pursued a strategy based on a tacit acceptance of unstable departmental truces rooted in highly personalized bargaining regimes. After 1957, shop stewards issued a more open challenge to the authority of trade foremen as they attempted to secure recognition at departmental level while building broader, factory-wide strategies. From 1957, shop steward bargaining weapons became more aggressive and better coordinated. Overtime embargoes became selective as stewards targeted key departments for tactical campaigns. Such selectivity spoke of more cohesive factory organization and of lay leaderships able to coordinate overall factory strategies whose effectiveness did not necessarily test the support of the entire workforce on every occasion. The discretion that lay at the core of the classical foreman's authority was rapidly eroded by shop stewards seeking to codify informal job controls. In this sense, the shop steward was a critical figure not just in the remaking of industrial relations but in the transformation of managerial structures and the gradual bureaucratization of the control processes of British manufacturers.

Notes

We wish to record our debt to the archivists of the Modern Records Centre, University of Warwick (MRC) and Glasgow City Archives (GCA) for their assistance in our research.

1. M. Burawoy, *Manufacturing Consent: changes in the labour process under monopoly capitalism* (Chicago, 1979); *The Politics of Production* (1985).
2. See D. Wrong, *Power: its forms, bases and uses* (Oxford, 1979).
3. Engineering Employers' Federation, *The Donovan Report: an assessment by the Engineering Employers' Federation* (1969), pp. 9–10.
4. T. Lupton, *On the Shopfloor: two studies of workshop organization and output* (Oxford, 1963), pp. 129–30.
5. H.A. Clegg and R. Adams, *The Employers' Challenge: a study of the national shipbuilding and engineering disputes of 1957* (Oxford, 1957), p.7.
6. Glasgow City Archives (GCA), Scottish Engineering Employers' Association (SEEA) Case Paper 44/125(2), EEF to SEEA, 'Status of Foremen', 22 May 1959.
7. See R. Croucher, *Engineers at War, 1939–1945* (1982) for a pathbreaking survey; W.W. Knox and A. McKinlay, '"Pests to Management": engineering shop stewards on Clydeside, 1939–1945', *Journal of the Scottish Labour History Society Journal*, 24, 1995; N. Fishman, *The British Communist Party and the Trade Unions, 1933–45* (Aldershot, 1995).
8. GCA, AEU Greenock District Committee, Minutes, 27 June 1946.
9. H.A. Clegg, A.J. Killick, and R. Adams, *Trade Union Officers: a study of full-time officers, branch secretaries and shop stewards in British trade unions* (Oxford, 1961), p. 162.
10. PEP, *British Trade Unionism: six studies by PEP* (1948), pp. 131–2.
11. See GCA, TD646/38, C. Ferguson, 'Pattern Shop Diary', March 1952–December 1957, for numerous examples; see E. Batstone, I. Boraston and S. Frenkel, *Shop Stewards in Action: the organization of workplace conflict and accommodation* (Oxford, 1977), pp. 100–12, for stewards' negotiated relationship with their constituencies.
12. See D. Roy, 'Efficiency and "the Fix!"', *American Journal of Sociology*, 60, 3, 1954, for a classic account of this process; see also B. Carter, 'Class and control at the point of production – foremen', in P. Armstrong, B. Carter, C. Smith and T. Nichols, *White Collar Workers, Trade Unions and Class* (1986), pp. 56–60.
13. Modern Records Centre, University of Warwick (MRC), MSS 237/1/13/84,

Mavor and Coulson (Creighton), Case Paper, May 1948.

14. MRC, MSS 237/1/13/78, Drysdales, Case Paper, January 1946.

15. A. McKinlay, 'Management and workplace trade unionism: Clydeside engineering, 1945–57', in J. Melling and A. McKinlay (eds), *Management, Labour and Industrial Politics in Modern Europe* (Cheltenham, 1996).

16. MRC, MSS 237/1/13/83, EEF, 'Central Conference notes', May 1948.

17. Ibid., Conference concerning a steward at Browns of Edinburgh, 11 June 1948.

18. See, for example, GCA, SEEA Case Paper 49/51, SEEA, Works Committees: Practice of Certain Members', April 1952; PEP, *British Trade Unionism*, p. 15; S. Lerner, 'Factory agreements and national bargaining in the British engineering industry', *International Labour Review*, 99, 1964, p. 6.

19. GCA, SEEA Case Paper 50/11(1), SEEA to Vactric, 2 February 1951.

20. S. Lerner and J. Marquand, 'Regional variations in earnings, demand for labour and shop stewards' combine committees in the British engineering industry', *Manchester School*, 31, 3, 1963.

21. MRC, MSS 237/1/13/98, Notes for Central Conference (Gloucester Aircraft), February 1948.

22. GCA, SEEA Case Paper 50/11(1), EEF to SEEA, 13 February 1956.

23. GCA, SEEA Case Paper 50/11(3), 'Memo of Interview, MD of Cochrane & Co', 1 August 1962. The Managing Director of Cochrane's was warned by an SEEA official that victimization of stewards would 'only increase the pressure' for the recognition of shop stewards.

24. MRC, MSS 237/1/13/101, Notes for Central Conference (Shelley Ltd), April 1955.

25. M. Terry, 'The development of shop steward organization: Coventry Precision Tools, 1945–1972', in M. Terry and P. Edwards (eds), *Shopfloor Politics and Job Controls: the post-war engineering industry* (Oxford, 1988).

26. GCA, SEEA Case Paper 50/11(2), SEEA to EEF, 24 June 1957.

27. MRC, MSS 237/3/1/267, EEF Enquiry into Shop Steward Recognition, June 1957.

28. Melling and McKinlay, *Management, Labour and Industrial Politics*.

29. N. Tiratsoo and J. Tomlinson, 'Restrictive practices on the shopfloor in Britain, 1945–60: myth and reality', *Business History*, 36, 2, 1994, pp. 65–82.

30. GCA, SEEA Case Papers 56/159; W. Brown, 'A consideration of "custom and practice"', *British Journal of Industrial Relations*, 10, 1, 1972, pp. 55–7.

31. T. Lupton and S. Cunnison, 'The cash reward for an hour's work under three piecework incentive schemes', *Manchester School*, 37, 3, 1957, p. 238; W. Brown, *Piecework Bargaining* (1973), p. 127, on increased steward surveillance and policing of times accepted by pieceworker.

32. GCA, SEEA Case Papers 56/159

33. GCA, SEEA, Circular Letter, 10 November 1954.

34. See R. Edwards, *Contested Terrain: the transformation of the workplace in the twentieth century* (1979); A. Friedman, *Industry and Labour: class struggle at work and monopoly capitalism* (1977).

35. GCA, AEU Greenock District Committee, Minutes, 15 November 1950.
36. GCA, SEEA Case Paper 54/228, NB Loco to SEEA, 31 May 1955; S. Lerner and J. Marquand, 'Workshop bargaining, wage drift and productivity in the British engineering industry', *Manchester School*, 30, 1, p. 33, for steward pressure and loosening bonus rates in mid-1950s.
37. GCA, SEEA Case Paper, 51/50(1), Rolls-Royce, Hillington, AEU, TGWU, Minutes of Works Conference, 5 March 1951.
38. GCA, Rolls Royce Convenor's Diary, May 1951.
39. GCA, SEEA Circular Letter, 3 April 1956.
40. MRC, MSS 237/3/1/267:S(5)44, EEF and General Iron Fitters' Association, Minutes of Central Conference, 14 September 1956.
41. A. Marsh and R. Jones, 'Engineering procedure and Central Conference and York in 1959: a factual analysis', *British Journal of Industrial Relations*, 2, 1964, pp. 228–50, stresses the resilience of engineering procedure and the increased importance of domestic level settlements.
42. P.J. Sloane, 'Wage drift: with reference to case studies in the engineering industry of central Scotland', *Journal of Economic Studies*, 2, 1, 1967, p. 62; A. Tatlow, 'The underlying issues of the 1949–50 engineering wage claim', *Manchester School*, 30, 3, 1953, p. 262; more generally, see A. Warner, 'British Trade Unionism under a Labour Government: 1945–1951', unpublished PhD thesis, Columbia University, 1954, esp. pp. 147–55.
43. See M. Derber, *Labor-Management Relations at Plant Level under Industry Wide Bargaining* (Champagne, Illinois, 1955); L. James, *Power in a Trade Union: the role of the District Committee in the AUEW* (Cambridge, 1984).
44. GCA, AEU Paisley District Committee, Minutes, 1 July 1954.
45. MRC, MSS 237/1/13/80, Notes for Central Conference, December 1946.
46. See GCA, SEEA Circular Letter, 27 June 1957, for a report of extraordinary scenes at Weir Valves.
47. Similarly, see Lupton, *On the Shopfloor*, pp. 114–5.
48. GCA, SEEA Circular Letter, 20 August 1957.
49. GCA, SEEA Circular Letter, 12 June 1958.
50. A. Marsh and E. Coker, 'Shop steward organization', *British Journal of Industrial Relations*, 1, 2, 1963.
51. GCA, Caterpillar, 3rd Shift Shop Stewards' Diary, entries for 7–11 May 1964.

CHAPTER NINE

'The Most Serious Crisis Since 1926': The Engineering and Shipbuilding Strikes of 1957

Nina Fishman

'This is the most serious crisis since 1926 and no one can tell how long it will last or how far it will spread'.[1] The *Observer* was describing the industrial situation on Sunday, 17 March 1957, the day after the first ever national strike organized by the Confederation of Shipbuilding and Engineering Unions (the Confed) had started. The *Observer* noted that all the 200,000 workers in UK shipyards answered the strike call, and anticipated that the Confed would now call out engineering workers: 'We now have to consider the possible cost, and it may prove to be much larger than anybody has calculated.' On Monday, the press reported that the General Secretary of the National Union of Railwaymen (NUR), Jim Campbell, had travelled back from the Continent in anticipation of a national railway strike. He told reporters, 'There are 200,000 out on strike now and by the end of the week there may be 500,000'.[2] On Tuesday 19 March, the Confed Executive called their engineering members out in three waves. The first, consisting of 10 Confed districts, 8 where shipbuilding workers were already on strike, together with Manchester and Sheffield, would come out on 23 March. A week later, 500,000 workers in the Confed's London district would strike. The final wave – 400,000 workers in the Birmingham district – would walk out after a further week.

In the event, the strikes ended on 4 April. The Conservative Minister of Labour, Iain Macleod, appointed a Court of Inquiry to hear the Confed's case for a 10 per cent increase in hourly wage rates for both sectors and he successfully appealed to the Confed Executive to call off the strikes whilst the inquiry was sitting. Comparatively short, certainly peaceful and settled by the Court of Inquiry awards, the strikes nevertheless had a significant impact on the 'post-war consensus'. In their wake, questions began to be asked in the press and inside the political establishment about the place of trade unions in British society. Just over a year later, London busworkers in the Transport and General Workers' Union (TGWU) went on strike for seven weeks. General Secretary Frank Cousins led the strike as a national trial of strength between the trade union movement and the Conservative government. By the end of 1958, the conviction had developed that some basic reform of industrial relations was necessary.

The erosion of the post-war industrial peace

Scholarly interest in the strikes of the mid-1950s has been notably lacking, even though 'the downward trend in strike activity was reversed in the latter part of 1953 and thereafter, despite an isolated fall in 1956, the overall trend was firmly upwards'. The period also witnessed 'the reappearance of the "set piece strike" in both token and total forms – i.e. industry-wide stoppages conducted with the support and approval of the trade unions concerned'. On 2 December 1953, the Confed staged a national one-day stoppage in support of its wage claim for a 15 per cent increase in basic wage rates. By 1959, there had been national strikes involving shipbuilding and engineering workers, train drivers, dockers, busmen and printers. It has been observed: 'The reoccurrence of national level confrontations, after a twenty year absence, is one of the most intriguing features of the whole post-war period.'[3]

National disputes had been conspicuously absent from British industrial relations since the early 1930s. Union leaders refrained from embarking on any national action, having drawn pragmatic lessons from the miners' failure in 1926. Employers' associations had no reason to resort to lock-outs. Pragmatic avoidance of national conflict was reinforced by the consensual approach to industrial conflict developed by Minister of Labour, Ernest Bevin, and his departmental officials during the Second World War. As General Secretary of the TGWU, Bevin's prominent role in the war effort invested the tripartism which his officials were promoting with a potent legitimacy. The image projected was that the British people were winning on the industrial front through voluntary cooperation between unions and employers underpinned by the wise counsels of the Ministry of Labour.[4]

The 1945–51 Labour government operated on the presumption that the post-war social order would include the positive, more orderly industrial relations which Bevin had inaugurated, with employers and unions acknowledging the legitimacy of each other's needs and demands. In 1946 the British Employers' Confederation and TUC agreed to the continuation of the wartime Order 1305 which required both sides to abstain from strikes and lock-outs and to accept binding arbitration in settlement of industrial disputes.

Order 1305 was hastily revoked in August 1951 as one of the last acts of the expiring Labour government anxious to satisfy the urgent pleas of right-wing trade union leaders. Lawful national industrial conflict became possible for the first time since May 1940. But the habits and expectations which its restriction had engendered over eleven years could scarcely vanish at the stroke of a pen. The expectation was that 1305's revocation would make little practical difference to the conduct of industrial relations. And the new Conservative government made it a priority to ensure that the return of 'free collective bargaining' did not resurrect unpleasant pre-war spectres. Churchill was anxious to avoid industrial strife and Sir Walter Monckton, as Minister of Labour, devoted his energies to reconciling both sides of industry, though the price was often inflationary settlements.[5]

The TUC leadership had acquiesced in the rejection by Congress in 1950 of Labour's wage freeze. They had done so without conviction. Most of them were younger than Churchill, but old enough either to bear personal scars from 1926 or to solemnly carry their unions' battle honours from it. They recollected the interwar period as one of steady retreat marked by the troughs of memorable defeats. The wartime consensus brokered by Bevin had yielded far better results. They were reluctant to accept that national disputes could return to being a normal part of a modern trade union's armoury of tactical weapons to gain better wages and conditions. None the less, the revocation of Order 1305 led ineluctably to the return of pre-war 'normality' with all its unpredictable trials of strength. With the retirement of Churchill in April 1955, the imperative to settle disputes through compromise no longer applied. Prime Minister Anthony Eden replaced Monckton in December 1955 with Iain Macleod. Eden, Macleod and the new Chancellor of the Exchequer, Harold Macmillan, agreed with their Labour predecessors that there must be some method of controlling inflationary wage demands. Eden 'began negotiations with the General Council in late 1955 in an attempt to secure support for ... some measure of wage restraint'.[6]

The move was partly prompted by pressure from the employers who considered themselves ill-used under Churchill and Monckton. The Engineering Employers' Federation (EEF) recalled that:

> The Government and the employers' organizations – notably the British Employers' Confederation, in a document 'Britain's Industrial Future', published late in 1955 – were in complete agreement in 1956 that further pay rises were not in the best interests of workers in a period of rising prices, when bigger pay packets would buy less and further aggravate the inflationary spiral.[7]

The government produced a White Paper, 'The Economic Implications of Full Employment' in March 1956 signalling their intentions to pursue a policy of wage restraint in the context of low inflation. This approach was strenuously rebuffed by the trade union movement at the September 1956 Trades Union Congress where Frank Cousins proposed a strongly-worded composite motion against wages policy:

> Congress asserts the right of Labour to bargain on equal terms with Capital and to use its bargaining strength to protect the workers from the dislocations of an unplanned economy. It rejects proposals to recover control by wage restraint and by using the nationalised industries as a drag-anchor for the drifting national economy ...[8]

After a spirited debate, notable for the number of left-wing union leaders who spoke in support, the motion was passed unanimously. Cousins' dramatic intervention caused a flurry of concern in the press about the state of health of the post-war consensus. Richard Crossman remarked later 'that the speech marked the end of "Butskellism" as far as the organized trade union movement was concerned'.[9]

The press could not get the measure of this new General Secretary. Cousins was forthright about having no time for Communism; and yet he was not anti-Communist in the sense that the press and political establishment had come to expect from his predecessor Arthur Deakin. Other union leaders, notably Ted Hill of the Boilermakers and Jim Figgins and Jim Campbell of the Railwaymen, were well known for holding similar militant left-wing views to Cousins. But they were content to occupy an established niche on the left flank of the movement. Cousins had inherited Bevin's mantle and aura as the pivotal figure on the political stage.

He had none of Deakin's prejudices, and was genuinely indifferent as to whether his views coincided with those of the Communists or not. Earlier in the summer, the TGWU had taken the lead at national level in a dispute with the British Motor Corporation on redundancies. It was the first time in the post-war period that a large company had declared extensive lay-offs. The blow fell without warning and without compensation. A strike ensued which was only partially successful. In a note on the dispute, the Ministry of Labour's Industrial Relations Department observed that Cousins and his Assistant General Secretary Harry Nicholas,

> are comparatively young (about 50) and are determined to show the world that under the new management the T. & G. W. U. can be as militant as any other union and are prepared, when necessary, to outbid the Communists. The B.M.C. dispute was their first major opportunity to demonstrate the union's 'new look' and their representative, Mr. Nicholas, was almost certainly the most extreme of the union negotiators, not excluding the Communists, Mr. Ambrose (A.E.U.) and Mr. Foulkes (E.T.U.).[10]

Nevertheless, there was not a hot autumn of heightened class conflict. On 19 November 1956, the circular letter to British Labour Attachés in foreign embassies from the Overseas Department of the Ministry of Labour began, 'I am happy to report that the industrial relations scene in this country is not unduly disturbed at the moment.' It concluded:

> You will not need me to tell you that we were much impressed with the responsible line of policy expressed by the trade union leaders … to the effect that workers should not take industrial action against the Government over the Suez crisis, and by the commendable reactions of the great body of British workers.[11]

The whole of the union leadership, including Communists and left-wing socialists, were habituated to dealing with the Conservative government in a highly pragmatic fashion. From the Communist-dominated ETU to that epitome of moderate rectitude, the NUGMW, union leaders did not allow party political considerations to interfere with their use of the Ministry of Labour's good offices to pressurize employers.

The background to the dispute

These same union leaders conspicuously refrained from any attempt to find or develop common ground with the Tory government. Right-wing leaders consistently spoke in favour of moderation, but would not be seen cutting a political deal with a Tory government on a matter of high national policy. Their contradictory response did not stem from simple expediency. They believed passionately in democratic socialism. They also recognized that their reflexive distrust of Tories was shared by most rank and file lay officials and activists. They spoke from their own hearts and for their active, committed membership when they expressed unalterable anti-Tory sentiments.

Typical of the right-wing's visceral anti-Conservatism was the leading article in the AEU *Journal* for January 1957, written by the right-wing President, Bill Carron:

> Hard times always hit the workers hardest. The latest [post-Suez sterling] crisis is one more galling reminder that this rule inexorably applies ... These days any wage claim has to surmount more than the customary hurdles of the employers' counter-arguments at the negotiating table. It has to find its way through the deliberate smoke-screen of propaganda against wage claims laid down by the Government and its allies in numerous newspapers and journals ... Since the war [workers'] restraint has been remarkable ... But since 1951 Government policies designed to these ends have been progressively abandoned.[12]

Macmillan, Prime Minister from January 1957, and Macleod were concerned that Carron's speech might signal a sea change. Neither was pleased by the prospect. Macmillan's attitude towards the possibility of heightened 'class war' was similar to Churchill's. His own memories of being MP for Stockton-on-Tees in the 1930s permanently influenced his political reflexes. Macleod was a man of the wartime generation who carried with him little of the emotional baggage of the 1930s. His Conservative outlook had been honed by participation in a levelling, democratic war effort. He wanted to make his mark at the Ministry of Labour with a progressive approach along the lines of the Industrial Charter, produced by the Conservatives' new Research Department in 1947, which proposed a substantial extension of rights for working men and women in return for their accepting new workplace responsiblities.[13]

Despite their unwillingness to countenance industrial conflict, both Macmillan and Macleod were subject to countervailing pressures from within the Conservative party and the government. There was concern about the

246

level of wage settlements in the context of Britain's problematic economy and the article of faith that wage increases must not be inflationary.[14] The government's policy of discouraging 'excessive' settlements remained official policy though its place near the top of ministers' priorities was displaced during the Suez crisis. On 19 December 1956 the circular letter to Labour Attachés noted that the situation had changed from being 'fairly quiet on the industrial relations front': ' ... a few black clouds are beginning to drift in due to repercussions of Suez, principally the sudden increase in the cost of motor fuel oils ... There are indications that trade unions will be more obdurate in pressing existing wage claims ...'.[15]

A battle was unlikely in coalmining. The Labour government had made significant concessions to the miners and the National Union of Mineworkers (NUM) had little reason to test the Conservative government's nerve. The railwaymen had more reason to be militant. They were key players in forcing the TUC General Council to back revocation of Order 1305 because they were frustrated by the meagre awards of the industry's arbitration machinery. When the NUR Executive voted unanimously in favour of national strike action in 1953 and 1954, they fared somewhat better. During Walter Monckton's tenure at the Ministry of Labour, reasonable advances in wage rates were gained.[16]

On 19 March 1957, the Railway Staff National Tribunal responded to an NUR demand for a 10 per cent increase in wages by awarding increases of no more than 3 per cent for most members. On 20 March, Jim Campbell led his Executive in rejecting the report as 'an insult to railwaymen'. The NUR case was strengthened by the fact that for the first time the Tribunal award had not been unanimous. The trade union member of the three-man body, E. Hall of the Lancashire NUM, issued a minority report stating that the NUR claim was '"fair and reasonable" particularly in view of the fact that productivity on the railways had increased'.[17]

The railway award was announced four days into the national shipbuilding strike and with a national engineering strike imminent. Instead of pressing home their policy of wage restraint in the face of these threats, the Cabinet on 18 March executed a dramatic *volte face*. Macleod informed his colleagues of his belief that 'the Government's own aim must be to prevent these three separate disputes from merging into a common struggle waged in three industries simultaneously, with the risk that the dispute would spread to other industries'. The immediate objective was to resolve the railway dispute and the necessary arrangements were being made. He reported that shipbuilding workers were 'showing little enthusiasm for the strike' and anticipated that conciliation would be possible here. In engineering, however, he was pessimistic about the efforts his department was making.[18]

That same day Macmillan made his first major public speech since becoming Prime Minister. It was highly pacific: 'In the long run, and for the common good, the umpire is better than the duel'.[19] On 19 March he met Eric Braby,

Director of the EEF, Sir John Hunter, President of the Shipbuilding Employers, Sir Brian Robertson of the British Transport Commission (BTC) and Sir
Colin Anderson, president of the British Employers' Confederation.
Macmillan was due to leave for Bermuda on the following day to meet Eisenhower. It was the first time that British and US heads of state had conferred
since Suez, and he had painstakingly prepared the ground for a favourable
outcome. Macleod supplied Macmillan with a briefing for the meeting with
the employers.

> [It] was designed to bring maximum pressure to bear on the employers and he
> couched the Prime Minister's appeal in appropriately spine-chilling terms ... [It]
> reveal[s] how desperately anxious Ministers were to avert industrial conflict on a
> scale that was likely to jeopardize the fragile confidence in sterling.[20]

The employers were pressed into accepting that the government's support
for 'sensible, realistic' wage settlements had to be subordinated to the wider
national interest. First on the agenda was a settlement of the railway dispute
which did not breach 'sensible' wage levels too openly. Robertson was freed
from taking the BTC's statutory duty to earn a profit into account. Negotiations were expedited and by 22 March the NUR had settled for 5 per cent.
The EEF and Shipbuilding chairmen, however, made no moves towards compromise. They promised only to present Macmillan's case to their respective
Executives.[21]

The protagonists

In contrast to the position in the railway dispute, neither the unions nor the
shipbuilding and engineering employers were ready to settle; in fact both
sides expected a set-piece battle. The shipbuilding employers reckoned they
were in a favourable economic position to withstand an all-out strike while
the EEF was determined to take a stand to end the unions' presumption of
annual wage increases. These two related industries comprised the largest
sector of privately owned capital, and were also amongst the most profitable. Since the First World War, negotiations had been informally, but
explicitly, coordinated by the two employers' federations.[22] Moreover, there
was a 'marked difference' between the approach of the EEF and the Shipbuilding Employers to the Confed. Due to the replacement of wartime losses,
British shipbuilding employers had had full order books since 1945, and
were currently highly profitable. The shipbuilding employers were prepared
'to discuss "off the record" and to try all means of reaching agreement'.[23]
Macleod's expectation of settling this dispute on its own was hypothetically
accurate, but the problem remained of the now traditional linkage with the
engineering dispute.

The middle-ranking employers who dominated the EEF's leadership conceived its principal duty as holding the line in the perpetual struggle with engineering unions. Relations between the EEF and engineering unions remained strictly adversarial, unlike other industries where unions participated as equals in joint consultation institutions and Joint Industrial Councils. In 1953, Clegg described the Federation's attitude towards unions as '"traditional" ... Trade unions have their place and their rights, which [engineering] firms and federation respect, but also wish to limit'.[24] For most of its history, the Federation had enjoyed the substantial advantage of facing a divided opposition: the largest engineering union, the AEU, refused to participate in the Confed. Engineering unions, and the AEU in particular, had old scores to settle with the EEF. Most full-time officials in the 1950s had bitter memories of the EEF's victory in the 1922 lock-out. In 1931, they had to endure another humiliating retreat when the EEF had imposed swingeing cuts in overtime and piece-rates. As young members they had listened to veterans who remembered the protracted lock-out in 1897 when the newly emergent EEF had seized the initiative from the union.[25] Many moderate AEU officials had been militant shop stewards in 1922. Executive Councillor, and later President, Bob Openshaw was typical of these veterans who shared the spirit of vendetta towards the EEF with left-wing and Communist colleagues.

The unions had taken the opportunity war offered to redress their weakness. In 1939, Jack Tanner won the election for AEU President. He was the leading member of a left-wing caucus, which had been operating effectively inside the union since the 1920s. His place on the Executive Council was taken by his close associate, the Communist Joe Scott.[26] The left were determined to improve the AEU's workplace organization and negotiating strength at all levels. Tanner's election enabled them to pursue aims which they had long cherished but had been frustrated from achieving by craft conservatives, notably the admission of women into the union. In the wartime atmosphere of radical optimism, they took stock of the union's position and recognized the AEU's failure to become the all-embracing industrial union for engineering which they had pursued as young revolutionary shop stewards.[27] The AEU's re-affiliation to the Confed was the obvious second-best option.

Tanner, Scott and their colleagues found willing allies inside the Confed. Its full-time General Secretary, Gavin Martin, a boilermaker, fully shared their left-wing activist outlook. His Assistant General Secretary, Maurice Kidd, was the son of the General Secretary of the Sheet Metal Workers. Hired for his shorthand and administrative skills, Kidd had been socialized into his father's left-wing craft trade unionism and was a keen Labour Party member. He was evidently indispensable to Martin who 'was not an administrator'.[28]

A motion was passed at the 1944 AEU National Committee by 38–12 in favour of affiliation to the Confed. Tanner welcomed the decision and predicted that it would 'yield important results'. Consequent negotiations led to agreement on terms which were approved in June 1946 by the AEU membership by a majority of 9–1.[29] The AEU returned to the Confed after a gap of twenty-eight years, becoming its largest and most powerful member. Changes to the Confed's constitution took account of the concerns of both the AEU and the smaller craft unions which had previously dominated the Confederation. In order to obtain a majority, the AEU either had to ally with some of the smaller craft unions or one of the two affiliated general unions which organized unskilled and semi-skilled workers. Tanner and his allies were content that the AEU should be treated by the thirty-six other craft unions as no more than an equal. All seven AEU Executive Councillors as well as the President and General Secretary had seats on the Confed Executive.[30] They were also confident of the coincidence of values and goals which they shared with the smaller unions.

Even though the AEU admitted semi-skilled members, the presumption by craft union activists of a coincidence of views with the AEU was not unrealistic. Critical numbers of AEU activists still shared a craft outlook, and had not adjusted to their union championing the interests of the growing number of semi-skilled members. In exceptional wartime conditions, a radical political climate had flourished and left-wing candidates, including many Communists, swept to victory in AEU elections to full-time office. Nevertheless, the new office holders were not anxious to challenge the craft mentality of the many union loyalists who had supported their election. They were also committed to the enlarged Confed, particularly its new district organization. They viewed the districts as the vital local expressions of the engineering unions' solidarity.[31]

The Confed's constitution provided for an Annual Meeting where delegates from affiliated unions' Executives and the new Confed districts gathered for an entire week. The meeting was an important occasion to cement relations. The election of a new and popular left-wing President in 1948, Harry Brotherton, greatly enhanced the Confed's standing. Brotherton had close, long-established working relations with Tanner, Ted Hill of the Boilermakers, Scott and the many Communist activists in his Sheet Metal Workers London district.[32]

The wage claim

The Confed used its new credibility to good advantage. Exploiting the conditions of full employment, its officers presented an unremitting and rapid succession of ambitious wage claims to the EEF. Despite the substantial increase in engineering earnings during the war, hourly rates remained low. The Confed case was that engineering workers deserved a reasonable basic rate, and in the post-war political climate this argument had strong reso-

250

nance.[33] The left in the Confed was not deterred by engineering workers' increasing prosperity. They based their arguments on morality. Low basic hourly rates and reliance on overtime were absolute evils for trade unionists. The EEF strongly resisted this basic premise. However, they were unable to sustain the argument that their members lacked the resources to pay a higher basic rate. Instead, the EEF hoped the unions, institutional inertia and a return to peacetime normality would prevail. As a result of the Cold War, the balance of power inside the AEU Executive moved towards a right-wing group which had coalesced during the war in response to the Communists' election successes.

Nevertheless, the changed national balance of power in the post-war period and Monckton's moral coercion forced the Federation into concessions which it greatly resented making. Between 1952 and 1956, the EEF actively resisted the Confed's claim for an increase in hourly rates on three out of four occasions but 'gave way in the end, twice because the Government and perhaps their own members could not face the struggle when the testing time came'.[34] In both 1955 and 1956, the Confed's wage claims had been settled without incident with the EEF conceding marginally higher amounts each time.[35]

The EEF leaders remained highly sceptical of the Confed's ability to mount an all-out attack based on opposition to low basic rates which affected few of their members. The Federation had successfully lobbied Eden into taking a stronger stand against 'excessive' wage demands in 1956. It now began to prepare its own members for the possibility of directly facing down the unions.

However, inside the AEU the left-wing continued its electoral success, with two members out of seven on the Executive Council, and strong representation at the policy-making annual National Committee. There Communist activists, particularly the young Reg Birch, put on dazzling displays of oratory to sway critical numbers of the fifty or so delegates.[36] The moderates lacked a realistic alternative strategy to counterpose to the militants' truism that basic rates were unacceptably low. The EEF remained implacably opposed to any suggestion of rationalizing the wages structure, despite the recommendations of a Court of Inquiry in 1954.[37]

At the end of April 1956 the AEU National Committee called for a 'substantial' wage rise. The EEF immediately responded by 'telling the public and member firms that they regarded the action of the AEU as wholly irresponsible and contrary to national policy. An immediate press statement was issued declaring that a new claim would have to be resisted'. The statement was insufficiently strong for the chairmen of the Midlands and West of England associations of the EEF. They met and organized a faction to ensure that this time round the Federation would actually fight.[38] *The Times* commented, 'it is hard to recall a previous occasion when determination to resist a new claim has been made public at such an early stage'.[39] There could be little doubt that the AEU National Committee motion would form the basis of the wage claim which would be discussed at the Confed Annual Meeting in August. With Cousins now its General Secretary, the TGWU was no longer automatically in favour of the moderate line. Nicholas, who represented the union on the Confed Executive, pursued an aggressively militant policy.

The Midlands and West of England chairmen successfully pressed the Federation's Management Board in May to make a direct appeal to the Confed 'not to bring forward a wage claim and to warn them that, if they did, the employers would have to reject it'. The EEF delivered the admonition on 28 June at a routine conference with the Confed. They held a Press Conference afterwards stating that they had appealed to the unions 'in a spirit of friendship and mutual respect'.[40] The hawks were greatly reinforced by a meeting between EEF officers and the Chancellor in early June, when Macmillan told them, 'So long as I have anything to do with the Government we will stand behind you'.[41] At the Confed's annual conference, Brotherton's presidential address referred to the EEF's manoeuvre in contemptuous tones.[42] Nicholas, proposing the vote of thanks to the President, applauded his militancy.

> His [Brotherton's] speech had emphasised the extent to which Government policies were presenting a challenge to the whole Trade Union Movement … It was opportune that the President should have reminded the delegates that those who supported these policies could not escape their responsibilities if the Unions showed their determination to challenge them.[43]

The AEU President, Bob Openshaw, moved the resolution on wages instructing the Executive to 'press a claim immediately for a substantial wage increase for all manual workers in the Engineering and Shipbuilding Industries'.[44] During the debate, Frank Foulkes commented: 'he could remember no other occasion when the Engineering Employers' Federation had made the position so simple … now all that remained was to give consideration on how to get any increase.' Nicholas seconded the motion which was carried unanimously.[45]

The Confed presented a claim for a 10 per cent increase in basic hourly wage rates to the EEF on 25 October, and the EEF rejected it outright on 29 November.[46] The Confed presented the same claim to the Shipbuilding Employers on 30 October and they rejected it on 11 December. At its meeting on 13 December the Confed Executive approved the action of the chairmen of the Engineering and Shipyard Sub-Committees, Carron and Hill respectively, in refusing 'to accept the rejection of our claims'. Arrangements were made for meetings in York on 9–10 January 1957.[47] Preparations to clear the decks for full-scale conflict had been made.

Strike preparations

The Confed Executive agreed unanimously on 9 January to recommend to the conference of executives of affiliated unions on 10 January that the claim be presented again to both employers' federations and 'that failing a satifactory conclusion, action will have to be taken to enforce the claim'.[48] The conference duly adopted the recommendation. The claim was re-presented to the EEF on 12 February, and the meeting concluded without a date for their reply being fixed.[49]

On 13 February, when the Shipbuilding Sub-Committee presented the claim to the Shipbuilding Employers, Hill secured a commitment from them that they would respond to the claim before the EEF. His move was part of an elaborate strategem. The union team was the same for both sectors, Hill, Brotherton, Martin and Scott, with the right-wing Carron, who joined it on becoming AEU President in September 1956. Carron was viscerally opposed to militancy. But he was also a rank outsider and cautious about making any moves in direct opposition to his colleagues.[50] Scott had been a member of the Confed's negotiating team since 1954. Jack Tanner had left the conduct of Confed Executive business to Scott and Openshaw in the latter years of his AEU presidency. The two had worked closely with their Confed colleagues despite the fact that Openshaw was more moderate than the others. Both remained on the Confed Executive through AEU custom, even though they did not hold AEU office. Scott was consequently not formally bound by the collective discipline of the AEU Executive.[51]

The AEU National Committee, recalled on 8 January, had approved a two-day national strike if the EEF rejected the claim. If the EEF rejected the claim before the shipbuilding employers, Carron as chairman of the Engineering Sub-Committee would propose a two day-strike and the negotiating team and the Engineering Sub-Committee were bound by custom to follow his lead. It was to pre-empt this outcome that Hill, Brotherton, Martin and Scott had contrived Hill's manoeuvre. They knew that the shipbuilding employers were likely to reject the claim. By ensuring that shipbuilding negotiations came to a head first, Hill as shipbuilding chairman could propose an indefinite national shipbuilding strike. By custom, his recommendation would be adopted by the negotiating team and Shipbuilding Sub-Committee. The militants anticipated that Carron would then be bounced into following the shipbuilding precedent for engineering.[52]

Their strategem succeeded. On 19 February, the Confed Executive was told that the Shipbuilding Employers would reply on 5 March. The Executive noted that if there was 'a breakdown of [the Shipbuilding] negotiations', their meeting scheduled for 7 March would 'require to determine what action is to taken to enforce the claim'. Contingency arrangements were made to bring the machinery for taking national action into readiness for a strike.[53]

The Shipbuilding Employers rejected the claim on 5 March. On 7 March the Confed Executive agreed unanimously to recommend an all-out indefinite strike to the conference of executives of affiliated unions to be held later that day. The strike would commence on Saturday 16 March, and was 'the only measure unfortunately available to us in face of the Employers' adamant attitude'. The conference adopted the recommendation unanimously.[54] Five days later on 12 March the EEF rejected the claim. The Confed Executive met later that day and considered a letter from Macleod offering to refer the shipbuilding dispute to arbitration as 'the best way to reach a peaceful settlement'.[55] However, the Executive voted to reject his offer. The militants then used the shipbuilding precedent to obtain agreement for a conference of affiliated executives on 15 March to approve strike action.[56]

Wilfred Neden, the Ministry of Labour's Chief Industrial Commissioner, met the Confed officers on 15 March to discuss the shipbuilding dispute. They told him 'the Confed was not agreeable to arbitration but were ready to negotiate' on the basis of the 10 per cent claim. The Confed Executive decided unanimously on 15 March to recommend strike action in engineering to commence on 23 March. However, they postponed the conference of affiliated Executives to approve the recommendation until 19 March.[57]

The reasons the Executive postponed the conference seem clear. The militants were determined to push the AEU Executive into calling an indefinite strike. The shipbuilding strike was scheduled to start the day after the conference of affiliated executives. But on 15 March, Brotherton, Martin, Scott and Hill were still uncertain of obtaining the overwhelming support they required to pressure the AEU Executive into support. By 19 March the shipbuilding strike would have been underway for four days. If it were 100 per cent solid, as the militants hoped, it would act as a magnet, irresistibly drawing the AEU Executive into emulation.

Events favoured the militants. On 16 March, 200,000 shipyard workers were on strike. The public face of the strike was the Boilermakers' leader, Ted Hill. His pledge to Merseyside strikers the following day was widely reported: 'I am prepared to die with you people in this struggle for justice'.[58] Another Hill strike epigram also lodged in collective memory: 'I am not concerned with the effect [of the strike] on the country; I am concerned only with our members, who come before the country'.[59]

On 19 March, the Confed Executive met and received reports that 'apart from apprentices and the members of the non-manual workers' unions, the strike in shipbuilding and ship-repairing establishments was complete'. A lengthy discussion followed without agreement on the form the engineering strike should take. The unidentified mover and seconder of a motion merely 'intimated they would pursue their proposal at the meeting of [affiliated] executive representatives to follow'.[60] However, the conference did not consider a detailed strike plan. It agreed only that action would commence on 23 March 'in units of the Engineering Industry to be specified', and that there would be a graduated withdrawal of labour to be completed by 6 April.

The next day, only three days before the strike was due to start, the Confed Executive finally decided on the form it should take. Workers in eight ship-building districts as well as Manchester and Sheffield would constitute the first wave.[61]

The protracted delay in agreeing arrangements was probably due to the need to balance the keen desire of AEU activists for an immediate all-out strike against the likelihood of achieving a 100 per cent response. Engineering workers were less well organized than shipyard workers and less committed to their unions. The ten Confed districts chosen represented the most credible threat to the EEF. Scott – allegedly the main architect of the plan – was probably confident that engineering workers in these areas would answer the call; and there were sufficient numbers to show the Federation that the unions meant business.[62]

Strike action and compromise

Because there had never been an engineering strike on this scale – and no ballots had been held to test rank and file support – neither union leaders nor employers could be certain of the response. However, the preparations made by local full-time officials had been thorough: 'Everywhere the impression was of a quiet but firm obedience to union instructions'.[63] Because of the uncertainty about which workers would be called out, most officials took the precaution of holding union district and Confed district meetings before the strike. They were attended by shop stewards, lay branch officials and other interested members, and passed resolutions supporting strike action. Smaller meetings discussed and arranged strike organization committees. Activists returned to their factories and branches prepared to pass on the call to strike.[64]

The Confed district committees were responsible for local strike organiza-tion. They normally met monthly, with affiliated unions sending representatives according to their local membership. The elected presidents and secretaries were typically full-time union district officials.[65] The ten striking districts made differing arrangements, but they all provided an ef-fective chain of command.[66] Though officials and lay activists were organizing district-wide strike action for the first time, they drew on the strong culture of engineering unionism and mounted picket lines, held meetings, organ-ized collections and generally kept their members busy.[67]

The *Daily Mail* reported on 28 March that the TUC General Council felt that 'Communist influence on many of these committees is strong. One of the TUC chiefs said that some of these bodies were becoming "little local Soviets" ... TUC chiefs agreed that the Communists are aiming at a repeti-tion of the General Strike of 1926'. Nevertheless, the strikes were uniformly orderly. Only 'a few clashes' with the police were reported.[68] Employers made no attempt to organize non-union labour to keep production running. Revenge for some came after the strike, when they refused to take back the shop stewards and conveners whom they considered 'ringleaders'.[69]

By the end of the first week of the engineering strike, the number of days lost through strikes in March 1957 'had been the highest in any month for about 30 years ... The total number was 3,646,000, of which 1,518,000 were in shipbuilding and 2,011,000 in engineering'.[70] Though the EEF had not yet been sufficiently bludgeoned by Macleod to come back to the negotiating table, the shipbuilding employers had made an offer in line with the railway settlement on 22 March, 5 per cent linked to a deal on 'conditions'. However, the Confed Shipbuilding Sub-Committee rejected the offer on 25 March. They were implacably opposed to 'conditions' linked to deals on 'restrictive practices'and also to a wage freezing undertaking not to make further wage claims for at least a year. The Confed Executive decided to report the breakdown in negotiations to the Ministry of Labour. The Confed officers met Wilfred Neden that evening.[71] Their evident intention was to bring government pressure to bear on the employers to make a better offer.

Neden subsequently met the shipbuilding employers and judged that there was no possibility of bridging the gap between the two sides in conciliation. Macleod then announced his intention to set up a Court of Inquiry, a course of action which he could take independently of both parties. However, he used the opportunity to request both the employers and the Confed to cooperate with the Court, and appealed for an end to the strike. The Confed Executive responded noncommittally, resolving merely to seek a meeting with him 'to discuss the situation as it is in both the Shipbuilding ... and the Engineering Industry'. They exerted pressure on Macleod to pressure the EEF leaders, who in contrast to the Shipbuilding Employers remained recalcitrant, refusing even to come back to the negotiating table. The Confed Executive were evidently determined to extract their pound of flesh from the Federation for its war of words against them during the summer of 1956.[72]

Macleod duly brought the government's full authority to bear, and the Federation finally made an offer on 29 March, but only for 3.5 per cent plus 'conditions', including a moratorium on submitting any further wage claims, 'either on a national, district, or establishment basis for an agreed period'.[73] As the EEF must have anticipated, the Confed Executive rejected the offer summarily and implemented their decision taken on 27 March to call out the second wave, 500,000 workers in the Confed's London district from Saturday 30 March.[74]

However, the Federation's offer enabled Macleod to extend the Court of Inquiry's brief to engineering in anticipation that the Confed would not only participate in it, but also call off the strikes in both sectors. He was receiving information from his Ministry officials, and probably also privately, that the Confed Executive could be so persuaded. On Friday 29 March he wrote informing them that the Inquiry would commence the following week. He appealed for an end to the strikes as being of 'the greatest assistance' to the Court's deliberations and 'in the interests of all concerned'. The Confed Executive arranged a meeting of affiliated Executives for the following Tuesday 2 April. The meeting had the authority to take a decision to call off the strikes.[75]

The Confed Executive met on 2 April to consider what recommendation to make to the meeting of affiliated Executives later that day. Two votes were taken, the first on an amendment declaring 'complete opposition to, and rejection of, the Employers' suggestion of a wage freeze' and urging that the strike continue 'until a cash settlement acceptable to the Unions is agreed upon'. This was rejected by 15–9. The second vote was on a motion which recorded 'appreciation for the loyalty and solidarity displayed' by the strikers whose 'action has resulted in both the Shipbuilding and Engineering Employers being ultimately forced to enter into direct negotiations and make cash offers'. It recommended 'an organized return to work; the position to be reviewed when the recommendation of the Courts are made known'. This was carried by 15–10 with three abstentions, from the TGWU, the Draughtsmen and the Furniture Workers. The ten opposing the resolution included Ted Hill and Danny McGarvey of the Boilermakers, Joe Scott, Frank Foulkes and the two Foundry Workers' representatives.[76]

The Executive's recommendation was accepted by the meeting of affiliated executives conference later that day. It was carried on a card vote, but only after Hill and Foulkes had moved an amendment to continue the strike, for which Frank Cousins had cast the TGWU's votes.[77] A united return to work was agreed for Thursday 4 April. By the next day it was public knowledge that the decision to end the strike had been carried through the efforts of one individual, Carron. He had used his casting presidential vote to break a 3–3 tie at a meeting of the AEU Executive Council in favour of a return to work.[78]

Judgements on the dispute

The decision to call off the strike was analysed succinctly in the Overseas Department's circular letter to Labour Attaches. It identified three factions: the moderates, 'the tough militants (and who can be more militant than shipworkers) [who argued] for a "real show-down"', and the 'Communists and fellow-travellers in some Union Executives and at factory level':

> The position of the wiser counsellors [moderates] was, however, gradually strengthened by the growing appreciation of the heavy costs of the strike to the trade unions themselves, and an awareness of the fact that more and more strikers were having serious doubts about the wisdom of the strike, with possible repercussions on the spread of the engineering snowball [*sic*] strikes. There was also a growing

realisation of the extent to which Communist trouble-makers were voicing the clamour for a 'class struggle'.[79]

There was notable disappointment amongst militant activists in the London area that their opportunity to engage in real struggle had lasted only three days. However, it was not only moderates who acknowledged that it was impractical to carry on with the strikes during the Court of Inquiry. Jack Jones, who was Secretary for the TGWU's large Midlands Region, recalled that he had not considered that the strike was sustainable.[80] It is, indeed, difficult to envisage the unions being able to hold workers on strike through the month while the Inquiry sat on their meagre strike pay, in most cases less than one-third of most engineering workers' average earnings.

The Court of Inquiry's reports were published on 2 May. The identical increases which they awarded represented a small advance on the shipbuilding employers' offer, and a sizeable advance on the EEF's: 5 per cent without strings, or about 6.5 per cent if the Confed would cooperate with initiatives to deal with 'restrictive practices' in their respective sectors. The Confed formally accepted the higher offer with strings for engineering on 23 May, and did the same for shipbuilding on 11 June, although only after strong protests from the Boilermakers. But in practice, the employers showed no enthusiasm in either sector for serious moves to root out 'restrictive practices'. The Inquiry's recommendation in this respect proved little more than a face-saving device to allow more than 5 per cent to be paid.[81]

The settlements represented excellent results for the unions. The 6.5 per cent increase they had won was above 'the going rate', when both employers' federations had been determined to offer nothing. There were also substantial non-monetary gains. The strikes had a decidedly positive effect on membership. Local union officials used the promise of strike pay to recruit new members from amongst those thrown out of work by the stoppage. Clegg and Adams reported brisk competition between the big unions to sign up new members on the best strike pay. The AEU and TGWU paid supplements to make their strike pay of £2 and £2 10s per week nearer to the NUGMW's £4 level.[82] The AEU Divisional Organizer (DO) for Merseyside reported that 'arising from the recent dispute a series of organizational meetings are being arranged at appropriate establishments'. His report is typical of information received by the AEU Executive Council.[83]

Equally important was the fact that for the first time the unions had got the better of the Federation in open conflict. This was reflected in the number of firms which made concessions either conceding recognition or even a closed shop, during the dispute, including large companies which had hitherto stood aloof. The comments of AEU Divisional Organizers are informative, not only for what they report but also for their proud invocation of the traditions of militant trade unionism. From Bristol, for example, E.A. Brown, a right-wing supporter of Carron, wrote:

> Arising from the Dispute, I have attended, together with other officials, meetings with the higher Management of BAC [British Aircraft Company], and we were successful in obtaining a Company Policy Statement approving of Trade Union membership ... the BAC at Filton, Rodney and Patchway, is now almost 100 per cent organized.

Bob McCallion, a Communist who was DO for Division 23 which included Southampton, reported that 'as soon as we received instructions for Strike Action, practically a 100 per cent came out in the Districts concerned, also a considerable number of new members were recruited'.[84]

The stoppages provided an indispensable opportunity to blood the younger generation of union members. For young workers in the ten striking Confed districts, participation in an all-out strike was an unusual and exciting experience. Not only were they off work and doing something out of the ordinary, there was also an element of 'showing the governor' that they were independent and could stand up for themselves. Some found a new and abiding interest in the dense, complex world of British trade union custom, practice and tradition. They became the rising generation of loyalists and activists in the 1960s.

The strike caused a crisis inside the Federation. The EEF officers could not forgive the government's 'betrayal'. They compared Macleod's conduct to Chamberlain's behaviour towards the Czechs in 1938. They drew heavily on the laconic prose and arguments of Clegg and Adams' book on the disputes, published in December 1957, to lay the blame at the government's door. Clegg and Adams described the EEF as the only party which had acted consistently and supported the worthy motive of a wages policy.[85]

Engineering employers were shocked and impressed by the strength of their workers' response to the strike call. The larger employers concluded that the Federation needed a different approach to industrial relations altogether. Their persistent efforts resulted in the EEF evolving a more positive policy towards trade unions, union recognition and workplace collective bargaining.[86] It is doubtful whether these changes could have been effected without the EEF's unexpected defeat by a combination of union solidarity and government pressure which had an unsettling, destabilising impact upon an institution whose attitude to unions had been unchanged and unchanging for the whole of its sixty years' existence.

No one on the union side doubted, at least officially, that they had won a total victory. The concluding paragraph of the Executive Council's Report to the 1958 AEU National Committee was typical:

> The great strike in Engineering and Shipbuilding in the Spring of 1957 proved that the spirit of solidarity is still as strong as ever in our ranks ... It is to be hoped that this lesson of the strike has been noted by the Employers, and also by the Tory Government, whose words and actions at present suggest it would like to provoke 'a show down' with the trade unions.[87]

259

However, left and right drew very different lessons from the victory. Carron and John Boyd, the moderates' strategists, determined to neutralize the Confed. The other skilled unions, in alliance with the TGWU, provided a dangerous critical mass, far too militant and susceptible to Communist influence. Carron had already utilized the AEU's voting strength to install George Barratt, a moderate AEU Executive Councillor, as Confed General Secretary, thus reneging on the unwritten agreement of 1946 that the AEU would not seek to dominate the Confed.[88]

With Barratt in office, the Confed could safely be counted on to do very little. The AEU continued to participate fully in the formal round of proceedings but showed no further interest in using the Confed as an instrument of policy. The Confed ceased pushing either for a rationalized wages structure or an Engineering Joint Industrial Council, both aims which the Court of Inquiry had emphatically endorsed.[89] It was not until Hugh Scanlon became AEU President in 1967 that the Confed was again taken seriously by the union.

The militants who had coalesced so effectively during the strikes used them as a concrete example. The Communist Party General Secretary, John Gollan, in his political report to the party Congress held a fortnight after the strikes, encapsulated their view:

> ... we have seen the new stage in the trade union struggle heralded by the historic strike of the shipyard workers and the engineers, the majority young people who have proved worthy of the pioneers of the movement. This official strike bears out the great importance of the break with Government policy shown at last year's TUC ...[90]

Brotherton used his Presidential Address to the 1957 Confed Annual Meeting to hit out in coded but unmistakable fashion against Carron's and Boyd's newly established ascendancy inside the Confed:

> We have permitted ourselves to be persuaded into expending a great deal more of our time combating the unrighteousness of Communism than the proved evils of Capitalism ... Can it be wrong to accept the dictates of Moscow if we accept dictation from Rome ... I hope we will take stock....with a view to a return to good old fashioned democracy and trade unionism with all its faults.[91]

Ambrose recalled that the Communists had 'known of course' that Brotherton would make his attack. Carron was a practising Catholic. Together with Boyd (a supporter of the Salvation Army) he was involved in mobilizing the right-wing vote inside the AEU through networks of Catholic laity and a shadowy group, the Industrial Research and Information Service (IRIS) which they formed in 1956 to influence union elections. Past AEU President Openshaw associated himself with Brotherton's sentiments when moving the vote of thanks. He referred to Brotherton's 'wise words ... on the industrial and political objectives of the Confederation and of the Trade Union Movement'. He praised his 'patience, tact and handling of the difficult situations' during the recent disputes as 'a lesson to us all'.[92]

The Cabinet also drew mixed lessons. Macmillan noted that 'there is an ugly feeling in the industrial world. This is political, and inflamed by the Communists and left-wingers'.[93] Though Carron had succeeded in pushing the Confed back to work, the margin of victory – his AEU Presidential casting vote – had been far too narrow for the government to feel secure about the balance of forces inside the trade union movement. Trevor Evans made a similar point in the *Daily Express*, noting that Communists 'have concentrated on key unions in the massive engineering group [the Confed], notably the Engineers, the Electricians, and the Foundry Workers ... They bring a quite disproportionate influence on wage trends and on the temperature of industrial relations'.[94]

Nevertheless, the government proceeded along a path recommended by the Court of Inquiry. In August, the Chancellor announced the appointment of an independent Council on Prices, Productivity and Incomes. They hoped the Council's regular reports would 'remove the wages issue from the political arena, partly by influencing arbitrators and Courts of Inquiry against ... "inflationary wage awards"'.[95] However, the reception of the 'Three Wise Men', as the Council was soon dubbed, by the TUC was dismissive. Whatever the private views of moderate and right-wing union leaders, they found it expedient to denounce the Council. Frank Cousins moved another resoundingly militant motion on wages and prices at the 1957 Congress which was again adopted unanimously. Carron found it politic to roundly dismiss the Council at the 1958 AEU National Committee.[96] Surveying the situation at the beginning of 1958, the Cabinet concluded 'the Government must ... seek to devise in collaboration with industry, means of securing a reasonable degree of wage restraint and of revising in certain respects the traditional procedure of wage negotiation and arbitration'.[97] Key players in the Macmillan government were determined to take a firmer line with the unions. They regretted that circumstances in the spring of 1957 had conspired against their intention to support the EEF, and they were resolved not to let the same sequence of events recur. The London bus strike in May 1958 gave them the opportunity they sought.[98]

Notes

1.   *Observer*, 17 March 1957.
2.   *Sheffield Telegraph*, 18 March 1957.
3.   J.W. Durcan, W.E.J. McCarthy and G.P. Redman, *Strikes in Post-War Britain: a study of stoppages of work due to industrial disputes 1946–73* (1983), p. 58.

4.   H.A. Clegg, *A History of British Trade Unions since 1889, Vol. 2, 1911–1933* (Oxford, 1985), p. 469; H.A. Clegg, *A History of British Trade Unions since 1889, Vol. 3, 1934–1951* (Oxford, 1994), pp. 257–9; A. Bullock, *The Life and Times of Ernest Bevin, Vol. II, Minister of Labour 1940–1945* (1967), pp. 98–123; T. Evans, *Bevin* (1946), pp. 170–222.

5.   For Order 1305, see O. Kahn-Freund, 'Legal Framework', in A. Flanders and H.A. Clegg (eds), *Industrial Relations in Great Britain* (Oxford, 1954), pp. 83–101; N. Fishman, 'The demise of wartime social partnership: the unexpected revocation of Order 1305 and unintended consequences of Order 1376', unpublished paper presented to the Annual Conference of the British Universities Industrial Relations Research Association, Keele University, 1998; A. Flanders, 'Collective Bargaining', in Flanders and Clegg, *Industrial Relations*, p. 317; S. Brittan, *The Treasury under the Tories 1951–1964* (Harmondsworth, 1964), p. 169; see also K.O. Morgan, *The People's Peace* (Oxford, 1992), pp. 114–15.

6.   D. Barnes and E. Reid, *Governments and Trade Unions: the British experience, 1964–79* (1980), p. 26.

7.   Engineering and Allied Employers National Federation, *Looking at Industrial Relations* (1959), p. 43. 'Britain's Industrial Future' was published in September 1955.

8.   R. Shepherd, *Iain Macleod: a biography* (1995), p. 108; Barnes and Reid, *Governments and Trade Unions*, p. 26; the White Paper is Cmd. 9725; TUC, *Report*, 1956, pp. 398–409.

9.   G. Goodman, *Awkward Warrior: the life and times of Frank Cousins* (1979), p. 136.

10.   Public Record Office (hereafter PRO), LAB 13/690, Z.G. Claro, 'Notes on the recent dispute arising from redundancy at the British Motor Corporation', 17 August 1956. For the dispute, see D. Lyddon, 'The car industry, 1945–1979: shop stewards and workplace unionism', in C. Wrigley (ed.), *A History of British Industrial Relations, 1939–1979* (Cheltenham, 1996), pp. 190–3.

11.   PRO, LAB 13/690, A. Greenhough to Labour Attachés, 19 November 1956.

12.   *AEU Journal*, January 1957, pp. 1–2.

13.   H. Macmillan, *Memoirs, Vol. 4, 1956–1959: riding the storm* (1971) p. 55–7; Shepherd, *Macleod*, pp. 49, 65–6, 110–12, 543–6; R. Blake, *The Paladin History of England: decline of power, 1915–1964* (1986), p. 336.

14.   Barnes and Reid, *Governments and Trade Unions*, p. 30.

15.   PRO LAB 13/690, A. Greenhough to Labour Attachés, 19 December 1956.

16.   Department of Employment and Productivity, *British Labour Statistics, Historical Abstract, 1886–1968* (1971), Tables 50 and 41; P. S. Bagwell, *The Railwaymen: the history of the National Union of Railwaymen* (1963), pp. 644–9.

17.   Bagwell, *Railwaymen*, p. 653.

18.   PRO CAB 128/31, Cabinet Minutes 18 March 1957, C.C.(57) 21, Minute 3.

19.   Quoted in E. Wigham, *Strikes and the Government 1893–1981* (1982) p. 115.

20. Macmillan, *Riding the Storm*, p. 346; Shepherd, *Macleod*, p. 125. The Labour Attaché in Washington DC wrote to A. Greenhough at the Overseas Department of the Ministry of Labour on 19 March: 'there is a great deal of concern here, amongst Americans ... about the outcome of [the disputes] and its effect upon Britain's efforts to recover the ground she has lost in recent months' (PRO LAB 13/690).

21. Shepherd, *Macleod*, pp. 124–6.

22. Clegg, *History, Vol.* 2, pp. 253, 326–7.

23. H.A. Clegg, 'Employers', in Flanders and Clegg, *Industrial Relations in Great Britain*, p. 232.

24. Ibid., p. 231.

25. H.A. Clegg, A. Fox and A. F. Thompson, *A History of British Trade Unions since 1889, Vol. 1 1889–1910* (Oxford, 1964), pp. 116–17, 130–1; J.B. Jefferys, *The Story of the Engineers* (1945), pp. 163, 192; Clegg, *History, Vol.* 2, p. 189, 496–7; N. Fishman, 'The British Communist Party and the Trade Unions, 1933–45' (unpublished manuscript, 1986), Modern Records Centre, University of Warwick (MRC), pp. 222–4, 229–31.

26. N. Fishman, *The British Communist Party and the Trade Unions* (Aldershot), 1995, pp. 262–7.

27. N. Fishman, 'Communist Party' MS, pp. 218–23, 264–5.

28. For Martin (1892–1958), see J.E. Mortimer, *History of the Boilermakers' Society, Vol. 3, 1940–1989* (1994), p. 21; information from Ian Aitken who worked as Research Officer to the Confed in 1945–6; interviews with Les Ambrose, 21 September and 14 October 1998.

29. *AEU National Committee Report*, 1945; *AEU Journal*, October 1946, p. 289.

30. In 1957 the Confed had an affiliated membership of nearly 1.25 million members. The AEU affiliated for 500,000 members; the TGWU, 100,000 members, and the NUGMW 95,000 (H.A. Clegg and R. Adams, *The Employers' Challenge: a study of the national shipbuilding and engineering dispute of 1957*, Oxford, 1957, p. 37). The terms of the AEU's affiliation to the Confed and a description of the revised Confed constitution are contained in *AEU Journal*, June 1946, pp. 170–4. Under the revised constitution there were two sub-commitees, one for engineering and one for shipbuilding to deal with negotiations in the two industries. The AEU President was the chair for engineering and the Boilermakers' General Secretary chair for shipbuilding; see also Clegg and Adams, *Employers' Challenge*, p. 36.

31. N Fishman, 'Communist Party' MS, pp. 302–10; interview with Les Ambrose, 28 March 1979. For Communists holding AEU offices see Fishman, *Communist Party*, Appendix 2.

32. Harry Brotherton was a member of the National Union of Sheet Metal Workers and Braziers. He served on the Executive of the union from London district from 1923–4 and 1927–43, and was London District Secretary from 1929–41. He was General President in 1934–5, and became General Secretary of the union in 1943; information on Communists' importance in the Sheet Metal Workers' Union from Charlie Hall.

33. Clegg and Adams, *Employers' Challenge*, pp. 43–5.

34. E. Wigham, *The Power to Manage: a history of the Engineering Employers' Federation* (1973), p. 170. For details of these settlements, see Clegg and Adams, *Employers' Challenge*, Appendix 3, p. 163.

35. Wigham, *Power to Manage*, p. 177.

36. Interview with Geoffrey Goodman, July 1998.

37. Clegg and Adams, *Employers' Challenge*, pp. 45–8.

38. Wigham, *Power to Manage*, p. 178.

39. Clegg and Adams, *Employers' Challenge*, p. 55, quoting *The Times*, 27 April 1956.

40. Wigham, *Power to Manage*, pp. 180–1.

41. Ibid., p. 180.

42. Confederation of Shipbuilding and Engineering Unions, *Report of Annual Meeting*, August 1956, p. 21.

43. Ibid., 1956, p. 26.

44. Ibid., pp. 67–8.

45. Ibid., pp. 69–70.

46. *AEU Journal*, December 1956, p. 360.

47. MRC, MSS 259/5/3, Confed Executive Minutes, Minute No. 4322, 13 December 1956.

48. Confed Executive Minutes, 9 January 1957, Minute No. 4354.

49. *AEU Journal*, February 1957, p. 38.

50. Clegg and Adams, *Employers' Challenge*, p. 73. Carron had been elected to the Confed Executive in 1950 after being elected to the AEU Executive Council; Scott and Openshaw had both participated in the negotiations for the AEU's re-affiliation to the Confed in 1944 and served on its Executive from 1946. Maurice Kidd also served on the Negotiating Team.

51. Members of the Confed Executive were elected by the Confed Annual Meeting. By convention, AEU officers who served on the Confed Executive kept their seats for the full term from one Confed Annual Meeting in August until the next. Openshaw retired as AEU President in September 1956 and Scott stood down from the AEU Executive Council in January 1957, but because both were elected to the Confed Executive in August 1956, they served their full term to August 1957. Scott served on the Confed negotiating team by virtue of the fact that he succeeded Openshaw as chairman of the Confed Railway Shops Sub-Committee when Openshaw became AEU President in April 1954 and became Chairman of the Engineering Sub-Committee. During 1956, Scott stood down from the AEU Executive to contest the election for AEU General Secretary but was decisively defeated. His vacant AEU Executive Council seat was taken by fellow Communist Claude Berridge (Interviews with Les Ambrose; *AEU Journal*, October and November 1956).

52. *AEU National Committee Report*, 1957; Clegg and Adams, *Employers' Challenge*, p. 72.

53. Confed Executive Minutes, 19 February 1957, Minute No. 4384.

54. Report of Conference of Executives of Affiliated Unions, 7 March 1957 in Confed Executive Minutes.

55. Confed Executive Minutes, 12 March 1957, Minute No. 4452.

56. Confed Executive Minutes, 12 March 1957, Minute No. 4453.

57. Confed Executive Minutes, 15 March 1957, Minute No. 4454.

58. *Sheffield Telegraph*, 18 March 1957.

59. *Annual Register,* 1957.

60. Confed Executive Minutes, 19 March 1957, Minutes No. 4455 and 4457.

61. Confed Executive Minutes, 20 March 1957, Minute No. 4458. The first plan of action discussed was much more ambitious. It called for stoppages in all marine engineering establishments as well as English Electric, Vickers, British Thomson Houston, Metropolitan Vickers, De Havillands, General Electric Company, AV Roe, Fairey, and Bristol Aviation Company. This plan was defeated by 16–8, and the more modest one was then carried unanimously.

62. *Observer*, 24 March 1957.

63. Clegg and Adams, *Employers' Challenge*, pp. 98–102, 112.

64. See *AEU Journal*, May 1957, p. 158.

65. In 1957 there were 48 Confed districts, whose boundaries 'bear very little relation' to the regional organization of the largest unions: 171 AEU districts, 13 TGWU regions and 10 NUGMW districts. This intricate institutional variation 'raised no unusual difficulties on this occasion [the national strike]' (Clegg and Adams, *Employers' Challenge*, p. 107).

66. There was an Emergency Committee and Central Strike Committee on Tyneside, the former probably the smaller, inner cabinet. In Manchester, the Confed District Secretary, Hugh Scanlon, reported that the Emergency Committee 'is in continuous session during the dispute, and all areas are operating their own strike Committees, pickets, etc.' In Sheffield there was a Central Strike Committee (*AEU Journal*, 12 April 1957, pp. 120–6).

67. See the reports from Divisional Organizers in *AEU Journal* for April 1957, pp. 120–6, and the reports of Confed District Committees to the 1957 Annual Meeting.

68. Clegg and Adams, *Employers' Challenge*, quoting the *Daily Mail*, pp. 112, 120.

69. See *AEU Journal*, May 1957, pp. 152, 155.

70. *Observer*, 31 March 1957.

71. Confed Executive Minutes, 25 March 1957, Minute No. 4460; 26 March 1957, Minute No. 4462.

72. Confed Executive Minutes, 26 March 1957, Minute 4462; 27 March 1957, Minute 4463. On 27 March the Executive stated its willingness to participate in the Shipbuilding Inquiry, but made no move to call off the strike. The successful motion on the engineering dispute spoke of the EEF's 'complete refusal ... to negotiate with us and what appears to be their utter indifference to the consequent results'.

73. Macleod had told the Cabinet that the engineering trade unions were unwilling to end the strike until the employers had taken direct wage negotiations to the point they had reached in shipbuilding. The employers were unwilling so far, 'but might be prepared to reconsider their attitude' (PRO CAB 128/31, Cabinet Minutes, 28 March 1957).

74. Confed Executive Minutes, 29 March 1957, Minute No. 4465. *The Times,*

30 March 1957. Wigham goes into considerable detail on the intense conflict inside the EEF (*Power to Manage*, pp. 186–7).

75. On 21 March, A. Greenhough's circular letter to Labour Attaches had reported: 'A few of us were told that Carron (AEU) has some hopes of a settlement of the Engineering dispute within a few days, but I am unable to evaluate his optimism (PRO LAB13/690). Macleod told the Cabinet on 2 April that the unions' response to his request was 'unpredictable. The attitude of the AEU would probably decide the issue' (PRO CAB 128/31, 2 April 1957). Confed Executive Minutes, 29 March 1957, Minute No. 4465.

76. Confed Executive Minutes, 2 April 1957, Minute No. 4468.

77. Clegg and Adams, *Employers' Challenge*, pp. 117–18.

78. *Sheffield Telegraph* 3 April 1957.

79. PRO LAB 13/690, A. Greenhough to Labour Attaches, 10 April 1957. Clegg and Adams noted that 'more than one union was contemplating drastic action to safeguard their remaining reserves if the decision had gone the other way ... on April 2nd' (*Employers' Challenge*, pp. 116–17). Macleod told the Cabinet that 'there were grounds for believing that they [the unions] were concerned about the financial implications of a protracted strike and might be prepared to ... suspend strike action in the interim [during the Inquiry]' PRO CAB 128/31, Minute No.2, Cabinet minutes, 26 March 1957).

80. Interviews with John Foster and Len Choulerton who were AEU District Secretaries for Kingston-upon-Thames and Southall, October 1995; interview with Jack Jones, 26 October 1998.

81. Bill Carron offered a jesuitical view of the final settlement to the recalled 1957 AEU National Committee: 'the Annex B [on restrictive practices], whilst it has validity, and it would be completely dishonest to deny its validity, is not written into the agreement ...' (Presidential Address, AEU Recalled National Committee, 4th June 1957, p. 29).

82. Clegg and Adams, *Employers' Challenge*, pp. 110–11.

83. *AEU Journal*, May 1957, p. 156. Hugh Scanlon reported from Manchester in the April *AEU Journal* that 'considerable numbers' had joined the union (p. 123).

84. *AEU Journal*, May 1957, pp. 153–8. Information about Divisional Organizers from Les Ambrose. For similar comments from the Boilermakers, see Report of the Sixth Annual Conference, 27–31 May 1957, Presidential Address, pp. 10, 12. See also reports from the Confed District Committees to the Confed Annual Meeting 1957: Sheffield (pp. 405–6); Bristol (p. 375); Clydeside (p. 427).

85. The Munich comparison is found in the EEF's pamphlet, *Looking at Industrial Relations*, p. 40. The pamphlet's conclusions (pp. 40–8) strongly resemble sections of 'Some Lessons from the Dispute' in Clegg and Adams, *Employers' Challenge*, pp. 142–51.

86. For the post-strike events in the EEF, see Wigham, *Right to Manage*, ch. 9.

87. *AEU National Committee Report*, 1958, p. 139.

88. Interview with Les Ambrose. See Mortimer, *The Boilermakers*, Vol. 3, pp. 110–11.

89. See PRO LAB 10/1503, Ministry of Labour.
90. Communist Party, *25th Congress Report*, 'Political Report', p. 7.
91. Confed *Report,* 1957, p. 26 and p. 28.
92. Ibid.; interview with Les Ambrose, 18 October 1998.
93. Macmillan, *Riding the Storm*, p. 347, quoting from his diary, 4 April 1957.
94. *Daily Express* 13 May 1957.
95. Barnes and Reid, *Governments and Trade Unions*, p. 30; they point out that a council of this kind had been recommended by three Courts of Inquiry since 1955.
96. Presidential Address, AEU National Committee Report, 1958.
97. CAB 128/32, Minute 3, Cabinet Minutes March 1958, p. 163.
98. Barnes and Reid, *Governments and Trade Unions*, pp. 30–1. Macmillan, *Riding the Storm*, p. 713.

CHAPTER TEN

'Spearhead of the Movement'?: The 1958 London Busworkers' Strike, the TUC and Frank Cousins

Nina Fishman

> Whatever the actual outcome may be in the monetary sense ... the London Bus-
> men have won a victory for every trade unionist with a wage claim pending. By
> their determination, they have at least placed a brake on Governmental Policy
> which has sought to ensure that wages shall not rise with the cost of living ... As
> the spearhead in the fight to maintain the living standards of the working-class of
> our country their display of solidarity is almost without example in the history of
> our Movement ... they are virtually fighting the battle of the whole of the British
> Trade Union Movement.[1]

This statement from the journal of the Transport and General Workers' Union (TGWU) represented the official position taken by the union and its
General Secretary Frank Cousins throughout the seven weeks of the London
busworkers' strike, from 5 May to 21 June 1958. Though the TUC officially
supported the strike, prominent members of the General Council were active behind the scenes in securing its defeat.

Cousins himself was pessimistic about the strike's chance of success. Nevertheless, he not only allowed the strike to go ahead, he led it vigorously.
The majority of General Council members were moderates who considered
his conduct reprehensible. They believed that he risked bankrupting the
TGWU and undermining its authority, as well as bringing the whole movement into dangerous disrepute. Yet Cousins was a shrewd tactician and
competent negotiator who had made strenuous efforts to pre-empt the strike.
He felt constrained to prove his militant credentials to the full-time officers
and lay activists who had promoted his successful bid for the general secretaryship. Geoffrey Goodman, who reported the strike as an industrial
correspondent, and later discussed it with him as his biographer, concluded:
'Cousins's purpose in the London bus strike was as much to rescue the union from its own internal strife and erosion of purpose as it was to fight a
wage claim for the busmen – or for the trade union movement as a whole'.[2]

It seems implausible that an incumbent of such force of character as Cousins was circumscribed by the union's internal balance of forces. Other unions,
notably the AEU, were perceived at the time as riven by internal political
conflict. But conventional images of the TGWU and its leader derived from
its first general secretary, Ernest Bevin, who was seen as possessing virtu-

ally unlimited power over his members and officers. However, Bevin's fabled strength was limited in reality. He acted with acute awareness of the need to strengthen the ties binding the union's disparate sections together and also to cement their loyalty to himself. Bevin's successor, Arthur Deakin, failed to recognize the internal tensions in the union and was consequently unable to control its parts. Deakin's powerful public facade was belied by his weakness when confronted by sections of the TGWU where activists refused to accept his and other full-time officials' authority.[3] Cousins' election in 1956 was the result of an internecine conflict conducted inside the TGWU's complex structures. His supporters, both left-wing and moderate full-time officials and lay activists, appreciated his commitment to bring the diverging interest groups inside the union back together and his determination to redress the grievances accumulated under Deakin's misrule.[4] The escalation of the London busworkers' dispute with the London Transport Executive (LTE) at the end of 1957 presented Cousins with a challenge. He had to respond to their call or be discredited as a general secretary in the Deakin mould who betrayed his members.

The militant traditions of the London busworkers

London busworkers possessed proud traditions of direct democracy and syndicalism, dating from the New Unionism in the 1890s. During the 1914–18 war, a rank and file movement with revolutionary syndicalist ideas appeared. In 1921, Bevin made important concessions to secure the London busworkers' adherence to the TGWU. Their garage branches elected ten representatives to a Central Bus Committee (CBC). The CBC was unique in being able to summon and treat with the union's General Executive Council (GEC) and General Secretary directly, going outside the national and regional passenger transport trade groups.[5] Ironically, London bus militants survived the 1920s and 1930s because they were cocooned by the corporatism pioneered by Bevin and actively promoted by London Transport's first chairman, Lord Ashfield. London Transport's largest private predecessor was run by Ashfield and he recognized the TGWU on favourable conditions, conceding a *de facto* closed shop in 1927.

In 1932, Bevin signed a rationalizing agreement with London Transport and presented it to the CBC for approval. London bus activists mobilized the membership to vote the agreement down, and re-formed the wartime rank and file movement involving Independent Labour Party, Socialist Party of Great Britain and Communist Party (CP) members. By loyal 'gingering', the movement would ensure that the TGWU carried out the membership's will. Rank and file leaders were soon elected to the majority of lay positions in the section, and decided in 1936 to embark on an all-out official strike against London Transport. The official strike began on 1 May 1937 and lasted four weeks. The GEC revoked their grant of plenary powers to the CBC. Bevin negotiated a reasonable settlement the next day. The GEC accepted the terms and ended the strike. Bevin was determined to punish the rank and file leadership whom he felt had betrayed the union's trust: the ensuing Executive report found that the movement was not only subversive but 'controlled' by the CP leadership.[6]

The rank and file leadership split irrevocably in the aftermath of the strike. The faction which remained loyal to the TGWU was led by Bill Jones and Bert Papworth and included CP activists. They were strongly supported and publicly applauded by the CP leadership. The other faction formed a breakaway union, the National Passenger Workers' Union (NPWU), committed to rank and file principles and the democratic traditions of their old union. Despite London Transport's hostility towards the NPWU, garage branches seceded from the TGWU and went into the new union.[7] The rank and file movement was found guilty of the charge of subverting the union by the TGWU Conference in July 1937: its principal leaders were expelled by the GEC. When the loyalist faction formally disbanded the movement in January 1938, Bevin recognized the need to conciliate. The GEC readmitted Papworth and Jones immediately on their pledge of loyalty, and declared them eligible to hold office from 1942. Bevin also found it expedient to reassure the bus activists of his intention to maintain their unique status inside the union. In 1943 Papworth was re-elected to the GEC, and in 1944 he was elected to its 'inner cabinet', the Finance and General Purposes Committee (F&GP). He was also chosen by the Executive to serve as the union's second member of the TUC General Council, alongside Deakin.[8]

The NPWU membership had increased during the war to between 4,000 and 5,000 members. Jones and Papworth responded by waging a vigorous campaign to bring NPWU members back into the TGWU. Despite some success, the NPWU retained its hold, and the TGWU eventually made common cause with London Transport to eradicate it. They concluded a closed shop agreement after the repeal of the 1927 Trades Disputes Act in 1946. The Board sacked 176 busworkers who refused to join the TGWU.[9]

Deakin's conduct towards the London bus militants in this period was diplomatic. He met the leaders of London bus unofficial strikes, and discussed their grievances. His persuasiveness was enhanced by London Transport's willingness to make material concessions. Relations between Deakin and the section dramatically worsened in July 1949 when he manoeuvred to obtain a ban on CP members holding union office from the TGWU Biennial Conference. The ban came into force on 1 January 1950. Though there were not many Communists on the London buses, they were disproportionately well represented in lay union posts. Papworth and Jones resigned their union positions. Papworth apparently had a nervous breakdown, and did not return to work until late in 1950, never resuming a union activist role. Jones returned to his work as a busdriver, continuing to play a prominent unofficial role in his garage union branch and the bus section.[10]

Non-communist left-wingers throughout the union were outraged by the ban. On the London buses, ex-rank and file movement leaders reorganized a dissident faction. A new paper, the *Platform*, appeared in November 1949 with the intention of fighting for union democracy and against the ban. The garages where the CP was strongest, notably Dalston (Bill Jones' branch) and Holloway, organized meetings calling for the restoration of democratic rights. The Regional Secretary, Charles Brandon, threatened to expel the dissidents and even disband their branches. He banned the *Platform* from circulating inside garages.[11]

Punitive actions redoubled the dissidents' will to resist. In the spring of 1951 they founded a new rank and file movement, the Passenger Workers' Unity Association. The formation of a 'democratic' breakaway union was freely discussed in the *Platform*. The CP leadership, alarmed by the dangers of secession and/or retaliation from the TGWU bureaucracy, convened an emergency meeting of London party busworkers. They carried their point. The Unity Association disappeared as quickly as it had come. Bill Jones played the principal role in winning over activists who had hoped for a final reckoning with Deakin.[12]

The threat of a breakaway was a powerful incentive for Brandon to reach a *modus vivendi* with the dissidents. When the Unity Association was disbanded, an informal accord evolved. Brandon did not interfere with either the *Platform* or the activities of left-wing garages like Dalston. The dissidents extended their influence inside the bus section, but remained loyal to the union. Moreover, communists continued to serve as lay officials in the section. Deakin evidently lacked the stomach for a witch hunt, and refrained from too close scrutiny of his full-time officers' conduct in enforcing the ban.[13]

The reformed *Platform* was full of garage and union news and provided a focus for London busworkers' discontents. The editor, George Renshaw, who left the CP in 1951, was a seasoned journalist. Its politics were keenly anti-Cold War. However, politics were not the staple diet of the paper which thrived on bread-and-butter 'economism'. In January 1954, *Platform* welcomed four new members who had been elected to the CBC: 'among the new members are those who have consistently argued for a more militant policy ... and for more democracy in the affairs of our union ... We shall judge the new CBC and Trade Group Committee strictly on their performance'. In November 1954, *Platform* anticipated Deakin's retirement the following summer and exhorted rank and file members and full-time officers 'who are so often left "holding the Deakin baby" [to] have the courage to stand up to the "big fella" and thus restore their own dignity in the eyes of the members'. Militant garages in the section were taking unofficial action regularly, and their hope was that a head of steam would build up behind a substantial wage claim. London busworkers' wages had been well above the

271

average for male manual workers in 1938. They 'had fallen back considerably' during the war. By 1948 'their earnings were only a few coppers over the national average', and they continued to fall further behind.[14]

The background to the strike

Cousins' victory as TGWU General Secretary in 1956 was a heady tonic. *Platform* reported his speech at the TUC in September which 'shocked Fleet Street' by its 'scathing denunciation of the Tory Chancellor' and his rejection of wage restraint which Deakin had previously supported. Cousins' peroration had even highlighted London busmen's own particular grievance.[15] In March 1957, against the background of the escalating wage dispute in the engineering industry and the CBC's consideration of a renewed claim, *Platform* declared on its front-page:

> ... to once again keep LTE staffs waiting in the queue while company and municipal bus sections are first dealt with – is to invite ... a settlement based on the weakest link. Trades unionism is under attack ... from an organized employing class – and a vicious Tory Government. Let our Trade Group Committee take up the challenge NOW.

The CBC was strongly pressing the Regional Passenger Trade Group to support a fresh wage claim for the section, even though their previous claim had only been settled in January.[16] Nevertheless, the substantial increase granted had been almost immediately negated by Chancellor Thorneycroft's deflationary measures. When the engineering conflict escalated into a national strike, *Platform's* front page article in April welcomed it:

> This is the first really massive strike action since the historic general strike of 1926. For the first time in thirty years the trade union giant is fully awake. ... When new troops enter the firing line for the first time, a great responsibility rests upon the 'old guard' with previous battle experience.

But Cousins declined to take up the London bus section's case. He was anxious to merge their wage negotiations into a comprehensive national passenger transport bargaining structure. London bus activists could hardly dismiss Cousins' arguments for unity in principle. But they nevertheless persisted in their separate claim.[17]

On 20 August 1957 the union's Regional Trade Group considered the CBC's motion for a London bus wages claim for the fifth time since March. The Group finally agreed to submit a claim for 25s per week increase in wage rates to the GEC for approval. The GEC sent Assistant General Secretary Harry Nicholas back to the CBC on 7 October. He proposed a unified claim to be submitted jointly to the LTE, private and municipal bus companies.

The CBC refused and 'overwhelmingly carried' another demand for their 25s claim. The CBC's militancy had been reinforced by the re-appearance of Bill Jones. Having left the Communist Party at the end of 1956, he became re-eligible to hold TGWU office, and was immediately re-elected to the CBC. Since 1952, Bill Waters, from Kingston garage, had led the militants on the CBC. Jones joined him, bringing humour and a formidable rhetorical skill. His presence at meetings made it much more difficult for officers to browbeat the bus section into compromise.[18]

Cousins and Nicholas made no further attempts to resist the 25s demand. They put it into play with the apparent intention of achieving a negotiated settlement. A written claim was formally approved by the union's F&GP and submitted to the LTE on 17 October. Nevertheless, there were clear indications that the claim would not be allowed to proceed smoothly to a compromise resolution.[19]

From the summer of 1957, the government's policy on wages was dominated by a hawkish faction in the Cabinet, including the Chancellor, Peter Thorneycroft, Heathcoat Amory, Enoch Powell and Harold Watkinson. They were keen to redress the hasty retreat over the engineering dispute executed by Prime Minister Macmillan in March.[20] The compromise settlement of the engineering and shipbuilding strikes reverberated through the Conservative party and business circles during the summer of 1957. Cabinet hawks and their allies in the party were not dogmatically anti-union. However, after the Cabinet's public loss of resolve in the face of union militancy, they sought an occasion to reassert the government's determination to resist. They were concerned about increasing 'extremist' tendencies amongst union leaders and the TUC General Council's apparent inability to curb militant industrial action.

The London bus section's claim for a 25s per week increase was fortuitous for the hawks. They considered Cousins a dangerous union leader liable to undermine the economy and the post-war political consensus. A double defeat for Cousins and the notoriously left-wing, if not Communist, London busworkers would provide a salutary lesson for the General Council to take a stronger stand against 'extremism'.

Nevertheless, Sir John Elliot, chairman of the LTE, was keen to negotiate a compromise settlement.[21] He recognized that once a strike had begun, it was likely to be protracted and to have potentially serious long-term consequences both for London Transport and its busworkers. Elliot knew that he would not be a free agent able to settle a high profile strike according to his own lights. Since 1948 the LTE had been responsible to the British Transport Commission (BTC), established by the Labour government to administer railways and road transport, enabling a strategic approach to national transport. The Labour Cabinet intervened regularly in the affairs of all nationalized industries, particularly in industrial relations and pricing policies. Successive Conservative governments' allegiance to *laisser faire* had not prevented them

273

from exercising scrutiny and intervention similar to their predecessors.

The LTE formally rejected the 25s claim on 25 November. On 9 December the union's three-section delegate conference 'resolved to request plenary powers [from the GEC to strike] should LTE refuse to continue negotiations'. They rejected Nicholas's proposal to submit the claim to arbitration by 105–25 votes. Nevertheless, Cousins and Nicholas persisted with a strategy of compromise. They met Elliot on 23 December, and he agreed to act jointly with the TGWU either in submitting the claim to arbitration or in requesting the Minister of Labour to appoint a Committee of Inquiry.[22] His agreement meant that the LTE would be bound 'in honour' to abide by an award from arbitrators or a Court of Inquiry by virtue of current custom and practice.

On 8 January 1958 the LTE rejected the 25s claim again, citing the government's strictures to nationalized industries to operate profitably. However, following Elliot's agreement, the LTE's labour director, Anthony Bull, met the Ministry of Labour's Chief Industrial Commissioner (CIC), Sir Wilfred Neden with Nicholas on 10 January. Neden explained conciliation was impossible because the LTE was adamant that no offer be made, but he also 'gave an indication of the various forms of arbitration and inquiry which were available'. Nicholas told him that the delegate conference had rejected such strategies, but nevertheless, the meeting ended with 'the suggestion that a Committee of Investigation be set up'.[23]

Neden's proposals for arbitration and inquiries were somewhat disingenuous. He had been telephoned before the meeting by Harold Watkinson, Minister of Transport, who told him not to make any arrangements for conciliation. 'This', said Watkinson, 'was a Cabinet instruction. No concession must be made to the busmen'.[24] Neden was not obliged to accept instructions from ministers other than his own. He immediately approached the Minister of Labour, Iain Macleod, who neither sanctioned nor repudiated Watkinson's instruction and Neden considered himself free to conduct the meeting. The CIC enjoyed virtual autonomy in dealing with conciliation issues, and he routinely acted without consulting Macleod. He now proceeded with arrangements for a Committee of Investigation, the option which Nicholas deemed most likely to be acceptable to the bus delegates.[25]

On 14 January Nicholas persuaded the busmen's negotiating committee to accept the Committee of Investigation. On 17 January, after six hours' debate, the delegate conference also agreed. When Nicholas, Bull and Neden met to agree final arrangements, Nicholas said the delegate conference had approved the Committee of Investigation by a majority of 6–1 but 'was emphatic that it would not agree to straight arbitration'. The committee was expected to start work on 4 February.[26] Macleod brought the question of a committee of investigation to Cabinet where it was discussed on 22 January. Watkinson tabled a paper which asked whether a committee would further the government's policy of wage restraint. He concluded:

It is always possible that if we do set up the enquiry and if it recommends an increase, the union might turn down the increase. In many ways this would be very convenient for us ... I think that it adds to the attraction of setting up the committee ... We must ensure that both the chairman and the LTE nominee of the proposed committee are likely to take a firm line.[27]

The discussion reached the view that a refusal to establish a committee '... would be liable to provoke widespread industrial unrest, directed ... against the Government'. However, the calculation that the claim was 'unlikely to command the support of public opinion generally' led to the conclusion that an enquiry would 'serve no useful purpose'.[28]

When Cabinet discussion resumed the following day, Macleod and Watkinson presented opposing memoranda, with Watkinson now arguing against a committee. Macleod disagreed: 'A refusal would almost certainly result in a strike, which would not be confined to the buses, and might cover the whole transport field ... More important still it would appear to be a strike against the Government'.[29] After lengthy discussion, resulting in support for Watkinson, Macleod prepared a draft letter suggesting to the TGWU that other means of settling the dispute would be more appropriate, either arbitration or 'an enquiry into the wages problem in the road passenger transport industry as a whole'. The Cabinet approved the letter as 'a reasoned refusal ... which the union would find it difficult to present as adequate justification for strike action'.[30]

Macleod's letter declining to establish the Committee of Investigation reached Cousins on 24 January. The TGWU leadership appear to have been genuinely shocked.[31] Macleod and Neden met Cousins and Nicholas on 28 January when Cousins tried to intimidate Macleod into changing his mind. Macleod denied that Neden had ever made a firm offer while Neden contradicted Macleod, a cardinal transgression for a senior civil servant.[32] Cousins and Nicholas now executed their own about-turn. Having previously rejected any form of arbitration – in line with the decision of their delegate conference – they now approached Elliot who joined them in requesting Macleod to refer the dispute to the Industrial Court. On 3 February, the busmen's Delegate Conference accepted Cousins' proposal for an Industrial Court reference, with the proviso that any arbitration decision 'against the interests of our members would not be accepted'.[33] Cousins was applauded by the press for his strong leadership in dissuading the busworkers from strike action.[34]

Macleod accepted this second joint request and the Industrial Court swiftly met. Its report recommended an increase of 8s 6d per week for the 36,000 central London busworkers, amounting to a 4.4 per cent increase for drivers and 4.5 per cent for conductors. However, the Court made no award for the other 14,000 workers included in the claim – maintenance men, country bus crews and Green Line workers whose bus routes straddled London and its environs.[35]

At first sight the Court's findings appeared perverse, since nearly one-third of the workers involved in the claim had received nothing. Ministry of Labour officials acknowledged, 'for a number of years awards and settlements have generally given something to all the workers involved'. However, they added that 'to some extent this course was forced upon him [the Industrial Court Chairman] by the Union's evidence which was effective on the point of worsening conditions of work of the central London people but unimpressive on the cost of living issue which was the main case for the country drivers, conductors and maintenance men'.[36] The award clearly fell short of Cousins' expectations. Watkinson, however, applied strong pressure on Elliot, both publicly and privately, to make no further concessions. The Cabinet expected to reap political advantage from the fact that the Court had broken with the post-war convention of offering something for everyone. Moreover, they believed that 'it was unlikely that the union would have recourse to strike action'.[37]

The *Platform* – written before the award appeared – anticipated bus delegates' mood more accurately: 'We are the spearhead of a great movement involving some seven million workers demanding wage increases ... We must demand plenary powers [to strike] – and let action speak where reasoned argument has failed'.[38] On 25 March the delegate conference unanimously rejected the award. Delegates then voted virtually unanimously to reduce their claim from 25s to 10s 6d week and to request powers to conduct a strike. A special session of the F&GP, attended by Cousins, Nicholas and Alf Chandler, the union's Chief Administrative Officer, approved the strike request, but granted Cousins the plenary powers to conduct it.[39] The leadership had clearly drawn important lessons from the 1937 strike when the CBC had been given plenary powers. Cousins duly tendered one month's notice to the LTE of a bus strike to commence on 5 May. The *Platform* declared:

> The amount necessary to include them [the other 14,000 workers] is so small as to represent peanuts to the British Transport Commission ... the award was dictated by the Tory Government in the interests of the employing class as a whole.[40]

Macmillan pondered a last minute intervention in the dispute. He sent a senior civil servant for a private meeting with the TUC General Secretary, Vincent Tewson. Tewson was asked whether he would persuade Cousins to accept a compromise based on the Court's award, presumably making some provision for the omitted workers. He refused, and Macmillan let events take their course.[41] The TGWU leaders had made thorough preparations for the strike, establishing a comprehensive chain of command. Two meetings were held between Region No. 1 officers and Nicholas and Chandler to discuss contingencies. On 15 April the first meeting noted 'a quiet determination to go ahead with the Strike'; many branches 'had already got down to the organization of the strike machinery in readiness, including picket rotas, arrangements for the pay-out of strike benefit, etc'.[42]

Despite inconclusive manoeuvres by both sides to gain tactical advantage, on 30 April the delegate conference declared their intention to strike for 10s 6d on 5 May. The TGWU went ahead with a rally where Cousins addressed an overflow crowd of 6,000 workers: 'He told them he was entering the strike with a heavy heart. They might well be alone in the struggle, which could drag on for weeks with little support from other unions and very little from the general public'. He finished by calling for a vote on the strike, a symbolic gesture since the rally had no official status. He may, nevertheless, have been buoyed up by the overwhelming vote in favour.[43] *Platform* was jubilant: 'Reports from the many special branch meetings held show attendances bigger than anything seen since pre-war days ... the busmen of 1958 will prove no less ready than those of 1937 to show their metal [*sic*]'.[44]

Renewing tradition: the strike on the road

From the outset, the strike was solid. Full pickets were mounted at all garages. Individual workers reported for work in isolated garages virtually every day but both union and LTE cooperated to keep them from coming to any physical harm.[45] In the first days of the strike, news reports conveyed surprise that 36,000 central London workers were the majority of the strikers since they would gain nothing from the action. The officers' meeting on 15 April had indeed reported self-interested sentiments in the weakest part of the battle line, the Clapham and Streatham district:

> One Branch Secretary had said the Strike would be a failure; a second that it was an unknown quantity; a third that the Branch members concerned would follow the crowd ... One point made was as to why the Central London Busmen should strike for the Country Services and Inside Staffs membership, as they had not been anxious, it was suggested, to render much help to the Central Busmen in the past.

The officers' response was that 'there must be an immediate concentration on all the weak spots in an endeavour to develop the right strike spirit'.[46]

On 15 May, Cousins successfully asked the F&GP to increase the busworkers' strike pay by 50 per cent 'on the understanding that this decision in no way constituted a precedent'. London busworkers' normal earnings were approximately £9 10s per week. After the increase, they received £3 per week strike pay, with an additional 15s for a wife and 7s 6d for each child. Strike pay was increased again on 6 June by a flat £1 per week per member, with no increase in wives' and children's allowances.[47] The first increase in strike pay was viewed in many quarters as a sign of weakness.

The *Manchester Guardian* observed:

> In a great cause men do not need an extra £1 a week to encourage them to stay on strike after being out for eleven days. But this is not a great cause ... The London strike has been called in the interests of perpetuating a system of wage-bargaining that is not only out of date but unfair to many groups of busmen ... it is a sad thing to see men's loyalties abused in such a shoddy cause.[48]

In fact, very few unions' strike pay was comparable to post-war earnings.[49] *The Times* Labour Correspondent noted: 'In the days when wages were little above subsistence level, workers would often hold out for months on next to nothing ... But workers to-day, with payments to keep up for rent and television and often cars, have a great deal to lose from a prolonged strike'.[50] London bus strikers also found casual work to supplement strike pay. The second officers' meeting discussed a *Sunday Pictorial* article about busmen 'seeking temporary jobs during strike period', and concluded 'it would seem that there is little we can do about it'.[51] Men took painting and decorating work; women did cleaning and ironing.[52]

It was evident that London busworkers had a limited capacity to inflict damage in a strike. In May 1937, neither the Baldwin government nor London Transport had been under serious pressure from the travelling public who had either taken the underground, walked or found lifts. In 1958 the increase in car ownership made a bus strike even less serious. Cousins faced a battle of attrition which he knew he was unlikely to win. He explored three ways to bring the dispute to a head. First, negotiations were proceeding for the railway workers' national wage claim, including London underground workers. If these were deadlocked, there might be a simultaneous railway and/or underground strike. The travel situation would become significantly worse, and the separate pay claims would be coupled together in the public's mind.

Second, other trade groups in the TGWU such as oil distribution workers and petrol lorry drivers could take action in support of the busmen. Third, if the TUC General Council gave strong support to the busworkers, the political stakes would escalate substantially – the Cabinet might be compelled to allow the Ministry of Labour to get on with its accustomed task of conciliation whatever the cost.

London busworkers' activists and the *Platform* were convinced that pursuing the first two options simultaneously would ensure victory. In anticipation, they had forged strong fraternal ties with the railway unions' London district organizations and the TGWU's oil distribution workers and petrol lorry drivers.[53] However, from mid-April it was clear that the Macmillan government was treating the railway pay claim more leniently than the London busworkers. Moreover, railway unions' national officials were keen to settle without a strike. Officers were told by Harry Nicholas on 15 April that 'we were not dependent upon the Railway Unions ... if there was any question of a link-up, it would necessarily come from the Railway Unions and not from us'. The second meeting noted that an inquiry to Sidney Greene, a moderate who had recently been elected National Union of Railwaymen (NUR) General Secretary elicited the reply 'That they are a long way from a stoppage yet'.[54] Greene's pacific intentions were abetted by Macmillan. The latter determined that the government would not be faced with a fight on two fronts and won his point in Cabinet. On 22 April Macmillan hosted a meeting with the railway unions and Sir Brian Robertson, head of the BTC, at which he suggested granting a wage increase in return for the unions co-operating with the BTC in 'making fresh economies with greater urgency'.[55]

The day after the bus strike began, the NUR National Executive scented their tactical advantage and Macmillan's intelligence was that the negotiations would break down.[56] He told the Cabinet on 11 May that they would have to choose between 'three possible courses of action' if there was a strike throughout the transport industry: they could oppose the unions 'until the unions themselves admitted defeat'; admit 'they were no longer capable of controlling the situation'; or reach a compromise which 'would represent to some extent a concession to their pressure'. Macmillan believed it would not be possible to defeat the unions 'unless public opinion was satisfied that the [railway] unions were making unreasonable demands'.[57] But the Cabinet believed that the public supported the railwaymen, and Macmillan obtained Cabinet agreement for further concessions, concluding that:

it would be be prudent to seek to deal separately with the various industrial disputes ... to avoid a conflict with organized labour on a wide front. There could be no certainty that, in such a conflict, the Government would retain the support of public opinion unless it was clear that the trade unions were deliberately organizing a conspiracy against the life of the Community.[58]

He felt 'immense relief' when a railway settlement was finally reached on 15 May.[59] On 20 May, the LTE granted the same increase to underground workers.[60] This made the second option, calling out the TGWU's members in oil distribution, more urgent for the busmen's leaders and those officers who believed that a maximum application of pressure from the union would secure victory. Cousins had countenanced sympathy action before in the 1956 British Motor Corporation dispute.[61] He now took the first steps down this road, but then hesitated and sought the TUC General Council's approval before proceeding.

Cousins had tried to involve the General Council in the strike from the outset. He sent a letter to Tewson on 4 May, which George Woodcock, deputising for Tewson, tabled at the TUC Finance and General Purposes Committee on 7 May. Woodcock presented a statement which reflected his views on the government's inequitable treatment of the busworkers and railwaymen. The Committee, sharing his indignation, approved the statement which expressed general support for the London busmen.[62] A week later, a special meeting of those General Council members in London was distinctly unhelpful to Cousins. The members present ruled out any further involvement by the General Council. Cousins could only obtain their agreement to sponsor a financial appeal. The moderate majority on the General Council, with fearful memories of 1926, were alarmed by the prospect of a confrontation with the government. To avoid such a possibility, a few of them 'maintained a regular and informal dialogue with the Prime Minister' and private contacts with Macleod.[63]

On 21 May a TUC circular launching the London Bus Dispute Appeal went to affiliated unions and trades councils. The amounts received were generous, but small compared to the TGWU's obligations for strike pay. Some members of the General Council, notably Bob Willis, General Secretary of the London Typographical Society, and Ted Hill, General Secretary of the Boilermakers, were sympathetic to Cousins' unspoken wish to escalate the strike, but they remained a comparatively silent minority.[64]

Had there been a groundswell of public sympathy for the busworkers, more moderate members of the Council might have swung behind Cousins. However, the busmen's case did not elicit palpable support outside the circles of union activists. Apart from London, there were no physical points of contact between strikers and other workers. There were no exciting incidents for radio and television news to report. The national press stories, with the exception of the *Daily Herald*, the *Daily Mirror*, and the *Daily Worker*, ranged from unsympathetic to implacably hostile. Despite left-wing activists' eager enthusiasm for displays of solidarity, numerous public meetings, marches and demonstrations drew scant response.[65]

On 27 May a special conference of TGWU officials 'decided to consider bringing out the drivers of petrol lorries and also power workers'. Although the TGWU informed Macleod and sought a meeting, he declined. His refusal was due to the Cabinet's determination that the LTE must go no further than the Industrial Court award. The government was prepared for the consequences of TGWU sympathy action and was willing to use troops to maintain petrol and electricity supplies.[66]

Macleod and Macmillan were assured privately by the moderate cabal of union leaders that the General Council would prevent Cousins extending the strike. Macleod recalled that they 'wanted Cousins taken down a peg'.[67] Cousins and Nicholas met Tewson on 28 May when they repeated their 'new threat', posing the question 'as to what the General Council would be prepared to do in view of the complete impasse in which the union found themselves and the possible spread of the dispute'.[68] Tewson convened the General Council on 29 May, reporting that 'the Government had dug its toes in and consequently it would be fair to assume that a deputation from the General Council to either the Minister of Labour or the Prime Minister might not be fruitful'. He wanted to avoid the 'possibility that the General Council would be faced with a show-down', and suggested 'informal talks' with the Government 'to see what could be done to secure a resumption of negotiations'. The General Council agreed and sent a delegation of five to see Macmillan the next morning. They were, he observed, 'desperately anxious that Cousins should be helped out of the position into which he has got, if HMG [the government] or Transport Board can do so ...'.[69] However, Macmillan followed the Cabinet's hard line, offering three points upon which negotiations could resume, which were only a very slender improvement on the LTE's 'final' offer: acceptance of the award of 8s 6d for the central London busworkers; inclusion of the Green Line busworkers in it; negotiations between the union and the LTE to fix a definite date for a pay review for all other workers.[70]

When the delegation reported back to the General Council meeting later that day, Cousins defiantly rejected Macmillan's terms:

> there would come a stage when the General Council would have to take a decision one way or the other. His union and the London busmen were the spearhead of trade union claims and resistance to lower living standards ... He did not think the Government would 'take on' the whole of the trade union Movement.[71]

However, Council members were determined to push Cousins towards acceptance of an orderly retreat. Willis observed that although the union and the LTE were refusing to budge, he wondered 'whether negotiations could not commence, and to try to agree on x amount to be paid on x date'. Cousins repeated: 'At some point he would have to come and ask the General Council a blunt question: are you with us or not?' Tom Yates, the TUC Chairman, asked him to give a lead to the busmen's negotiating committee but he refused and would undertake only to 'express to them the varied views which had been expressed from the General Council'.[72]

The TUC Press Release after the meeting was notably candid, stating that 'the gap [between the LTE and TGWU] was too small to warrant a general strike' and the five-man delegation considered there was still scope for negotiation.[73] Although he had denied the General Council the satisfaction of knowing he would begin preparations for a retreat, Cousins recommended to the busmen's negotiating committee on the morning of 31 May 'that attempts be made to re-open negotiations'. They immediately agreed and negotiations resumed that afternoon, before breaking down the following day.[74] The problem was that Elliot was observing the government's strictures, insisting there could be no question of something for everyone. Cousins tried in vain to move him, declaring that a resumption of work before negotiations on the pay could start for the remaining 14,000 was 'worse than anything a hard-riding, Victorian employer would have put up'.[75] The busmen's negotiating committee fully expected that Cousins would now call out the oil distribution and electricity workers. A special edition of the *Plat-form* predicted 'after four weeks of "folded arms" strike action, the fight is to be hotted up ... oil tanker drivers will be withdrawn from the roads and T&GWU members from power stations supplying the LTE railway system'.[76]

However, on 2 June, having taken stock of the General Council's refusal to sanction sympathy strikes, Cousins duly led his Executive back from the brink. They decided that 'having regard to the whole of the associated implications, it would be inadvisable at this time to seek to extend the scope of the dispute to involve other sections of the membership of the Union'.[77] Having taken the first steps of a retreat, Cousins then proved viscerally incapable of agreeing a settlement with Elliot which did not yield up substantial concessions. He was perhaps still keen at this point to save his own face, and evidently convinced himself that he could reverse the General Council's negative decision of 30 May. Macmillan's memoirs noted that:

> It was now clearly a contest of will ... To Cousins's threat to withdraw the petrol distribution workers ... our only overt reply was to cancel the weekend leave for the selected troops and the announcement that we would take immediate action if vital services to the community were threatened.[78]

On 4 June Cousins bluntly informed the General Council:

> He had a delegate conference on Monday [9 June] and on that basis [Elliot's proposals] the men would not be got back to work with a machine gun. They knew they were right and they would stay out ... [M]ass meetings of petrol drivers at Stratford and Battersea had pledged their support to take action when called upon. So had the power workers. The question which arose now was what was the General Council going to do about it.[79]

The General Council delegation of five had met Macmillan before the meeting. They reported that he had refused to pressurize Elliot to make further concessions and had reiterated his three points of 30 May as a basis for negotiation. After Yates called for an expression of views, most Council members voiced impatience and anger at Cousins. Bill Webber of the Transport Salaried Staffs Association was typical:

> this strike was not the spearhead of any wages movement ... it was doubtful even if the General Council agreed to an extension of the strike whether the members ... would undertake to extend the strike.[80]

Tewson bluntly stated: 'the views of General Council members were that negotiations to get a settlement would have to take place but would it be any easier in three weeks' time than it would be at this stage?'[81] Harold Collison was frankly pessimistic: 'He did not think it was good that men should be led into a massacre, especially where there was no possibility of a successful conclusion being reached'.[82] Yates summarized the consensus of opinion as 'overwhelmingly against any extension of the strike' and urged the limitation of the dispute 'within its narrowest confines'. Though Cousins accepted the accuracy of this characterization, he refused to say whether he would honour the feeling of the meeting.[83] The TUC press statement issued after the meeting stated baldly that the General Council 'decided to advise ... [the TGWU] against any extension of the stoppage to other groups of workpeople'.[84]

But the union was paying a substantial price for the busmen's stand. The TGWU had spent over £1 million on the strike by 4 June. Cousins sought help from the General Council, hoping to avoid the TGWU selling its less liquid investments at a loss, and was given to understand that once he took steps to end the strike, loans from other unions would be forthcoming.[85] He recommenced negotiations with Elliot once again, but failed to persuade the busworkers' negotiating committee to abandon their demand for something for all 50,000 workers. They voted 7–6 to recommend an extension of the strike. Cousins finally found the will to go over their heads. He convened the delegate conference three days early on 6 June, and argued against extending the strike. He succeeded 'after a four hour battle which he had waged to get that decision', and the conference supported him by 71–60. But delegates then voted unanimously to continue the strike.[86] Cousins had evidently declined to stake his credibility on recommending Elliot's meagre terms.

On 12 June, the General Council delegation of five approached Macleod, but returned with little new. Nevertheless, Tewson told the General Council, 'With the guarantee now that negotiations could start twenty-four hours before a resumption, there was a basis of an appeal which could be made to end the strike and after this length of time it could be an honourable settlement'.[87] It seemed that Cousins was now proceeding backwards along the road to compromise. A special meeting of the TUC Finance and General Purposes' Committee issued an appeal for loans to the TGWU on 13 June and affiliated unions responded immediately. The TGWU was loaned a total of £364,000, with the largest contribution coming from their sister general union, the Municipal Workers.[88]

That same day, one individual on the bus negotiating committee changed his mind and the vote reversed to 7–6 in favour of recommending a return to work.[89] Cousins also had a sweetener for the delegate conference. He reported he had been assured by Elliot that the LTE would make a definite wage offer for the excluded 14,000 workers once they voted to call off the strike. Honour having been salvaged, delegates voted by a large majority to recommend a return to work.[90]

In the subsequent garage ballot, 64 branches to 54 voted against a return to work, confounding the expectations of many, including Cousins.[91] The *Platform* was unrepentant:

> Here is the verdict that sank Sir John Elliot – Mr. Ian MacLeod [*sic*] – and the whole motley, Tory crew. Here is the voice of men and women who, in the seventh week of a strike, made answer to employers, Government, Fleet Street, and the heroic gentlemen of the General Council of the TUC ...[92]

The result is less surprising when considered against the background of militancy in the section and its activists' strong commitment to fight to the last ditch. Before 4 June, Cousins had hardly mentioned retreat. His abrupt change of tack was being obscured by vigorous propraganda from branch activists and the *Platform* in support of his previous hard line.[93]

The vote was also influenced by a notice posted by the LTE in garages stating that the Board's financial situation would necessitate a 10 per cent cut in bus schedules once work was resumed.[94] The notice had evidently been composed more with Harold Watkinson's scrutiny in mind than facilitating a speedy return to work.

Elliot now acted decisively to end the stalemate. He and Brian Robertson saw the Chancellor and sought his approval to make a firm interim money offer for the 14,000 excluded busworkers, following an immediate resumption of work and pending a pay review. Heathcoat Amory saw them with Watkinson. The two ministers flatly refused the request. Having held the line for seven weeks, they were not going to be denied the unconditional surrender of Cousins.

Elliot and Robertson eventually convinced them that a firm money offer had to be made. But Heathcoat Amory would concede no more than 3s 9d per week. Elliot knew that more was required, and he persuaded the Chancellor to refer the question to Macmillan. Fortuitously, Macleod was in Geneva and Macmillan therefore exercised his doveish inclinations freely. When Heathcoat Amory telephoned Elliot the following evening, he said the 3s 9d limit no longer applied. Elliot's only constraint was that the figure 'must be kept below the 8s 6d offered to Central London busmen by the Industrial Court'.[95]

On 19 June, Elliot told Cousins that 'the country busmen would receive an "agreed increase" from the resumption of work and that other excluded grades would have their pay reviewed – a retreat from their earlier position'. He made a 'promise' that the figures for the 14,000 would be between 6s 6d and 7s 6d per week.[96] Cousins put the improved offer to the delegate conference on the same day and it was overwhelmingly accepted. A branch vote followed on 20 June; it confirmed the acceptance by a large vote and a general return to work followed on 21 June.[97]

The left were evidently concerned to avoid a repetition of the 1937 breakaway, and most militants now accepted the need to end the strike. The money promised by Elliot was a substantial concession, and they could tell their members that they had achieved their objective, a just settlement for the 14,000 excluded workers. The LTE also withdrew its notice about 10 per cent cuts to services, issuing a vague warning that cuts would follow in the light of an anticipated fall in demand after the strike and the Board's straitened finances. Here was another concession enabling activists to fight future cuts another day.

The aftermath of the strike

On the busworkers' return, hawkish ministers learned of Elliot's money 'promise' from the press. They were furious and determined to force him to renege. Abetted by Macleod, they won their point in Cabinet. Though Macleod had been a dove in January, he had trimmed in deference to the Cabinet decision to refuse a committee of investigation. He had then become an enthusiastic hawk out of political opportunism during the first week of the strike. Gaitskell had tabled an Opposition motion of censure against the government's handling of the dispute in the Commons on 8 May. In reply, Macleod delivered a withering assault on the Opposition leader for his slavish courting of Cousins and his failure to advise a course of wage restraint and compromise.[98] His speech was reckoned a stunning political success.

Macleod concluded that he had much to gain from pressing the attack against Cousins. He let his displeasure be known when he arrived back from Geneva and found that Macmillan had allowed Elliot to make a money offer:

Indeed so annoyed did Macmillan become with Macleod's carping criticism of the busmen's settlement that the Prime Minister's private office suggested that St James's Square [Ministry of Labour] officials should drop a hint to their Minister to desist. One brave member of Macleod's staff who sought to carry out Downing Street's request was snapped at for his pains.[99]

Macmillan made no attempt to restrain his Cabinet hawks now the busmen were back at work. Elliot was compelled to publicly deny ever making a money offer. Cousins insisted he had. On 17 July, after many attempts by the union to claim the 6s 6d–7s 6d figure and amid much acrimony, Cousins and the negotiating committee accepted 5s for most of the 14,000 workers and 7s 6d for Green Line single-deck drivers. An improvement on Heathcoat Amory's 3s 9d, the settlement was nevertheless viewed by the union as a rank betrayal of their good faith in Elliot.[100]

This unseemly *coda* was the source of considerable embarrassment for the TUC General Council. The cabal who had privately encouraged the Cabinet to be hawkish were nevertheless angered at the spectacle of the government forcing Elliot to go back on his word to Cousins. The Council's sense of fair play was offended by the Cabinet encouraging what they viewed as sharp practice. Their anger probably eased Cousins' passage back into cordial collegiality on the General Council. Cousins himself made no attempt to play the victim of a Tory plot. He was the General Secretary of the country's largest union, and would not court sympathy as leader of a once proud organization laid low by the Tories. He also refused to engage in personal recriminations with his General Council colleagues, even though he was well aware they had gone behind his back to Macmillan and Macleod.[101]

At Congress in September, the President of the Fire Brigades' Union challenged the section of the General Council's Report on the bus strike because it contained 'a most serious omission': 'Nowhere in this Report is there a single word ... showing appreciation of the epic struggle of the London busmen'. Cousins came to the rostrum and remonstrated with him: 'Inquests on certain things usually only reveal the cause of death. We do not think that there is any death in this affair'.[102] However, much later in the week, Cousins dwelt on the bus strike again. In his speech proposing the TGWU's motion against the government's wage freezing policy, he recalled, 'We feel, and I am sure there are many in this Congress hall who feel likewise, that the busmen were fighting the battle for most of us'.[103]

By the end of Congress week, the movement had apparently returned to business as usual. Neither Cousins nor the TGWU suffered damage to their reputations. The TGWU continued to be seen as the strongest, most powerful union. Cousins apparently gloried in the 'strong man' persona with which the right-wing press invested him. Nevertheless, there were adverse lingering consequences for the union. A left-wing TGWU full-time official writing in 1985, felt constrained to observe:

> For the London Bus Section ... there is no escaping the fact that it [the strike] was a defeat of major proportions. Hereafter, the ... Section would become cautious in its approach to major industrial action and the negative lessons of 1958 would be retailed in garage canteens for years to come.[104]

After the strike Cousins never put either his union or the General Council to the test again. He resolutely forbore to make any form of political contribution to the General Council and focused on 'business as usual'.[105] Bevin had not designed his organization to fight the battles confronting unions in the post-war world of consensus and full employment. Nor did Cousins possess Bevin's creative flair. He failed to draw the lesson from the bus strike that the union required a radically different approach to questions of wages policy and nationalized industries.

The net political result of the strike was apparently a strong revival of the Conservative goverment's fortunes. Macmillan noted the sea change: 'from the political aspect the bus strike seemed to be a turning point'.[106] On 15 July 1958, Richard Crossman noted in his diary that Roy Jenkins 'who was one of the great addicts of the theory that we were bound to win, now admits that we are faced with a possibility of defeat'.[107] Nevertheless, Macleod deemed it prudent to dissuade the Conservative Research Department from holding an inquiry into arbitration and collective bargaining, 'especially in the nationalized industries', where it was undesirable that evidence might be given of 'constant communications between minister and Chairmen of nationalized Boards'.[108]

The Conservatives won the general election in October 1959, gaining votes in 'the prosperous west Midlands, the home of the booming car industry'. Peter Clarke concludes that working-class voters combined support for unions with voting Tory because these apparently contradictory allegiances secured the same object.[109] But the Cabinet hawks were hardly given their head to initiate punitive action against unions. Macmillan remained strongly committed to the post-war consensus, and continued to seek a tripartite resolution to questions of wages and prices.[110] In the sixteen months between March 1957 and June 1958, the trade unions had led two large-scale strikes. The national engineering and shipbuilding strikes and the London busworkers' strike brought into sharp relief the fundamental and unsettled issues of how a strong trade union movement should conduct its affairs and whether it should be regulated. Before March 1957, these questions were hardly considered seriously by the political establishment. When they were asked, it was *sotto voce* for fear of upsetting the post-war social equilibrium which was perceived as being somewhat delicate.

After March 1957, Clegg and Adams were certain that the engineering employers had been right to resist the engineering unions to the last ditch. In the absence of a fully fledged wages policy which would render costly industrial conflict unnecessary, they claimed it was the employers' duty to fight.[111] The following summer the Cabinet accepted the challenge thrown down by the London busworkers, and over the seven weeks exposed their principled, altruistic militancy as hubris. The responses of the main players to these dramatic events proved critical to the way in which the questions of trade union power and the state's role in upholding the post-war consensus were resolved. If the terrain and its contours remain largely unexplored by British labour historians, there is a growing feeling that we must begin to chip away at the dusty stereotype of the 1950s as a tranquil, moderate interlude between the action-packed 1940s and 1960s and a growing understanding that the years 1957–58 marked an important watershed in industrial relations.

Notes

1. *Record*, July 1958.
2. G. Goodman, *The Awkward Warrior. Frank Cousins: his life and times* (1979), p. 174.
3. V. L. Allen, *Trade Union Leadership. Based on a Study of Arthur Deakin*

(1957), p. 250; and see also Jim Phillips' chapter in this volume.

4. Goodman, *Awkward Warrior*, p. 120.

5. N. Fishman, *The Communist Party and the Trade Unions 1933–45* (Aldershot, 1995), pp. 51–3; H.A. Clegg, *Labour Relations in London Transport* (Oxford, 1950), pp. 14–15.

6. Fishman, *Communist Party*, pp. 54, 122–7; Clegg, *London Transport*, pp. 16–17.

7. Clegg, *London Transport*, pp. 127–9; *Record*, June 1964.

8. Allen, *Union Leadership*, p. 73.

9. National Museum of Labour History, Manchester, Communist Party Archive, CP/CENT/IND/12/1 and 3, Bill Jones papers, miscellaneous leaflets; K. Fuller, *Radical Aristocrats: London busworkers from the 1880s to the 1980s* (1985) pp. 166–7; Allen, *Union Leadership*, pp. 160–4.

10. Allen, *Union Leadership*, pp. 168–70; Fuller, *Radical Aristocrats*, pp. 190–2.

11. *Platform*, May 1951, September 1952; G. Stevenson, 'Anti-communist bans in the TGWU 1949–68', in G. Stevenson (ed.), *The Life and Times of Sid Easton*, (n.d.), pp. 36–8. Stevenson states that the Dalston garage had a 'large' Communist branch of 40 members.

12. *Platform*, December 1950; CP Archive, CP/CENT/PERS, George Renshaw and Bill Jones files.

13. *Platform*, September 1951, November 1951, January 1952, October 1953, November 1953, January 1954; CP Archive, CP/CENT/PERS, Renshaw file, letter from Renshaw to John Mahon, 8 November 1951; Stevenson, 'Anti-Communist bans', p. 44; J. Jones, *Union Man* (1986), p. 133.

14. H.A. Clegg and R. Adams, *The Employers' Challenge: a study of the national shipbuilding and engineering dispute of 1957* (Oxford, 1957) p. 67.

15. *Platform*, October 1956; TUC, *Report*, 1956, p. 400.

16. Clegg and Adams, *Employers' Challenge*, p. 68; Goodman, *Awkward Warrior*, p. 164.

17. Goodman, *Awkward Warrior*, pp. 164–5. In March 1958 Cousins' report to the GEC referred to 'the problem of the coordination of wage policy as between the three trunk sections of the [Passenger Services] Group – London Transport, Municipal and Company-Owned Undertakings. This, in my view, is fundamental so much so that we shall fail to make effective progress until the problem is resolved' (GEC minutes, p. 53); *Platform*, November 1956.

18. CP Archive, Bill Jones Papers, TGWU Region No. 1 duplicated paper, 'LTE Wages Negotiations (25s per week claim)', n.d.; *Platform*, November 1953, stated that Waters began union activity in 1928, and that he was 'One of the few who had courage to give evidence on behalf of the Rank and File leaders expelled from the union in 1937. Always declined office until 1950 when he became branch chairman'. Waters was a member of the SPGB. Jones announced his resignation from the Communist Party in the *Platform* in January 1957 in response to the events of 1956, but he remained a committed 'fellow traveller', serving on the TGWU GEC (re-elected 1957).

19. 'LTE Wages Negotiations'.

20. D. Barnes and E. Reid, *Governments and Trade Unions* (1982), p. 29.
21. For details of Elliot's career, see *Who Was Who, 1981–1990* (1991).
22. 'LTE Wages Negotiations'; Goodman, *Awkward Warrior*, p. 165. The three sections comprised the whole of London Transport's workforce – central buses, trolleybuses and country buses. The CBC's special status inside the union made it necessary for each to have separate lay machinery.
23. PRO LAB 10/1512, Note of Meeting held at 8 St. James's Square, 10 January 1958; Assistant General Secretary's Seventh Quarterly Report, TGWU GEC Minutes, Appendix II, 10 March 1958.
24. Goodman, *Awkward Warrior*, p. 166.
25. G. Ince, *The Ministry of Labour and National Service* (1960), p. 23; Goodman, *Awkward Warrior*, pp. 166–7.
26. TGWU Minutes, Appendix II Assistant General Secretary's Report, 10 March 1958; Goodman, *Awkward Warrior*, p. 167; PRO LAB 10/1512, Note of a meeting held at 8 St. James's Square on 20 January 1958; PRO LAB 10/1512, Press Notice.
27. PRO CAB 129/91, C.(58)15, 21 January 1958, 'British Transport Commission: Bus Wages. Memorandum by the Minister of Transport and Civil Aviation.
28. PRO CAB 128/32, C.C.8(58), Minute 7 Cabinet Minutes, 22 January 1958.
29. PRO CAB 129/91, C.(58)20, 23 January 1958, 'London Bus Dispute. Memorandum by the Minister of Transport and Civil Aviation'; PRO CAB 129/91, C.(58)17, 23 January 1958, 'London Bus Dispute. Memorandum by the Minister of Labour and National Service'.
30. PRO CAB 128/32, C.C.9(58), Minute 2, Cabinet Minutes 23 January 1958; CAB 128/32, C.C.10(58), Minute 1, Cabinet Minutes 23 January 1958. See also R. Shepherd, *Iain Macleod: a biography* (1995), pp. 134–5; Goodman, *Awkward Warrior*, pp. 166–70; N. Fisher, *Iain Macleod* (1973), p. 125.
31. Goodman, *Awkward Warrior*, p. 168.
32. Ibid.
33. TGWU Assistant General Secretary's report, 10 March 1958.
34. Goodman, *Awkward Warrior*, p. 171.
35. PRO LAB 10/1512, 'London Bus Strike. 5th May, 1958–20th June 1958. Chronological Record of Events'. The exact numbers were: 36,616 central busmen; 5,997 country busmen; 7,387 maintenance and other grades (TGWU GEC minutes, 10 March 1958, Assistant General Secretary's report).
36. PRO LAB 10/1512, Note from St. John Wilson to CIC, 4 June 1958. The award is set out in *The Industrial Court. (2680) London Transport* (1958).
37. PRO CAB 128/32, C.C.23(58) Minute 2, Cabinet Minutes, 13 March 1958; Goodman, *Awkward Warrior*, pp. 171–2.
38. *Platform*, March 1958.
39. TGWU Finance and General Purposes Committee minutes, special session, 2 April 1958, minute 221.
40. *Platform*, April 1958.
41. Goodman, *Awkward Warrior*, p. 173.
42. CP Archive, Bill Jones Papers, 'Memorandum, 16.4.1958. London Trans-

port Executive (Wages Position)', no. 8, p. 2. The second meeting is summarized in 'Note by A. J. C. [Alf Chandler], London Transport. April 22nd 1958'. Region One included Greater London and its suburbs.

43.   'LTE Wages Negotiations'; *Labour Research*, July 1958; Goodman, *Awkward Warrior*, pp. 173–4.

44.   *Platform*, May 1958.

45.   Information from Mary Williams who was a bus conductress at Edgware Road Garage; Fuller, *Radical Aristocrats*, pp. 226–7; Goodman, *Awkward Warrior*, p. 196.

46.   'Memorandum', 16 April 1958, p. 3.

47.   F&GP Minutes, 15 May 1958, Minute no. 283; GEC Minutes, 6 June 1958, Minute No. 426.

48.   *Manchester Guardian*, 16 May 1958.

49.   Clegg and Adams, *Employers' Challenge*, p. 110.

50.   *The Times*, 16 May 1958.

51.   CP Archive, Bill Jones Papers, 'Note by A.J.C.', no. 3, p. 1.

52.   Information from Mary Williams, and from Vicky Johnson about her father who was a bus conductor in Croydon.

53.   *Platform*, March and April 1958.

54.   CP Archive, Bill Jones Papers, 'Memorandum' no. 2, p. 1 and 'Note by A.J.C.', nos. 6 & 7, pp. 1–2.

55.   H. Macmillan, *Memoirs Vol. 4, Riding the Storm: 1956–1959* (1971), p. 711.

56.   Ibid. p. 713. The NUR Executive increased the pressure by adopting a motion on 8 May calling for strike action on Whit Sunday 25 May (P.S. Bagwell, *The Railwaymen: the history of the National Union of Railwaymen*, 1963, pp. 654–5).

57.   C.C.39(58) Minute 3, Cabinet Minutes, 11 May 1958. I am grateful to the Cabinet office for supplying me with a photocopy of this minute which was not available at the Public Record Office.

58.   PRO CAB 128/32, C.C.40(58), Cabinet minutes, 13 May 1958.

59.   Macmillan, *Riding the Storm*, p. 715.

60.   Cousins was ingenuously sanguine that the NUR – at least the underground drivers – would come out with the busmen (Goodman, *Awkward Warrior*, p. 174).

61.   See N. Fishman, 'The most serious dispute since 1926', in this volume.

62.   Goodman, *Awkward Warrior*, p. 181: TUC *Report*, 1958, p. 130.

63.   Goodman, *Awkward Warrior*, p.182.

64.   The appeal brought in £28,183 18s 3d (TUC General Council F&GP minutes, 23 June 1958).

65.   See, for example, the *Daily Worker* report on 12 May 1958 and leaflets in the Bill Jones Papers.

66.   PRO LAB 10/1512, 'London Bus Strike ... Record of Events'. On 22 May Macleod told the Cabinet about discussions the CIC had conducted with both sides in the disputes on 21 May. The Cabinet concluded that 'it was likely to become increasingly difficult for the union leaders to sustain the bus strike and it would be unwise for the Government to appear to weaken in

the firm attitude which they had hitherto maintained'. They 'invited the Minister of Transport to inform the Chairman [Elliot] that ... he should adhere to his earlier offer ...' (C.C.45(58)2. 22 May 1958). There had been preparations made early on in the strike to deal with its spreading, up to and including a general transport strike (Report from Home Secretary to the Cabinet on 11 May, C.C.39 (58) 3).

67. Goodman, *Awkward Warrior*, pp.184–5.
68. Modern Records Centre, University of Warwick, MSS 292/24.1/19 TUC General Council Minutes, 29 May 1958.
69. General Council Minutes, 29 May 1958; Macmillan, *Riding the Storm*, p. 716.
70. This description of the meeting is contained in the TUC's press release, quoted in TGWU GEC minute No. 313, 2 June 1958.
71. TUC General Council Minutes, 30 May 1958, p. 75.
72. Ibid.
73. PRO LAB 10/1512, 'Chronological Record'.
74. Cousins outlined the negotiations at the General Council meeting on 4 June (General Council minutes, 4 June 1958, pp. 82–3).
75. Ibid, p. 83.
76. *Platform*, 'Special Strike Edition', June 1958. The headline was 'Extend It – And End It'.
77. TGWU GEC Minute No. 313, 2 June 1958.
78. Macmillan, *Riding the Storm*, p. 718.
79. TUC General Council minutes, 4 June 1958, p. 84.
80. Ibid., pp. 86–7.
81. Ibid., p. 89.
82. Ibid., p. 91.
83. Ibid., p. 93.
84. TUC, *Report*, 1958, p. 137.
85. TUC General Council Minutes, 4 June 1958; Goodman, *Awkward Warrior*, pp. 187–8.
86. TUC General Council Minutes, 12 June 1958, p. 40; Goodman, *Awkward Warrior*, p. 188.
87. TUC General Council Minutes, 12 June 1958, p. 41.
88. TUC, *Report*, 1958, pp. 137–8. The total cost of the strike to the TGWU was £1.17m (Goodman, *Awkward Warrior*, pp. 188–9).
89. The vote is given in PRO LAB 10/1512, 'Chronological Record of Events'; the text of the motion is given in TGWU GEC Minute No.428, Special Session of GEC, 13 June 1958.
90. Goodman, *Awkward Warrior*, p. 189.
91. Ibid.
92. *Platform*, July 1958. There are no available figures for the numbers of busworkers participating in the garage branch ballot. Activists probably concentrated on mobilizing a 'no' vote rather than ensuring a full 100 per cent turnout.
93. See, for example, leaflet from the Holloway bus garage in the Bill Jones

papers.

94. Goodman, *Awkward Warrior*, p. 190.
95. Goodman, *Awkward Warrior*, pp. 190–1. The meeting was probably held on 18 June. The three extant accounts of this episode, by Goodman and Shepherd (*Macleod*, pp. 140–1) and Elliot (Sir John Elliot, *On and Off the Rails*, 1982, pp. 97–8), differ in detail, being vague and sometimes aesopian about dates, participants, and sequences of events.
96. Goodman, *Awkward Warrior*, p. 190.
97. Ibid.; TGWU F&GP Minutes, Minute No. 449, 3 July 1958, pp. 121–2.
98. Shepherd, *Macleod*, pp. 138–9.
99. Ibid., p. 141. Shepherd's source is notes from Ministry of Labour officials.
100. PRO LAB 10 /1512, 'Chronological Record of Events'; see also Goodman, *Awkward Warrior*, pp. 190–2.
101. Goodman notes that Tom O'Brien told Cousins on 25 May about seeing Macmillan and Churchill on the eve of the strike when they had asked him 'whether Frank Cousins was trying to start a civil war or a revolution...' (*Awkward Warrior*, p. 185 quoting Cousins' diary kept sporadically during the strike).
102. TUC, *Report*, 1958, pp. 332–3. The challenge was supported by Frank Haxell, General Secretary of the Electrical Trades Union. The Fire Brigades Union had been exemplary in its assistance to the London busworkers. See Bill Jones article thanking the union in their journal, *Firefighter*, July 1958.
103. TUC, *Report*, 1958, pp. 432–3.
104. Fuller, *Radical Aristocrats*, pp. 228–9. Fuller was a London bus driver for eleven years.
105. Goodman, *Awkward Warrior*, p. 194.
106. Macmillan, *Riding the Storm*, pp. 719–21.
107. J. Morgan (ed.), *The Backbench Diaries of Richard Crossman*, (1981), p. 689.
108. Shepherd, *Macleod*, p. 148.
109. P. Clarke, *Hope and Glory: Britain 1900–1990* (1997), p. 271.
110. Barnes and Reid, *Governments and Unions*, pp. 33–4.
111. Clegg and Adams, *The Employers' Challenge*, pp. 142–56.

CHAPTER ELEVEN

Democracy and Trade Unionism on the Docks

Jim Phillips

With post-war recovery dependent on the rapid outward despatch of manufacturing exports and the swift inward flow of food and raw materials which kept manufacturing industries afloat, the docks were central to Britain's economic performance. This chapter focuses on the character of trade unionism in this vital economic sector. The analysis centres on the question of democracy, always a controversial issue in the docks. Right-wing critics of trade unionism generally felt that there was too much democracy in the ports, objecting to the joint industrial character of the National Dock Labour Board, the body responsible for administering a range of employment issues. Trade union membership of the Board was the alleged source of the ill-discipline which many observers regarded as characterizing the industry. Left-wing critics generally asserted the opposite: it was the absence of practical democracy which caused so much trouble on the waterfront. Unofficial strikes recurred frequently only because the leadership of the dockers' main organization, the vast Transport and General Workers' Union (TGWU), paid insufficient attention to its 70,000 or so dock members. The TGWU, unsurprisingly, believed that there was democracy in the ports, and made a virtue of the constitutional features which connected union leaders and fulltime officials with their working dockers. In the 1940s and 1950s, however, the TGWU leadership did not define democracy solely in terms of the branch meeting or the National Docks Delegate Conference. Democracy also involved defending the interests of other occupational groups of members, providing support for the Attlee governments and the Labour leadership, and promoting domestic and international Cold War opposition to Communism. These broader concerns often brought the TGWU leadership into conflict with sections of its dock membership, particularly in the ten years that immediately followed the Second World War.

In this essay, trade union politics in the docks are viewed through these conflicting conceptions of democracy, indicating that the TGWU's failure to respond to a popular demand for a more militant policy led to an attempted exodus of members to a rival organization, the National Amalgamated Stevedores and Dockers (NASD), in 1954–5. The chapter divides chronologically with the death of Arthur Deakin in 1955, often characterized as a turning point in TGWU history. Like Ernest Bevin, his predecessor as the union's

General Secretary, Deakin earned a reputation as a loyal supporter of the Labour Party leadership and a stridently intolerant opponent of dissent. Frank Cousins, Deakin's successor but one in 1956, was a very different political figure, whose commitments to expanding public ownership and unilateral nuclear disarmament brought him into sharp conflict with the Labour leadership in the late 1950s and early 1960s. Cousins also differed from his predecessors in seeking to alter the relationship between the union leaders and members, sympathizing with the argument that this had deteriorated in the 1940s because of the undemocratic behaviour of Deakin and his officials. The most visible indication of the TGWU's new approach in the docks came in 1962. Responding to the mood of his members, Cousins took the union to the brink of the first official national strike in the ports since 1926. This incident offers a particularly vivid contrast with Deakin's resolute condemnation of a string of popular unofficial strikes in the 1940s and 1950s.

There were other explanations, besides the change in leadership, for improving relations within the union. The most important, perhaps, was the relaxation of industrial discipline in the ports as general economic pressures eased from the mid-1950s onwards. International developments were also significant. The Cold War inflated the impact of unofficial strikes, which the anti-Communist Deakin typically characterized as Communist-inspired plots to undermine trade union democracy and western economic recovery. International tension diminished after the Korean War ended in 1953, and although Deakin continued to insist that unofficial representatives in the docks were politically-motivated, anti-Communist rhetoric declined and was decreasingly effective. Hence the emphatic nature of Cousins's victory in 1956, despite Deakin's persistent attempts to portray him as a Communist sympathizer. The new leadership, while retaining Deakin's 1949 ban on Communists holding union office, did not react to unofficial action in the docks with allegations about political subversion.

Trade union democracy in the docks, 1945–55

The Transport and General Workers' Union, the largest trade union in postwar Britain with around 1.3 million members in the mid-1950s, was formed in 1922 as an amalgamation of fourteen separate unions in a number of different trades. To 'prevent loss of identity', in the words of its founding General Secretary, Ernest Bevin, the new union's constitution included trade groups as well as regional divisions.[1] Reflecting the character of pre-1922 waterfront organization, the Docks Trade Group had incorporated a large number of small unions without dismantling their administrative structures. Each of these had a large number of full-time officials, owing to the need to have an official at the side of a ship whenever a dispute arose. This meant that after 1922 dockers were served by a disproportionate number of full-time officials: in 1954 the Docks Group had about 5 per cent of the union's members but 15 per cent of its full-time officials.[2]

The Docks Trade Group and the large number of full-time officials, buttressed by the National Docks Delegate Conferences that were required to endorse major agreements on pay and conditions, ought to have ensured that the TGWU was responsive to its dock membership. However, within its first decade, the union had lost several thousand members in London and on the Clyde amid allegations that it was ignoring dockers' interests and wielding power in too centralized a manner. The Londoners who left the TGWU in 1923 and 1924 formed the Dockers' Section of the new National Amalgamated Stevedores and Dockers Union (NASD). In subsequent decades the existence of this separate organization was to be a constant source of difficulty for the TGWU. It developed a reputation for being more democratic than its large rival, and therefore operating as a pole of attraction for disenchanted TGWU dockers. The NASD's full-time officials were elected rather than centrally-appointed, and served fixed terms rather than for life. And while agreements negotiated by the TGWU were subject to ratification by Delegate Conferences, the smaller scale of the NASD – confined to 7,000 London members until the inter-union dispute of the 1950s – allowed it to approve decisions at a single mass meeting of all members.[3] Bevin's Scottish dissentients, the Clydeside branches of the TGWU, disaffiliated *en masse* and established a separate Scottish Transport and General Workers' Union in 1932, although the UK-wide union managed to stabilize its position on the Scottish east coast.[4]

It is only within this tradition of powerful localized resistance to centralized union directives that the frequency and character of unofficial strike action between 1945 and 1955 – when the average dock worker was on strike six times more often than the average coal miner – can be fully understood. A number of distinctive factors contributed to this militancy, which has been analysed in detail elsewhere.[5] It was, in part, a rebellion against the intense economic pressures of the period. Having worked through the dangers of the Blitz and intensified their efforts during the Battle of the Atlantic, dockers were poorly rewarded in peacetime. The Labour government's export drive renewed pressure on the ports and the 1948 pay freeze prevented the workforce from reaping the material rewards its unusually strong position in the labour market merited. Dock militancy was also rooted in the character of the 1947 Dock Labour Scheme. Very much the creation of Bevin, who had campaigned relentlessly for 'decasualisation' since the 1920 Shaw Inquiry, the Scheme was seen as a major advance for dockers, eliminating the harsh human costs of casual recruitment by offering guaranteed payment when work was unavailable. Its arrival was duly celebrated as a fitting climax to the TGWU's 25th birthday in July 1947: 'The Long Fight for Decasualisation Ends in Victory!' headlined the cover of the union journal's special Silver Jubilee issue.[6]

In two aspects of its practical operation, however, the Scheme tended to sharpen rather than alleviate tensions. First, it left the traditional system of competitive casual recruitment unreconstructed. With piece-rates still in place, and determined by a cargo's market value rather than the physical effort involved in moving it, the relative attraction of different jobs continued to vary immensely. As a result favouritism and petty corruption – bribery of foremen for more lucrative jobs – were not eradicated, and those who were denied a share of 'the cream' harboured significant and understandable resentment.[7] Second, and perhaps more seriously, as the Scheme was motivated by considerations of economic efficiency as well as social justice, it incorporated a tough disciplinary code.[8] Dockers who failed to comply with their new obligations, to report to the docks twice daily, even if there were no ships to be worked, and to accept any job, no matter how unattractive, could be fined, suspended from the Scheme's benefits, or even dismissed. As TGWU officials were responsible for administering the new regime, through the joint industrial local dock labour boards, many dockers increasingly saw their union as an instrument of discipline rather than democratic representation. James Callaghan, Parliamentary Secretary at the Ministry of Transport from 1947–50, sympathized strongly with this view, contending that in disciplinary hearings the union official had become the 'judge' rather than the 'advocate' of his dock members. Writing to Attlee and Bevin in July 1949, Callaghan suggested that disciplinary questions be handled by a body independent of union and employers.[9] The National Association of Port Employers exploited the TGWU's discomfort on this issue by seeking an end to joint industrial control in the docks. In 1949 and 1955 the Association unsuccessfully attempted to persuade the government to alter the basis of the Scheme by excluding the unions from its administration.[10]

An alternative idea, that local dock labour boards of appointed employers and union officials be bolstered with delegates directly elected by the workforce, was put forward by the unofficial London Port Workers' Strike Committee during the 1948 stoppage.[11] This proposal was as unsuccessful as those devised by Callaghan and the port employers, but it typified the self-consciously democratic and directly representative character of the worker committees which organized the various unofficial strikes and struggles from the 1940s to the 1960s. The deep dissatisfaction with the official union machinery was demonstrated by the establishment of rank and file committees with lay delegates elected from each control point on the docks. These assumed a semi-permanent existence throughout the post-1945 period on Merseyside and in London, collecting contributions and publishing newspapers, such as *Portworkers' Clarion* and *Portworkers' News*. The London committee claimed a circulation of around 5,000 for the latter in 1950.[12] Links with ports where rank and file organization was more sporadic were formed by the London and Mersey committees, whose main efforts were expended in coordinating activity during major industrial disputes, although some dockers also turned to recognized unofficial leaders for advice and support on more routine questions.[13]

With the TGWU leadership firmly behind pay restraint and the export drive, unofficial representation assumed particular relevance in the 1940s. In October 1945, a local piece-rate dispute on the Mersey escalated into a huge national stoppage, with around 50,000 dockers protesting about the union leadership's conduct of pay negotiations with employers. Significant inter-port links were formed during this dispute, with members of the Mersey committee journeying to London and other dock areas. Police in Edinburgh, for example, believed that the presence in Leith on 18 October of one of the Mersey leaders, Phil Callanan, had been decisive in prolonging the strike on Scotland's east coast at a time when rank and file support for the stoppage appeared to be waning.[14] The final decision to bring the strike to an end was taken, moreover, by a 'national' conference in Liverpool of delegates from each affected port area, including Dundee, Leith, Glasgow, Wearside, Humberside, Preston, Manchester and the Avon as well as Merseyside and London. The 1945 strike for improved pay anticipated the character of subsequent unofficial action, usually triggered by disputes over pay and conditions where TGWU officials had failed to provide adequate leadership. In this respect the unofficial movement was industrially militant rather than politically radical, seeking a much sterner confrontation with employers in order to secure for dockers a fuller realization of their market strength, although unofficial pamphlets did make reference to the need for nationalization without compensation of port transport.[15]

Another important feature of unofficial activity in London was its 'inter-denominational' character. Strike committees drew representatives from the TGWU, the NASD and the port's other main trade union, the Watermen, Lightermen, Tugmen and Bargemen's Union (WLTBU). The more prominent TGWU members were Harry Constable, Ted Dickens and Tom Cronin, the NASD presence regularly included Albert Timothy and Tom 'Sandy' Powell, and WLTBU representation featured E.C.W. Thomas and W.J.R. Brooks.[16] With the unofficial movement characterized by inter-union as well as inter-port cooperation, its activities were punctuated by periodic threats – from Liverpool and London – that a separate port trade union might be established. Powell and Timothy, both members of the NASD's Dockers' Section, were especially keen on this idea. During the 1945 strike Powell claimed that a new union could be formed at a moment's notice.[17] After the 1949 strike, addressing a meeting at Canning Town Hall, Timothy argued that the establishment of a separate Port Workers' Union would strengthen the workforce's ability to shape the operation of the Dock Labour Scheme.[18] This emphasis on the potential benefits of 'breakawayism', in terms of enhanced democracy and sharpened militancy, anticipated the attempted mass transfer of northern TGWU members which the NASD Dockers' Section encouraged in 1954 and 1955.

The TGWU rejected entirely the notion that unofficial committees were democratic expressions of rank and file opinion. Union leaders responded to each unofficial strike by emphasizing the benefits of patient negotiation and the democratic nature of the union's constitution which allowed members to influence the conduct of these negotiations. In December 1954 the Transport and General Workers' *Record*, the union's monthly journal, carried an editorial entitled 'A Job Worth Doing'. Characteristic of the period, this asked members to contemplate the 'progressive improvement in standards of living' that had been achieved through negotiation with employers since the war, and detailed the highly democratic character of these negotiations, conducted on motions passed from branch meeting to trade group committee to joint industrial talks. Agreements at these talks were then reported back to members through the trade group committee and branch meeting. 'If any member is unaware of what is being done on his behalf', the editorial continued, 'it is because he does not attend his branch meeting. That, as an excuse for (a) complaining that the leadership is out-of-touch with the rank and file; (b) breaking an agreement negotiated for him, appears singularly inadequate'.[19]

Rhetoric apart, the TGWU's response to unrest was limited. Following the 1948 strike Deakin was forced into a significant concession on the question of discipline, negotiating with employers a reduction in the maximum allowable period of suspension from the benefits of the Dock Labour Scheme from three months to four weeks. Otherwise the union's positive action was confined to disciplining leaders of the unofficial strikes. Early in 1949 seventeen London dockers were given an official warning for shaping the 1948 strike. Following further lengthy stoppages in the spring and summer of 1949, the activities of seven unofficial London representatives were the subject of an official inquiry at Transport House in 1950. Three of these individuals, Constable, Dickens and Bert Saunders, were expelled from the union as a result.[20] Tom Cronin, present at this hearing but merely reprimanded, went on to become one of the TGWU's most respected full-time officers in London.[21]

There were, of course, constraints, both structural and political, on the TGWU's behaviour in the docks. In structural terms, TGWU officials were often unable to respond quickly to developments in the ports because of the physical distances involved. Fred Lindop has argued that until the shop stewards system was introduced in the late 1960s, established procedures for dealing with disputes actively increased rather than reduced the likelihood of strike action. Most disagreements between workers and management centred on the nature, and therefore the wages to be paid for a particular cargo. To resolve these disagreements a full-time official had to be brought down to the ship. This could take time, during which the dockers involved had to choose between stopping work altogether or weakening their case by finishing the job and 'removing the evidence'.[22] The origins of the 1948 strike provide a good illustration of this general point, the relevant TGWU official angering his members by siding with the employer in piece-rate negotiations which he conducted by telephone, without ever seeing the disputed cargo of zinc oxide himself.[23]

In political terms the TGWU was constrained by its wider commitment to supporting the Labour government through pay restraint and industrial conciliation. Key personnel in the union's Docks Group, including successive National Secretaries Jack Donovan and Arthur Bird, shared Deakin's support for this strategy. Donovan was particularly hard on strikes and unofficial action, especially after the adoption of the Dock Labour Scheme. Through the pages of the union *Record*, in 1947 he warned dockers that as the Scheme was based on an Act of Parliament, any future strikes 'would not be against the employers but against the Government'.[24] The union's conduct of important crises, including each of the large strikes between 1945 and 1954, was in any event dominated by the General Secretary, who attended Docks Group meetings in an *ex officio* capacity. Deakin's opposition to unofficial action was based, in the first instance, on the belief that it threatened union rules and established agreements with employers. He also felt that unofficial strikes undermined the work of Attlee's governments, which he sought to defend by supporting the pay freeze. This made Deakin deeply unpopular among dockers, but he was prepared to trade personal popularity and short-term pay increases for dockers for the longer-term economic, social and welfare benefits which he believed the Labour government was bringing to all of his members.[25] Unofficial dock strikes, in his view, threatened the delivery of these benefits, by choking the economic recovery and the security of the government on which they were contingent. 'We are fortunate to have a Labour Government', he told union officials during an unofficial dispute in 1949, and 'we should be more fortunate still to have a Labour Government in 50 years. All this refusal to accept the policy and discipline that democratic trade unionism provides was another nail in the coffin of Labour and Government in this country'.[26] Defending union democracy in these terms meant that Deakin was not prepared, as he saw it, to allow the short-term interests of some dockers to cut across the long-term needs of larger numbers of workers, including non-dockers.

This crude version of utilitarian democracy was perhaps understandable in the late 1940s, given the extent of the economic emergency. Deakin's intolerance of dissent was less justifiable as economic conditions improved, particularly after 1951 with Labour out of office. In the 1950s, however, Deakin persisted with his belief, formed in the early period of the Cold War, that dissent in the trade union movement was an expression of support for Communism, designed to weaken the labour movement and undermine economic recovery. Deakin's interpretation of international developments from 1945 onwards was clearly influenced, if not entirely directed, by Ernest Bevin, Foreign Secretary in the Attlee governments. Both believed that anti-

Communism was in the interests of independent trade unionism, observing clear parallels between the manner in which both fascism and Stalinism had crushed workers' rights and autonomous organization.[27] The anti-Communist commitment in the 1940s and 1950s was thus a logical extension of the anti-Nazi rearmament strategy which Labour had adopted in the 1930s.[28] Despite this reasoning, however, the TUC's anti-Communist campaign concentrated more on the allegedly subversive character of domestic Communist activists than the anti-working-class character of the Soviet Union.[29] Anti-Communism's most visible consequence in the TGWU was the 1949 ban on Communists from holding official positions within the union.[30] This weakened the union by forcing able and committed individuals out of office at every level and in almost every geographical area and trade group.

Deakin's obsession with Communism had particularly damaging consequences for the TGWU in the docks, where unofficial strikes were routinely characterized as Communist plots.[31] During the huge unofficial strike of October 1954 he reiterated what had become a tediously familiar charge, that dockers in London and Liverpool were being duped by Communist workmates acting in 'furtherance of the policy of international Communism'. As ever, he insisted that the assault on trade union democracy merely prefaced Communism's larger anti-democratic design, describing the strike as 'a conspiracy to create chaos and confusion as a prelude to securing revolutionary change in the political nature of our government in this country'.[32] Communism certainly enjoyed some degree of influence in the docks, especially in London, where party members like Ted Dickens, Ted Kirby, Vic Marney and, in the 1950s and 1960s, Jack Dash, assumed great prominence in unofficial struggles. In other ports, however, the CP was deeply unpopular. This stemmed largely from the fact that its national leadership was sometimes as sharp a critic of unofficial action as the TGWU. Anxious about preserving its position in the wider labour movement, the CP opposed the great strikes of 1945 and 1955, and lost much of its influence as a result.[33]

With the CP forfeiting its reputation as a party of struggle, Trotskyists came to play a significant minor role in the ports. This began during the huge 1945 strike, when Deakin and Donovan claimed that the tiny Trotskyist Revolutionary Communist Party (RCP) – which had less than 500 members – was behind the national stoppage.[34] RCP activists on the Mersey were certainly involved to the extent of publicizing dockers' grievances in advance of the strike, and helping to develop links between dockers in Liverpool and London. There was also Trotskyist activity in Leith, where the detective constable responsible for monitoring developments described one of the local strike leaders, Robert Gardner from Granton, as a member of the RCP. In a separate bulletin the same detective spoke luridly of spotting three nationally-prominent Trotskyists – Willie Tait (from nearby Portobello), Roy Tearse and John Archer – in conversation with small numbers of dockers and unofficial leaders in the vicinity of Leith's Eldorado Ballroom, where several mass meetings were held during the strike. With apparent disappointment, however, he also observed that none of the Trotskyists had been allowed into the ballroom to address the strikers as a body.[35] On the whole, in fact, the TGWU's assertion that the RCP was behind the strike – as opposed to simply supporting it – was hugely overblown. Even on the Mersey, once the strike was under way, dockers were hostile rather than amenable to the RCP's politics.[36] Trotskyists effected a much closer engagement with dockers in the 1950s. The vehicle for this activity was 'the Club', Gerry Healy's entrist group in the Labour Party, and its newspaper, *Socialist Outlook*. The Club's breakthrough was strengthened by the Labour government's botched prosecution in 1951 of seven dockers under Order 1305, the emergency regulation which forbade strikes and lock-outs. The most charismatic of the seven, Harry Constable, became a supporter of *Socialist Outlook* around 1950.[37] Constable was one of many politically-conscious dockers who became hostile to the CP over its conduct of docks policy and, with comrades in London and Liverpool, later joined the Club. Having been expelled from the TGWU in 1950, Constable joined the Dockers' Section of the NASD in 1954. Along with other ex-Communist Trotskyists in the small union, notably Bert Aylward, Constable was thus in a position to direct the inter-union dispute which began later that year. The transfer of members from the TGWU to the NASD began in Hull, where relations between TGWU officers and members had been particularly rancorous in the 1930s and 1940s. After local officials refused to support the workforce's demand for the mechanization of grain unloading and packing, an unofficial committee invited the NASD to start a branch in Hull.[38] The NASD responded to this and similar requests which followed from dockers in Manchester and on the Mersey.[39] In May 1955 the NASD held an official strike, in London and the northern ports, pursuing the right to represent its new members in joint industrial negotiations. On the orders of the NASD's established London leadership, this was called off, without achieving its aim, at the start of July.[40]

It has been suggested that Trotskyists played the crucial organizational role in this dispute, developing the tactic of striking for recognition. In his recent autobiography Bill Hunter, the Trotskyist organizer and journalist, was keen to dispel any notion of conspiratorial behaviour, ascribing the story that Healy engineered the breakaway to 'the gossip which some middle-class "revolutionaries" have substituted for Trotskyist history'.[41] This story emanates, in fact, from the NASD's inquiry into the origins of the 1955 strike, held in November 1956, when dockers from Manchester and Liverpool claimed that the policy of striking for recognition had been shaped by Constable and another Trotskyist docker, Peter Kerrigan, after a meeting at the Stork Hotel in Liverpool (on 16 April 1955) with Healy and Hunter. According to a docker who attended this meeting (a Mancunian called Walsh), Hunter had said 'that the time was now ripe to go forward for recognition. He formulated policy for strike action and handed it to Kerrigan'.[42]

This story fitted in with Deakin's view that industrial unrest in the docks was artificially stirred up by politically-motivated opponents of moderate trade unionism. But this position overlooked the fairly obvious practical point that any unofficial leader, whether Communist, Trotskyist or mainstream Labour, commanded a following only when he articulated popular grievances which full-time officials had been unable or unwilling to address. So it was, surely, with Constable and Kerrigan in 1955. The strike only proceeded because almost 10,000 northern dockers believed that the TGWU was incapable of responding to their demands, and perceived the NASD to be a far more responsive, democratic and militant organization. The conspiratorial view of the move to the NASD also overlooks the powerful traditions of 'breakawayism' in the ports. This had been present from the very earliest days of dockers' trade unionism, was revived in London in 1923, featured on the Clyde in 1932, and punctuated the 1945 and 1949 strikes.[43] In attacking the motives of individual unofficial leaders, while largely ignoring the substance of the grievances which they articulated, Deakin and his dock officers merely intensified their union's difficulties in 1954 and 1955. The union's huge losses, one-sixth of its docks membership, were entirely self-inflicted, resulting from the absence of practical democracy in the ports.

The TGWU and the docks after Deakin, 1955–64

Frank Cousins became leader of the TGWU at the start of 1956, following the sudden death of Deakin's successor, Jock Tiffin, in December 1955. Deakin had also died prematurely, collapsing at an election rally on 1 May 1955, several months before his planned retirement. The election of Cousins clearly had an important impact on Labour politics. Under Deakin the TGWU strictly observed what Lewis Minkin has described as 'the rules' of the Labour Alliance: in party–union debates the TGWU took a lead only on industrial issues, such as wages and productivity, leaving 'political' matters to the 'politicians' – in other words, the Parliamentary leadership. And it was the union's duty to support loyally the policies adopted by this leadership – hence the justification for Deakin's attacks on the Bevanites who repudiated Labour foreign policy in the early 1950s.[44] Under Cousins, it is commonly assumed, the TGWU abandoned this approach, challenging the Labour leadership on non-industrial 'political' issues. The TGWU's advocacy of unilateral nuclear disarmament, opposed bitterly by Gaitskell and bulk of the Parliamentary leaders, has been presented as the most vivid example of this departure.[45] A departure it certainly was, but the extent of the political changes wrought by Cousins has been exaggerated. The new leader's behaviour was inhibited by existing union policy and the generally cautious and moderate character of the full-time officers and executive whom he inherited from Deakin and Tiffin.[46] He, too, was bound, it should be emphasized, by Minkin's 'rules'. Despite his involvement in the debates over unilateralism, after 1956 Cousins' main priorities were always industrial questions and, particularly, vigilant opposition to government wage controls. Ever the reluctant politician, even after he joined Harold Wilson's Labour government in 1964, Cousins joined no political grouping and turned down an invitation to join the editorial board of *Tribune*.[47]

The new leader's actions were particularly constrained in the docks, where Cousins inherited the long-running dispute with the NASD. Although shocked by the departure of so many dock members, Deakin had admitted no wrongdoing on the part of the TGWU, attributing sole responsibility for the episode to the NASD's predatory behaviour.[48] Operating through the TUC, he initiated an attempt to regain the lost members by charging the NASD with breaking the TUC's 1939 Bridlington Agreement on poaching of members.[49] Cousins viewed matters differently, seeing the dispute as a crisis which illustrated the general gulf that had emerged between union leadership and membership. The remedy, he believed, was to restore practical democracy in the TGWU, making the union more responsive to the demands of its members. Conscious that the union's continued presence in the docks was in jeopardy, Cousins was also aware that the campaign to regain members would be long and hard.[50] The union's National Docks Secretary, Tim O'Leary, was instructed to devote particular attention to Liverpool and Birkenhead. A local broadsheet, funded by the union nationally, was established to publicize the benefits of TGWU membership and compete with the NASD's popular *News of the Blues*.[51]

In seeking to restore its position the union was greatly assisted by the loosening of the economic and disciplinary pressures which had complicated Deakin's task in the docks. In 1956 an official inquiry into the operation of the Dock Labour Scheme, chaired by the then Mr Justice Devlin, reported that increased discipline had been a major source of tension.[52] In the years which followed, according to Gordon Phillips and Noel Whiteside, dock labour boards took a less rigid approach to discipline. As a result working days lost to stoppages between 1956 and 1964 were approximately half of the 1945–55 total.[53] Yet so long as the dispute with the NASD remained unresolved, this was not enough to restore the TGWU's former strength. In October 1954, at Deakin's bidding, the TUC suspended the NASD for poaching TGWU members. This suspension was lifted in June 1955, when the NASD promised to relinquish the northern members and accept the findings of a TUC Disputes Committee. Responding to these findings, on 4–6 July 1955 the NASD brought its lengthy recognition strike to an end, expelled its northern members, and pledged that no further attempt to organize outside London would be made.[54]

But this apparent conclusion merely prefaced a lengthy and increasingly complicated episode. Many of those who left the TGWU before July 1955 regarded their actions as a 'prison break', freeing them from a rigid and undemocratic bureaucracy.[55] Having subsequently been on strike for six weeks in order to gain recognition for their new union, many of these dockers were understandably determined to remain outside the TGWU. In 1956 one of the Merseysiders, Francis Spring, took the NASD to court, claiming that its action in expelling him had been unlawful. Like many others, Spring greatly resented the manner in which his personal status was being determined by various ranks of union officialdom, and felt he was being arbitrarily passed from the NASD back to the TGWU regardless of his own wishes. His case was upheld and the NASD forced to re-admit all who had been expelled in July 1955. Spring's actions were, it should be added, encouraged by a split within the established London ranks of the NASD. The Dockers' Section, which had organized the northern men, wanted to keep them. The Stevedores' Section, which feared being dominated by the potentially more militant northerners, wanted to be rid of them, an outcome that would yield the additional advantage of restoring the union's position in the TUC. This sectional division was compounded by political differences, with Trotskyist dockers like Constable and Aylward confronted by stevedores with CP associations, including Dickie Barrett, the NASD General Secretary.[56]

The outcome of the Spring case required the TUC to resume its defence of the Bridlington Agreement. The 1956 Congress, where Cousins, according to the *Economist,* 'spanked the NASD with all of Deakin's paternal arrogance', ordered the smaller union to negotiate an agreement that would enable the TGWU to represent its northern members.[57] The NASD failed to do so, fearing further legal action by northern dockers, and was suspended in 1958 and then finally expelled from the TUC in 1959.[58] In the period which followed the TGWU attempted to disprove Deakin's 1954 insistence that it was 'impossible to carry on any relationship' with the NASD.[59] O'Leary regularly held informal discussions with Barrett, who had opposed the northern recruitment in the first place. These talks centred on how the NASD could give up its northern members and be readmitted to the industry's National Joint Council and the TUC, but were frustrated by the determined actions of Mersey activists, who continued to operate as if they were Dockers' Section officials.[60]

This lengthy postscript to the inter-union dispute delayed the start of the TGWU's recovery in the docks, which was in the end extremely limited under Cousins. Many dockers who left in 1954 and 1955 remained hostile to the TGWU, as the General Secretary discovered when canvassing in Liverpool during the 1959 General Election. Angrily heckled by a large group of NASD dockers at Sandhills, Cousins was forced to abandon his speech, although he characteristically made light of the incident, saying 'if I get no worse than this I will have had a feather-bed trip'.[61] With so many northern dockers reluctant to return to the TGWU, but unable to enjoy official representation from the NASD, a high incidence of non-unionism was the inevitable result. In 1963 about one-third of dockers in Hull, Birkenhead and Liverpool belonged to no union.[62] This was perhaps the most serious legacy of the absence of practical democracy in the docks in the 1940s and 1950s.

Besides the inter-union dispute, there were two other main impediments to recovery for the TGWU after 1959. First, the point of contact between the TGWU and its members had been undermined as union branch life was further weakened under the impact of long-term social change. TGWU branches were organized geographically, in waterfront communities. Many of these communities had been broken up by war-time bomb damage and post-war housing developments, a problem acknowledged by Deakin when giving evidence to an official inquiry on the 1954 strike, but branches were not subsequently restructured and many were moribund by the 1960s.[63] There was thus an air of unreality about the union's insistence, articulated in the *Record*, that members should take grievances to branch meetings rather than unofficial representatives.[64]

Secondly, the officials who oversaw the union's decline under Deakin largely remained in place. Despite the contempt with which some of his members and most of his former members regarded him, Jimmy O'Hare remained the union's Merseyside district secretary until his death in September 1964. Having earned the unfortunate sobriquet of 'Crusty' for suggesting in 1955 that the NASD strikers would be forced to live on crusts, in January 1964 without consulting members O'Hare suddenly announced that he and local employers had agreed a plan for greater permanency of employment.[65] Several branches immediately passed motions of no confidence in the local leadership, which possibly influenced the selection and subsequent behaviour of his successor, Lew Lloyd, characterized by one Labour correspondent as 'acting more as a servant of his members'.[66] O'Hare's authoritarianism was exceeded by officials in Hull. Following several unofficial disputes, the union's Acting Assistant Secretary, Jack Jones, visited the port in 1966 with Tim O'Leary. Jones's official record notes that he 'toured the Docks with a view to exploring the possibilities of improving our officering and representation arrangements'.[67] His memoirs are more revealing, indicating that he asked dockers why grievances had not been taken to branch meetings. The reply, that officials rarely attended branch meetings, shook him. It was this, more than anything else, which finally forced the union to address the question of democracy in the docks. To investigate the union's behaviour in Hull, Jones engaged a London official, Tom Cronin, rebuked by Deakin for his unofficial activities in 1950. Following Cronin's inquiry three of the Hull officials were dismissed and the union regained 137 former members. In the longer term, stimulated also by fresh signs of unofficial militancy in Liverpool and London, the Hull episode encouraged Jones to revive the union's organizational structure by establishing the shop stewards system in the late 1960s. Rooting the union more firmly in the workplace, this innovation briefly threatened to embarrass the TGWU. London dockers challenged Deakin's Cold War ban on Communists by electing several CP members as their shop stewards. David Wilson suggests that the ban was lifted in 1968 to avert a confrontation on this issue, although Geoffrey Goodman – writing several years later – indicates that Frank Cousins had resolved to take this action at a much earlier date. Cousins had long opposed the ban as undemocratic and, in any event, counter-productive, forcing Communist activity underground and rendering it harder to detect.[68]

From this it would be unfair to imply that the TGWU had done nothing to mend its undemocratic ways in the docks before 1964. The single most positive sign in this respect was the threatened national strike in May 1962, arising from a dispute between the TGWU and the National Association of Port Employers over an increase in basic pay and a decrease in normal working hours. This was a major incident, for the concessions eventually offered by the employers were interpreted by contemporary observers, including Conservative MPs, as an early breach in the Macmillan government's pay policy.[69] Cousins certainly regarded the outcome as an important victory for dockers and the TGWU, 'an emphatic reminder to the Government of the injustice of the methods through which they are attempting to impose a restrictive Incomes Policy bearing harshly upon the lowest paid'.[70] The fact that employers could offer concessions was, of course, an indication that Cousins was not facing the same economic and financial constraints as Deakin. Nevertheless, Cousins' handling of the situation still bears favourable comparison – from a democratic perspective – with Deakin's conduct of comparable national pay dispute in October 1945. Having gained no basic pay increase since before the war, the 50,000 dockers who participated in the month-long strike were impatient with the perceived delay in negotiations between the TGWU and employers. Instead of sympathizing with his membership's plight, Deakin had reacted defensively, arguing that the strike was the product of Trotskyist agitation rather than genuine material grievances.[71] Cousins took a far more sober view when dockers expressed a willingness to challenge employers on pay. Reluctant to sanction a strike in 1962, he attempted to postpone the intended action by organizing a last-minute special Delegate Conference. But when this reiterated the commitment to strike, Cousins acknowledged 'the very strong feeling that procrastination has gone as far as it ought', and authorized the stoppage.[72]

In responding to his dock members in this manner, as equally he had done in the case of the London Busmen's strike in 1958, Cousins offered a far more democratic brand of union leadership than his predecessors.[73] In terms of the impact of trade unionism on national economic performance, it was arguably also a more responsible brand of leadership. The National Employers' chairman, Sir Andrew Crichton, conceded as much when explaining the reasons for conceding defeat in 1962, speaking of his concern that, without an early settlement, 'the dockers might repudiate Mr Cousins and take matters into their own hands'.[74] Where Deakin had frequent cause to lament the fact that agreements between the union and employers were broken by unofficial action, Cousins sought to protect 'the constitutional machinery' by brokering only those agreements which his members genuinely supported. The outstanding difficulties he inherited, most notably the inter-union dispute with the NASD, constrained the emergence of the TGWU as a more fully democratic and representative organization, but the 1962 episode highlighted the union's increasing sensitivity to the needs of ordinary members. It certainly anticipated the more pronounced efforts which Jones made to base official union policy on the views and support of his docks membership. At least as far as the ports are concerned, Geoffrey Goodman's appraisal, that Cousins 'opened the door' which Jack Jones pushed 'wide open and walked through', seems reasonably apt.[75] In the docks, as perhaps elsewhere, the 'Cousins era' was one of transition, a period when the absence of democracy was recognized if not decisively redressed by the TGWU.

Notes

1   K. Coates and T. Topham, *The Making of the Labour Movement: the formation of the Transport and General Workers' Union, 1870–1922* (Nottingham, 1994), pp. 3, 804.

2.   V. L. Allen, *Trade Union Leadership. Based on a study of Arthur Deakin* (1957), p. 188.

3.   A. Bullock, *The Life and Times of Ernest Bevin, Volume One: trade union leader, 1881–1940* (1960), pp. 212–18; S. Hill, *The Dockers* (1976), p. 131.

4.   Allen, *Trade Union Leadership*, pp. 60–3.

5.   J. Phillips, *The Great Alliance: economic recovery and the problems of power, 1945–1951* (1996); J. Phillips, 'Decasualization and disruption: industrial relations in the docks, 1945–1979', in C.J. Wrigley (ed.), *A History of British Industrial Relations, 1939–1979: industrial relations in a declining economy* (Cheltenham, 1996), pp. 165–85.

6.   *Transport and General Workers' Record*, July 1947.

7.   F. Lindop, 'Unofficial militancy in the Royal Group of Docks, 1945–67', *Oral History*, 11, 2, 1983, p. 27.

8.   D. Delay, *Myths About the Origins and Effects of the National Dock Labour Scheme* (1986).

9.   Public Record Office (hereafter PRO), FO 800/519, Callaghan to Attlee, 15 July 1949; Bevin–Callaghan correspondence, 19–20 July 1949. This correspondence, in which a junior minister challenged the validity of Bevin's views and policy in the docks, has been presented by Callaghan's biographer as a significant episode in his early Parliamentary career (K.O. Morgan, *Callaghan: a life* (Oxford, 1997), pp. 85–6).

10.   Museum of London Library, Limehouse (hereafter MLL), BPA 244, J.R. Hobhouse (NAPE) to Alfred Barnes, Minister of Transport, 11 August 1949;

MLL, LEDEA 278, NAPE Executive Committee, 24 November 1955.

11. PRO, BK 2/72, London Port Workers' Strike Committee, *Reflections on the Strike*, July 1948.
12. *The Times*, 27 January 1950.
13. B. Hunter, *They Knew Why They Fought: unofficial struggles and leadership on the docks, 1945–1989* (1994).
14. J. McIlroy, '"The First Great Battle in the March to Socialism": dockers, Stalinists and Trotskyists in 1945', *Revolutionary History*, 6, 2/3, 1996; Scottish Record Office (hereafter SRO), HH 56/46, note by Detective Constable Andrew Crosbie, 'Unofficial Strike of Dockers at Leith', sent by Assistant Chief Constable, City of Edinburgh Police, to Scottish Home Department, 18 October 1945.
15. TGWU Transport House, London, TGWU National Docks Trade Group Committee, National Secretary's Quarterly Report, 30 October 1945; Modern Records Centre (hereafter MRC), MSS 15B/40, National Port Workers' Committee, *The Enquiry and YOU!*, May 1947.
16. PRO, BK 2/76, National Dock Labour Board memo, 'Brief Particulars of Dock Workers known to have been more or less prominent during the Strike', August 1949.
17. *Manchester Guardian*, 17 October 1945.
18. PRO, BK 2/76, London Dock Labour Board minute, 'Meeting of London Central Lock-Out Committee', 7 August 1949.
19. 'A Job Worth Doing', *Transport and General Workers' Record*, December 1954.
20. MRC, MSS 126/T&G/1/1/28, TGWU General Executive Council, 6–10 March 1950.
21. D.F. Wilson, *Dockers: the impact of industrial change* (1972), p. 193.
22. Lindop, 'Unofficial militancy', p. 27.
23. Phillips, *Great Alliance*, pp. 95–6.
24. *Transport and General Workers' Record*, February 1947.
25. V.L. Allen, 'Arthur Deakin', *Dictionary of National Biography, 1951–60* (Oxford).
26. TGWU Transport House, London, TGWU Docks National Trade Group Committee Minutes, 21 July 1949.
27. A. Bullock, *Ernest Bevin: Foreign Secretary* (Oxford, 1985), pp. 105–7.
28. P. Weiler, *Ernest Bevin* (Manchester, 1993), pp. 92, 96.
29. See R. Stevens, 'Communism and anti-Communism in the trade unions', in this volume.
30. MRC, MSS 126/T&G/1/4/13, Proceedings of the Thirteenth Biennial Delegate Conference, 11–15 July 1949, para. 10. The motion banning Communists – along with fascists – was carried by 426 votes to 208.
31. Phillips, *Great Alliance*, pp. 78–88.
32. *Transport and General Workers' Record*, November 1954.
33. McIlroy, 'The First Great Battle', pp. 125–33.
34. *Manchester Guardian*, 13 October 1945.
35. McIlroy, 'The First Great Battle', p. 138; SRO, HH 56/46, notes by Detective

Constable Andrew Crosbie, 'Unofficial Strike of Dockers at Leith'.

36. McIlroy, 'The First Great Battle', pp. 138–48.
37. B. Hunter, *Lifelong Apprenticeship: the life and times of a revolutionary, 1920–1959* (1997), pp. 279–93.
38. K. Sinclair, *How the Blue Union came to Hull docks* (Hull, 1995), pp. 6–10.
39. National Museum of Labour History, Manchester (hereafter NMLH), National Amalgamated Stevedores and Dockers, Main Executive Committee Minutes, 11 October 1954; the NASD records are now kept at the Modern Records Centre.
40. J. Phillips, 'Inter-union conflict in the docks, 1954–1955', *Historical Studies in Industrial Relations*, 1, March 1996, pp. 107–30.
41. Hunter, *Lifelong Apprenticeship*, p. 291.
42. NMLH, NASD Joint Executive Council, 23 November 1956.
43. For the early history, see J. Lovell, *Stevedores and Dockers* (1969); the most recent account of the 1923 strike is T. Topham, 'The unofficial national docks strike of 1923: the Transport and General Workers' Union's first crisis', *Historical Studies in Industrial Relations*, 2, 1996, pp. 27–64.
44. L. Minkin, *The Contentious Alliance* (Edinburgh, 1992), pp. 27–40.
45. P.M. Williams, *Gaitskell*, (Oxford, 1982), p. 307.
46. G. Goodman, *The Awkward Warrior. Frank Cousins: his life and times* (1979), pp. 157–9.
47. Minkin, *Contentious Alliance*, pp. 83–4.
48. MRC, MSS 126/T&G/1/1/32, TGWU General Secretary's 58th Quarterly Report, 20 September 1954.
49. S.W. Lerner, *Breakaway Unions and the Small Trade Union* (1961), pp. 66–81.
50. Goodman, *Awkward Warrior*, pp. 115–16.
51. MRC, MSS 126 T&G/1/1/34, General Secretary's 1st Quarterly Report, 4 June 1956.
52. *Port Transport Industry, Report of a Committee of Inquiry* (Cmnd 9813, 1956), p.17.
53. G. Phillips and N. Whiteside, *Casual Labour: the unemployment question in the port transport industry 1880–1970* (Oxford, 1985), p. 253.
54. TUC, *Report*, 1959, p. 111.
55. Hunter, *They Knew Why They Fought*, pp. 33–4.
56. Phillips, 'Inter-union conflict', pp. 123. This perspective was formed during an extremely helpful conversation on 10 April 1995 with Andrew Flinn at the NMLH in Manchester. Andrew's heroic achievement in sorting the NASD files before they were transferred to the MRC is gratefully acknowledged.
57. *Economist*, 8 September 1956.
58. TUC, *Report*, 1959, pp. 112–15, 326–9.
59. MRC, MSS 126 T&G/1/1/32, General Secretary's 58th Quarterly Report, 20 September 1954.
60. MRC, MSS 126 T&G/1/1/40, General Secretary's 24th Quarterly Report, 5 March 1962.
61. *The Times*, 7 October 1959.

62. *Final Report of the Committee of Inquiry under the Rt. Hon. Lord Devlin into Certain Matters concerning the Port Transport Industry* (Cmnd 2734, 1965), p. 38.
63. *Transport and General Workers' Record*, November 1954; Wilson, *Dockers*, p. 197.
64. 'A Job Worth Doing', December 1954.
65. Hunter, *They Knew Why They Fought*, p. 41; Wilson, *Dockers*, p. 171.
66. *Devlin Report*, pp. 80–2; Wilson, *Dockers*, p. 193.
67. MRC, MSS 126 T&G/1/1/44, Acting Assistant General Secretary's 6th Quarterly Report, 8 March 1966.
68. J. Jones, *Union Man* (1986), pp. 182–3; Wilson, *Dockers*, pp. 192–8; Goodman, *Awkward Warrior*, pp. 561–4.
69. *The Times*, 14 and 18 May 1962.
70. MRC, MSS 126 T&G/1/1/40, General Secretary's 25th Quarterly Report, 7 June 1962.
71. *Manchester Guardian*, 13 October 1945.
72. *The Times*, 12 May 1962.
73. See N. Fishman, '"Spearhead of the movement"? The 1958 London busworkers' strike, the TUC and Frank Cousins', in this volume.
74. *The Times*, 14 May 1962.
75. Goodman, *Awkward Warrior*, p. 598.

Afterword

Eric Hobsbawm

In the history of the British trade unions the twenty years after the Second World War were a period of obscurity. How little was known about what had been really happening in British industrial relations only became evident in the second half of the 1960s when the Royal Commission on Trade Unions and Employers' Associations (the Donovan Commission) set out to discover the state of affairs on British shopfloors by means of its invaluable programme of research under W.E.J. McCarthy.[1] The present volume shows how much historians have since learned.

At first sight the obscurity of the industrial scene in the 1960s is surprising. Never had the unions had a more prominent position in public life, with greater access to the highest levels of government, Labour or Tory. Indeed, given the size of the public sector, governments had never been more directly involved with the unions. Cabinets discussed their affairs, politicians – Conservative ministers as well as opposition Labour leaders – noted down their thoughts about union leaders and crises in their diaries. Strike news was front-page news, especially when it could be presented as a red plot, and, as Geoffrey Goodman reminds us in his essay in this volume (Chapter 1), industrial correspondents were the princes of Fleet Street. Commentators wrote at length about the political and ideological divisions within the union movement, although they did not write much about the involvement of the British union movement in the Cold War (on which Anthony Carew's contribution on the TUC and the international throws some unexpected light).

And yet, what was happening on the ground, in the Donovan Commission's 'informal system created by the actual behaviour of trade unions and employers associations, of managers, shop stewards and workers', had simply not entered public consciousness.[2] It had been known only to those involved in or concerned with shopfloor negotiations, to a few specialists in labour relations and conciliation (to which all governments were committed) and a few journalists and union or Communist Party (CP) functionaries. Even they probably saw only particular bits and pieces of it, and failed to recognize just how rapidly and dramatically the system of industrial relations was changing. For even they lived through and were part of these changes, which nobody had intended or even planned. Consider the evolution of shop stewards and informal rank and file bodies growing into power-centres of sectionalism in the Rolls-Royce plant at Hillington, as described in Alan McKinlay and Joseph Melling's illuminating chapter on 'The shop floor politics of productivity' (Chapter 8). It was a development nobody foresaw or even welcomed (certainly not the CP stewards, opposed to fragmentation, who wanted a disciplined, factory-wide organization) but which happened all the same – and which contained the roots of the trade unionism of the 1970s.

In short, what characterizes the history of the British labour movement after the Second World War is not that the plans and policies of protagonists had unintended consequences, but that those who were in a position to shape it had no relevant intentions at all for its post-war development. Industrially the movement was committed to unrestricted free bargaining, except where loyalty to Labour governments required self-control. For, as David Howell's chapter (Chapter 4) and a number of other studies in this book remind us, politically, the group of leaders who counted were, as sincere democratic socialists, totally and passionately committed to Labour in government, and later – in spite of the friendliness of Tory Ministers of Labour – to their party in opposition. Apart from the Communists of 1941–5, they had no plans for the role of unions in post-war society. Even the old dream of a systematic structural reform of the union movement had faded away: the only force that now shaped it was the 1939 Bridlington Agreement's ban on poaching members. It is a pity that there is no discussion of the decline and fall of TUC reform to set beside John McIlroy's decline and fall of socialist union education (Chapter 2).[3] The union movement still looked substantially as it had before the war. In the middle 1960s it was still possible for this historian to write: 'Except for the merger of the distributive unions (1947) there have been no major rationalizations of union structure since the Second World War, though a tendency for smaller craft unions (e.g. in shipbuilding and printing) to merge made itself felt in the early 1960s ... '.[4]

In retrospect it is clear that, with few exceptions, all concerned with industrial relations – unions, employers, governments of both parties – were more or less satisfied with, or reconciled to, the situation of trade unionism as it emerged out of the war. Or at least felt that nothing much could be done about it, a view that always sounds more convincing to those who believe that nothing very fundamental need be done about it. Did the multi-union structure need simplifying? Of course, thought Donovan, but 'the really decisive objections to industrial unionism' were that it could not be done, and anyway 'the natural growth pattern' of British unions would eventually make things easier.[5] Were industrial relations organized differently elsewhere? The Donovan commissioners were not unaware that this was the case, but only Sweden figures briefly in their Report; their visit to Federal Germany left no apparent trace. They note that, since this was Britain and not Sweden, their system wouldn't work here.[6]

Nor was there a sense of crisis in the unions. Why should there have been? As Campbell, Fishman and McIlroy's survey, 'The post-war compromise: mapping industrial politics, 1945–64' (Chapter 3) reminds us, as far as unions and their members were concerned, the 'Forward March of Labour' had not halted with the end of the Labour government. It continued well into the

1950s, through the freak electoral defeat of 1951, which saw the all-time peak in Labour's vote, as the ensuing period saw the party's highest ever individual membership. As the authors note, even allowing for the defeats of 1955 and 1959, 'the two post-war decades were far from years of unprecedented working-class decomposition or political defeat'.[7] The unions could see no cause for worry, even as the politicians, to whose lack of contact with what was happening on shopfloors all over the country this book bears witness, argued about how much of Labour's luggage they had to drop to win another election. But, however loyal union leaders and their members were to Labour, politics was not their business and elections only happened every few years. Industrial relations was, and they happened every day.

How little politics impinged on the activities of unions is clear, not least from Richard Stevens' essay on Communism and anti-Communism in the unions (Chapter 6). The tiny band of Communists – even in the CP-dominated ETU and Fire Brigades Union comprising less than 0.4 per cent of the membership – could not have otherwise exercised so substantial an influence in the face of the overwhelming and unremitting hostility of the Cold Warriors. Nor could the party have recovered so much of its influence as rapidly as it did after the much more damaging *internal* upheavals of 1956. As Stevens says, 'they continued ... to win respect for their industrial and workplace activities, if not necessarily for their politics. This had always been the key to Communist influence in the unions'.[8] And yet, may not this very stability or resilience of Communist influence in the unions have led the party to overlook the developments which in the next twenty-five years, were to lead to its disappearance? In the meantime there did not seem to be much doubt about what party members in the unions should be doing and they went on doing it. Just as they, together with the non-Communist Labour left, had no doubt about what should be done by the next Labour government: nationalize more industries and 'keep left'.

That does not mean that the movement of these years should be blamed for what it did not and could not achieve. The editors of this volume argue in their survey (Chapter 3) that, if there was a moment for radical transformation it was in 1944–5, when it was possible 'to mobilize, nurture and institutionalize the real, if not to be exaggerated, desire for change; to ensure the planning and mobilization of the war economy was developed not displaced; to break down the barriers between the industrial and political sphere; to politicize the unions and extend industrial democracy'. That is probably right, though one must also agree with them, that the chances that this would happen were negligible. It is clearly true that 'Attlee, Morrison, Bevin, Dalton, Cripps, Deakin, Williamson and Lawther, for all their virtues, were not the men for such a project', and the Labour government was, in any case, soon derailed by post-war economics and politics.[9] After that the opportunities were no longer there to lose. And yet, as we look back on the history, not just of British Labour and British trade unionism in the twenty years after

1945, but of Britain as a whole, we must be struck, even more than by the failure of action, by the failure to understand the nature of the post-war world and of Britain's predicament within it.

However, the core of the book lies not in its general reflections on much-debated themes, but in what its editors, with excessive modesty, describe as 'first accounts of neglected byways', namely the 'case-studies' of Part Three. Not the least merit of these invaluable explorations is that they open perspectives on future research. One thing that emerges from them is the need to set the text of trade union history into the wider context of social change. How did the massive rehousing effort after the war affect trade unionism and industrial relations? Thus Jim Phillips' study of the docks (Chapter 11) observes the problems of TGWU branches, organized geographically in waterfront communities, after these communities had been broken up by wartime bombing and post-war housing developments. Where else did home and work separate? How did the massive demobilization affect the structure of workshops? McKinlay and Melling cite the case of a young, ex-service-man unduly promoted in the opinion of his fellow foundry workers. How, more generally, did young workers, in the 1950s, when 'youth' became a culture, market and a self-conscious group, fit into what they describe as the 'shared, if implicit, notion of seniority' so typical of skilled work-groups – but not only of these?[10] How did a West Indian immigrant come to set foot on the ladder that eventually led to the top of the TGWU? Could it have happened in another union?[11] How did the post-war educational changes affect the recruitment to union leadership of those bright, reading, working-class, youngsters whose pre-war schools – apprentice group discussions in big Manchester or Glasgow engineering works and Marxist, CP or Plebs classes – did not remove them from the workshops to the common-rooms of colleges and universities? And when did the South Wales miners cease to use their libraries?[12] Such questions will enable us to go beyond the analysis of what happened behind the factory gates and the narratives of unjustly forgotten battles, and they open perspectives on the next phase of that inexhaustible subject, the history of labour. To read this volume is to reflect on them.

Notes

1. Eleven research papers covering diverse aspects of trade unionism and industrial relations were published between 1966 and 1968; see Royal Commission on Trade Unions and Employers' Associations 1965–68, *Report* (Cmnd 3623, 1968), Appendix 4.
2. Royal Commission on Trade Unions, *Report*, para. 46.
3. But see R. Taylor, '"What are we here for?" George Woodcock and trade union reform, 1960–69', in J. McIlroy, N. Fishman and A. Campbell (eds), *British Trade Unions and Industrial Politics, vol. 2: The high tide of trade*

unionism, 1964–79 (Aldershot, 1999).

4.   E.J. Hobsbawm, *Industry and Empire* (Harmondsworth, 1969) p. 250.
5.   Royal Commission on Trade Unions, *Report*, para. 677.
6.   Ibid., paras 481–4, 673, 748–9.
7.   A. Campbell, N. Fishman and J. McIlroy, 'The post-war compromise: mapping industrial politics, 1945–64', in this volume, p. 99.
8.   R. Stevens, 'Cold War politics: Communism and anti-Communism in the trade unions', in this volume, p. 177.
9.   Campbell, Fishman and McIlroy, 'The post-war compromise', p. 100.
10.   A. McKinlay and J. Melling, 'The shop floor politics of productivity: work, power and authority relations in British engineering, c. 1945–57', in this volume, p. 228.
11.   Campbell, Fishman and McIlroy, 'The post-war compromise', p. 93.
12.   J. McIlroy, 'Making trade unionists: the politics of pedagogy, 1945–79', in this volume.

Index

Aaronovitch, S., *The Ruling Class: a study of British finance capital* 107

Abrams, Mark, *Must Labour Lose?* 89, 110, 143

Ackers, P., *The New Workplace and Trade Unionism* 14

ACTU (Association of Catholic Trade Unionists), and the CP 170–71

Adams, R. 61, 112, 239, 258, 259, 263, 264, 265, 266, 287, 288, 290, 292

Addison, P., *The Road to 1945: British politics and the Second World War* 106

Aden 156

AESD (Association of Engineering and Shipbuilding Draughtsmen), and the CP 178

AEU (Amalgamated Engineering Union)
affiliation to the Labour Party 119, 120
affiliation to the TUC 119
and the Confed 249–50
and the CP 171, 174, 175, 178, 179, 180
membership growth 104
organization 83, 86
politics 130–31
shop stewards 94, 234
trade practices 222–3

AFL (American Federation of Labour) 147
and the ICFTU 149, 150
and the WFTU 201, 216
see also AFL-CIO

AFL-CIO (American Federation of Labour - Congress of Industrial Organizations)
and Africa 157–60
formation 165
and the ICFTU 151, 152, 153, 161–2, 165
and the TUC 146, 157
see also AFL

Africa
and the AFL-CIO 157–60
trade union training centre 158
trade unions 157–65

African Mine Workers' Union (N. Rhodesia) 156

African-American Labor Centre 162

Ahlstrand, B., *The Quest for Productivity: a case study of Fawley after Flanders* 212

Aitken, Ian 263

Aldrich, R.J., *British Intelligence, Strategy and the Cold War* 186

Alford, B.W.E., *British Economic Performance 1945–75* 106

Allan, Willie 176

Allen, Alf 86

Allen, V.L. 11, 308
The Militancy of British Miners 110, 189, 191
The Sociology of Industrial Relations 14

Trade Union Leadership: based on a study of Arthur Deakin 18, 60, 108, 109, 141, 165, 186, 287, 288, 307
Trade Unions and Government 110

Amalgamated Society of Railway Servants 117
see also NUR

Ambrose, Les 260, 263, 264, 266, 267

Anderson, Sir Colin 248

Anderson, J.R.L. 29, 65, 188, 191

The Angry Silence (film) 101

Annan, N., *Changing Enemies: the defeat and regeneration of Germany* 216

Archer, John 300

Armstrong, M. 18

Armstrong, P. 14
Capitalism since World War II 106, 107
White Collar Workers, Trade Unions and Class 239

Army Bureau of Current Affairs 38

Arnot, R. Page 112

Ashfield, Lord 269

Ashworth, Martin 186, 188, 189

associations, employers' 73

ASTMS (Association of Scientific Technical and Managerial Staffs), education programmes 55

ASW (Amalgamated Society of Woodworkers), membership growth 104

Atkinson, A.B.
Distribution of Personal Wealth in Britain 107
Poverty in Britain and the Reform of Social Security 107

Attlee, Clement 25, 100, 127, 201, 313

Attlee government 4, 23, 25, 27, 75, 99, 119, 199
domestic programme 125–6

AUCCTU (Soviet All Union Central Council of Trade Unions) 146, 147, 148
and the TUC 150, 151, 153, 163

AUEW (Amalgamated Union of Engineering Workers) 63
conflicts in 10–11

Aylward, Bert 301, 304

Babcock and Wilcox (Renfrew) 227

Bagley, Bob 176, 178

Bagnall, G.H. 154

Bagwell, P.S.
The Railwaymen, the history of the National Union of Railwaymen 262, 290
The Railwaymen, Volume 2: the Beeching era and after 144

Bain, G.S.
The Growth of White Collar Unionism 109
Industrial Relations in Britain 103, 106

Bain, P. 15

Baker, Bill 178
Baker, Harry 179
balance of payments, crises 71–2
Baldwin government 118
ballot-rigging, in ETU 30–31, 84, 87, 177, 182
Bank of England 26
Banks, J.A., *Trade Unionism* 14
Barker, Bas 185, 190
Barnes, Alfred, Minister of Transport 307
Barnes, D. 108
  *Governments and Trade Unions: the British
    experience 1964–79* 109, 220, 262, 267,
    289, 292
Barnsby, George 187
Barou, N., *British Trade Unions* 112
Barratt, George 260
Barrett, Dickie 304
Batstone, E. 55–6, 94
  *Shop Stewards in Action: the organization of
    workplace conflict and accommodation*
    239
  *Working Order: workingplace industrial
    relations over two decades* 64, 112
Bayliss, F. 64
Bean, R. 191
BEC (British Employers' Confederation) 48, 73
Bechofer, F. 111
Becker, H., *Erziehung und Politik: Minna
    Specht zu ihrem 80 Geburtstag* 212
Becu, Omer 160, 167
Beeching Report (1963) 138
Beer, S.H., *Modern British Politics* 141, 143
Behan, Brian 176
Belanger, J. 112
Belchem, J. 16
Belcher, Percy 180
Bell, J.D.M. 109
Bellamy, Joyce 12
  Dictionary of Labour Biography 142, 218
Berridge, Claude 264
Bescoby, J. 107, 112
Bevan, Aneurin 124, 127, 128, 132, 142
  resignation 25, 127
Bevanism 90–91, 100–101
  and the Cold War 126–8
Beveridge Report 73
Bevin, Ernest 24–5, 37, 85, 86, 100, 130, 211,
    299, 313
  career 124
  and Dock Labour Scheme (1947) 295
  and education programmes 40
  General Secretary of TGWU 269, 286, 293,
    294
  and London busworkers 269–70
  Minister of Labour 76, 77, 210, 218, 243
Beynon, H., *Working for Ford* 14, 113, 191
Bidwell, S. 60, 111
Birch, Alan 143
Birch, Reg 251

Bird, Arthur 299
Birkenhead, Lord, *Walter Monckton* 109
Birmingham Trades Council, and the CP 179
Black, L. 218
black workers, and trade unions 4, 92, 93–4
Blair, Tony 1
Blake, R., *The Paladin History of Britain:
    decline of power 1915–1964* 262
block votes, and trade unions 86
Blumler, Jay 201, 218
BMC (British Motor Corporation) 178–9
  dispute (1956) 245, 279
  see also British Leyland
Bonfield, John 152
Booth, A.L., *The Economics of the Trade Union*
    14
Boraston, I. 239
Boston, S., *Women Workers and the Trade
    Union Movement* 16, 111
Bowers, D. 107
Bowman, Jim 85
Bowry, Doug 180
Boyd, John 260
Boyfield, Ray 171, 179
Braby, Eric 247
Brandon, Charles 271
Branson, Noreen 4, 185, 187
  *History of the Communist Party in Britain
    1941–1951* 16, 108, 185
Bridlington Agreement (1939) 303, 312
Briggs Motor Bodies, inquiry 95, 112
British Control Commission (Germany) 197
British Guiana 156
*British Labour Statistics, Historical Abstract
    1886–1968* (Dept of Employment) 262
British Leyland
  and the CP 8
  and shop stewards 8
  study 7–8
  see also BMC
British Trade Fair, Moscow 151
Brittan, S., *The Treasury under the Tories 1951–
    1964* 262
Brivati, B., *Hugh Gaitskell* 143, 217
Brody, David 9, 15, 17
Bromley, George 186
Brooke, S. 219
Brooks, W.J.R. 297
Brotherton, Harry 250, 252, 253, 254, 260
  career summary 263
Brown, E.A. 258–9
Brown, F.J. 172
Brown, George 32, 34, 130, 139, 142
Brown, Henry Phelps 2, 12
  The Origins of Trade Union Power 14
Brown, M. Barratt 63
  Adult Education for Industrial Workers 64
Brown, W., *Piecework Bargaining* 240
BTC (British Transport Commission) 248, 273

Bull, Anthony 274
Bullock, A.
  Ernest Bevin: Foreign Secretary 308
  *The Life and Times of Ernest Bevin, Volume
    One: trade union leader 1881–1940*
    218, 262, 307
Bullock, Herbert 148, 166
Burawoy, Michael 223
  *Manufacturing Consent: changes in the
    labour process under monopoly
    capitalism* 239
  The Politics of Production 239
Burge, A. 61, 62, 63, 64
Burkitt, B., *Trade Unions and the Economy* 107
bus strike, London (1958) 129, 177, 242, 261
  background 272–7
  Industrial Court 275–6, 280, 289
  and public opinion 280
  settlement 283–5
  strike pay 277–8
  see also busworkers
busworkers
  and the CP 269–70, 271
  traditions 269–72
  see also bus strike
Butler, D.E. 90, 91
  The British General Election of 1955 111
  The British General Election of 1959 61, 111
  The British General Election of 1964 111
  British Political Facts 1900–1985 185, 187
  *Political Change in Britain: forces shaping
    electoral choice* 111
Butler, G. 185, 187
Butler, H.W. 172

Caborn, George 180
Callaghan government
  and shop steward training 54
  and trade unions 34–5
Callaghan, James 139, 197, 296
Callanan, Phil 297
Cameron, Lord, inquiry into Briggs Motor
    Bodies 95
Campbell, Alan 16, 17, 18, 62, 63, 108, 109,
    113, 144, 312, 314, 315
  Miners, Unions and Politics 1910–1947 17,
    110
Campbell, Jim 84, 131, 242, 245, 247
Cannon, Leslie 30, 176
Cannon, O., *The Road from Wigan Pier: a
    biography of Les Cannon* 65, 188, 191
Cannon, Wilf 117, 118, 121, 139, 140
capitalism 72
Carew, Anthony 87, 165, 166, 167, 216, 311
  Labour Under the Marshall Plan 186, 215, 216
Carlsson, G. 109
Carr, F. 106
Carron, Bill 83, 86, 93, 96, 130–31, 158, 185,
    246, 252, 253, 258, 260, 261, 264, 266

cars, ownership 72
Carter, B. 239
Carthy, Albert 171
Castle, Barbara, *In Place of Strife* 33, 62
CAWU (Clerical and Administrative Workers'
    Union), and the CP 170, 171
CBC (Central Bus Committee) 269, 271, 272–3,
    276
Central Office of Information 175
CGT (Confédération Générale du Travail) 146
Chandler, Alf 276, 290
change, and trade unions 312–14
Chapman, Tom 179
Chapple, Frank 176
Chase, M. 15
Chester, George 170
Chester, T.E. 221
Child, J., *Man and Organization* 64
Chipchase, Ethel 93
Choulerton, Len 266
Church, R., *Strikes and Solidarity: coalfield
    conflict in Britain 1896–1966* 113
Churchill government, and trade unions 78
Churchill, Winston 78, 206, 243, 244, 292
CIA (Central Intelligence Agency), anti-
    communist activity 217
CIC (Chief Industrial Commissioner) 274
CIR (Commission on Industrial Relations) 33,
    50, 192
  Report No. 33 Industrial Relations Training
    62, 64
Citrine, Walter 25, 35, 202, 211
  joins National Coal Board 85
  President of the WFTU 146, 200, 201
  and trade union education 38–9, 58, 65
  TUC General Secretary 200
Civil Service Clerical Association 201
Clack, G. 112
Clarke, Peter 287
  Hope and Glory: Britain 1900–1990 292
Clarke, T., *Trade Unions Under Capitalism* 63
Claro, Z.G. 262
Clause Four, attempts to revise 99, 133
Clay, Harold 41
Clegg, Hugh 9, 73, 85, 94, 96, 107, 108, 109,
    192, 201, 211, 220, 221, 225, 226, 249,
    258, 259, 262, 263, 287
  on Allan Flanders 212
  Autobiography 221
  *The Changing System of Industrial Relations
    in Britain* 108, 109
  *The Employers' Challenge: a study of the
    national shipbuilding and engineering
    disputes of 1957* 239, 263, 264, 265,
    266, 288, 290, 292
  General Union in a Changing Society 110,
    112, 142, 185, 217
  A History of British Trade Unions 3, 15, 59, 65,
    108, 109, 110, 112, 113, 215, 262, 263

318

Industrial Democracy and Nationalization 221
Labour Relations in London Transport 288
Trade Union Education. A report for the
    WEA 61
Trade Union Officers: a study of full-time
    officers, branch secretaries and shop
    stewards in British trade unions 112, 239
Clements, L. 63
Cliff, T., *The Employers' Offensive - productivity*
    deals and how to fight them 63, 107, 212
closed shop 81
Clydeside, shop stewards 95, 223, 226, 235
CND (Campaign for Nuclear Disarmament) 91
coal industry
    disputes 27, 98
    nationalization 26
    see also miners
Coates, D.
    The Economic Decline of Modern Britain:
        the debate between left and right 19
    Industrial Policy in Great Britain 19
Coates, Ken 13, 53
    The Making of the Labour Movement: the
        formation of the Transport and General
        Workers' Union 1870–1922 15, 307
    Trade Union Register 63
    Trade Unions in Britain 109
    Workers' Control: a book of readings and
        witnesses for workers' control 110
Cockburn, C., *Brothers: male dominance and*
    technological change 16
Coker, E. 241
Cold War, The 69, 77, 100
    and Bevanism 126–8
    and trade unions 86–7, 136, 138, 139, 169, 294
Cole, G.D.H. 199, 211, 214
Cole, John 29
Cole, Margaret 214
    The Life of G.D.H. Cole 220
Coleman, P., *The Liberal Conspiracy: the*
        Congress for Cultural Freedom and the
        struggle for the mind of postwar Europe
    217
collective bargaining 56, 73–4, 76, 80, 192, 209
    engineering industry 223–6
    and inflation 203–4
    and monopoly 204–5
    and public interest 205–6
Collins, H. 188
Collison, Harold 86, 282–3
Colonial Development Fund, and the TUC 155
Colonial Economic Development Council, and
    the TUC 154
Colonial Labour Advisory Committee, and the
    TUC 154, 155
Cominform 147, 200, 201
Common Cause 171, 181
Common Cause Bulletin 187
Commonwealth Trade Union Conference

(1949) 154
communism
    anti-communist organizations 171–2
    events of 1956–7 176
    and the ICFTU 151
    and trade unions
        influence 168–9
        statistics 168, 183
    and the TUC 150–51, 171–2, 299–300
    see also CP (Communist Party)
Confed/CSEU (Confederation of Shipbuilding
        and Engineering Unions) 248
    and the AEU 249–50
    membership numbers 263
    organization 264
    Report of Annual Meeting (1956) 264
    strike (1957) 242, 254–7, 265–6
    and training 47–8
    wage claims 250–53
Confederation of British Industry 73
Conference Campaign Committee 201
Congress for Cultural Freedom (CCF) 217
Conservative Party
    General Election win (1959) 287
    and trade unions 69–70
Constable, Harry 297, 298, 301, 302, 304
consumer goods, increase 72
Cook, C. 2, 12–13, 14, 108, 110
Cooper, Jack 84, 86
Cope, Elmer 165
Corfield, A.J. 43–4, 61
    Epoch in Workers' Education 59, 63
Corr, H. 113
Cosgrove, F. 64
Council on Prices, Productivity and Incomes 261
Cousins, Frank 33, 80, 83, 86, 93, 132, 134–5
    and African policy 158
    biography 65
    and the docks industry 303, 304, 306
    General Secretary of TGWU 129–30, 242,
        245, 252, 261, 269, 272, 294, 302
    and London bus strike (1958) 129, 268, 273,
        274, 275, 276, 277, 279, 280, 281, 282,
        283, 284, 285–6, 288, 291, 292
    and wages policy 136, 244
Cox, Sir Geoffrey 24
CP (Communist Party) 39, 41
    and the ACTU 170–71
    and the AESD 178
    and the AEU 171, 174, 175, 178, 179, 180
    and the Birmingham Trades Council 179
    and British Leyland 8
    and the CAWU 170, 171
    compared with ISK 198
    Czechoslovakia 201
    Economic Committee 174
    and education programmes 42, 48
    and engineering industry strike (1957) 260, 261
    and the ETU 84, 121, 171, 174, 175, 176, 313

and ETU ballot-rigging 30–31, 84, 87, 177, 182
events of 1956–7 176–7
and the FBU 175, 176, 177, 178, 313
formation 168
and the GMWU 126
Industrial Department 174
Industrial Organizer 174
and industry 4, 13
and the Labour Party 91, 200
and London busworkers 269–70, 271
membership figures 168, 176, 177, 181, 183, 184
Men and Motors 178, 189
and the motor industry 178–9
and the NSP 170, 171
and the NUBSO 170
and the NUGMW 170
and the NUM 84, 126, 141–2, 175, 178, 181–2
organization 173–6
Organization Department 174
role in industry 4, 13
role in unions 87
and shop stewards 179–81
Soviet Union
20th Congress 131
24th Congress 172
and strikes 29–30, 173–4, 300
and the TGWU 126, 294
and trade union hostility 170–73, 181–2
and the TWU 180–81
and USDAW 171
and wages policy 78, 204
see also communism
CPSA (Civil and Public Services Association), education programmes 65
Craig, F.W.S., *British Parliamentary Election Statistics 1918–1970* 110, 111
Crawley, Aidan 172
The Hidden Face of British Communism 186
Creech-Jones, Arthur 216
Crichton, Sir Andrew 306
Cripps, Sir Stafford 25, 100, 313
Cripps Wage Bargain (1948) 125
Cronin, James 18
Industrial Conflict in Modern Britain 102, 113
Labour and Society in Britain 1918–79 12, 16, 107, 111
Cronin, Tom 297, 298, 305
Crook, S., *Post-modernization: change in advanced societies* 17
Crosbie, Det Constable Andrew 308, 309
Crosland, C.A.R. 217
Can Labour Win? 89, 111
The Future of Socialism 106, 143, 221
Crossman, Richard 132, 141, 197, 245, 286
Crouch, Colin 70
Class Conflict and the Industrial Relations Crisis 14

The Politics of Industrial Relations 18, 106
Trade Unions: the logic of collective action 14
Croucher, Richard, *Engineers at War* 8, 16, 112, 239
Cruikshank, Robin 24
Crump, Jim 178
CSEU *see* Confed
Cumings, B. 217
Cunningham, M. 108
Cunnison, S. 240
Curtice, J. 111
Cyprus Confederation of Labour 156

Dalley, Fred 154
Dalton, Hugh 100, 219, 313
Daly, Lawrence 176, 188
Daniel, W.W., *Workplace Industrial Relations in Britain* 64
Darlington, R., *The Dynamics of Workplace Unionism* 14
Dash, Jack 300
Davies, A.J., *To Build a New Jerusalem: the labour movement from the 1880s to the 1990s* 216
Davies, K. 61, 62, 63, 64
Davies, P., *Labour Legislation and Public Policy* 108, 109
Davison, Stan 187
DEA (Department of Economic Affairs)
activities 33
formation 32
Deakin, Arthur 25, 29, 77, 83, 88, 100, 126, 130, 165, 172, 269, 294, 303, 305, 313
anti-communism 164, 300, 302, 306
biography 18, 308
death 129, 293, 302
and Dock Labour Scheme 298, 299
and education programmes 40
and London busworkers 270, 271, 306
President of the WFTU 147, 148, 149, 200
and wages policy 78, 135, 136, 204, 245
Dean, Frances 186
defence, expenditure 71
Defence of Democracy Trust 171
Freedom First 170
Delay, D., *Myths About the Origins and Effects of the National Dock Labour Scheme* 307
Derber, M., *Labor-Management Relations at Plant Level under Industry Wide Bargaining* 241
devaluation 71–2, 78
Devine, Don 189
Devine, F., *Affluent Workers Revisited: privatism and the working class* 14
Devlin Inquiry, Dock Labour Scheme (1947) 303, 309, 310
Dickens, Ted 297, 298, 300
Dicks-Mireaux, L.A. 107

320

Dictionary of National Biography 1951–1960
141, 308
Dictionary of National Biography 1971–1980 212
Dintenfass, M., *The Decline of Industrial
Britain 1870–1980* 19
DMA (Durham Miners' Association) 124
Dockers
and GMWU 28–9
shop stewards 298, 305–6
and the TGWU 28–9, 293–307
and Trotskyists 300–301, 304
Dock Labour Scheme (1947)
adoption 295, 299
Devlin inquiry 303, 309, 310
drawbacks 296
docks industry
Bristol 29
conflict 28–9
Glasgow 28, 29
Hull 28, 29
Liverpool 28, 29
London 28, 29
Manchester 29
and RCP 300–301
Southampton 28
strikes 295, 297, 298, 300, 301
wages system 296, 298–9
Donovan Commission 33, 49, 54, 62, 81, 192,
210, 211, 222, 238, 311, 312, 314, 315
Donovan, Jack 299, 300
The Donovan Report: an assessment by the EEF
(EEF) 239
Dorfman, G.A.
British Trade Unionism against the TUC 18
Wage Politics in Britain 1945–1967 219
draughtsmen 257
Dubinsky, David 165
Dukes, Charles 84
Durbin, Evan 199
Durcan, J.W. 97
*Strikes in Post-War Britain: a study of
stoppages of work due to industrial
disputes 1946–73* 105, 112, 113, 261
Dyers and Bleachers' Union 154

economic growth, UK 72
The Economic Implications of Full Employment
(White Paper) 244
Economic League 172, 179
Edelstein, J.D., *Comparative Union Democracy*
186, 187, 188, 191
Eden, Anthony 79, 244
Edinger, L.J., *German Exile Politics: the social
democratic executive committee in the
Nazi era* 214
education, and training 46
education programmes
and Arthur Deakin 40
ASTMS 55

Communist Party 42
CPSA 65
and Ernest Bevin 40
ETU 43, 65
GMWU 43, 55, 63
and Hugh Scanlon 53
impact 56
and industrial relations 49
and Jack Jones 53
London School of Economics 39, 61
NALGO 55
NCLC 40–41, 42, 43, 44
NGA 55
NUM 44, 55
NUPE 38, 55
NUR 55
NUT 55
POEU 55
rationale 39, 58–9
South Wales Miners 44
TGWU 38, 55, 57, 63, 65
and trade unions 37–59
TUC 39–40
USDAW 43, 55
and Walter Citrine 38–9
WEA 41–2, 43–4
WETUC 41, 43
see also training
Education and Science, Department of 56
Edwardes, M., *Back from the Brink* 17
Edwards, P.K. 3, 15, 17, 107, 112, 113
Edwards, R., *Contested Terrain: the transforma-
tion of the workplace in the twentieth
century* 240
EEF (Engineering and Allied Employers' National
Association) 73, 224, 228–9, 244
attitude to unions 248–9
*The Donovan Report: an assessment by the
EEF* 239
and engineering industry strike (1957) 258,
259
Looking at Industrial Relations 262, 266
Egelnick, Max 175
Eichler, Willi 194, 197, 216
Eisenhower, President Dwight D. 248
electricity industry, nationalization 26
Eley, G. 15
Elliot, Sir John 273, 274, 276, 281, 282, 283,
284, 285, 289, 291
On and Off the Rails 292
Ellis, Frank 189, 191
Ellis, Les 178, 181, 182
Ellison, N., *Egalitarian Thought and Labour
Politics: retreating visions* 218
embourgeoisement, and the Labour Party 89–
90, 132
employment, full 72
growth 75
Employment, Department of 56

Employment and Productivity, Department of, *British Labour Statistics, Historical Abstract, 1886–1968* 262
Employment Protection Act (1975) 54
Enever, R.J. 61
engineering industry
  collective bargaining 223–6
  post-war expansion 94
  shop stewards 222–39
  strike (1957) 225, 236–7, 254–61, 265–6
    Court of Inquiry 256, 258, 261
  and wage rates 74
The Enquiry and YOU! (National Port Workers' Committee) 308
Etheridge, Dick 178
ETU (Electrical Trades Union) 25
  ballot-rigging episode 30–31, 84, 87, 177, 182
  and the CP 84, 121, 171, 174, 175, 176, 313
  education programmes 43, 65
  membership growth 81, 104
ETUC (European Trade Union Confederation)
  formation 145
  and the TUC 145
European Plan Recovery Conference (1948) 147
Evans, Lincoln 25, 85, 165, 170, 204
Evans, R.J., *In Defence of History* 17
Evans, S. 112
Evans, Trevor 29, 261
  Bevin 262
Ewing, K.D. 108
exports
  Germany 72
  UK 72

Fabian Colonial Research Bureau 202
Fabian Society 197
  and Allan Flanders 197
  Reports 214
Fabianism 35
Falber, Reuben 187
Fawley refinery agreement 74
FBI (Federation of British Industries) 73, 79
FBU (Fire Brigades' Union) 38, 286, 292
  and the CP 175, 176, 177, 178, 313
Feather, Victor 33, 171, 172, 179
Feminist Review, *Waged Work: a reader* 16
Ferguson, Colin 227, 239
Fieldhouse, R. 59
  Adult Education and the Cold War 60, 216
  A History of Modern Adult Education 60
Fielding, S. 15
  England Arise! The Labour Party and popular politics in 1940s Britain 60, 110, 111
Figes, Orlando, *A People's Tragedy* 6
Figgins, Jim 84, 131, 138, 144, 245
films, portrayal of trade unions 101
Fimmen, Edo 166–7

Fisher, Nigel, *Iain Macleod* 289
Fishman, Nina 17, 18, 79, 83, 97, 108, 109, 110, 142, 144, 263, 290, 310, 312, 314, 315
  Arthur Horner: a political biography 110
  The British Communist Party and the Trade Unions, 1933–45 16, 17, 109, 185, 214, 216, 239, 263, 288
Flanders, Allan 9, 48–9, 80, 212, 213, 216, 217, 218
  The Alternative to Monopoly Capitalism 219
  anti-communism 193, 199–200, 214
  The Battle for Production 192, 198, 215, 218
  British Trade Unionism 215, 218, 220, 221
  The Churches and Their Politics 213
  and collective bargaining 205–6, 209
  Collective Bargaining: prescription for change 192
  early writings 196
  and ethical socialism 199, 202, 203
  and the Fabian Society 197
  The Fawley Productivity Agreements 106, 107, 192, 211
  and incomes policy 207–8
  Industrial Relations in Great Britain 262, 263
  influence on industrial relations 209–11
  and the ISK 193–8
  Management and Unions: the theory and reform of industrial relations 108, 192, 211
  and monopolies 204–5, 208, 219
  Monopoly is the Enemy 198, 215, 219
  and nationalization 205
  A Policy for Wages 218, 220
  and shop stewards 208
  and strikes 206–7
  The System of Industrial Relations in Great Britain 107, 108, 109, 220, 221
  Trade Unions 62, 209, 221
  in TUC Research Department 198, 202, 218
  Wage Policy in Wartime 198, 202, 215, 218, 219, 220
  and the WFTU 201
  writings about 212
Flanders, Annemarie 220
Fletcher, R. 217
  Bernstein to Brandt: a short history of German social democracy 214
Flett, K. 15
Flinn, Andrew 309
Foote, G., *The Labour Party's Political Thought: a history* 213
Ford, B., *The Bureau of Current Affairs* 59
Ford, Sid 86, 182
Ford Motors, Dagenham strike (1962) 177, 182
foremen, and shop stewards 227–9, 232–3
Foster, John 266
Foulkes, Frank 25, 252, 257
foundry workers 257
The Foundry Workers: a trade union history (H. J. Fyrth) 188

Fox, Alan 64, 70–71, 212, 263
  History and Heritage 3, 9, 10, 12, 15, 17, 106, 107
  A History of the National Union of Boot and Shoe Operatives 1874–1947 185
  A Sociology of Work and Industry 14
Francis, H. 110
Freedland, M. 108, 109
Freedom First (Defence of Democracy Trust) 170
Freeman, John, resignation 127
Frenkel, S. 239
Friedman, A., *Industry and Labour: class struggle at work and monopoly capitalism* 240
Friends of Socialist Commentary 218
Frow, Edmund 18, 109, 112, 179, 186, 189
Frow, Ruth 189
  Engineering Struggles: episodes in the story of the shop stewards' movement 109, 112, 186
Fryer, B.
  The Battle for Socialism 112, 113
  A Century of Service: an illustrated history of the National Union of Public Employees 1889–1993 110
Fuller, Ken, *Radical Aristocrats: London busworkers from the 1880s to the 1980s* 189, 288, 290, 292
furniture workers 257
Fyrth, H.J.
  The Foundry Workers: a trade union history 188
  Labour's High Noon: the government and the economy 1945–51 15, 106, 108, 110, 215
  Labour's Promised Land: culture and society in Labour Britain 1945–51 59

Gaitskell, Hugh 25, 88, 89, 91, 99, 127, 206, 217, 218, 302
  Labour Party Leader 131, 132, 133, 134
  Labour Party Treasurer 128
  and London bus strike (1958) 285
  and trade union affiliation to Labour Party 120–21
Gallie, B. 61
Gallie, D., *Trade Unionism in Recession* 14
Gamble, A., *The Free Economy and the Strong State* 18
Gardner, Robert 300
gas industry, nationalization 26
Geddes, Charles 164
General Strike (1926) 34, 76, 118, 255
General Union in a Changing Society (Hugh Clegg) 110, 112, 142, 185, 217
Gennard, J. 221
  A History of the National Graphical Association 15

A History of the Society of Graphical and Allied Trades 15
Germany, exports 72
A Giant's Strength (pamphlet) 80
Gill, Ken 189
Gill, Vi 62
Glees, A. 214
  Exile Politics During the Second World War: the German social democrats in Britain 212
Glynn, A. 107
  The British Economic Disaster 106
GMWU (General and Municipal Workers Union)
  and the CP 126
  and docks industry 28–9
  education programmes 43, 55, 63
  and unilateralism 134
Godwin, Anne 93
Goldman, L., *Dons and Workers: Oxford and adult education since 1851* 60
Goldstein, J., *The Government of British Trade Unions* 112, 187
Goldthorpe, J. 63, 90
  The Affluent worker: industrial attitudes and behaviour 14
  The Affluent worker: political attitudes and behaviour 111
  The Affluent Worker in the Class Structure 14
Gollan, John 260
Goodman, Geoffrey 77, 97, 110, 268, 306, 307, 311
  The Awkward Warrior: Frank Cousins: his life and times 65, 109, 110, 142, 143, 262, 287, 288, 289, 290, 291, 292, 309, 310
Goodman, J.F.B., *Shop Stewards in British Industry* 112
Gorst, A., *Post-war Britain, 1945–64* 106
Gospel, H., *Markets, Firms and the Management of Labour in Modern Britain* 106, 107
Gourvish, T.R.
  Britain since 1945 108
  British Railways 1945–1973: a business history 144
Grahl, Jack 38, 176
Grant, R.M., *The Confederation of British Industry* 107
Grant, W., *Business and Politics in Britain* 18
Grebing, H., *The History of the German Labour Movement* 214
Green, George 201
Greene, Sid 84, 86, 131, 279
Greenhough, A. 262, 263, 266
Gregory, R., *The Miners and British Politics 1906–1914* 113
Griffin, Alan 189
Griffith, J.A.G.

Coloured Immigrants in Britain 111
The Politics of the Judiciary 107, 109
Griffiths, James 197, 216
   Minister of National Insurance 124

Hackett, Ida 189
Hall, Charlie 263
Hall, E. 247
Hall, P.A., *Governing the Economy: the politics*
   of state intervention in Britain and
   France 109
Halliday, J., *Korea: the unknown war* 217
Hallsworth, Joseph 85
Halpin, Kevin 113
Halsey, A., *Trends in British Society since 1900*
   106
Halstead, J. 15
Halverson, Ron 186
Hammond, Jim 176
Hancock, Florence 61, 93
Harries, Edgar 171
Harris, Fred 189
Harrison, A.J. 107
Harrison, J. 106, 107
Harrison, Martin 84, 91, 111
   Trade Unions and the Labour Party since
   1945 104, 111, 122, 123, 140, 141, 142
Haseler, S., *The Gaitskellites: revisionism in the*
   British Labour Party 218
Haxell, Frank 292
Hay, C. 17
Hayday, Fred 164
Hayek, F.A.
   Constitution of Liberty 73
   Road to Serfdom 73
Healey, Denis 197, 217
   The Time of My Life 214
health and safety, training 55
Healy, Gerry 301
Heath, A., *How Britain Votes* 111
Heath government, and trade unions 33–4
Heathcoat Amory, D. 273, 284, 285
Heery, E. 14, 18, 109
Henderson, Arthur 125
Hennessy, P., *Never Again: Britain 1945–1951*
   108
Hill, Christopher 5
Hill, S.
   Competition and Control at Work 14
   The Dockers 307
Hill, Ted 86, 245, 250, 252, 253, 254, 257, 280
Hillard, J. 19
Hinden, Rita 89, 110, 197, 202, 216, 217
   biography 218
Hindess, B. 110, 111
Hindle, K. 143
Hinton, J. 4, 7, 110
   Labour and Socialism 106, 110
   Shop Floor Citizens 16, 17, 108

historians, view of trade unionism
Hobhouse, J.R. 307
Hobsbawm, Eric 5, 11, 18, 92, 98, 106, 111, 113
   Industry and Empire 315
   On History 14, 16, 17
Holford, J., *Union Education in Britain - A TUC*
   Activity 59
Hollis, P., *Jennie Lee: a life* 142
Holmes, C. 108
Home, Earl of 101, 135
Hood, Walter 167
Hoover Institute 166
Horner, Arthur 84, 85, 88, 142
Horner, John 176
Hose, John 189
houses, owner-occupation 72
Howarth, Herbert 179
Howe, Sir Geoffrey 35
Howell, David 6, 15, 16, 17, 84, 86, 110, 113, 312
   British Social Democracy: a study in
   development and decay 111, 113, 221
   Respectable Radicals: studies in the politics
   of railway trade unionism 140, 144
Howlett, P. 106
HRM (Human Resource Management) 3
Hudson, K.J. 188
Hungary, uprising (1956) 87, 131, 176, 177,
   178, 179, 180
Hunter, Bill 301
   Lifelong Apprenticeship: the life and times of
   a revolutionary 1920–1959 309
   They Knew Why They Fought: unofficial
   struggles and leadership on the docks
   1945–1989 308, 309, 310
Hunter, Sir John 248
Hutt, A., *British Trade Unionism: a short*
   history 220, 221
Hyman, R. 4, 15, 18, 64, 193, 215
   Industrial Relations: a Marxist introduction
   14, 18, 109, 212
   Marxism and the Sociology of Trade
   Unionism 14
   Strikes 113

ICFTU (International Confederation of Free
   Trade Unions)
   and the AFL 149, 150
   and the AFL-CIO 151, 152, 153, 161–2
   and Africa 157–65
   and communism 151
   formation 145
   philosophy 149
   and the TUC 87, 145, 146, 148–53, 156
IGF (International Graphical Federation) 152
ILO (International Labour Organisation) 154
ILP (Independent Labour Party) 269
I'm All Right Jack (film) 101
In Place of Strife (White Paper) 33, 62
   and shop steward training 50

Ince, G., *The Ministry of Labour and National Service* 289
incomes policy 207–8
Declaration of Intent (1966) 32, 34
introduction 79

industrial action, and politics 9–10
industrial correspondents, role 23–36
Industrial Court, London bus strike (1958) 275–6, 280, 289
industrial democracy, and the NUR 138
industrial policy, and voluntarism 76, 77
industrial relations
  and education programmes 49
  influence of Allan Flanders 192
  and state intervention 71
  writings about 2–3, 4
Industrial Relations Act (1971) 33–4, 35
  TUC opposition 51–2
Industrial Relations Training (Report No. 33) (CIR) 62, 64
industry, and the CP 4, 13
Industry Act (1972) 34
Industry and Society 131, 143
inflation
  and collective bargaining 203–4
  and wages 203–4
Information Research Department (IRD) 172
inheritance, and wealth 75
Inozemtsev, I., *The International Working Class Movement* 216
Institute of Contemporary British History 5
Interim Report on Postwar Reconstruction (TUC) 199
International Institute for Social History 166
International Socialists 173
International Solidarity Fund (ISF) 160–61
IRIS (Industrial Research and Information Services) 171, 179, 181, 190, 260
Iron Curtain speech (Churchill) 200
Iron and Steel Board 85
Isaacs, George, Minister of Labour 85
ISK (Internationaler Sozialistischer Kampfbund)
  and Allan Flanders 193–8
  in Britain 198, 214
  compared with CP 198
  origins 193–4
  philosophy 195, 207
ITF (International Transport Workers Federation) 148
ITS (International Trade Secretariats) 146, 148, 162, 163
  expelled from WCFTU 152
IWC (Institute for Workers Control) 53, 63

Jack, Prof Daniel, London Airport Inquiry (1958) 95, 112
Jackson, R. 63

Jacobs, Lionel 189
Jacques, M., *The Forward March of Labour Halted?* 106
Jagan, Cheddi 156
James, L., *Power in a Trade Union: the role of the District Committee in the AUEW* 18, 241
Jamieson, L., *State, Private Life and Political Change* 113
Janosik, E.G., *Constituency Labour Parties in Britain* 111
Jay, Douglas 219
  Change and Fortune 143
Jefferys, J.B., *The Story of the Engineers* 263
Jefferys, K., *The Attlee Government 1945–51* 106
Jefferys, S. 17
Jelf, George 178, 189
Jenkins, Mark 90
  Bevanism: Labour's high tide 104, 111, 113
Jenkins, Roy 217, 286
  A Life At The Centre 211
Jodoin, Claude 166
John Brown Engineering 232
Johnman, L. 106, 219
Johnson, Barry 189
Johnson, Vicky 290
Johnston, P., *Twentieth-Century Britain: economic, social, and cultural change* 16, 106
Joint Industrial Councils 73, 249, 260
Jones, Aubrey 32
Jones, Bill 177, 270–71, 273, 288, 292
Jones, Ernest 85, 142
Jones, H., *The Myth of Consensus: new views on British history 1945–64* 106
Jones, Jack 186, 189, 266, 305
  biography 11
  and education programmes 53
  General Secretary of TGWU 33, 258, 307
  Union Man: an autobiography 19, 62, 63, 109, 112, 288, 310
Jones, R. 241
Jones, Ted 85
Jowett, R. 111
Joyce, Patrick 6
JPC (Joint Production Committee) 77, 208
Jupp, J., *The Radical Left in Britain 1931–1941* 59

Kahn, P. 187, 189
Kahn-Freund, O. 108, 262
Kalecki, Michal 202, 204
Kampala College project 158, 160
Kandiah, M. 106
Kane, J., *No Wonder We Were Rebels* 187
Kaplansky, Kalmen 166
Kavanagh, D., *Thatcherism and British Politics* 18
Keating, J.E. 185

Keely, Leo 176, 178, 188, 189
Keithley, G.R. 64
Kelly, John 16, 17, 80, 109
  Rethinking Industrial Relations 14
  Social Democracy and Anti-Communism:
    Allan Flanders and the development of
    British   industrial relations 221
  Trade Unions and Socialist Politics 18
  Working for the Union: British trade union
    officers 14
Kenny, M., *The First New Left: British*
    intellectuals after Stalin 143
Kerrigan, Peter 174, 180, 190, 301, 302
Keynes, John Maynard 71
  How To Pay for the War 198, 203
KFL (Kenya Federation of Labour) 159
Khruschev, Nikita 87, 164
Kidd, Maurice 249, 264
Kidron, M., *Western Capitalism since the War*
    106
Killick, A.J. 112, 239
Kimeldorf, H. 4, 15, 19
King, A. 18, 111
Kirby, Ted 300
Kirk, N., *Social Class and Marxism: defences*
    and challenges 16
Klugmann, J. 60, 62
Knox, W. W. 239
Kolakowski, L., *Main Currents of Marxism: its*
    origins, growth and dissolution 213
Korean War 25, 78, 201, 294
Kumleben, Gerhard 193, 213

labour history
  and politics 10–11
  post-modernist approach 6–7, 16–17
  reasons for neglect 5
  and trade unionism 3
Labour, Ministry of
  Industrial Relations Department 245
  Overseas Department 245, 257–8
Labour Party
  Clause Four 99, 133
  Conference (1944) 75
  Conference (1948) 88
  Conference (1952) 127, 140
  Conference (1958) 136
  and the CP 91, 200
  electoral defeat 132–3, 313
  electoral fortunes 99
  and *embourgeoisement* 89–90, 132
  general election votes 89, 99–100
  and meritocracy 135
  and trade unions 69, 90–91, 117–40
  and the TUC 58
  working class support 88–92
  see also Labour Representation Committee
Labour Representation Committee
  formation 117

  see also Labour Party
Lane, T.
  Strike at Pilkingtons 14, 110
  The Union Makes Us Strong 63, 65
Law, Ted 180
Lawther, Sir William 25, 27, 77, 84, 85, 100,
    126, 127, 140, 156, 170, 204, 313
Laybourn, K. 4
  A History of British Trade Unions 1770–1990
    15
leadership, and trade unions 209
Leeson, R.A., *Strike: a live history* 187, 189
Leier, M., *Red Flags and Red Tape: the making*
    of a labour bureaucracy 18
Leonard Nelson: philosopher, politician,
    educationalist (MSI) 212, 213
Lerner, S.W. 74, 107, 112, 240, 241
Lewenhak, S., *Women and Trade Unions: an*
    outline history of women in the British
    trade union movement 16, 111
Lewis, W. Arthur 217
Lewis, W.S. 106
Liberal Democrats 140
Lindop, Fred 298, 307, 308
Link, W., *Die Geschichte der Internationalen*
    Jugendbendes und des Internationalen
    Sozialistischen Kampfbundes 212–4
living standards 72
Lloyd, J., *Liberty and Light: a history of the*
    EETPU 110, 141, 191
Lloyd, Lew 305
Lloyd, Selwyn 32, 79, 136
Loach, Harry 189
Lockwood, D. 111
London Airport Inquiry 95, 112
London Bus Dispute Appeal, and the TUC 280
London Port Workers' Strike Committee 296
  Reflections on the Strike 308
London School of Economics, and education
    programmes 39, 61
London Typographical Society 280
Looking at Industrial Relations (EEF) 262, 266
Loughlin, Anne 93
Lovell, J., *Stevedores and Dockers* 309
Lowe, R., *Adjusting to Democracy: the role of*
    the Ministry of Labour in British
    Politics 1916–1939 108
LTE (London Transport Executive) 269, 273, 274
Lucas, W.S. 186
Lunn, K. 108, 112
Lupton, Tom 224, 240
  On the Shopfloor: two studies of workshop
    organization and output 239, 241
Lyddon, D. 4, 8, 9, 15, 17, 107, 112, 262

McCallion, Bob 259
McCarthy, W.E.J. 97, 105, 112, 192, 261, 311
  Legal Intervention in Industrial Relations:
    gains and losses 13

The Role of Shop Stewards in British Industrial Relations 64
McCullough, Ellen 61, 93
MacDonald, Ramsay 132
McGarvey, Danny 257
Machen, Alwyn 182
McIlroy, J. 13, 18, 19, 60, 61, 62, 63, 64, 92, 96, 111, 113, 220, 308, 309, 312, 315
   British Trade Unionism and Industrial Politics, vol 2: the high tide of trade unionism 1964–79 108, 109, 144, 314
   Trade Unions in Britain Today 15
MacIntyre, Alasdair 144
Mack, J. 61
Mackay, Ian 24
McKenzie, R., *British Political Parties* 140, 142
McKinlay, Alan 18, 19, 95, 106, 108, 239, 240, 311, 314, 315
Macleod, Iain
   Minister of Labour 79, 129
      and engineering industry strike (1957) 242, 244, 246, 248, 254, 256, 259, 265, 266
      and London bus strike (1958) 274, 275, 280, 283, 284, 285, 286–7, 290
Macmillan government 30–31
   and London bus strike (1958) 273, 276, 278, 279, 281, 282, 284, 292
   and strikes 246–8
   and trade unions 80–81
Macmillan, Harold 79, 80, 244, 246, 248, 261
   Memoirs, Vol 4, 1956–1959: riding the storm 262, 263, 267, 290, 291, 292
MacShane, D., *International Labour and the Origins of the Cold War* 215, 216
Maguire, P. 109, 221
Mahon, John 288
Major, P., *The Death of the KPD* 216
Marney, Vic 300
Marquand, D. 106, 139, 140
   The Progressive Dilemma 144
Marquand, J. 107, 240, 241
Marsh, A. 241
   The Carpet Weavers 15
   Industrial Relations in Engineering 62
   Managers and Shop Stewards 112
   The New Politics of British Trade Unionism 14, 18
   The Seamen: a history of the National Union of Seamen 1887–1987 15
   Workplace Industrial Relations in Engineering 62
Marsh, David 10, 14, 18, 107
Marsh, Harold 178
Marshall Aid 147, 148, 163, 200
Marshall, B., *The Origins of Post-War German Politics* 216
Martin, D.E. 15
   Ideology and the Labour Movement 113
Martin, Gavin 249, 253, 254, 263

Marwick, A., *British Society since 1945* 106
Marxism 40–41, 101
Matthews, George 187
Mboya, Tom 159, 161
Mee, G., *Adult Education and Community Service* 64
Melling, Joseph 95, 106, 311, 314, 315
   Management, Labour and Industrial Politics in Modern Europe 18, 19, 108, 240
Members of Parliament, sponsorship by trade unions 121–4
Memoirs, Vol 4, 1956–1959: riding the storm (Harold Macmillan) 262, 263, 267, 290, 291
Men and Motors (CP) 178, 189
Mercer, H. 108
meritocracy, and the Labour Party 135
metalworking industries 95
Middlemas, K. 69, 70
   Politics in Industrial Society 18, 59, 106
Mikardo, Ian 117
   Back-Bencher 117, 140
Miles, A. 16, 113
Miles, R. 16
   The TUC, Black Workers and New Commonwealth Immigration 1954–1973 111–12
   White Man's Country: racism in Britain 111
Miliband, Ralph 53
   Parliamentary Socialism: a study in the politics of Labour 110
The Militant Socialist International: its aim, methods and constitution (MSI) 212, 213
Millar, J.P.M. 41, 61
   Education and Power 60
   The Labour College Movement 59, 60, 62
Millard, Charles 157, 160, 166, 167
Miller, S., *A History of German Social Democracy. From 1848 to the Present* 212, 214
Millward, N. 64
Milne, S., *The Enemy Within* 186
Milne-Bailey,, *Trade Unions and the State* 199, 215
Milward, A.S., *The Reconstruction of Western Europe 1945–51* 215–16
miners
   decline in numbers 99
   strike of 1973–4 34
   strike of 1984–5 28
   see also coal industry
Miners' Federation of Great Britain 27
   see also NUM
Minkin, Lewis 2, 18, 302
   The Contentious Alliance: trade unions and the Labour Party 14, 61, 63, 111, 140, 144, 219, 221, 309
   The Labour Party Conference 14, 141, 142, 143, 144
Mock, Vernon 191

modernization, railway industry 138
Moffat, Alex 176, 178, 181, 182
Monckton, Sir Walter, Minister of Labour 78, 79, 80, 129
  and engineering industry 243–4, 247, 251
Monks, John 13
monopoly, and collective bargaining 204–5
Montgomery, D. 9, 12, 19
  The Fall of the House of Labor: the workplace, the state and American labor activism 1865–1925 19
Moore, Bill 180, 187, 188, 190
Moral Rearmament 172, 181
Moran, M.
  The Politics of Industrial Relations 14
  The Union of Post Office Workers: a study in political sociology 14
Morgan, J., *The Backbench Diaries of Richard Crossman* 141, 143, 292
Morgan, K.O.
  Callaghan: a life 307
  Labour People: leaders and lieutenants, Hardie to Kinnock 218
  Labour in Power 1945–1951 108, 217
  The People's Peace 262
  The Red Dragon and the Red Flag 141
Morris, Bill 93
Morris, C.J. 186
Morrison, Herbert 60, 88, 100, 124, 127, 131, 206, 219, 313
Mortimer, J.E. 110
  History of the Boilermakers Society 15, 263, 266
Moss, Jack 186, 187
motor industry
  and the CP 178–9
  training 47–8
Mowatt, J. 65
MSI
  Leonard Nelson: philosopher, politician, educationalist 212, 213
  The Militant Socialist International: its aim, methods and contstitution 212, 213
  Russia and the Comintern 214, 219
Mulhern, F. 106
Mullaney, Tom 189
Murray, Len 62, 156, 172, 186
Murray, Phillip 165
Museum of London Library 307
Myant, M., *Socialism and Democracy in Czechoslovakia 1945–1948* 216

NALGO (National Association of Local Government Officers)
  affiliation to TUC 84
  education programmes 55
NAPE (National Association of Port Employers) 296, 306
NASD (National Amalgamated Stevedores and Dockers) 28–9, 297, 309
  conflict with TGWU 29, 295, 298, 301, 302, 303, 307
  expelled from TUC 304
  formation 293, 295
  internal conflict 304
National Council of Labour 135
National Docks Delegates Conference 293, 295
National Enterprise Board 8
National Federation of Building Trade Employers 73
National Health Service, creation 26
National Plan (1965) 33, 101
National Port Workers' Committee, *The Enquiry and YOU!* 308
National Unemployed Workers' Movement 4
nationalization 26–7, 75–6
  and Allan Flanders 205
  and the NUM 88
  and the NUR 88
  railway industry 26
  and the TGWU 88
  and the UPW 88
Nazi-Soviet Pact (1939) 198, 199
NBPI (National Board for Prices and Incomes) 192
  origins 207
NCB (National Coal Board) 85
NCLC (National Council of Labour Colleges) 38, 39, 53
  and education programmes 40–41, 42, 43, 44, 46, 92
NDLB (National Dock Labour Board) 293, 308
NEDC (National Economic Development Council) 79, 80
  formation 31–2
  TUC opposition 80
Neden, Sir Wilfred 254, 256, 274
Nedzynsky, Stefan 166
Neild, K. 15
Nelson, Leonard 194–5, 207, 209
  The Better Security: Being the heresies of a revolutionary revisionist 212, 213
  biography 212
  Politics and Education 212, 213
Neufeld, M. 15
New Unionism 2
News of the Blues (NASD paper) 303
News Chronicle 24, 29, 30
Newton, John 86
NGA (National Graphical Association) 86, 152
  education programmes 55
NIC (National Incomes Commission) 79, 80
Nicholas, Harry 245, 252, 272, 273, 274, 276, 278, 280
Nicholas, Peter 178
Nichols, T. 239
  Workers Divided 14
Nickolay, Laurie 186, 191

NMLH (National Museum of Labour History) 60, 63, 185, 288, 309
Northern College 57
Notting Hill riots (1958) 94
NPWU (National Passenger Workers' Union) 270
NSMM (National Society of Metal Mechanics) 93
NSP (National Society of Painters), and the CP 170, 171
NUAW (National Union of Agricultural Workers), membership 104
NUBSO (National Union of Boot and Shoe Operatives)
  and the CP 170
  history 185
NUDAW (National Union of Distributive and Allied Workers)
  membership 104
  see also USDAW
NUGMW (National Union of General and Municipal Workers) 86
  affiliation to the Labour Party 119, 120
  affiliation to the TUC 119
  and the CP 170, 174
  membership growth 104
  organization 83–4
  politics 130
  shop stewards 94, 96
NUM (National Union of Mineworkers) 86
  affiliation to the Labour Party 119, 120
  affiliation to the TUC 119
  and the CP 84, 86, 126, 141–2, 175, 181–2
  education programmes 44, 55
  formation 27, 84
  and Manny Shinwell 27–8, 77
  membership decline 81, 104, 137
  and nationalization 88
  Nottinghamshire coalfield 178
  organization 84
  politics 130
  and TUC General Council 85
NUPE (National Union of Public Employees)
  and members education 38
  membership growth 81, 84
NUR (National Union of Railwaymen) 86
  affiliation to the Labour Party 119, 120
  affiliation to the TUC 119
  education programmes 55
  and industrial democracy 138
  membership decline 81, 104
  and nationalization 88
  politics 84, 131
  see also Amalgamated Society of Railway Servants
NUT (National Union of Teachers), education programmes 55
NUTGW (National Union of Tailors and Garment Workers) 86
Nutt, H., *Education Schemes with the WETUC* 60

NUVB (National Union of Vehicle Builders), and the minimum wage 77

O'Brien, Sir Tom 86, 123, 141, 171, 292
O'Day, A. 108
Office, Shops and Railway Premises Act (1963) 93
O'Hare, Jimmy 305
oil crisis 34
Oldenbroek, J.H. 157, 160, 166
O'Leary, Tim 303, 304, 305
Openshaw, Bob 249, 252, 253, 260, 264
Oppenheimer, Franz 195, 204
Order 1305, and strikes 76–7, 78, 243, 244, 247, 262, 301
The Origins of Trade Union Power (Henry Phelps Brown) 14
Osborne, Walter 118
Outram, Q. 113
Overseas Employers' Federation 155
Oxford Delegacy for Extra-Mural Studies 42, 48

Padley, Walter 142, 143
Panitch, L., *Social Democracy and Industrial Militancy* 141, 144
Pannell, Charles 142
Papworth, Bert 177, 270
Park, T. 63
Parker, S., *Workplace Industrial Relations, 1973* 64
Parsons, S.R. 185, 188, 189
Paynter, Will 51, 86, 142
  My Generation 110
Pelling, Henry
  The British Communist Party: a historical profile 188
  A History of British Trade Unionism 15
  A Short History of the Labour Party 111
Penceval, J.H., *Labour Markets under Trade Unionism* 14
Penn, R. 14
PEP (Political and Economic Planning), *British Trade Unionism: six studies by PEP* 61, 239, 240
personnel management 72–3
Phillips, Gordon 303
  Casual Labour: the unemployment question in the port transport industry 309
Phillips, Jim 83, 97, 98, 142, 288, 309, 314
  The Great Alliance: economic recovery and the problems of power 1945–1951 307–8
Phillips, Morgan 41, 60
Phizacklea, A. 16, 111
Pimlott, Ben 2, 12–13
  Harold Wilson 62, 144
  Trade Unions in British Politics: the first 250 years 14, 108, 110
pit closures 138
Plant, Cyril 86

329

Platform (busworkers paper) 271, 272, 276, 277, 278, 282, 283–4, 288, 290, 291
Platt, J. 111
Platts (Barton) Ltd, closure 11, 18
POEU (Post Office Engineering Union), education programmes 55
politics
  and industrial action 9–10
  and labour history 10–11
  and wages policy 136–7
Pollard, S., *The Development of the British Economy 1914–50* 106
Pollert, A., *Girls, Wives, Factory Lives* 14
Poole, M.
  The IBM Handbook of Human Resource Management 212
  Theories of Trade Unionism 212
post-modernism, and labour history 6–7, 16–17
Potthoff, H. 212, 214
poverty 74
Powell, Enoch 273
Powell, Tom 297
Praetorian Guard (alliance of trades union leaders) 126–7, 129
Price, John 60
Price, Richard 9, 15, 17, 18, 103
Prices and Incomes Board 32
prices and incomes policy 33
Prior, Jim 35
productivity, and wages 136, 208
public interest, and collective bargaining 205–6
public opinion, and trade unions 101
Purcell, J. 106, 107

racism, and the TUC 93–4
railway industry
  modernization 138
  nationalization 26
  strike threats 247–8
Ramdin, R., *The Making of the Black Working-class in Britain* 16
Ramelson, Bert 182, 190
Ramsay, R. 185, 186
  The Clandestine Caucus: anti-socialist campaigns and operations in the British labour movement since the war 217
rationing 72
Ratner, H., *Reluctant Revolutionary: memoirs of a Trotskyist 1936–60* 18
RCP (Revolutionary Communist Party), and docks industry 300–301
Redman, G.P. 97, 105, 112, 261
redundancy, and strikes 95
Reflections on the Strike (London Port Workers' Strike Committee) 308
Reid, E. 108, 109, 220, 262, 267, 289, 292
Reid, H., *The Furniture Makers* 186
Renshaw, George 271, 288
Report of Annual Meeting (1956) (Confed) 264

Resler, H. 107
restrictive practices 95, 231–2
Rewley House Papers 61
Rhodesia, Northern 156
Rhydderch, David 142
Richter, I., *Political Purpose in Trade Unions* 141, 186
Rigg, P. 64
Roberts, Alfred 164
Roberts, Ben 211, 218
  The Price of TUC Leadership 109
Roberts, Bryn 84, 173
Roberts, E., *Strike Back* 186
Roberts, G. 112
Roberts, K. 14, 110
Robertson, Sir Brian 248, 279, 284
Robertson, D. 64
Robinson, Derek 8, 62, 178, 185, 186, 187, 189
Robinson, Joan 199, 202, 218
Rolph, C.H., *All Those In Favour?* 191
Rookes v. Barnard case, and strikes 81
Roper, Joe 215
Rose, E., *Colour and Citizenship* 111
Rose, J. 60
Rose, M. 14
Rose, Richard 61, 89, 110, 111, 143
Routledge, P., *Scargill: the unauthorized biography* 19
Rowley, C. 212
Roy, D. 239
Roy, W., *The Teachers' Union* 185
Royal Commission on the Distribution of Income and Wealth 107
Royal Commission on Trade Unions and Employers' Associations 1965–1968 *see* Donovan Commission
Rubinstein, D. 113
Runciman, W.G. 90
  Relative Deprivation and Social Justice 111
Ruskin College 57
Russia and the Comintern (MSI) 214, 219
Ryan, K. 19
Ryan, V. 15

Saillant, Louis 146, 147, 165, 200
Salmon, J. 112
Saran, Mary 215, 217, 218
  Never Give Up. Memoirs 212, 215
Saunders, Bert 298
Savage, Bernard 189
Savage, M. 113
  The Remaking of the British Working Class 1840–1940 16, 113
Saville, John 4, 12, 15, 19, 98, 100, 108, 142, 218
  The Labour Movement in Britain 15, 106, 113
Saville, R. 110
Scanlon, Hugh 260, 265, 266
  biography 11, 19
  and education programmes 53

leader of AEUW 33
Scargill, Arthur, biography 11, 19
Schneer, J., *Labour's Conscience: the labour left 1945–51* 110, 113, 141
Schuller, T. 64
Schumacher, Kurt 200
Scott, J., *The Upper classes: property and privilege in Britain* 107
Scott, Joe (AEU) 77, 249, 250, 253, 254, 255, 257, 264
Scottish Engineering Employers' Association (SEEA) 229
Scottish Record Office 308
Scottish Transport and General Workers' Union 295
Screpanti, E. 220
SDP (Social Democratic Party, Germany) 193, 194, 197, 200
Seamen and Dockers' Union (Trinidad) 156
Sedgwick, P. 212
Shane, T.N. 171
Shanley, Jock 48
Sheet Metal Workers 249, 250
Shepherd, J.R. 107
Shepherd, R., *Iain Macleod: a biography* 142, 262, 263, 289, 292
Shinwell, Manny 26
    and the NUM 27–8, 77
Shipbuilding Employers 248, 252, 253–4, 256
shipbuilding industry, strike (1957) 254–61
shop floor, dynamics 231–7
shop stewards
    in the AEU 94
    and British Leyland 8
    Clydeside 95, 223, 226
    communist influence 179–81, 306
    docks industry 298, 305–6
    employers' attitudes 229–31
    engineering industry 222–39
    and foremen 227–9, 232–3
    increase in numbers 56, 94, 311–12
    inter-union committees 229–30
    in the NUGMW 94, 96
    and official structures 96
    organization 95–6
    and strikes 95–8
    in the TGWU 94
    training 47–56
        and the Callaghan government 54
        content 55–6
        rationale 57
        and The Social Contract 54
        and the TUC 49, 54–5, 62–3
        and the Wilson government 54
    and wage rates 74, 208
    writings about 4
Simon, B., *The Search for Enlightenment: the working class and adult education in the twentieth century* 60, 61, 63, 220

Sinclair, K., *How the Blue Union came to Hull docks* 309
Sisson, K. 106, 107
Skidelsky, R., *Thatcherism* 18
Sloane, P.J. 241
Smith, B. Abel 107
Smith, C. 239
Smith, D., *Aneurin Bevan and the World of South Wales* 141
Smith, George 176
Smith, J. Davis 77
    The Attlee and Churchill Administrations and Industrial Unrest 1945–1955 108, 109
Smith, P. 8, 17, 18, 109
Smith, T. 64
Social Contract, The 8, 59
    and shop steward training 54
    and trade unions 34–5
Socialism: a new statement of principles (Socialist Union) 206–7, 215, 220
socialism, ethical 199, 202, 203, 218
Socialist Labour League 173
Socialist Party of Great Britain 269
Socialist Union 197
    dissolution 205
    formation 201, 203
    Socialism: a new statement of principles 206–7, 215, 220, 221
    Twentieth Century Socialism 211, 220, 221
Society of Industrial Tutors 53, 63
sociologists, view of trade unionism 2
South Wales Miners, education programmes 44
Spencer, B. 64
spin doctors 26
Spoor, A., *White Collar Union: sixty years of NALGO* 110
Spring, Francis 304
Squires, Len 186
Stalinism 5, 86–7, 300
state intervention, and industrial relations 71
Statement on Personal Incomes, Costs and Prices (White Paper, 1948) 136
steel industry, nationalization 88
Stephenson, P. 217
Stevens, Richard 17, 87, 91, 97, 141, 143, 186, 188, 308, 313, 315
Stevens, Walter 25
Stevenson, G., *The Life and Times of Sid Easton* 288
Stewart, Margaret 24
Stokes, D. 90, 91, 111
strikes
    bus strike, London (1958) 129, 177, 242, 261
    and the CP 29–30, 173–4, 300
    docks industry 295, 297, 298, 300, 301
    engineering industry (1957) 225, 236–7, 254–61, 265–6
    Ford, Dagenham (1962) 177, 182
    and Macmillan government 246–8

miners, 1973–4 177; 1984–5 28
and Order 1305 76–7, 78, 243, 244, 247, 262, 301
post-war 243
and redundancy 95
and *Rookes v. Barnard* case 81
shipbuilding industry 254–61
and shop stewards 95–8
statistics 97, 105
unofficial 206–7
and wage increases 98
Suez crisis (1956) 178, 247
Supple, B., *The History of the British Coal Industry* 113
Supplementary Evidence to the Russell Committee on Adult Education 1970 (TUC) 63
SVG (Socialist Vanguard Group) 193, 197, 198, 199, 201, 202, 203, 209, 212
finance 217
Sworakowski, W. S., *World Communism: a handbook 1918–1965* 217

Tait, Willie 300
Tanner, Jack 83, 85, 170, 249, 250, 253
Tatlow, A. 241
Tawney, R.H. 202
Taylor, A.J. 109, 186
Trade Unions and the Labour Party 14
Taylor, Robert 5, 12, 13, 19, 71, 109, 144, 314
The Future of the Trade Unions 14
The Trade Union Question in British Politics 16, 19, 102, 106, 108, 113
Tearse, Roy 300
Terry, M. 3
Shopfloor Politics and Job Controls: the post-war engineering industry 15, 17, 107, 112, 113, 240
Tewson, Sir Vincent 61, 85–6, 141, 148–9, 150, 158, 164, 171, 204
and the ICFTU 160, 161
and London bus strike (1958) 276, 279, 280–81, 283
TGWU (Transport and General Workers Union) 25, 148
and the CP 126, 170, 294
and docks industry 28–9, 293–307
Docks Trade Group 294–5
education programmes 38, 55, 57, 63, 65
Labour Party, affiliation 119, 120
membership growth 82, 104, 294
NASD, conflict with 29, 295, 298, 301, 302, 303, 307
and nationalization 88
organization 83
shop stewards 94, 234
TUC affiliation 119
and unilateralism 134, 302–3
and the Wilson government 33

Thatcher government 26, 35
Thatcher, Margaret 34
Thatcherism 1, 69
Theatrical and Kine Employees 86, 171
Third Way 6
Thomas, E.C.W. 297
Thomas, Jimmy 117–18
Thompson, A.F. 263
Thompson, Edward 5
The Making of the English Working-class 3
Thompson, Harry 186
Thompson, K., *Under Siege: racial violence in Britain today* 111
Thompson, N., *Political Economy and the Labour Party* 219
Thompson, P. 60, 110, 111
Thompson, W. 4, 188
The Good Old Cause: British Communism 1921–91 16, 185, 188, 191
Thornett, A., *Inside Cowley. Trade union struggle in the 1970s: who really opened the door for the Tory onslaught* 17
Thorneycroft, G. 61
Thorneycroft, Peter, Chancellor of the Exchequer 272, 273
Thornton, A.H., *Adult Education and the Industrial Community* 64
Thornton, C. 188
Tiffin, Jock 83, 303
death 129, 302
The Times House of Commons 1951 109
Timothy, Albert 297
Tiratsoo, N. 60, 110, 111, 112, 240
The Attlee Years 15, 108, 219
Reconstruction, Affluence and Labour Politics, Coventry 1945–60 113
Tocher, John 179
Tolliday, S. 4
The Power to Manage? Employers and industrial relations in comparative-historical perspective 18
Shop Floor Bargaining and the State: historical and comparative perspectives 15
Tomkins, Alf 173
Tomlinson, J. 4, 15, 77, 112, 240
Topham, T. 15, 60, 63, 109, 110, 307, 309
Townsend, P., *The Poor and the Poorest* 107
Tracey, Herbert 171
Trade Disputes Act
(1927) 76–7, 270
(1965) 81
Trade Union Education (WEA) 61
trade unionism
and historians 2
and labour history 3
and social change 314
and sociologists 2
see also trade unions
Trade Unionism (TUC) 64

Trade Unionism and the New Social Order
(WEA) 215
trade unions
acceptance by political parties 70
affiliation to Labour Party, statistics 119–20
in Africa 157–65
anti-communism 86–7, 170–73, 181–2
and black workers 4, 92, 93–4 ·
and block votes 86
and the Callaghan government 34–5
and change 312–14
and the Churchill government 78
and The Cold War 86–7, 136, 138, 139, 294
and communism
influence 168–9
statistics 168, 176, 183, 184
and the Conservative Party 69–70
films, portrayal 101
and the Heath government 33–4
and the Labour Party 69, 90–91, 117–40
and leadership 209
legal status 80–81
and the Macmillan government 80–81
members' education 37–59
membership decline 99
membership growth 54, 81, 101, 103
MPs, sponsorship 121–4
political classification 104
and public opinion 101
purpose 202–3
Royal Commission on 33
and The Social Contract 34–5
statistics 104
and training 48
and unilateralism 134
and the Wilson government 33–4
and women 4, 82, 92–3, 123
Yugoslavia 149–50, 151
see also trade unionism
training
and the Confed 47–8
and education 46
health and safety 55
motor industry 47–8
shop stewards 47–56
and trade unions 48
see also education programmes
Training Shop Stewards (TUC) 62
Transport Salaried Staffs Association 282
Trotskyists 13, 173, 179
in the docks industry 300–301, 304
Truman Doctrine (1947) 200
TUC Charter for Women (TUC) 93
The TUC and Communism (TUC) 150
TUC (Trades Union Congress) 13
and AFL-CIO 146, 157, 164
and the AUCCTU 150, 151, 153, 163
Colonial Advisory Committee 157, 166, 167
and the Colonial Development Fund 155

and the Colonial Economic Development
Council 154
and the Colonial Labour Advisory Commit-
tee 154, 155
and communism 150–51, 164, 171–2, 299–300
Congress (1945) 38
Congress (1946) 77, 87–8, 109
Congress (1950) 24–5, 78
Congress (1956) 244
Congress (1960) 47, 96
Congress (1961) 45
Congress (1962) 80
Congress (1964) 58, 93–4
Congress (1965) 152–3
and developing countries 153–6
Economic Committee 78, 199
Education Committee 46, 61, 62
Education Department 56
education goals 45–6
education programmes 39–40, 42–3, 50–51,
54–5
and ETUC 145
General Council 85–6
and the ICFTU 87, 145, 146, 148–53, 156–60
conflict 160–63
influence 31
of major unions 82–3
Interim Report on Postwar Reconstruction 199
International Committee 152, 154, 167
International Department 155
international policy 145–82
and the Labour Party 58
London Bus Dispute Appeal 280
membership 55, 82
and the NASD 304
opposition to Industrial Relations Act (1971)
51–2
opposition to NEDC 80
Organization Committee 82
and post-war reconstruction 87, 88
post-war strategy 1
and racism 93–4
Research Department 198
and shop steward training 49, 54–5, 92
*Supplementary Evidence to the Russell
Committee on Adult Education 1970* 63
Trade Union News for Overseas 154
Trade Unionism 64
and trade unions overseas 156
training college 45
Training Shop Stewards 62
TUC Charter for Women 93
The TUC and Communism 150
and the WFTU 87, 145, 147–8, 152, 169
Why We Have Left the WFTU 166
Turner, H.A. 11
Labour Relations in the Motor Industry 112
*Trade Union Growth, Structure and Politics:
a comparative study of the cotton*

unions 18
The Trend of Strikes 113
Turner, I., *Reconstruction in Post-War Germany* 216
Turner, J. 106
Twentieth Century Socialism (Socialist Union) 211, 220
TWU (Tobacco Workers' Union), and the CP 180–181

UGSOB (Union of German Socialist Organizations) 197
UK, exports 72
Undy, R., *Managing the Unions: the impact of legislation on trade unions' behaviour* 14
unemployment, and wages 102
unilateralism
  and the GMWU 134
  and the TGWU 134, 302–3
  and trade unions 134
UPW (Union of Post Office Workers)
  membership growth 104
  and nationalization 88
USDAW (Union of Shop Distributive and Allied Workers) 86, 93
  and the CP 171
  education programmes 43, 55
  membership growth 81, 82, 104
  politics 84, 131
  see also NUDAW

Vernon, James 6
Volker, D. 110
voluntarism, and industrial policy 76, 77
von Beyme, K., *Political Parties in Western Democracies* 216

Waged Work: a reader (Feminist Review) 16
wage(s)
  claims 250–53
  drift 74
  freeze, and the CP 204
  increases 72
    and strikes 98
  and inflation 203–4
  minimum 77
  and productivity 136, 208
  rates
    and the engineering industry 74
    and shop stewards 74
  and unemployment 102
Wages Council Act (1945) 73
wages policy
  and Arthur Deakin 78, 135, 136
  and the CP 78
  docks industry 296, 298–9
  and Frank Cousins 136
  and politics 136–7

Walker, Peter 34
Walsh, L., *CIA Infiltration of the Labour Movement* 217
Ward, F. 60
Warman, Bill 178
Warman, Lorna 189
Warner, A. 241
Warner, M. 186, 187, 188, 191, 212
Warren, A. 64
Waters, Bill 273, 288
Watkinson, Harold, Minister of Transport 273, 274–5, 276, 284
Watson, Sam 136, 141, 209
Watters, Frank 189, 191
  Being Frank 187, 188
WEA (Workers' Educational Association) 38, 39
  Annual Report (1948) 60
  education programmes 41–2, 43–4, 92
  Trade Union Education 61
  Trade Unionism and the New Social Order 215
  Workers' Education and the Trade Union Movement 59
wealth
  distribution 74–5
  and inheritance 75
Webb, Sydney & Beatrice 9
Webber, W. 61, 282
Wedderburn, K.W., *The Worker and the Law* 64, 109
Weiler, P.
  British Labor and the Cold War 216
  Ernest Bevin 141, 221, 308
Welfare State, formation 23
Westacott, Fred 185, 187, 188, 189, 190, 191
Westergaard, J., *Class in a Capitalist Society* 107
WETUC (Workers' Educational Trade Union Committee), and education programmes 41, 43, 46
WFTU (World Federation of Trade Unions)
  and Allan Flanders 201
  and Arthur Deakin 147, 148, 149, 200
  expells the ITS 152
  formation 145, 200
  Information Bulletin 165
  Soviet bias 146–7, 200
  and the TUC 87, 145, 147–8, 152, 169
  and Walter Citrine 146, 200, 201
Whelan, Joe 178
Whiteley, William, Chief Whip 124
Whiteside, Noel 106, 113, 303, 309
Whittingham, T.G. 112
Why We Have Left the WFTU (TUC) 166
Widden, W. 171
Widgery, D., *The Left in Britain, 1956–68* 109, 144, 188
Wigham, E.
  From Humble Petition to Militant Action: a

history of the Civil and Public Services Association 1903–1978 216
The Power to Manage: a history of the Engineering Employers' Federation 107, 264, 266
Strikes and the Government 1893–1981 262
What's Wrong with the Unions? 107, 113, 186, 187, 216
Wilkinson, Ellen 41, 123
Williams, F., *Magnificent Journey* 140
Williams, Len 41
Williams, Mary 290
Williams, P.M.
  The Diary of Hugh Gaitskell 1945–1956 141, 142, 143, 144
  Gaitskell 309
  Hugh Gaitskell: a political biography 143, 144, 218
Williams, S. 110
Williams, W.E. 59
Williamson, Tom 25, 83–4, 85, 100, 126, 142, 204, 313
Willis, Bob 86, 173, 280, 281
Willman, P., *Innovation and Management Control: labour relations at BL cars* 7–8, 17
Wilson, A. 16
Wilson, D.F., *Dockers: the impact of industrial change* 306, 308, 310
Wilson government 99
  and shop steward training 54
  and the TGWU 33, 303
  and trade unions 33–4
Wilson, Harold 32, 71, 101, 139
  Labour Party Leader 134–5
  President of Board of Trade 77
  resignation 127
Winch, G. 17
Winnard, Dennis 46, 60
Winstone, R., *Tony Benn - Years of Hope: diaries, papers and letters 1940–1962* 143

WLTBU (Watermen, Lightermen, Tugmen and Bargemen's Union) 297
women
  trade union leaders 93
  and trade unions 4, 82, 92–3, 123
Woodburn, Arthur 41
Woodcock, George 33, 45, 46, 49, 57, 58, 65, 80, 82, 109, 202, 215, 218
  and the ICFTU 160, 161, 162, 163, 165
  and London busworkers strike (1958) 279–80
  TUC General Secretary 86, 135, 151, 152, 153
Wootton, G. 189
Workers' Education and the Trade Union Movement (WEA) 59
working class
  culture 100, 101
  identity 90, 100
  Labour Party support 88–92
Workplace Industrial Relations Survey (1980) 55
Wray, J. 61
Wright, A.W., *G. D. H. Cole and Socialist Democracy* 214, 219, 221
Wright, Bob 189
Wrigley, Chris 4, 19, 107, 111
  British Trade Unions 1945–95 16
  A History of British Industrial Relations 1939–1979 5, 12, 16, 19, 109, 215, 221, 262, 307
  A History of Industrial Relations 1940–79 107, 113
Wrong, D., *Power: its forms, bases and uses* 239
Wyatt, Woodrow 172, 181
  The Peril In Our Midst 186
Wynn, Bert 176, 177

Yates, Tom 164, 281, 282, 283
Young, Jim 156
Yugoslavia, trade unions 149–50, 151

Zeitlin, Jonathan 3–4, 8. 9, 15, 17, 18
Zilliacus, Konni 127

Lightning Source UK Ltd.
Milton Keynes UK
UKOW07f1208191214

243414UK00004B/111/P